Selecting by Origin

Selecting by Origin

*Ethnic Migration in
the Liberal State*

Christian Joppke

Harvard University Press

Cambridge, Massachusetts, and London, England | 2005

Copyright © 2005 by the President and Fellows of Harvard College
All rights reserved
Printed in the United States of America

Library of Congress Cataloging-in-Publication Data

Joppke, Christian.
　　Selecting by origin: ethnic migration in the liberal state / Christian Joppke.
　　　　p. cm.
　　Includes bibliographical references and index.
　　ISBN 0-674-01559-2
　　1. Emigration and immigration—Government policy. 2. Ethnic groups—
Government policy. 3. Multiculturalism. 4. Nationalism. I. Title.
　　JV6038.J65 2005
　　325′.1—dc22　　　　2004052276

For Benjamin and Nicolas

Contents

Preface

In a world divided into mutually exclusive sovereign states, each encaging a distinct national subset of the human species, international migration constitutes a fundamental anomaly and disturbance. As Aristide Zolberg (1999:84) describes the source of the trouble, "modern nations have come to be perceived by most of their members as family-like bodies, with a common ancestry and a common destiny." International migration stirs up the national order of things, as people do not just break out of their own ancestry and destiny nexus but, by necessity, break into another one, which is always differently configured. No wonder that, to cushion the impact of migration, there is an intrinsic inclination in modern nation-states to select newcomers in light of their proximity to the particular ancestry and destiny definitions they happen to adhere to. The result is ethnic migration.[1]

The purpose of this book is twofold: to map out the different forms that ethnic migration has taken in different geographic-historical constellations, from "settler state" to "postcolonial" and "diaspora"; and to point to a general trend away from ethnically selective toward nonethnic, universalistic immigration policies across Western states. This trend is due to the fact that such states are not just nation-states, embodiments of historically particular collectivities with distinct ancestry and destiny definitions, but also liberal states in which public policies that distinguish between people, be they citizens or aliens, along the ascriptive lines of ethnicity, national origin, or race are in conflict with fundamental liberal precepts, such as public neutrality and equality. This raises the question of why these liberal precepts, born in the European Enlightenment three centuries ago, became unambiguously embodied in Western states only much later, arguably not before the 1960s. The answer is both simple and complex (and, as a complex one, lies outside the purview of this study):

the rise of a world-spanning human rights culture after the Holocaust and decolonization.

Ethnic migration is a prominent site in which the tension between the national and liberal vocations of the modern state has come to a head. On the one hand, this is a migration that is everywhere waged for national "identity" reasons, and the policies that enable it are decoupled from the interest-driven political economy matrix in which the contemporary immigration function is usually located (for the latter, see Freeman, 1995a). On the other hand, if the diminishing scale of ethnic migration across Western states is any measure, liberal-universalistic principles and forces are steadily gaining ground over the parochially national ones. This leads to a paradox: Although it is notionally the foremost expression of a state's sovereignty, immigration (as well as citizenship) policy is no longer at the service of reproducing historically particular nationhood.

This does not mean that ethnic migration has come to an end, nor that it will come to an end any time soon. The contemporary state is in the crossfire of countervailing trends and forces, some furthering its "de-ethnicization," others instead pushing for its "re-ethnicization." Both trends, as opposite as they are, are often generated by the same global processes. An example is globalization-induced migration itself, whose immigration and emigration sides work toward the involved states' de- and re-ethnicization, respectively. Whether ethnic migration happens then depends on the contingent concatenation of de- and re-ethnicizing forces in a certain time and place. However, *when* it happens, ethnic migration is likely to be constrained by liberal norms: that is, it is likely to be based on a positive discrimination that redresses a disadvantage to a "minority" group; to be nested within a nonethnic frame of immigrant selection *or* to be notionally decoupled at all from "immigration" policy; and not to generate a concrete loser in domestic society who is capable of effective mobilization.

In looking at state policies and laws in the context of societal contestation, this book lies at the intersection of sociology, political science, and legal studies. Because the focus is on the policies and legal provisions that generate ethnic migration, the book will disappoint the sociologist who expects to hear more about the migration and the migrants themselves. Because it gives much to the cultural factor of nationhood (in, however, critical and qualified ways) and to the justifications and sociopolitical pressures surrounding ethnic migration policies, it will disappoint the political scientist who may expect a more technical and rigorous account of the policy process. Not to mention that the legal scholar will immediately recognize the dilettante. Some twenty-five years ago Aristide Zolberg and Gary Freeman started to look at international migration as a process shaped by states, within a broad historical and cross-national perspective. This book is meant to be a contribution to that program. There are signs that, in light of new kinds of circular and market-regulated migration, especially in Europe, "nation-state"-centered conceptions of immigration and citizenship have run their course (see Favell and Hansen, 2002). Then this book may be one of the last of its kind. However, in shifting the focus from the "nation-state" to the "liberal state," it comes to a quite similar conclusion, though from a statist angle.

I began working on this book during my last three years in service at the European University Institute in Florence and finished it as a Visiting Scholar at the Russell Sage Foundation in New York. At the European University Institute, I am grateful to the EUI Research Council for generously funding this project between 2000 and 2002. At Russell Sage, my thanks go to Eric Wanner, without whose kind invitation I might have spent many more years on a seemingly endless project. A group of extremely capable, amazingly multilingual research assistants in Florence helped me to compile and sift the primary parliamentary and legal documents on which much of this study is based. Elia Marzal, Mercedes Fernandez, Pablo Jáuregui, and Oscar Molina were indispensable for getting especially the Portuguese and Spanish cases done; Emmanuelle Ryon procured and organized the parliamentary records and documents on which the discussion of the French and Italian citizenship debates in Chapter 5 is based; and Elke Viebrock provided me with tall stacks of German parliamentary and government materials. Zeev Rosenhek of the Hebrew University, Jerusalem, familiarized me with the Israeli case. The architecture of Chapter 4 owes much to an article we conceived and published together (Joppke and Rosenhek, 2002), but it is based on a second round of independent research done at Russell Sage in the fall of 2002. My thanks go to Sabina Neem and the superb library service at Russell Sage for getting this chapter done. As so often in the past, I profited from a razor-sharp report on the entire manuscript by Rogers Brubaker. Rainer Bauböck is also to be thanked for a meticulous reading of Chapter 1.

Because it takes so long to write a book, it is always a period in one's life. This period coincided with the arrival of Benjamin at the beginning and that of Nicolas toward the end. This book shall be dedicated to them, big boys by now, bigger travelers still, *fiorentini per la vita*.

Selecting by Origin

1

The Problem of Ethnic Selectivity

In the 2000th anniversary year of Christianity, the Archbishop of Bologna, Cardinal Giacomo Biffi, suggested that for the sake of "saving the identity of the nation" the Italian state should privilege the entry of Catholic immigrants.[1] After all, "Italy is not an empty land, without history and without traditions, to be populated indiscriminately." Of course, Italy was a secular state in which state and religion were officially separated,[2] but Catholicism still remained the "historical religion of the nation," and respecting this was nothing less than a question of "respect for the majority."[3] As one would assume, in the year 2000 and in a heartland of uniting Europe, the churchman's digression on immigration policy did not find much applause, to put it mildly—at least not in "polite" society, which included the Catholic Church establishment itself. This was "a discrimination, a negation of human rights," fumed the left-liberal *la Repubblica*, and at a European Commission meeting on a future European immigration policy the cardinal's curious recovery of the preliberal *cuius regio eius religio* principle was in all mouths, as the proposal that should and would clearly *not* see the light of day anywhere in Europe.[4]

This response, understandable (even required) as it is from a liberal point of view, should let us pause for a moment. Are not states the sovereign arbiters over territorial entry and membership, and should not the state's decisions in this critical domain reflect a concern for the "identity" of the political community from which it derives its legitimacy? At least, would it not be prudent, because less costly for society, to admit preferentially people who are likely to adapt better to the culture of the majority? In sum, is not immigration policy, next to nationality law, the one domain in which not just "states" but "*nation*-states"—historically singular collectivities here and not elsewhere—are centrally involved, so that heeding

1

the liberals' rejection of Cardinal Biffi's prescriptions would amount to a momentous self-abdication of the nation-state?

As I shall argue in this book, liberal states indeed no longer can explicitly and directly reproduce and reinvigorate particular nationhood through immigration policy. However, this claim applies with important nuances, variations, and exceptions that will be explored in the chapters to follow.

If one compares past and present criteria of immigrant selection in Western states, one notices a significant contraction: the roles of ethnicity, national origin, and race, which were all-dominant when the first explicit, national immigration policies were forged at the turn from the nineteenth to the twentieth century in the Americas, Australia, and Europe, have been dramatically narrowed. The "comprehensive" immigration policy that is currently being prepared in the European Union will include only the three selection criteria that exhaust the realm of the legitimate today:[5] skills or economic need, the recognition of family ties, and a human need for protection, the latter channeled into the legally separate asylum and refugee domains. These selection criteria incorporate in different ways two opposite principles: state interests and individual rights—the latter expanding only recently and stirring up the orthodoxy of immigration as the prerogative of the sovereign state.[6] Selecting according to human need is not selecting at all, because here an inviolable, natural right of the individual cancels out all interests of state—this is the one achievement of the postwar human rights regime built under the auspices of the United Nations Organization (UNO). Selection according to family ties combines the principles of state interests and individual rights, with interesting variations between states that situate this right either in the family member abroad or in the immigrant already admitted (see Guendelsberger, 1988). Interestingly, family ties (between children and parents) are the only ascriptive element that is universally recognized in contemporary immigrant selection, because it is couched as an individual right and carried by a consensus that the family is the fundamental building block of society. Finally, selection according to skills or economic need, which is currently having a historical revival in Europe, is the only domain in which state interests reign supreme: here no rights of the individual have to be respected (except those of basic fairness and due process).

The reduction of unfettered state interests to skill-based or economic selection epitomizes the contraction of state sovereignty in immigration policy more generally: the state may consider the individual only for what she *does*, not for what she *is*. In the language of Talcott Parsons' pattern variables, the individual is selected according to "achievement," not "ascription," that is, according to her agency rather than according to what she is immutably born with.[7] For Parsons the transition from ascription to achievement was the hallmark of modernization, and in this sense one could argue that an immigration policy under the sign of skills and achieved individual characteristics, rather than primordial givens, has finally caught up with modernity.

However, there are exceptions to this trend. An important class of these exceptions is discussed in this book as "ethnic migration."[8] It is engendered by immigration policies (sometimes also by nationality laws and policies as "second" admissions), in which immigrants (or applicants for citizenship) are selected on the basis of their ethnicity, race, or national origins.

What Is "Ethnic"?

A fundamental ambiguity of the notion of *ethnic* is to be either generic or specific, sometimes "embodying" but at other times being "differentiated from" related markers (such as race or national origins) (see Jackson, 1984:230). The *Oxford English Dictionary (OED)* defined *ethnic* in a generic way, as "pertaining to or having common racial, cultural, religious, or linguistic characteristics." For the purposes of the broad historical comparisons aimed at in this book, this is an appositely wide definition. However, it is mute on the common denominator of these characteristics. What makes all of them "ethnic"? I suggest what makes them "ethnic" is the reference to perceived common origins or descent. Ethnicity is fundamentally a notion of origins, indicating certain ascribed characteristics of individuals *qua* their membership in the group into which they are usually (but not necessarily) born and which they usually (again not necessarily) leave only at death. This minimal content of ethnicity is captured by Anthony Smith (1981:66), who argues that "it is the myth of a common and unique origin in time and place that is essential for the sense of ethnic community." In a similar vein, Emerich Francis (1965:57) defined "ethnic formations" *(ethnische Gebilde)* through the "criterion of origins," adding the important qualification that "origins" was not to be conflated with "biological descent": "Only in a limiting case is a sociological communality of descent identical with a biological communality of descent [*Blutsverwandtschaft*]. This is because even kinship is socially defined, and thus highly variable."

In defining ethnicity in reference to perceived origins and descent, but including race, language, religion, nationality, or even a joint political history as possible markers of ethnicity, I follow in principle Max Weber's (1976:234–244) brief but complex discussion of ethnicity, which remains unsurpassed in the sociological literature. Weber defines an "ethnic group" as "a group of people who, on the basis of similarities of exterior habitus, of customs, or of both, or of memories of colonization and migration, share a subjective belief in a communality of descent . . . whether an objective consanguinity [*Blutsgemeinsamkeit*] exists or not" (p. 237). This definition stresses the artificial—today one would say *constructed*—quality of ethnicity. The markers (as well as conditioning factors)[9] of ethnicity are multiple and exchangeable—physical traits, language, religion, ways of life or customs, even joint political experiences or struggles in the past *(politische Schicksale)* (p. 238). Conversely, none of these markers per se constitutes ethnicity. For instance, ways of life or customs become explicit only through migrations, wars, or colonial expansion: "The resulting contrast of different ways of life tends to feed the belief of mutual differences of biological descent [*Blutsfremdheit*], quite independently of the objective fact" (p. 240). Most interestingly, Weber stresses the fluidity between political and ethnic conceptions of community: "[T]he political community everywhere tends to create a belief of ethnic communality" (p. 237), a trend he sees confirmed by nothing less than "the entire course of history" (p. 240), from ancient Hellas to the strengthening of subnational state identities in early twentieth-century America. Here is the nucleus for a debunking of the more recent "civic" versus "ethnic" distinction in the nations-and-nationalism literature.

Weber was aware of the price of his notion of ethnicity, which is descent-based yet elastic in its expressions and conditioning factors: it includes "phenomena that a truly exact sociological investigation would have to distinguish carefully" (p. 242). The same holds true for his concept of nation, which he introduces at the tail end of his discussion of ethnicity. The nation shares with ethnicity its "usual" *(normalerweise)* reference to a (variably conditioned and expressed) "communality of descent." A difference is that for the nation the "reference to political power" is constitutive (p. 244); that is, a nation is always allied (or aspiring to be allied) with a state. Conversely, one could infer from this that ethnic groups differ from nations through the more or less conscious "renunciation of power" (p. 243).[10] As previously intimated, Weber anticipates a transcending of the "civic" versus "ethnic" distinction in the nations-and-nationalism literature: a nation *qua* nation is an origin- or descent-based community—this is already implied in the Latin root word *natio*, "something born" (Greenfeld, 1992:4). A non–descent-based "civic nation" is an impossibility, because a nation by definition is an intergenerational unit. David Hollinger, a leading advocate of liberal nationalism in the United States, has acknowledged this in conceding that even the United States is a "'descent-community' of a kind: the kind produced by ethnoracial mixing" (Hollinger, 1998:324).

It is incontrovertible that only the reference to origins and descent makes ethnicity distinct from other cultural formations. This is why gay or other lifestyle cultures are not ethnic; they are not "encompassing" (Margalit and Raz, 1990:448), that is, lacking the power of self-reproduction. However, there is disagreement about the biological component in this. For Weber, common descent clearly meant consanguinity *(Blutsgemeinsamkeit)*. But he immediately pulled the primordial sting by making this more a matter of "subjective belief" than objective fact, and then confining himself, strictly sociologically, to investigating the multiple sociocultural conditioning factors and expressions of such beliefs. By contrast, Pierre Van den Berghe (1981) opted for a biological interpretation of the common-descent core of ethnicity. According to him, ethnicity is an extended form of kinship, geared toward "maximiz[ing] the individual inclusive fitness . . . through the operation of nepotism," and thus it has to be accounted for in terms of nonsociological, genetic behavior (p. 252). This view should not be quickly cast aside for its sociobiological underpinnings. In fact, it tackles head-on the "why ethnicity" question that Weber's constructivist approach carefully avoided and that, perhaps, requires an evolutionary and behavioral explanation that transcends the boundaries of sociology.

However, the drawback of a biological notion of descent is that such "ethnicity" is radically different from the way it is commonly understood today, which is more in terms of cultural belonging and voluntaristic self-identification than of biological pedigree (the debates on "who is a Jew" and "who is an ethnic German" in Chapter 4 will provide ample evidence for this). Donald Horowitz (1975:113–114) has usefully suggested that ethnicity, while "generally acquired at birth," cannot be sharply set apart from "voluntary affiliation" but that both "occupy different positions in a continuum" (p. 114), citing the examples of linguistic or religious conversion. At least, if narrowly defined in terms of biological descent, "ethnicity" would shade into (one way of understanding) "race," which the *OED* notably defined as "[a] group of persons, animals, or plants, connected by common descent or origins"—only here an origins reference appears that had been absent from the *OED*'s definition of *ethnic*. Ever since UNESCO's classic recommendation to use the notion of "ethnic group" in lieu of "race" (1953), there has been a thorough cleansing of all biological or racial connotations from the notion of *ethnic*. If one is looking for an "ethnic group" into which one literally has to be born in order to be considered a member, one is increasingly forced to locate it on the nondeveloped, non-Western periphery (as in Francisco Gil-White's [1999] intriguing account of Mongolians as practicing primordialists). Closer to home, Britain's highest court, the Law Lords in the House of Lords, defined as an "ethnic-origin" group entitled to protection under the 1976 Race Relations Act, in a deliberate distancing from notions of biological ancestry, any group that had a "long shared history" and a "cultural tradition of its own."[11] This broad and cultural definition of ethnicity was actually influenced by the *OED* definition cited in the beginning of this section (Poulter, 1998:304).

The cultural, self-identification turn of ethnicity reflects the rationalist individualism that has come to permeate identity and group formation in contemporary "world society."[12] This trend has also affected material state practices, for instance, the making of the "ethnicity" and "race" entries in the census a matter of self-identification rather than of objective classification by census enumerators (see Kertzer and Arel, 2002). At times this leads to paradoxical results, such as the quadrupling of the U.S. "American Indian" population between 1960 (the first census to use self-identification) and 1990, which certainly is not compatible with the birth and mortality rates of the population in question (Goldscheider, 2002:84). In fact, self-identification undermines the entire ethnicity construct, because one's descent and origin surely constitute the one thing in life that is not subject to choice, "characterizing what the individual *is* rather than what [s]he *does*," as Talcott Parsons (1975:56) put it. The tension between ascription and self-identification is inherent in the notion of ethnicity and perhaps accounts for the notorious difficulties of defining the term, giving all such attempts the air of pointless casuistry. I suggest that the best way to proceed is simply to recognize this tension at the conceptual level and then to investigate how in practice it is differently resolved in different situations (at least this is my procedure in Chapter 4).

Interestingly, some contemporary liberal theorists have defined ethnicity narrowly in terms of biological descent, thus abstracting from its increasingly cultural and voluntaristic connotations. This leads to instructive inconsistencies and contradictions. From such a perspective, ethnicity is set apart as an inborn characteristic from language, religion, or cultural belonging, all of which are in a sense acquired rather than innate. This allows for a distinction between "ethnic" and "cultural" group, and, by implication, between ethnic and cultural nationalism. Acknowledging only chosen, or at least choosable, community is in the interest of rescuing cosmopolitanism (see the good discussion by Eric Kaufmann [2000a]). That course, however, is marred by difficulties. Will Kymlicka (1999:133), for instance, distinguishes between ethnic and cultural nationalism and corresponding models of nationhood, the former defined by descent and closure to the outside, the latter by language and history and a corresponding openness to the outside. As he starkly put it, "descent-based approaches to national membership have obvious racist overtones, and are manifestly unjust" (Kymlicka, 1995:23). This way of putting it has the clear rationale of calling Quebec "in" and calling a (stereotyped) Germany "out" of the universe of liberal nationalism.[13]

However, such a narrow definition of ethnicity, which sets it sharply apart from the cultural realm of language and history, makes the exorcised descent beast strangely reappear in unwanted parts of the theory. In fact, Kymlicka's key concept of "societal culture," which liberal individuals require as a "context of choice," is fundamentally a notion of origins and descent. First, why must it be—as Kymlicka (1995:84–93) insists— "one's *own*" societal culture, and not one, or several, acquired later on in life? His answer is that attachment to this culture is a matter of "belonging, not accomplishment," a "fact" residing "deep in the human condition" (p. 90).[14] In other words, societal culture is ascribed, not achieved, and thus fundamentally a matter of (nonchosen) descent and origins. Furthermore, reference to descent is what distinguishes societal culture from mere lifestyle cultures, which are (quite rightly, in my view) not seen as entitled to minority rights. Only consider Kymlicka's definition of societal culture as "synonymous with 'a nation' or 'a people'—that is, as an intergenerational community more or less institutionally complete, occupying a given territory or homeland, sharing a distinct language and history" (Kymlicka, 1995:18). How can an "intergenerational community," a "people," a "nation" *not* be defined by descent? The reference to descent (and the possibility of biological reproduction and "institutional completeness") is key to Kymlicka's (1998:6) unambiguous "No" to the question "Can Multiculturalism be extended to non-ethnic groups?" Gays cannot reproduce themselves; the deaf can, but then they face the problem of what to do with their nondeaf children; and so on.

The quintessence of this discussion is this: in selecting on the basis of ethnicity, a state selects immigrants on grounds of their perceived descent or origins. Such origin perceptions, however, are broader than in terms of immigrants' biological descent and variably refer to their race, national origins, language, religion, or cultural-historical belonging. In colloquial terms, ethnic selectivity means selecting newcomers on the basis of "where they are coming from" (which is not the same as "of whom they are born").

A further assumption, not discussed so far but self-evident for a meaningful notion of "ethnic," is that these markers are taken by the state as indicators of alleged *intrinsic* characteristics of the individual, making her *as such* more or less worthy to be accepted as an immigrant. Accordingly, the "racial profiling" to which U.S. immigration authorities have recently resorted with respect to Muslim visa applicants does not amount to an ethnically selective immigration policy, at least not in the sense considered in this study. This is because the involved national-origin screening is agnostic about the intrinsic worth of Muslims as an ethnic category and serves the *extrinsic* purpose of identifying potential terrorists that (for probabilistic reasons) are believed to be concentrated in certain populations.[15]

State, Community, and Immigration in Political Theory

Even more than "ordinary" immigration policies, ethnically selective immigration policies inevitably raise normative questions about their legitimacy and permissible scope in a liberal state. A good way to explore these questions is to turn to political theory. Unfortunately, much of the normative-theoretical discussion on immigration policy in the liberal state has centered on the general question of whether the liberal state is entitled at all to restrict the movement of people. Such restriction, as Joseph Carens has most succinctly argued, contradicts the universalistic liberal creed of the equal moral worth of all persons, and drawing a line on the basis of (usually) randomly attributed citizenship would sanction a "modern equivalent of feudal privilege" (Carens, 1987:25). On the opposite side from pure liberalism stand more practically minded liberal theorists, who accept the world as one divided into states and who derive the legitimacy of restricting free movement from the apparent paradox that liberal values can be realized only in bounded settings (see, for example, Wheelan, 1988). In this debate on the general legitimacy of immigration restriction the more relevant question of *what kinds* of selectivity are permissible in the liberal state has faded from view.

Easily the most prominent and influential of all normative reflections on immigration policy is the one by Michael Walzer in his book *Spheres of Justice* (1983). This is a defense not just of the right of states to restrict immigration but also of the nearly unfettered right of state-constituting political communities to select newcomers in their own particular image—which may (but does not have to) imply ethnic selectivity. According to Walzer, individuals derive their sense of self from the particular community in which they grow up—call it their political community. This political community is the site of distributive justice, which is (as canonized by Rawls, 1971) the one criterion for evaluating social and political institutions. Distributive justice does not reach beyond political communities; states, for instance, do not have a moral obligation to take in immigrants. Though usually presupposed, one important good that a community has to distribute is membership itself. Because justice is possible only within a political community, the community's very composition cannot itself be the subject of justice. Accordingly, the admission of new members is constrained only by whatever may be the self-image of the community: "[W]e who are already members do the choosing, in accordance with our own understanding of what membership means in our community and what sort of a community we want to have" (p. 32). Without such sovereign choices, "there could not be *communities of character*, historically stable, ongoing associations of men and women with some special commitment to one another and some special sense of their common life" (p. 62).

Except with respect to settled guest workers, who can claim a "right of place" and have to be admitted into the citizenry as a matter of justice (p. 61), most implications of Walzer's defense of communal self-determination are stunningly illiberal. This is not trivial. The rationale of this type of practical philosophy is to leave the world as it is and, instead of holding the abstract mirror of reason against it, to reconstruct the historical forms of reason and normative justifications that are already in this world. What Walzer indeed captures is the formal principle of state sovereignty according to international law. What he leaves out is the ubiquitousness of liberal constraints on its unfettered exercise—not just in liberalism's historical heartland, the United States, but elsewhere too.

Consider some of Walzer's dubious judgments that flow from his theory yet clearly violate contemporary sensibilities. If the United States had indeed been an Anglo-Saxon nation-state in the 1920s, Walzer speculates at one point, its old regime of selecting immigrants according to their national origins, whose purpose was to exclude southern and eastern Europeans, would have been unobjectionable; only the random fact that "earlier Americans . . . had created a pluralist society" made it an "unjust" policy (p. 40). If this holds true, why does none of the (for Walzer by definition ethnic) "nation-states" of Europe wage such a policy today?[16] Similarly, the "White Australia" policy, whose purpose was to exclude Asians, would be unobjectionable for Walzer if Australia ceded portions of its vast and uninhabited territory: "White Australia could survive only as Little Australia" (Walzer, 1983:47). This was incidentally understood by Australian leaders in terms of their desperate "populate or perish" policy after World War II. As this policy was successful in its own terms (see Chapter 2), why was this not enough to save "White Australia"? Finally, refugees, who are not helped by ceding territory but who are in need of elementary membership itself, have "no right to be successful" (p. 50). When their numbers are small, the principle of "mutual aid" commands the host country to let them in. However, this principle "can only modify and not transform admissions policies rooted in a particular community's understanding of itself" (p. 51). Accordingly, when the numbers are up, "and we are forced to choose among the victims, we will look, rightfully, for some more connection with our way of life" (p. 49). This formulation falls notably short of international refugee and asylum law and practice, in which the very abstraction from communitarian concerns defines the refugee as the Human Being in need of elementary protection.

The problem with Walzer's theory is the assumption that "political communities" do the choosing.[17] This is admittedly a necessary assumption for the purposes of democratic theory. Otherwise a state's decisions could not be democratic. However, as an empirical statement it has at least two shortcomings. First, liberal states are not "owned" by any one political community (for this, see Kymlicka, 2001; Joppke, 2005). Liberal states are also constitutional states, in which the respective political community has self-limited its possible choices in light of universal principles that are considered valid across all political communities. Second, in differentiated, pluralistic societies, there is never a perfect correspondence between the state and any one "community." Instead, there is at best a multiplicity of "communities," divided by multiple markers such as political ideology, culture, and economic interests, to name just a few. The notion of a master "community" united by a "way of life," which stands to be defended at the immigration front, does not adequately describe the fragmented, chaotic, and multiple worlds we live in; it is sociologically naïve. The only agreement one is likely to find in a pluralistic society is on formal procedures and rules, not on substantive forms of living. This rules out the possibility of using an immigration policy for reproducing "our way of life" in anything more than a thin, procedural sense.

In liberal theory, since John Stuart Mill, such concerns have been articulated as the public neutrality obligation of the liberal state. According to this, the liberal state is a state that imposes no conception of the good life on its citizens but allows them to pursue their own goods in their own ways. Among contemporary writers, the most concise formulation of this position is by Ronald Dworkin: "[G]overnment must be neutral on what might be called the question of the good life . . . or of what gives value to life. Since the citizens of a society differ in their conceptions [of the good life], the government does not treat them as equals if it prefers one conception to another, either because the officials believe that one is intrinsically superior, or because one is held by the more numerous or more powerful group" (Dworkin, 1978:127). Note that from this point of view Cardinal Biffi's laconic reference to "the majority" in society does not justify a preference for Catholic immigrants. Note also that Dworkin's statement refers only to the government's treatment of its own citizens. However, one could infer from it that if there is no domestic agreement about the "good life," related concerns of religion, culture, and customs cannot be made a criterion of immigrant selection. This becomes shockingly evident if one compares liberal states with Islamic or Communist states, in which one religious creed or political "truth" ideology, respectively, is made binding for all. Such states never had explicit immigration policies (they do not need such policies, because no one is seeking to immigrate to them), but one may assume that if they had such policies, they would be strictly in the service of reproducing Walzerian "communities of character."

Unfortunately, liberal theory has rarely addressed immigration policy explicitly, presumably because issues of boundary drawing and exclusion have always sat uneasily with its universalistic precepts. No surprise, therefore, that some of liberal theory's first explicit statements on immigration policy entailed the wholesale rejection of any such policy, and a call for "open borders" (Carens, 1987).[18] However, one could equally argue that liberal theory has simply taken for granted that bounded societies, cultures, or nations are its unit of analysis. Rawls (1993:12), for instance, assumes that the liberal principles of freedom and equality are effective only in a "closed society" that people "enter . . . only by birth and leave . . . only by death."[19]

Will Kymlicka (1989a, 1995) was the first to address systematically the relationship between liberalism, on the one hand, and community and culture, on the other, and not just to presume and quickly leave aside the paradox that liberal principles can be realized only in bounded settings, as most liberals had done before him. For Kymlicka, a "societal culture," constituted by language, history, and territory, provides a "context of choice" without which an individual could not make free and meaningful choices: "[F]reedom involves making choices amongst various options, and our societal culture not only provides these options, but also makes them meaningful to us" (Kymlicka, 1995:83). States are the protectors of these cultures. However, a complication arises from the fact that in any given state, because of migrations and colonization, there is likely to be not only one, but a variety of coexisting societal cultures, carried by immigrant and national minority groups. Liberalism's blind spot was to assume a one-to-one correlation between state and culture, which allowed it to relegate the entire topic to the status of an implicit background assumption, but at the cost of ignoring the problem of minorities. If the latter was addressed nevertheless, the traditional liberal answer was "public neutrality": in the public sphere, there were only citizens, subject to the same universal laws, whereas cultural difference was relegated to the private sphere and associational life. For Kymlicka, such "benign neglect" of cultural difference is not enough. The state cannot be culturally neutral; it "unavoidably promotes certain cultural identities and thereby disadvantages others" (p. 198), for instance, through government decisions on official languages, holidays, anthems, flags, and so forth. The analogy sometimes drawn between religion and culture is flawed in his view: the state cannot (and, indeed, should not) dissociate itself from culture in the same manner as it had once dissociated itself from religion. Accordingly, if equality is to prevail, states must endow minorities with special rights to and protection of their culture, in addition to universal citizenship rights.

This theory rests on a problematic assumption, interestingly the same that had already marred Walzer's theory: the assumption that states, even liberal states, are the tool of the majority culture in society, and in this sense unambiguous "nation-states."[20] Contemporary Western states are conceived of as unabashed "nationalizing states" (Brubaker, 1996), much as they were during nineteenth-century industrialism and imperialism, and as they still are in many parts of the world today, forging populations and individuals into linguistic and cultural standard copies of a hypostasized "nation." Is this the world in which homosexual marriages are officially recognized (actually commanded by the neutrality obligation of the liberal state), school curricula are multiculturalized, and—more on the farcical side—a British Foreign Minister sought to improve the electoral chances of his (Labour) party by pronouncing that chicken *tikka masala* had replaced fish and chips as the Britons' favorite dish?

Kymlicka's implicit picture is that of a "pact" with the state: states are granted the right to protect and further majority culture but are asked in turn to grant special rights for minority groups. As he says, "the orthodox liberal view about the right of states to determine who has citizenship rests on the same principles which justify group-differentiated citizenship within states" (p. 124). Only, the premise of this "pact" is faulty. The contemporary liberal state has already ceded most of the "sovereign," classic nation-building prerogatives that are notionally still attributed to it. This raises the question, For what, exactly, are minority group rights to be a compensation (see Joppke, 2001b)? To the degree that Kymlicka's theory of minority rights is not just descriptive but prescriptive, the liberal state is asked to deliver a second time around what it has in fact already delivered; upon watering down the imprints of the majority culture on its forehead, the state shall mark on itself, glaringly, those of the minority groups.[21]

What are the implications of Kymlicka's account of liberal states and culture for immigration policy? More concretely, can the liberal state take culture (and thus ethnicity) into account when selecting immigrants? There is no clear answer. His realism would say "Yes." If "liberal states exist . . . also to protect people's cultural membership," as he concedes in a defense of "some limits on immigration" (Kymlicka, 1995:125), why couldn't the ensuing "limiting" measures take into account that some immigrants are closer to, while others are more distant from, the particular societal culture that is subject to protection, and favor the former over the latter? This is simply the price to pay for the "pact" with the Gellnerian nation-building state. However, the opposite answer is possible too. Kymlicka, after all, is a liberal, who previously had even defended a version of the "liberal neutrality" principle (1989b). There he had stressed the autonomy of the "cultural marketplace" against the imposition of "good ways of life" by the "perfectionist state" (p. 895): "Neutrality requires a certain faith in the operation of nonstate forums and processes for individual judgment and cultural development, and a distrust of the operation of state forums and processes for evaluating the good" (p. 899). In this context, he distinguishes between the "structure" and the "character" of a culture, the first referring to the essential principles without which a culture would cease to exist, and the latter to their historically variable incarnations (Kymlicka, 1989a:164–178).[22] Crucially, only cultural structure provides a "context of choice" and stands to be protected by the state, whereas in a liberal setting the concrete and historically variable "character" of a culture can only be the "product of people's choices" (p. 178), which requires the state to stay out.

What does this mean concretely? Consider the example of Quebec. Before the "Quiet Revolution" in the 1960s, French-Canadian culture was Catholic, rural, and traditionalist. Not much of this is left today, even though a Quebecois identity continues to exist, to say the least. As a result of people's choices, French-Canadian culture's "character" has changed, while its "structure" has remained the same. However, this cultural structure is so thin—excluding virtually no one as long as she bows to the "French Fact" (see Carens, 1995:24)—that by implication the scope for bolstering this culture through the state's immigration policy is severely limited too. In Quebec's autonomous immigration policy more points are awarded for French- than for English-language competence, in contrast to their equal consideration at federal level. Only such a weak form of ethnic selectivity seems to be endorsed by Kymlicka (1989b:903), when he argues that "immigration policy should give consideration to the consequences of immigration on the cultural structure." However, what this means outside the highly particular context of Quebec—an assertive minority nation within a multinational state, unambiguously defined by the French Fact—is unclear. What if religion, not language, constitutes a culture's "structure," as Cardinal Biffi (however wrongly) suggested for the case of Italy? Moreover, who decides what is invariable "structure," how can it be clearly delineated from variable "character," and can there ever be agreement?

Due to this ambivalence in Kymlicka's normative theory, both a defense and a rejection of ethnically selective immigration policies are equally possible on its basis (for a defense, see Coleman and Harding,

1995; for a rejection, see Perry, 1995). A pragmatic middle position, which perhaps reflects best how ethnic selectivity is actually processed in liberal states, has been proposed by Joseph Carens (1992). It is in principle legitimate to "preserve a distinct culture or way of life" (p. 25) by means of a culturally or ethnically selective immigration policy.[23] However, two additional conditions must be met. First, this culture must be "compatible with respect for all human beings as free and moral persons" (p. 37). Carens thus puts his finger on a central problem in Kymlicka's theory, which presumes that any culture, as long as it qualifies as "societal," could serve as a "context of choice" and thus be subject to legitimate state support. But what about illiberal cultures? How could they be at the service of individual "choice" if their whole point is to destroy freedom of choice?[24] Second, cultural or ethnic selectivity should not be "a disguised form of racial or ethnic prejudice" (p. 44), that is, it should be positive, never negative. Accordingly, for Carens the context decides whether ethnic migration is legitimate from a liberal point of view. For British patriality his answer is "no," because it implies the exclusion of (nonwhite) New Commonwealth immigrants; for the "grandparent" clause in Irish citizenship law the answer is "yes," because here no one is excluded or discriminated against by readmitting the third-generation descendants of Irish emigrants. Carens reasonably eschews a priori judgments and thus builds a bridge to the empirical investigation of concrete cases of ethnic migration in liberal states. However, one still might argue that the Irish case is rather exceptional and that it would be difficult to come up with more cases of ethnic migration that pass the liberal test (as defined by Carens)— it would require finding a country with a (minimally) liberal culture and not sought out by any other but the ethnically favored migrants.[25]

What does this discussion of normative political theory leave us with? First, there is no agreement, not even among liberal theorists, sometimes not even within the same liberal theorist, on the normative status of ethnic selectivity in immigration policy. No one has really thought it through, and scattered reflections on ethnic selectivity appear only at the margins of other concerns, most notably about the status of minority cultures in liberal states. But perhaps an a priori judgment is the wrong thing to strive for. I take this to be Carens's useful suggestion: seek a judgment within the individual case, not across cases or before any one case.[26] States in the real world have in any case always deviated from the precepts of political theory. Liberal rules are multiply violated even by unambiguously liberal states, and this in the pursuit of putatively liberal goals, as Desmond King (1999) has incisively shown, in his investigation of illiberal social policies in the United States and Britain at the twentieth century's beginning and end. While King may overstate the degree in which illiberal policies "appear to be part of liberalism itself" (p. 27), one should not be surprised to find illiberal elements in a policy that is already notionally at odds with pure liberalism: the state's immigration policy.

In this spirit, the purpose of the following analysis is not to evaluate violations of, or a correspondence with, liberal precepts from the vantage point of normative theory, but to identify, empirically and from a sociological point of view, the justifications, mechanisms, and pressures surrounding ethnic migration. This empirical analysis will show that ethnic migration has appeared in radically different guises, some more, others less reconcilable with liberal principles.

The "Nationhood" and "Liberal State" Vectors of Immigration Policy

The foregoing discussion of normative theory revealed one dead end of conceptualizing immigration policy: as reflective of the self-definition of a political community or nation. One could call this the "nationhood" model of immigration policy. It stipulates that "ethnic" nations have ethnic immigration policies, whereas "civic" nations have nonethnic, universalistic immigration policies (most explicitly in Coleman and Harding, 1995:48–51).[27] This nationhood model is misleading in several respects. First, it suffers from what Rogers Brubaker has aptly called "realism of the group": "the social ontology that leads us to talk and write about ethnic groups and nations as real entities, as communities, as substantial, enduring, internally homogenous and externally bounded collectivities" (Brubaker, 1998a:292). There are no such "groups" acting in society, neither "minority" nor "majority," but only competing entrepreneurs and organizations seeking to create and act on behalf of such collectivities, employing the assets, resources, and symbols that are differently developed and arranged in different social spheres or fields.[28] A "political community" or "nation" not only does not exist anywhere, it is also a potentially illiberal idea, because it conceives of the society as one and undivided, a "personality writ large" in Ruth Benedict's terms (1934).

Problematic also is the nationhood model's main tack on ethnic migration, according to which the latter is a prerogative of "ethnic nations," whereas "civic nations" have a universalistic immigration policy. As intimated earlier, the distinction between "ethnic" and "civic," if reified as markers of entire nations that are either one or the other, is misleading (among the many good recent critiques of the ethnic-civic distinction, see Peters, 2002). All nations are fundamentally defined by descent and origins; this makes them different from, say, class, age, sex, or lifestyle as alternative (and often competing) forms of allegiance and group organization. Conversely, all nations have a "civic" element, because they are by definition associations of strangers that transcend the immediate kinship nexus. Nevertheless, a "civic nation" as being voluntary and contractual only, without reference to origins, is a fiction, meaningful only in the polemical contrast with an "ethnic nation." At a minimum, the ethnic component comes in through the "diachronic continuity" that is a necessary component of any nation (Das Gupta, 1975:467). Consider that the purpose of Ernest Renan's famous notion of the civic nation as the "plebiscite of all days" had been to reject Germany's rivaling claims for Alsace and Lorraine, which had only the objective reference to German language and culture going for it, but crucially *not* the expressed will of the people living there. Outside of this polemical contrast, Renan was well aware that "*two* things" made the nation, not just the (civic) "consent" of the present, but also the (lastly ethnic) "memories" of the past: "The nation, like the individual, is the culmination of a long past of endeavors, sacrifice, and devotion" (quoted in Yack, 1996:198).

Even if one retains the distinction between civic and ethnic nation for the sake of argument, the confining of ethnic migration to "ethnic" nations would face empirical difficulties. As we shall see, proverbially "civic" nations such as France, Britain, or the United States had ethnically selective immigration policies too (see Chapters 2 and 3), and the proverbially "ethnic" nation, Germany, has in principle phased out its open-door policy for "ethnic Germans" from Eastern Europe and Russia (see Chapter 4). The only way of accounting for these anomalies within the nationhood model is to allow for the coexistence of ethnic and civic strands in any one nation and then to relate policy changes to shifts in the ethnic-civic balance. In this vein, one could argue that the phaseout of ethnic migration in Germany reflects a gradual strengthening of civic over ethnic nationhood after World War II (see Levy, 1999); for the U.S. case, one could argue on the opposite that its pre–World War II national-origins regime reflected a moment in which an ethnic conception of nationhood had taken precedence over a civic conception. Such reasoning is possible, but it faces the pitfall of being post hoc and circular: the respective prevalence of ethnic or civic strands of nationhood is read from the rise or fall of ethnic migration, which—in turn—is explained by the prevailing strand of nationhood.

Instead of construing a symmetry between types of nationhood and immigration policy, a more adequate root image is to assume a built-in tension between universalistic and particularistic elements in all liberal nation-states, the liberal component commanding nonascriptive, universalistic criteria and equity in the selection of immigrants, the national component (sometimes) commanding the opposite, in the name of reproducing the particular beliefs that constitute a political community. Nationhood and liberal stateness are then seen as vectors that impinge on immigration policies, *countervailing* vectors if an ethnic understanding of the nation prevails, *conjoint* vectors if a civic one is dominant. Bringing in the factor of liberal stateness helps account for the general trend toward nondiscriminatory immigration policies across all types of nations (the predominantly "ethnic" as much as the predominantly "civic"), as a result of which ethnic selectivity will always be a critically guarded and strenuously justified exception.

What is it in the liberal state that conflicts with ethnic selectivity? First, there is the principle of public neutrality. In contrast to the former Communist states or some contemporary Islamic states, liberal states are agnostic vis à vis truth doctrines and substantive forms of living or cultures (of which ethnicity is one important expression), except the very thin and procedural culture that goes along with liberalism itself. One can observe that liberal states, even at the point of distributing citizenship, no longer require immigrants to become "assimilated" in a cultural sense, except in the procedural sense of accepting the rules of liberal democracy. Where thick cultural screening is ruled out internally, its external maintenance would be contradictory. The public neutrality principle rules out the possibility of ranking and selecting immigrants according to their ethnic fit with the domestic population. At least this cannot be done in the open, because public discourse has become constricted in this respect. Stephen Holmes spoke in this context of "gag rules" by means of which liberal democracies remove from the public agenda "certain emotionally charged and rationally irresolvable issues" (Holmes, 1995:10). In the field of immigration policy, Gary Freeman (1995a) called the "antipopulist norm" a gag rule that prohibits "argument over the ethnic composition of migrant streams" (p. 884). Pointing to the end of ethnically selective immigration policies in the English-speaking settler states, Freeman argues: "Having foregone the prerogative to control the ethnic composition of flows, elites in these countries adopted the position that questions about the wisdom of the unselected flows that resulted from universalism were illegitimate as well" (ibid., n. 4).

This raises the interesting question of whether such constrained discourse is a structural feature of liberal-democratic states, as Freeman (1995a) argues, or whether it is only "a historically specific and contingent feature of public discussion at certain times and places," as Brubaker (1995:905) suggested against Freeman. Here one has to consider that the ethnic selectivity discussed by both is only the primarily negative selectivity of the settler states, which stigmatized and excluded certain groups on grounds of their ethnicity, race, or national origins. The discussion does not refer to the more resilient cases of positive selectivity, in which presumed coethnics are granted privileged treatment, as in the Israeli or German Laws of Return. This adds plausibility to Freeman's (1995b) "Tocquevillian" response to Brubaker, according to which a return from universalism to ethnic selection would contradict the "forces of equality and individualism" that are constantly gaining ground in liberal democracies (p. 909). Indeed, negative ethnic selectivity has so fundamentally been stamped out, with no example left in contemporary Western states, that this is unlikely to be merely "a cultural-political story about particular times and places" (Brubaker, 1995:905). While the temptation to go populist is always there in immigration matters, the terrain for this is increasingly narrow: "Appeals to ethnic bases of identity, national hierarchies and racial homogeneity, easy and natural before 1945, are now politically unacceptable" (Hansen, 2001). We shall see that even positive ethnic selectivity did not remain immune from this trend. Although its origins are certainly contingent, the antipopulist norm has come to resonate with the ethos of liberal democracy and thus is revocable only at the price of a wholesale civilization break or regression.

The effectiveness of the antipopulist norm is not negated by Kymlicka's observation that the liberal state is not, and cannot be, culturally neutral (1995, ch. 6). Neutrality is never the *is* condition but always the *ought to* imperative of liberal states. As historically particular states, identified by a name and history that do not happen twice in the world, even liberal states are necessarily couched in particular cultures and ways of life. However, this does not imply that the reproduction of this particularity can become the measure of the state's immigration policy. If the state risks immigration, its cultural particularism is at risk too—there is nothing the liberal state can do about it. When conceding the impossibility of cultural neutrality, Kymlicka does not sufficiently distinguish between the state's minimalist "by default" preferencing and a maximalist "by design" preferencing of the majority culture—if the former inevitably occurs, a license for the latter does not necessarily follow. Applied to immigration, conceding that complete cultural neutrality is impossible does not entail the legitimacy of culturally or ethnically selective immigration policies.

A second, closely related (even implied) component of the liberal state that conflicts with ethnic selectivity is the principle of equality. Whereas the public neutrality principle is a "pull" factor emanating from the nature of the liberal state itself, the equality principle is a "push" factor emanating from societies that, under the roof of liberal states, are necessarily pluralistic and pluralizing—as a result of previous immigration, for example. The public neutrality constraint is to a certain degree raised on the liberal theorist's armchair, multiply violated in the real world, and marred by the paradox of asking the state to abstract itself from the ethnic group whose name it—most of the times—carries. By contrast, equality concerns have been unambiguously central to all concrete episodes in which ethnic migration has come under pressure or has even been phased out. In the United States, the descendants of southern and eastern European immigrants revolted in the mid-1960s against the racially motivated national-origin quotas that prioritized British, German, and Scandinavian over all other immigrants. In Britain, the liberal advocates of nonwhite New Commonwealth immigrants attacked the racially discriminatory "patriality" provision in British immigration law, which prioritized the descendants of white Old Commonwealth settlers. In the German case, liberal opinion turned against the privileged entry of "ethnic Germans" from Russia and southeastern Europe, when—in the early 1990s—asylum seekers began to be excluded through a restriction of the constitutional asylum clause and the children and grandchildren of Turkish guest workers continued to be excluded by a blood-based citizenship law. And so on. Once a society is ethnically heterogeneous and individuals of many an ethnic origin knock on its doors, the state's ethnic preference-setting loses its innocence and becomes socially scandalized.

If one looks closely, one sees that there are two different reference groups for the equality norm: citizens (or residents) in domestic society and "other migrants" as subset of the universe of all human beings. Depending on which is the reference group, the liberal opposition to ethnic migration is couched in different terms: in communitarian membership terms if citizen or resident interests or identities are affected; in abstract human-rights terms if migrants are capriciously excluded because of presumed inherent ethnic or racial characteristics. Good examples for these different reference possibilities are the U.S. and Australian oppositions to ethnoracial immigration policies in the 1960s. In the United States, significant domestic citizen interests and identities were affected by the national-origin regime, as the sizeable group of descendants of southern and eastern European immigrants saw their ethnic identities denigrated and their family-reunion interests harmed by a policy that prioritized northern and western Europeans. By contrast, White Australia had been uniquely successful in *preventing* the ethnic pluralizing of domestic society that could then become the basis for citizen-based equality claims. Consequently, the opposition to White Australia, next to being motivated by a pragmatic foreign-policy rationale, was led in abstract human-rights terms, not in the concrete terms that this was a policy that hurt citizens. This partially explains the relative longevity of White Australia, because even its liberal critics found this to be a policy that was *less* pernicious than a policy (such as the American one) that discriminated against a part of domestic society.

Whatever the reference group is—citizens or "other migrants"—one sees in these real-world conflicts that the immigration and naturalization domain *is* subject to perceived and acted-upon justice considerations, even though this domain is peopled by noncitizens and nonresidents whose treatment is generally deemed exempt from such considerations. An often-quoted license for the exemption of immigration and naturalization from justice considerations is Article 1(3) of the UN Convention on the Elimination of All Forms of Racial Discrimination. It states that nothing in the Convention "may be interpreted as affecting in any way the legal provisions of States Parties concerning nationality, citizenship or naturalization, provided that such provisions do not discriminate against any particular nationality." This free pass on immigration and naturalization explicitly excludes only direct negative discrimination, presumably of the racial kind. However, we will see that the realm of the permissible in a liberal state is much more narrowly drawn, excluding (via effective sociopolitical mobilization) also positive discriminations that produce concrete losers, especially in domestic society.

Forms and Features of Ethnic Migration

Ethnic migration has appeared in a variety of forms, with sharply differing (1) discriminatory directions, (2) justifications, (3) selection mechanisms and legal infrastructures, and (4) pressures and types of conflict surrounding it. Explicating these dimensions will provide us with a classificatory grid for the concrete cases to be investigated in this study and will help us understand why some instances of ethnic migration have proved more resilient or compatible with the exigencies of liberal stateness than others.

1. The most fundamental distinction is with respect to the *discriminatory direction* underlying the policy: positive or negative. An example of negative selectivity is the exclusion of Asian immigrants, which has been explicitly or implicitly practiced in most settler states well into the mid-1960s.[29] Of course, it is meaningless to speak of "ethnic migration" here, because the whole point of the underlying policy was *not* to make it happen. However, the exclusion of some (Asian) ethnic groups has always been accompanied by the inclusion of other (European-origin) groups, which occurred likewise on ethnic or racial grounds. In this sense the settler states' immigration policies, though they were primarily negatively selective, have still generated ethnic migration. In contrast to negatively selective policies, which target specific groups for exclusion, positively selective policies operate on a floor of equal treatment for all noncitizens (or aliens), from which positive derogations are made for certain ethnic or national-origin groups. Prominent examples of this type are the German and Israeli Laws of Return, which provide automatic access to territory and citizenship to ethnic Germans and Jews (see Chapter 4); less prominent, though no less interesting, examples are privileged immigration and nationality rules for "Hispanic" (Ibero-American) and "Lusophone" (Portuguese-speaking) immigrants in Spain and Portugal, respectively (see Chapter 3).

Both types of ethnic immigration policies are evidently made from starkly different moral cloth, and they have sharply different survival chances in a liberal state. We will see that the legacy of negative selectivity in the settler states has cast a long shadow on all cases of positive selectivity too. Conversely, the positively selective policies of some European states have never been marred by a similar legacy of racial exclusion, which helps explain their relative longevity.

However, the distinction between positive and negative selectivity is not as watertight as many have claimed (see, for example, Weil, 1998; Carens, 1992). In the orthodox view, only negative selections, whereby a concrete group is singled out for exclusion, are to be rejected on liberal grounds, whereas positive selections, if operating on a floor of equality, are not just justifiable but in effect practiced everywhere. This distinction is not as clean and clear as it seems. The reverse side of prioritizing some is discriminating against all others, particularly in the European context of zero-immigration policies sitting on top of ethnically pluralized societies. As Thomas Sowell (1983:161) put it, "'[p]references' and 'discrimination' are . . . simply the same act expressed in different words. Preferences for A, B, and C constitute discrimination against X, Y, and Z." If the Portuguese government decides to legalize preferentially illegal immigrants from Portuguese-speaking countries (as it did twice in the 1990s), this constitutes de facto discrimination against non–Portuguese-speaking immigrants. Conversely, the negatively selective immigration policies of the settler states, which are now routinely (and rightly) branded as "racist," busily tried to present themselves as positively selective. Witness that the notorious "White Australia" policy indicated who was to be in, not who was to be kept out, even though the exclusion of Asians was its primary intention. In the U.S. national-origins system, the intent of negative selection, to the degree that it was directed against unwanted southern and eastern European immigrants, was even less visible, because newcomers were positively selected on the basis of the relative representation of their respective nationality group at a certain point in time. In this sense, most ethnically selective immigration policies have presented themselves as positively selective policies, even if their primary intent was the exclusion of particular groups.

2. Regarding *justifications*, the fundamental distinction is between ethnic migration as in the interest of the receiving society, or as based on a right on part of the ethnic migrant. According to the first, ethnic migration is justified in terms of its easier "assimilability" to domestic society. This was the main justification of the national-origins regime in place in the United States between 1924 and 1965. On the opposite side, some policies of ethnic migration are couched in the language of individual rights. Examples for this are the German and Israeli Laws of Return, which invest some immigrants with constitutional (Germany) or natural law entitlements (Israel). Of course, the existence of "rights" as such does not yet answer the question how these rights are justified. One prominent justification, found especially in the German and Israeli cases, is the assumption that coethnics abroad are subject to "persecution," which triggers a moral-historical claim to protection by their homeland state.

Underlying these different (assimilationist versus rights-based) justifications is a different phenomenology of immigrants in both cases. In the assimilationist discourse, immigrants are conceived of as culturally or ethnically "similar to" but essentially different from the state-bearing nation; in the rights-based discourse, immigrants are conceived of in terms of "sameness" and a priori membership in the state-bearing nation. We shall see that both justifications are differently resilient in liberal states. Assimilationist justifications and the related immigration policies blatantly violate contemporary "multicultural" sensibilities and have mostly succumbed to the verdict of "discrimination" or "racism." By contrast, rights-based justifications and related immigration policies, as they make the individual and her need for elementary protection key, are fully compatible with liberal-state principles and thus have proved more resistant to attack.

Next to the assimilationist and rights-based justifications, there is a third way of justifying ethnic migration: to give expression to a historical-cultural community that encompasses more than one state. States (and individuals *qua* membership in these states) are the constitutive units of this "panethnic" community.[30] This communitarian justification can be found in the historical context of (some versions of) European colonialism, in which the settlement of Europeans in (presumably) uncharted lands overseas has led to a transfer of language and culture, as well as the creation of genealogical ties, that call for expression even after the formal independence of the new settlements. In pure form, in which the individual-rights dimension especially is rather submerged, the notion of state-transcending community can be found in the Spanish and Portuguese justifications of immigration policies and nationality laws that give preference to Ibero-Americans and Lusophones, respectively.

It is important to see that these justifications often overlap in concrete cases. In the Spanish case, for instance, governments have often mixed communitarian and assimilationist justifications of prioritizing Ibero-American immigrants, while some Spanish courts have interpreted bilateral conventions as creating rights for some Ibero-American immigrants against a lately more restriction-minded government. In the German and Israeli cases, presumed membership in a state-transcending ethnic community is of course the condition for invoking the constitutional right to immigrate, though the strong individual-rights component is grounded in the additional assumption that the individual is "persecuted" for her coethnicity; and in its latest version the ethnic German immigration policy became heavily influenced by assimilation concerns that had not originally been a part of it. And so on. Fluidity and lack of explicitness regarding their justifications have been a mark of many ethnic immigration policies, with the exception perhaps of those that pertain to what I shall call the "diaspora" constellation (including Germany and Israel).

3. Regarding *selection mechanisms* and *legal infrastructures,* some ethnic immigration policies select on citizenship (in the formal sense of state membership) or country of birth, whereas others select on ethnicity proper. Both are difficult to do for the liberal state, because they force the latter "to define and constitute social groups" (Starr, 1992:156), something that the liberal state usually leaves to the free play of society. However, even more difficult than citizenship- or country-of-birth–based screening is ethnicity-based screening, because it drags the state into the murky terrain of examining individual "identity" claims. By contrast, selecting on citizenship or country of birth is categorical and generic, based on the simple presence or absence of the requisite state membership (or birth certificate). This raises the question of whether such citizenship-based screening has any ethnic component at all. The answer is, It depends. States have always entered into special contractual relations with other states, based on the international law principle of reciprocity, granting "most favored nation" status also to states not linked by historical and cultural ties, out of sheer self-interest and "reasons of state." An early example of an obviously nonethnic preference regime is the 1868 Burlingame Treaty between the United States and China, which (among other things) established reciprocal free movement rights for U.S. and Chinese citizens (and was infamously abrogated by the 1882 Chinese Exclusion Act). By contrast, the reciprocity formula that underlies the Portuguese and Spanish preference regimes for citizens of Lusophone and Ibero-American states, respectively, has certainly injected these regimes with an element of self-interest, namely to protect Portuguese and Spanish emigrants in the contracting states. However, I shall demonstrate that this nonethnic dimension of reciprocal privileges is nested within essentially panethnic constructs of state-transcending community in both cases.

Closely linked to the distinction between citizenship-based and ethnicity-based screening are fundamentally different understandings and uses of ethnicity: some ethnic immigration policies select immigrants according to their putative *proximity* to (but essential difference from) the state-bearing nation, whereas others select according to the putative *sameness* of immigrant group and state-bearing nation. Examples of selection based on proximity are the U.S. national-origins quotas and the informal ethnic hierarchies in early postwar French immigration policy, which selected immigrants on the basis of their assimilability to the host society. Examples of selection based on sameness are the Laws of Return favoring ethnic Germans and Jews, who are believed to be not similar to but identical with the state-bearing nations.

In between proximity and sameness are the Spanish and Portuguese ethnic immigration regimes. Max Weber argued that "memories of colonization and migration" were a major factor in feeding a "subjective belief in a communality of descent" (1976:237). Portugal and Spain are good examples of this, helped by unique colonial histories that included a mixing and blending between colonials and colonized. Lusophone and Hispanic immigrants are defined as "same" via membership in a state-transcending community yet also as "different" via membership in another state (after all, a certain foreign citizenship triggers a preference claim). Lusophony and Hispanism are panethnic constructs, denoting in Weber's terms a broadly defined "communality of descent." However, this does not mean that the Portuguese and Spanish states were not capable of distinguishing more or less clearly between these panethnic schemes and ethnic-return schemes proper, which target the descendants of former emigrants and generally offer more advantages than the former (for the case of Spain, see Joppke, 2003:452–454).[31]

The following chapters will reveal that ethnic proximity constructs proved less tenable in the liberal state than ethnic sameness constructs. Whereas it would be impossible for a state today to select immigrants according to an ethnic rank-order (with citizenship or country of birth as proxy), as the settler states did well into the 1960s, the German and Israeli Laws of Return are still in place (though the former in starkly reduced form). The decline of ethnic proximity constructs is an indicator for the increasing de-ethnicization of contemporary states: states no longer stand for homogenous collectivities, and inferences from membership in a state to the quality and behavior of the individual are now considered improper and stigmatizing, at least in liberal opinion (see Chapter 5). Intrastate ethnic differences have both increased and become legitimate in the guise of multiculturalism and minority rights, whereas interstate ethnic differences have decreased and lost the legitimacy they once enjoyed in the guise of nationalism.

Within his formal sociology, Georg Simmel captured this in the "phenomenological formula" that "the elements of a differentiated circle are undifferentiated, [whereas] those of an undifferentiated circle are differentiated" (Simmel, 1992:797–798). To the degree that a society becomes more differentiated, Simmel argues, the "individualism" of its parts increases (as well as their contacts with similar parts in other societies—called "transnationalism" today), whereas as bounded units all societies increasingly come to resemble one another and in this sense lose their collective personality. In this optic, the delegitimation of nationalism in contemporary liberal states, and of an immigration policy that treats individuals as standard copies of a national "personality writ large" (Benedict, 1934), is the result of the increasing differentiation of society.

4. Finally, what can we say about the types of *pressure* and *conflict* surrounding ethnic migration? A distinct feature of ethnic migration is its susceptibility to a "liberal" challenge, in which the inequity between differently privileged immigrant groups and minority groups within the citizenry is contested. Particularly in the context of ethnic-sameness schemes, the state often seeks to deflect this challenge by denying that "immigration" is occurring at all, preferring to speak instead of the "return" of coethnics. Relabeling the latter as "immigration" is thus part and parcel of the liberal challenge, because it creates the possibility of comparing coethnic with other, less privileged immigrants. The liberal often comes in conjunction with a "restrictive" challenge that addresses the fact that ethnic migration is still *immigration* that entails economic or cultural costs for (usually disadvantaged groups of) domestic society. Although their thrusts are obviously different, there is always the possibility of odd coalitions between liberal and restrictive challengers, and where ethnic migration schemes have been visibly knocked down, such odd coalitions have often been key to it—such as in (one round of) the British patriality debate, or in the 1990s restrictions of ethnic German immigration.

While the possibility of a liberal challenge is shared by all instances of ethnic migration, the latter differ regarding the site and level at which pressure is generated. The fundamental watershed for the rise of the liberal challenge has been the discrediting of racism after World War II. Before Nazism and the Holocaust, it was legitimate for states to be guardians of ethnic homogeneity and racial exclusivity, often in combination with "high modernist" ambitions of "engineering whole societies" (Scott, 1998:91); thereafter, this sort of reasoning was no longer legitimate. Moral universalism and the eschewing of ethnic and racial discrimination became institutionalized in an international human-rights regime under the auspices of the United Nations Organization. This has led some scholars to argue that the pressures toward universalistic immigration policies and immigrant rights have mostly been external, originating from the norms and actors of the international regime (Soysal, 1994). There is much to this view, but it neglects the domestic resources, mechanisms, and justifications that push toward universalistic and nondiscriminatory policies.[32] In the United States, for instance, Chinese exclusion was abolished because China had become a military ally during World War II, and the national-origins regime was pincered by the domestic "civil" (not "human"!) rights revolution and foreign policy concerns, which made this regime an obstacle to America's global leadership aspirations. The focus on domestic mechanisms (including foreign-policy interests) is not to deny that, especially today, the prohibition of racial discrimination is first and foremost an international human-rights norm. However, initially it was not this way. As Chapter 2 will show, not an international regime but domestic society pressures led to the demise of settler states' ethnoracial immigration policies.

The role of domestic-level pressure is even more pronounced in the case of positively discriminatory immigration policies, in whose contestation universal human-rights considerations are almost entirely absent. In a world of porous borders and intensified and diversified migrations, positive discriminations are bound to produce losers, in terms of similarly situated migrant and minority groups that do not partake in the privileges bestowed on the preferred group(s). This is the moment in which such policies come under pressure. In this case, even more than in that of negatively discriminatory policies, not the top-down pressure of an international human-rights regime but the bottom-up pressure emanating from group conflict in domestic society has pushed states toward de-ethnicized and liberalized membership policies.

Finally, there is a third site and level of pressure on ethnic migration, which may result from the supranational integration between states, especially in Europe. As we shall see, neither international human-rights norms nor domestic equality pressures but the Europeanization of the immigration function has forced Portugal and Spain to cut down their panethnic ties to the Hispanic and Lusophone worlds. One could of course argue that the European free-movement regime, which privileges the citizens of member states, is yet another case of ethnic migration. However, at the moment of its creation it was certainly not perceived this way. As we will show in the British and Portuguese cases, states gave in to the European immigration regime for the sake of economic "interest," not of cultural "identity." The proverbial absence of a European identity has been nowhere more visible than in the reluctance of Britain and Portugal to grant to other Europeans the privileged status that had previously been granted to Old Commonwealth or Lusophone immigrants.

Case Selection

Ethnic migration has appeared in at least three distinct geographic-historical constellations: settler state, postcolonial, and diaspora.[33] Each of these constellations is covered in this book along a detailed analysis of several national cases, in order to capture both between- and within-type variations of ethnic migration.

The *settler state* constellation, discussed along the examples of the United States and Australia, refers to the racially motivated immigration policies in place until the mid-1960s and early 1970s, respectively (Chapter 2). The chapter discusses how and why such policies were set up at the turn of the twentieth century and what brought them down after World War II. After the turn to source-country universalism, concerns about the ethnic or racial texture of immigration can be raised only in muted and indirect forms, as I show in a section on contemporary challenges to what is called in these states "nondiscriminatory" immigration policies. The case of Australia serves as an important control. Australia never adhered to a "civic" model of nationhood but, instead, understood itself well into the early 1970s as the implantation of ethnically conceived British nationhood on new soil. If it nevertheless abandoned its White Australia policy, other factors than "civic" nationhood have to be responsible for this. Incidentally, I shall show that foreign policy and liberal neutrality and equality concerns similar to those in the United States have been driving the abolition of White Australia.

The *postcolonial* constellation in Europe is perhaps the most complex of all three, because it ranges from the rejection to the embracing of postcolonial immigrants in ethnic terms (Chapter 3). I seek to capture these extremes with the distinction between "northwestern" and "southwestern" constellations. In the northwestern constellation (Britain and France), postcolonial immigrants were generally rejected in ethnic terms and accepted only for the political interest in retaining empire. By contrast, the distinct mark of the southwestern constellation (Spain and Portugal) is that postcolonial immigrants were perceived as belonging to a state-transcending historical-cultural community and were embraced in the panethnic terms of Hispanism or Lusophony. These other European empires and their panethnic approach to postcolonial immigration have so far escaped scholarly attention, especially in the English-speaking world.

Most commonly associated with the notion of ethnic migration is the *diaspora* constellation, in which perceived coethnics are lastingly stranded as precarious or oppressed minority groups in other states (Chapter 4). This is also the most resilient of all three constellations, resonating with self-definitions of receiving states as national homelands of their diasporas abroad, and endowing the latter with the right of "return." The Israeli-German comparison is attractive for obvious historical reasons, but also because in one case (Germany) diaspora migration has come to be severely restricted, while in the other case it continues unabated. I shall argue that, because of the religiously closed, nonterritorial self-definition of the titular nation and the deep division of society, Israel is a limiting case of a liberal state; it is certainly the only state discussed in this book that remains firmly and formally committed to an exclusively ethnic immigration.

A concluding chapter reconsiders why some types and instances of ethnic migration are more resilient than others. Instead of stating a linear decline of ethnic migration in the liberal state, I conceive of the contemporary liberal state as in the crossfire of countervailing trends and forces, some pushing for its "de-ethnicization," others instead pushing for its "re-ethnicization." The latter tendency guarantees that certain types of ethnic migration will continue to exist in the future, but within liberal constraints.

2

Toward Source-Country Universalism in Settler States: The United States and Australia

The states that were born as Anglo-European overseas settlements, most notably the United States, Canada, and Australia, are today firmly committed to nondiscriminatory immigration policies, eschewing the selection of immigrants along ethnic, racial, or national origin criteria. However, they arrived at the now dominant principle of "source-country universalism,"[1] according to which immigrants are selected as individuals and not as representatives of ascriptive groups or countries and regions, only after having most blatantly violated it, in the form of racially exclusive immigration policies that were put in place in the late nineteenth century and lasted well into the second half of the twentieth century.[2]

This chapter discusses the rise and demise of racially exclusive immigration policies in the American and Australian cases. These cases are especially interesting, because—underneath the common Anglo-European origins—both countries are set apart by sharply distinct immigration experiences, political developments, and ensuing national self-definitions. The United States was built by highly diverse (though predominantly European) migration flows and gained political independence at an early stage—it is "the first new nation" (Lipset, 1963). By contrast, Australia is a predominantly British settlement that lacks a political founding myth and has remained a loyal member of the British Commonwealth to the present day.[3] In preferring Britons as immigrants, Australia has been somewhat like Israel, which sees itself as an ethnic state of Jews. An ethnically selective immigration policy is thus fundamentally aligned with an ethnic nation-building project: "The fundamental reason for the adoption of the White Australia policy is the preservation of a British-Australian nationality," says a classic study on the subject (Willard, 1923:188–189). Conversely, the parallel American policy has subsequently been denounced as a fundamental aberration from an essentially nonethnic, political project of American nation building. "[W]e cannot be true to the democratic faith of our own Declaration of Independence in the equality of all men and at the same time pass immigration laws which discriminate among people because of national origin, race, color or creed," argues an influential government report in the early 1950s (President's Commission on Immigration and Naturalization, [1952] 1971:xiv).

This linking of immigration policy with national self-definition is not just an academic construct but has arguably been present in the mindset of policy-making and -contesting elites. However, it raises two obvious questions: Why did the United States set up an ethnic immigration policy at the start; and why did Australia give it up eventually? With respect to the first question, one must realize that the United States did only what all immigrant-receiving states were doing at the time: to select (or exclude) immigrants on ethnic or racial grounds.[4] In addition, the United States was intrinsically enabled to do so because of a home-grown tradition of ethnoracial self-definition that goes back to the founding of the republic.[5] With respect to the second question, this chapter will show that, despite its close linkage with an ethnic nation-building project, Australia had to give up its ethnic immigration policy for much the same reasons as the United States did: an epistemic shift after World War II outlawed "race" as a legitimate principle of ordering the social world; foreign policy interests, in combination with (variously strong) domestic society pressures, then commanded to expunge "race" from all domestic policies, including immigration policy. The one difference is that this liberalization proceeded in the United States in terms of a "return" to presumably race-neutral founding principles. By contrast, in Australia, where such founding principles were not available, it entailed the invention of something new: "multiculturalism," along with persistent doubt and uncertainty about national self-definition.

Before ferreting out these different trajectories in more detail, it is important to identify some common elements of the ethnic immigration policies of settler states. They were "ethnic" in the sense of selecting immigrants according to their descent or origins. However, they were imbued with the negative thrust of excluding some immigrants as members of other-(rather than self-)defined groups that were deemed intrinsically (in the extreme: biologically) inferior. Following Max Weber (1976:234), such other-directed, descent-based classifications with a negative intent are "racial," and they have also been perceived as such by the political elites engaged in such classification.[6] It is difficult to imagine today that the race concept once had the dignity of a scientific fact, so much that "even for self-proclaimed egalitarians, the inferiority of certain races was no more to be contested than the law of gravity to be regarded as immoral" (Barkan, 1992:2–3). At the same time, even at its "scientific" prime the race concept was extremely malleable, denoting highly variegated phenomena, some of which we would call "ethnic group" or "nation" today.[7] However, a constant in its many uses was the assumption that the moral and cognitive qualities and capacities of a person were determined by the physical endowment of his or her origin group and the ordering of these groups in terms of a hierarchy.[8]

However, their declared purpose to exclude immigrants on the basis of race does not exhaust the ethnic immigration policies of new settler states. Somebody was to be included too, because immigration was always deemed indispensable for nation building. Sometimes the inclusive and exclusive dimensions were combined in one policy, which then functioned like a *filter* to separate the wanted from the unwanted incomers. An example is the extraordinarily complex national-origin quota policy in the United States, which combined the inclusion of wanted northwest European immigrants with the relative (not absolute) exclusion of unwanted southeast European immigrants. Only regarding Chinese (and, later, all Asian) immigrants a separate policy was set up that explicitly singled out this group for total exclusion, thus not filtering but *blocking* the entire flow.[9] Asian exclusion was common to the ethnic immigration policies of all settler states,[10] and no other element of these policies expressed more blatantly their racial underpinnings. White Australia, though ironically naming who was to be included rather than who was to be excluded, was essentially a blocking policy, whose purpose was to keep out Asians. Because of Australia's remote geographic location, and corresponding low attractiveness for British-European immigrants,[11] the latter had to be proactively *pulled* by a separate policy of "assisted passage" schemes, land grants, and prearranged housing and employment. Though a costly matter, this pulling allowed Australia to hand-pick her wanted ethnic intakes to an extraordinary degree. In sum, the ethnic immigration policies of settler states combined elements of inclusion and exclusion in highly variegated arrangements of "filtering," "blocking," or "pulling" different classes of ethnic immigrants.

Notably absent from the target groups of settler states' ethnic immigration policies are the "patrials" or coethnics proper, which figure prominently in the postwar ethnic immigration policies of some European states and Israel (see Chapters 3 and 4). These patrials and coethnics are the descendants of former emigrants or settlers, or perceived members of the state-bearing nation clustered or dispersed under foreign jurisdictions. Even such an avowedly "nonethnic" nation as France has carved out such patrials as a privileged group in its nationality law quite recently (see Chapter 5). In a way, the ethnic immigrants targeted by settler states are the reverse of patrials, not descendants of emigrants or settlers abroad but descendants of those who stayed behind, replenishment from the source country for the dominant ethnicity of the settler society. By the same token, the notion of "conational" without citizenship abroad has remained foreign to American and Australian immigration and nationality laws,[12] and still today relatively low hurdles to citizenship acquisition are accompanied by the easy and irrevocable loss of citizenship for later-generation emigrants.[13]

This chapter proceeds in three parts. First, it briefly delineates the setting-up of racially exclusive immigration policies at the turn of the last century. Second, it identifies the "liberalizing" factors and forces that brought them down after World War II. Third, it discusses some contemporary challenges to the universalistic immigration policies established since the mid-1960s.

Building the Racial "Ring Fence"

A British demographer wrote in the mid-1930s that "there are few gaps in the ring fence which has been erected in the last 50 years by the United States and the Dominions in order to exclude non-Europeans" (Carr-Saunders, 1936:186) This statement captures two important features of the restrictive immigration policies of the time: their interactive nature, in which a change in policy in one place would be closely monitored and quickly adopted in other places too (see Zolberg, 1997:292); and their thrust to block the entry of non-Europeans, especially Asians. Before mapping out their variations, one must realize the common context that conditioned the setup of strikingly similar restrictive policies in all new settler (and, to a certain degree, other immigrant-receiving) states.

First, these policies were part of a larger response of assertive nation-states to the perils of the first, nineteenth-century "globalization." Under the aegis of imperial Britain, much of the nineteenth century had been a "universal age" of free trade, unregulated capital movements, unrestricted migration, and the shrinking of time and space through the invention of new transport and information technologies such as railroads, steamships, telegraphs, and telephones (James, 2001:10). The nation-state as we know it, with tariffs, central banks, national currencies, and social insurance schemes, is a response to the "challenges of the first wave of globalization" (ibid., p.13). One of the new protective measures was the shielding of "national" labor markets from cheap foreign labor. A European example is Prussia's exclusion of Polish seasonal migrants in 1885. As Max Weber aggressively addressed in one of his first academic writings, the employment of low-skilled Polish workers, because of their "different propensities to consume," had endangered the higher living standards of domestic workers in the German Reich: "There is a certain situation of capitalistically disorganized economies, in which the higher culture is not victorious but rather loses in the existential fight with lower cultures" (ibid., p.16). Restrictive immigration policies were evidently put together in terms of the cultural repertory available at the time, which was one of Social Darwinism and "official nationalism," pitting rivaling nation-states against one another in a presumed struggle for survival.[14]

If the hierarchical ordering of "higher" and "lower" cultures had infested the relationship between neighboring people in Europe, how much more ferocious the will to exclude had to become when concerted "Europeans" faced people from an entirely different civilization. This points to a second factor influencing, especially, the racially restrictive immigration policies of new settler states: the perceived supremacy of Europeans over non-European subject peoples in the age of empire. The entire project of European overseas expansion and settlement had been driven by a sense of superiority over other cultures, religions, and races. Though sharing with Max Weber's case against Polish workers the economic fear of cheap-labor competition, the peculiarly vitriolic defamation of Chinese immigrants in the Western frontier states also fed on something more. "[T]he men the most degraded slaves upon earth . . . the women slave-prostitutes . . . the children the product of the most promiscuous miscegenation on earth," one can read in a report on San Francisco's Chinatown by the California state legislature in 1887 (cited in Coolidge, [1909] 1969:191). This was the populist coda to five centuries of European conquest, which ended at their westernmost point in the first-time encounter between European and non-European migrants. As Alan Cairns (1999:34) aptly summarized, "[a] global politics of empire and subject peoples, complemented by a generalized hierarchical view of the world's people, supported racially restrictive immigration policies."

Thirdly, if Asians were singled out for exclusion, this also had a demographic dimension, a fear of pending "inundation" by faster-growing alien populations. Not just a sense of superiority (which on its own would hardly provide an incentive to act), but one of superiority and inferiority at the same time drove the new settler states toward racially exclusive immigration policies. The European colonization of the world had so far rested on massive population growth, the European share of the world population increasing from one-fifth to one-fourth in the nineteenth century. By 1900, declining birth rates in Europe, in combination with declining mortality rates in Asia (a result of Western medical intervention), shifted the demographic balance against Europe. As Geoffrey Barraclough (1967:80) wrote, there was "an almost neurotic awareness of the precariousness of (the European) position in the face of an expansive Asia." Nowhere was this more extreme than in Australia, where—according to a turn-of-the-century observer—"a population less than the depleted population of Scotland (was) pathetically struggling to hold a continent as a white man's land against the congested millions of coloured peoples just across the sea" (ibid., pp. 81–82). Indeed, in a vast and underpopulated continent of barely 3 million Anglo-European settlers in 1900, separated from over 400 million Asian neighbors in overcrowded lands by just a stretch of water, the fear of invasion was real, so much that one author even denied that any sense of "superiority" had been driving the White Australia policy at all.[15]

Racial exclusion did not exhaust the ethnic immigration policies of new settler states. In addition, there was also the attempt to include wanted Anglo-European migrants. The following sections discuss the different combinations of including and excluding ethnic migrants in the United States and Australia.

Asian Exclusion and National-Origin Quotas in the United States

When Tocqueville visited Jacksonian America in the 1830s, he observed a society divided into "three races": the "white man" or "European," which he subsequently identified with "Anglo-American" or "American" as such; "Negroes," and "Indians." Their relationship was one of subordination, if not destruction, of the latter two by the first: "[T]he European is to the other races what man is to the animals. . . . He makes them serve his convenience, and when he cannot bend them to his will he destroys them" (Tocqueville, [1835–1840] 1969:317). Along such lines,

Pierre Van den Berghe characterized the United States as a "*Herrenvolk* democracy,*"* in which the people enunciated in the great founding documents, such as the Declaration of Independence and the Constitution, were a priori understood to be white: "There is little evidence of an 'American dilemma' during most of the 19th century and the first third of the 20th century."[16] This rebuts the canonical reading of American history since Gunnar Myrdal's *An American Dilemma* (1944), according to which a race-neutral, universalistic founding act was only temporarily tainted by African slavery (and to a lesser extent the extinction of Native Americans), and in which a "return" to the universalistic founding principles provided the normative horizon of liberal-democratic politics.[17] This was a very European optic on the United States, placing class conflict (or the absence thereof), and not race, into the center of analysis. Ironically, this view was informed by Alexis de Tocqueville as well, namely his central argument in *Democracy in America* that, because of the absence of European feudalism and class politics, a unique "equality of conditions" could prevail in America. As he famously wrote, "the Americans have this great advantage, that they . . . were born equal instead of becoming so" (Tocqueville, [1835–1840] 1969:509); note that "Americans" in this context could hardly have included blacks or Native Americans.

This view, subsequently most fully elaborated in Louis Hartz's (1955) vision of the United States as a "liberal society," is silent on the other two "races" and, generally, how the boundaries of the liberal society were to be determined.[18] Boundary drawing was a problem for all emergent nation-states subscribing to the new doctrine of popular sovereignty—the self-governing "people" had to be defined and set apart from other "people." In Europe, these boundaries, to a certain degree, could be taken for granted in the context of settled populations marked by distinct linguistic, religious, and cultural features.[19] In the chronically fluid context of a new settler state, such preset boundary-markers were available to a much lesser extent.[20] Moreover, liberal-democratic principles as such were no substitute. As Rogers Smith (1997:38) pointed out, the latter "offered few reasons why Americans should see themselves as a distinct people, apart from others." This void was filled by what Smith has called "ascriptive Americanism," which coexisted from the start as the boundary-defining complement to the "liberal" and "republican" traditions in the United States.

Immigration history has long been empirical grist to the "liberal society" (or "civic nation") mill. This is because this history could be read as one of fusing a variety of ethnic groups into an "ethnically anonymous"

American mold (Walzer, 1990:596). In this vein, Oscar Handlin (1951:3) could famously say that "immigrants were American history." Still today, the liberal immigration imagery subtly informs "liberal nationalism," which finds in the United States "a national culture less dependent on any one, particular community of descent than . . . most other comparable national . . . solidarities" (Hollinger, 1998:314). However, recent revisionist historians have put their fingers at the fact that, before 1965, the proclaimed "nation of immigrants" had been a nation of "white" immigrants only. As Matthew Frye Jacobson (1998) argued forcefully against the liberal orthodoxy, "the civic story of assimilation . . . is inseparable from the cultural story of racial alchemy" (p. 8), race being no mere lapse from liberal founding principles but "among the central organizers of the political life of the republic all along" (p. 43). This claim finds support in the first naturalization law of 1792, which allowed only "free white persons" into the citizenry and was abolished not before 1952.

As the new revisionist historians have brought to the fore, it is the silences as much as the explicit exclusions that show the workings of race. Even for the cultural pluralists of post–World War I America, who rejected the assimilationist narrowing of the melting pot in the 1920s "Americanization" campaign, the "nations" that constituted the American "nation of nations" were European only. Horace Kallen, often taken as a precursor to later-day multiculturalism, established the "ethnicity" that was to be preserved rather than abolished in the American context only by excluding from it the groups that were defined by race. As one author characterized this move, "[o]ne is an ethnic in the American context to the extent that one's difference is not configured in racial terms" (Hattam, 2001:12).

Turning to immigration policy, one must distinguish three separate policies and legal frameworks that were established at national level from 1875 on: individual-level screening (for health, character, destitution, etc.), which is in principle (though not always in practice)[21] racially neutral and, in modified form, still exists today; and two group-level selections: the "blocking" of Asians and the "filtering" of Europeans according to national origins. Asian exclusion stands to this day as the only example in U.S. immigration history that particular groups were named in law as barred from entry. At one level, there was an obvious reason for setting up a separate policy for excluding Chinese (and other Asians) as groups rather than individuals: individual-level screening would have had little effect on them. In this regard, the Chinese were excluded because of "their virtues, not their vices" (Coolidge, [1909] 1969:488). Note that the first Chinese Exclusion Act of 1882 targeted only (skilled and unskilled) "laborers," thus carrying the imprint of the populist, working-class cause that the case against the Chinese had originally been in California.[22] As Mary Coolidge ([1909] 1969:180) emphasized, the hostility to capital and to the Chinese tended to go hand in hand, but "it was much easier and safer for the politicians to fight the Chinese than to make war upon the great monopolies." However, to the economic rationale one must add the racial animus, which consequently broadened the anti-Chinese into a cause against all Asians. Here the deviously circular root charge was that the Chinese could not or would not assimilate, and that their despotic background made them "utterly unfit for and incapable of free or self-government" (in Salyer, 1995:16).

A third policy, which likewise followed the principle of group selection, if in a less exclusive and categorical way, came to be directed at European immigrants. As late as 1882, about 87 percent of the 650,000 European immigrants entering were from northwestern Europe. By 1907, 81 percent of the 1,210,000 entering Europeans were from southeastern Europe (King, 2000:50–51). This was the backdrop to a restrictionist movement that differed markedly from the anti-Chinese cause. It was elitist, not populist, originating in the educated New England establishment, not the "alien class" of the unsettled frontier lands, and it centered almost exclusively on the cultural (rather than economic) consequences of the new immigration (see Solomon, 1956).

The amateur scientist Madison Grant's influential treatise, *The Passing of the Great Race*, offers unsurpassed insight into the elite restrictionists' key ideological tenet: that even the Europeans were divided by race. For Grant, there were three European races: "Nordic," "Mediterranean" (or "Iberian"), and "Alpine," each endowed with a distinct skull shape, eye color, hair color, and stature.[23] However, Mediterraneans and Alpines were really "western extensions of Asiatic subspecies," so that only the Nordics figured as "purely European type," "Homo europaeus," "the white man par excellence" (Grant, 1924:167). The main problem was that, as a matter of the "law of nature," the mixing of "higher" and "lower" races would always result in a lower type, so that—in combination with the greater fertility of the latter—"one type gradually breeds the other out" (ibid., p. 46). Luckily there was the new discipline of eugenics to the rescue: "[T]he most practical and hopeful method of race improvement is through the elimination of the least desirable elements in the

nation by depriving them of the power to contribute to future generations" (ibid., p. 53).

The prominent role of eugenics experts in the crafting of the 1924
National Origin Quota Act (see King, 2000, ch. 6) brought to a peak the
prominent role that "science" (or rather what passed as that at the time)
had played all along in the post-1880s restrictionist movement. Immigration restriction had been a "paradigmatic Progressive cause," the rational
planning of society on the basis of "massive fact gathering and complex
regulation" (Keller, 1994:223). The prankish antics of race theory should
not distract from the fact that turn-of-the-century immigration restriction
was part of a larger project of designing society *more geometrico*, project-
ing the mastery of nature that had been achieved through modern physics
and biology into the realm of human affairs, and thus perversely realizing
the "absolute perfection of the human race" as laid out in Antoine Nicolas de Condorcet's famous "Tenth Stage" of his European enlightenment
manifesto ([1795] 1955:184). In this vein, an observer at the time characterized the 1924 immigration act as "a scientific plan for keeping America American" (Warner Parker, 1924:740).

Four features of the national-origin quota regime, which would last
from 1929 to 1965, stand out. First, the discriminatory impulse against
southern and eastern European immigrants, which had been driving the
development from the 1917 literacy test to the 1924 National Origins Act,
was obscured by the formula of preserving the "racial homogeneity" of the
United States. Instead of constituting negative discrimination, this objective could be couched as a cause of justice to everybody's ancestors. Note
that the first Quota Act of 1921 had been deficient in this respect: in appor-
tioning future intakes according to the distribution of foreign nationality
groups in the 1910 census, immigration was made the property of the foreign nationality groups that had contingently dominated inflows at a relatively late point: southern and eastern Europeans. If the purpose of
restriction was to "preserve . . . the racial status quo in the United States,"[24]
what better method to realize this than distributing quotas on the basis of
the national origins of the entire American population, and not just of the
foreign nationality population?[25] This was a policy whose discrimination
was hidden under the cloak of nondiscrimination.

It is important to stress that the leaders of immigration restriction in
the House and the Senate, Albert Johnson and David Reed, respectively,
did not espouse theories of Nordic superiority, at least not openly.[26] For
them, national-origin quotas were nondiscriminatory, and a corrective to

the previous quota scheme that had unduly discriminated in favor of the foreign-born, especially from southern and eastern Europe. As David Reed, sponsor of the national-origin bill in the Senate, put it, "[w]hat we want to [make] is . . . a quota law that is nondiscriminatory. We do not want to discriminate against some nation, but we want to end the discrimination that now obtains."[27] Restrictionists framed their insistence on nondiscrimination within a dichotomy between "American" and "alien" interests. Only the national-origin principle, or its proxy of using the 1890 census in the 1924 Act, served the "American" interest. As a restrictionist put it in the House debate, "[t]he idea which I am trying to impress is, that it is not the aliens who are entitled to a quota, but it is the American people who are entitled to a quota. [Applause]."[28] Conversely, opponents of moving the census date from 1910 to 1890 could be dismissed as serving the interests of foreigners and foreign states, which was a powerful and ever-present motif in this debate.

Second, the imperative of nondiscrimination applied only to the European-origin population and the immigrants "owned" by them. Not included in the calculation of the population baseline for the national-origin quotas were "aliens ineligible to citizenship" (that is, Asians), descendants of slave immigrants,[29] descendants of American aborigines, and Western Hemisphere immigrants.[30] This meant that quotas were available only for white European immigrants, as the population baseline from which quotas were calculated included only the white, European-origin population. The 1924 Act, despite fracturing the European immigrants into a variety of "races," also "constructed a white American race" (Ngai, 1999:70). Incidentally, the 1924 Act completed the process of Asian exclusion by making all "aliens ineligible to citizenship" ineligible for immigration too.[31]

Even on the side of the antirestrictionists in the 1924 debate, their strategy of revealing the discriminatory intent underneath the allegedly nondiscriminatory national-origin principle stopped short of addressing the fact that Asians had been excluded all along, and much more categorically than any Europeans ever were to be excluded. On the contrary, antirestrictionists often wholeheartedly supported Asian exclusion. Their restrictionist opponents took a delight in expounding this contradiction. Consider the following exchange in the House:[32]

> *Mr. Jacobstein:* . . . Nothing is more un-American (than the belief that there is such a thing as a Nordic race). Nothing could be more dangerous in a land the Constitution of which says that all men are

created equal, than to write into our law a theory which puts one race above another, which stamps one group of people as superior and another as inferior . . .

Mr. Perkins: Does the gentleman favor the exclusion of the Chinese?

Mr. Jacobstein: Yes.

Mr. Perkins: Does the gentleman favor the exclusion of the Japanese?

Mr. Jacobstein: Yes.

Third, the computation of the national-origin quotas implied a peculiar freezing of society. The formula was an annual cap of 150,000 immigrants to be divided in national quotas according to how many Americans (in the 1920 census) could trace their origins to the respective nationality. That is, identical total numbers and national quotas prevailed year after year, with no change of number whatsoever. The goal was to foreclose for all times any ethnic change to the American population as it existed in 1920. No more grandiose yet also ludicrous "high modernist" population policy has ever been ventured by a modern state (Scott, 1998).

Fourth, and most surprisingly given the declared purpose of the law, the national-origin quotas were not based on the immigrant's race or ethnicity proper but on his or her place of birth, and this place as defined by the state to which it "belonged" at the time of visa application. This meant that an immigrant's citizenship, ancestry, residence, or the state to which her place of birth "belonged" at the time of her birth, were not relevant factors in the determination of which national quota she was to be charged to (see Auerbach, 1955:53). For example, a person born in Dublin was chargeable to the Irish quota, even if she was of Italian ancestry, held French citizenship, perhaps resided in a fourth country, and was born while Dublin was still a part of the United Kingdom. Strictly speaking, this definition of national origin militated against the purpose of the law, because it could not capture a possible disjunction between place and ethnicity—not an unlikely event given the fluctuations of borders and population movements in postimperial Europe. Technical considerations of identifying and classifying immigrants are the reasons for the use of the "place of origin" proxy to their ethnic or national origins proper.[33]

Interestingly, the Immigration Bureau classified entering immigrants between 1899 and 1952 according to a "List of Races or Peoples," which included some ethnic or racial categories. Italians, for instance, were now divided between "Iberics" (from the south) and "Celtics" (from the north), and Jews—not explicitly mentioned in any of the quotas—figured as "Hebrew race." While the Labor Department assured that this list was for statistical purposes only and without any "political significance" (quoted in Weil, 2001a:639), it became a bone of repeated domestic and international contention, had to be revised many times, and tended to be kept in the shadows.[34] This hints at the—not just technical but political— difficulties for a national-origin policy that *really* would have been based on race or ethnicity.

White Australia

If the United States is characterized by "multiple traditions" of national self-definition (Smith, 1993), only one of which fed the racially exclusive immigration policies, the White Australia policy was the very fulcrum of Australian nation building and self-definition. The perceived need to exclude Asian immigrants was the driving force behind federating the six Australian colonies into the Commonwealth of Australia. Its very first leg- islation was the Commonwealth Immigration Restriction Act of 1901, which enunciated the White Australia policy. During the parliamentary debate over this act, Alfred Deakin, Australia's leading politician in the early federation years, identified national unity with racial exclusion: "[N]o motive power operated more powerfully in dissolving the technical and arbitrary political divisions which previously separated us than the desire that we should be one people, and remain one people, without the admixture of other races . . . The unity of Australia is nothing if it does not imply a united race."[35]

The "unity of Australia" was in a twisted way premised on and in opposition to identification with Britain. The former was premised on the latter because Australia defined itself as a "nation of the British type" (Willard, 1923:201), and the very exclusion of Asians came to be consid- ered the *sine qua non* for this. Conversely, a British-type nation building implied a policy of "pulling" predominantly British immigrants. Econom- ically, Britain remained federated Australia's major export market and source of finance, and geopolitically Australia remained dependent on Britain's naval protection. Because of the uniquely generous and flexible approach of the British colonial government, which was eager to avoid a United States–style independence drive of the Dominions, most Austra- lian colonies were self-governing by the 1850s, with Westminster-style parliaments that had jurisdiction over most domestic matters. Only for- eign policy and defense remained firmly under British authority, even after federation. With respect to self-definition, a "distinctive 'Australian' national identity was considered entirely consistent with and even dependent on British attachments" (Spillman, 1997:26). This was paradoxical, and in effect the latter had to be at the cost of the former. Accordingly, an English visitor in 1910 found a "national spirit" practically "non-existent": "You drop from Imperialism to something like parochialism in Australia, with little of the real national spirit intervening—though it exists and must increase" (quoted in Birrell, 1995:161–162). When Australia opened itself up to non-British, European immigration in the immediate post–World War II period, there was still a characteristic slippage as to what the society was into which these immigrants were to be "assimilated": "They will all be Australians, they will all be British, and they will all be, as we are, the King's men, and the King's women."[36]

However, the "unity of Australia" also was in opposition to identification with Britain. The very White Australia policy was central to this opposition—an ironic fact, because the policy's racial thrust of protecting the "white race" is nationally anonymous and could have provided an imperial identification with Britain and other white settler states that were equally beleaguered by the "yellow peril." White Australia contained Australia's distinct national self-definition as a "land of toilers" (Rosecrance, 1964:276). In Hartz's (1964) terms, Australia is the "radical fragment" of Europe implanted overseas, the convicts and paupers of Britain being its earliest settlers. They could hardly be celebrated as heroic founders and patriots, American-style. Instead, as Richard Rosecrance (1964:295) observes, "'Waltzing Matilda,' a song that glorifies the theft of a sheep from a squatter, has become Australia's only truly national song." Accordingly, Australian nationalism, to the degree that it existed at all, expressed itself in social, not political and territorial, terms as the leveling of the class hierarchies and social distinctions that prevailed in Britain.

Crucially, this social nationalism, in which Australia finally differed from Britain, came to crystallize in the White Australia policy. To the degree that the latter had a positive content, it was to preserve the social equality and "dignity of work" that was threatened by cheap labor competition from Asia. Prime Minister Deakin expressed this motif in 1903: "[T]he White Australia policy covers much more than the preservation of our own people here . . . It means the maintenance of social conditions under which men and women can live decently. It means equal laws and opportunities for all . . . [I]t means social justice and fair wages. The White Australia policy goes down to the roots of our national existence . . ." (quoted in Willard,

1923:204). In this respect one could even say, with Robert Birrell (1995:12), that "the White Australia doctrine embodied civic ideals." More than that, the ultimate touchstone of national belonging—sacrifice—was in it too. "[W]e may sacrifice in the way of immediate monetary gain . . . [and] we may retard the development of the remote and tropical portions of our territory," conceded Alfred Deakin in the debate over the 1901 Commonwealth Immigrant Restriction Act, with an eye on the consequences of renouncing the use of indentured Asian workers on the sugar plantations of tropical Queensland.[37] Conversely, this renunciation allowed preserving the dignity of toil, that distinctly Australian value. No wonder that even an impeccably liberal author such as Rosecrance (1964:317) would not completely condemn the White Australia policy: "White Australia was an understandable reaction of a coercive radical society in the 19th century."

Not only the symbolic content but also the political enactment of the White Australia policy occurred in opposition to Britain. Imperial Britain was committed to racial nondiscrimination and free movement within the Empire and beyond, which collided with the racially exclusive "ring-fence" building of her self-governing Dominions. However, the "Imperial philosophy of equality" was only skin deep, because "Whitehall was interested more in the letter of any particular piece of legislation [in the white settler colonies] than in the spirit" (Huttenback, 1973:271). A case in point is how the most salient feature of the White Australia policy— racial exclusion by subterfuge—came into being. At the 1897 Imperial Conference in London, the British Secretary of State for the Colonies, Chamberlain, pointed out to the Australian delegates how they could exclude racially without appearing to do so: "What I venture to think you have to deal with is the character of the immigration. It is not because a man is of different color to ourselves that he is necessarily an undesirable immigrant, but it is because he is dirty, or he is ignorant, or he is a pauper, or he has some other objection which can be defined in an Act of Parliament, and by which the exclusion can be managed with regard to all those whom you really desire to exclude" (quoted in Willard, 1923:112–113). More concretely, Chamberlain suggested Natal's "education test," which had enabled this white South African settler colony to exclude non-whites (from India) without being explicit about doing so.

The most astonishing feature of the 1901 Immigration Restriction Act is that neither the word "race" nor national-origin terms appear anywhere in it. All that is "White Australia" is contained in section 3(a) of the act. It defines a "prohibited" immigrant as "[a]ny person who when asked to do so by an officer fails to write out at dictation and sign in the presence of the officer a passage of fifty words in length in an European language directed by the officer."[38] In contrast to the legal explicitness of the ethnoracial immigration policy in the United States, the White Australia policy was entirely discretionary, and thus uniquely flexible. It has to be read and evaluated from actual government practices rather than statute books (see Palfreeman, 1957:26–27). The dictation test was key to this flexibility. It was a trick test, applied only when the government, or its agent at the port, had decided beforehand that an immigrant was not to be admitted. Confidential instructions on how to apply the dictation test, which were forwarded to the immigration officers only orally, prescribe that, should the officer deem a particular immigrant "undesirable," the test should be held in a language that he or she surely would not understand (Yarwood, 1964:46). The underlying logic is maliciously circular. Formally, one became a "prohibited" immigrant only by failing the dictation test, but in reality the government decided beforehand that an immigrant was to be prohibited, sealing this with a dictation test that would end always negatively. Further, only one factor conditioned the *ex ante* decision on admission: not ancestry or place of birth, as determined or evidenced by objective criteria, but subjective racial appearance, crude and simple, as determined by the physical gaze of the officer at the port.

Since the meaning of "White Australia" is nowhere enunciated in the letter of the law, even courts have resorted to the parliamentary debates surrounding it when forced to define the range of exclusion in their case law. The language of these debates is clear and loud, with some disagreement about the "how" to exclude but not at all about the "whom" to exclude. When an early version of the bill still foresaw a dictation test in English, Prime Minister Barton assured its critics that the test would not be applied to Europeans (Yarwood, 1964:27). For all who might doubt that any sense of racial superiority was implied in the exclusion of non-Europeans, the Prime Minister clarified: "I do not think that the doctrine of the equality of men was really ever intended to include racial equality" (ibid., p.24). On the opposition bench, Labor Party members described the goal as a "snow white Australia" in which the threat of "racial contamination" arising from "the mixing of the coloured people with the white people of Australia" was banned (ibid., p.25).

Overall, the White Australia policy was remarkably successful on its own terms. The Chinese population dropped from 29,907 in 1901 to

9,144 in 1947 (Palfreeman, 1967:145). Foreign-born non-Europeans declined from 47,017 in 1901 to 9,973 in 1954, most of the latter being temporary migrants only (Palfreeman, 1958:50). This implied that the Asian share of the total population fell from an already miniscule 1.25 percent in 1901 to close to zero (0.28 percent) in 1954 (Palfreeman, 1967:151). The "foothold" to Asian immigrants had indeed been denied and the mission of a "snow white" Australia fulfilled.

While the "blocking" of Asian immigrants was similar to that in the United States (and all settler states, for that matter), there was no parallel in Australia to the highly salient "filtering" of European immigrants that embroiled the United States in protracted debate and policy innovation in the first two decades of the twentieth century. The reason is simple: geographical distance, which made Australia the remote third choice for European immigrants, after the United States and Canada. The immigrants that Australia wanted to have would not come on their own (at least not in sufficient numbers) and thus had to be proactively "pulled" by offering them positive incentives. How much this pulling occurred separately from blocking is epitomized by the fact that it remained under the authority of the colonies (or "states") until 1920, when blocking had long since been federalized in terms of the 1901 Immigration Restriction Act.

"Pulling," by definition, allowed Australia an extraordinary degree of control over the size and composition of migrant flows. Until World War II, assisted passage was available only for Britons, 1,068,000 of who entered this way between 1831 and 1947.[39] Through the Empire Settlement Act of 1922 (periodically renewed until 1962), the British government cofinanced the assisted passage scheme, in the interest of "build[ing] up the strength and wealth of the Empire as a whole by the better distribution of its population" (quoted in Paul, 1997:28). However, one should not think that the recruitment of Britons was ever a smooth process. "All distrusted each other," one historian described the process in the early 1920s (Roe, 1995:31). On the part of the Australian government there was persistent suspicion that Britain, in continuation of the convict transport legacy, wanted only to relieve herself of her own worst elements and potential troublemakers. In addition, the (Irish-dominated) Australian Labor Party was worried not only about imported labor competition in general but about its Protestant-British texture in particular. On the British side, especially after World War I, there was apathy, even hostility, among potential migrants, because the act of emigration was equated with the desertion from country and class alike (ibid., p. 184). There was also resentment of Australia's harsh and rigorous selection procedures. To be British was not enough to qualify for assisted entry; nonwhite British, of course, were excluded from the start, and all others were subjected to positive and negative individual screening.[40] On the positive side, Australia preferred agricultural workers and domestics, who incidentally were in high demand in post–World War I Britain also. On the negative side, applicants who did not meet the preferred age, skill, or physical criteria were not admitted for assisted passage, though they were mostly free to go at their own expense.

A different policy applied to other Europeans, who first entered in noticeable numbers after the first American quota act in 1921[41] and who came to be classed as "white aliens." This notion camouflages the fact that southern European immigrants, especially, were perceived as nonwhites. In 1925 the *Manchester Guardian* described the Australian racial hierarchy in these terms: "The average Australian, of whatever class, does in effect, limit the term 'white' to British stock, allows American and Canadian, tolerates Scandinavian or Dane or French, but is doubtful about Central Europeans and satisfied that Southern Europeans are coloured" (quoted in Langfield, 1991:1). In the interwar period, with Asian exclusion safely established, the "white aliens" were increasingly perceived as a threat, and all of them were subjected to a special regime that was different from the one applied to British immigrants. They were exempted from assisted passage (until 1947), had to be "sponsored" by close relatives, and had to possess prearranged landing permits and financial resources (Jordens, 1997:49). Interestingly, Australia followed closely the quota debates in the United States at the time and even emulated for a while an unofficial national quota system for some southern and eastern European countries (see Langfield, 1991:3). Moreover, Europeans were screened according to race. Against the promise given by Prime Minister Barton in 1901, the dictation test was increasingly applied to European immigrants of mixed race. After the landing-permit procedure was put into place, photographs allowed officials in Canberra to screen candidates for skin color and "typically Jewish" characteristics (Langfield, 1995:413). As in the American Immigration Bureau's "List of Races or Peoples," a distinction was made between northern and southern Italians, the latter being characterized as "dark in colour and . . . showing evidence of black blood" (ibid.). Even when they became proactively recruited after World War II, European immigrants were still subjected to racial screening (see Jordens, 1997:48–58; London, 1970:125–126). The reach of White Australia evidently extended wide beyond the unwanted Asians.

The End of Racial Exclusion

World War II, which was fought on the winner's side for "the supremacy of human rights everywhere"[42] against a regime that stood for the supremacy of a race, brought about a fundamental epistemic shift whose consequences are still with us today. "Race" was outlawed as a legitimate ordering principle of the social world. Because "race" once had the status of a scientific truth, it was crucial that scientists were at the forefront of demolishing it. In 1950 UNESCO, the educational branch of the newly created United Nations Organization, published a declaration on race, branded as "the most authoritative statement of modern scientific doctrine on the controversial subject of race ever to be issued."[43] Drafted and signed by a panel of eminent social scientists and anthropologists from four continents (including French anthropologist Claude Levi-Strauss), the UNESCO declaration on race hammered out what is still the dominant view today: the mental capacities and characters of individuals are independent of their race; race mixing does not produce biologically inferior results; national, religious, and cultural groups do not constitute races; and "race is less a biological phenomenon than a social myth" (UNESCO, 1953:111). In light of this, the panel recommended to drop the "erroneous" term "race" in favor of "ethnic group."

Positively phrased, the novelty of the post–World War II period was the rise of a "world human rights culture" (Skrentny, 2002:23–27), which was driven by the United States and became embodied in the United Nations institutions and conventions. However, it was not the international regime but foreign policy interests that initiated the change to nondiscriminatory immigration (and other domestic) policies. This is an important difference. Much of the current literature conceives of the international human rights regime, with its own norms, institutions, and actors, as confronting monolithic states from the outside. This view is certainly valid with respect to contemporary human-rights violations in some autocratic states in Africa or Asia (see Risse, Ropp, and Sikkink, 1999). However, for the immediate post–World War II period, in which this regime was still nascent, and with respect to the Western countries that crafted it in their image, the "international regime" versus "state" duality is inappropriate.

John Skrentny (1998; 2002, ch. 2) even argues that the framing of racial equality as a "national security" concern was key to America's turn to racial nondiscrimination in the mid-1960s (see also Dudziak, 1988). Although this claim somewhat downplays the domestic society pressures that were *also* involved in this change (particularly in its later phases), the thrust of the argument is correct. Moreover, as Skrentny effectively suggests, for a proper understanding of the turn to nondiscrimination one has to disaggregate the state. Those sectors of the state that faced a "world audience" (the presidency and the Department of State) were pushing for it, whereas the sector committed to a domestic audience only, Congress, long tried to block change. In the United States, the rise of a universalistic immigration policy is thus also the story of intragovernmental conflict, with the foreign policy–oriented presidency (strengthened by the war and the need to handle its consequences) asserting itself over a parochial Congress that had dominated immigration policy from the 1870s to the early 1940s.[44]

Foreign-policy interests were driving the turn to universalistic immigration policies in all settler states after World War II.[45] However, this occurred with important internal variations. In the United States this turn was a prerequisite for credible world leadership, particularly toward decolonizing Africa and Asia. In Australia, the turn was a prerequisite for successful integration in the Asian region, occurring not in a position of strength (as in the United States) but of demographic weakness and geopolitical vulnerability. Moreover, interactive effects with the other settler states mattered. Once Canada and the United States had dismantled their "ring fence" in the early and mid-1960s, respectively, it was ever more difficult for Australia to stand alone—with the exception of South Africa, the internationally ostracized apartheid state.

With respect to institutional dynamics, there could not be a parallel in Australia to the public conflict in the United States between President and Congress over the course of immigration policy: there is no space for such conflict in the Westminster system, where power is concentrated in the Cabinet. Rather, liberalization occurred by administrative stealth, with foreign policy–oriented reformers at the head of the newly created Department of Immigration quietly pushing for change. "Stealth" was commanded by the fact that, well into the 1960s, all parties and public opinion stood solidly behind White Australia. However, liberalization by stealth had an inherent limitation: because the government had to deny in public that change was going on, Asian states could not know about it either. This constraint forfeited the whole purpose of liberalization and called for a further, symbolic rupture with the White Australia policy, which occurred only in 1973.

Foreign policy considerations were not the only factor conditioning the turn to universalistic immigration policies. In addition, domestic actors pointed out that racial exclusion was discriminatory and harmful to society. The strength of domestic mobilization differed significantly in the United States and Australia. In the United States, immigration became tagged as a "civil rights" issue in the early 1960s. This is also because there was a clear domestic loser of the restrictive immigration policy, a group that had gained increasing electoral clout over the preceding decades: the descendants of southern and eastern European immigrants. Now constituting a major urban voting bloc within the Democratic Party, the European "ethnics" attacked a national-origin quota policy that discriminated not just against certain immigrants but against all Americans of these ethnic origins. The national-origin quota policy was appropriately buried by the first Congress in U.S. history in which Roman Catholics constituted the majority.

By contrast, in Australia, whose restrictive policy had been more successful in preventing the entry of groups that later could raise equality claims, domestic pressure was more vicarious and intellectual than ethnic constituency–based; it ebbed and flowed with harsh individual deportation or exclusion measures by a tough-minded government; and, overall, it remained fixed on the negative external (rather than domestic) implications of the White Australia policy.

In both cases the turn to source-country universalism was more the result of cumulative ad hoc measures than of premeditated change, and the de facto demise of racially exclusive immigration policies long preceded their de jure demise. In a very different context, Peter Sahlins (1989) has described how local actors responded to a sudden change in their environment chameleonlike, with pragmatic adjustments at first, until these adjustments grew into an identity that later could not be disposed of at will. Something quite similar happened in the settler states' abandonment of racial exclusion, which at first was interest-based and partial and only later turned into a matter of identity and principle.

The fundamental communality of both cases is obscured by the American rhetoric of a "return" to an allegedly race-neutral founding myth, according to which America was at heart an "asylum for the oppressed" that only temporarily had been subverted by a race ideology "utterly unworthy of our traditions and our ideals."[46] "When was *that?*" one is tempted to ask (with Jacobson, 1998:133–134). Not the recovery of an old conception of the nation, but the new liberal imperative of racial nondiscrimination, which had not existed before in this form,[47] drove the turn to source-country universalism. The case of Australia, whose sense of nationhood had been unequivocally aligned with racial exclusion, but which followed a path parallel to that of the United States, is proof of that.

The United States

The pragmatic-geopolitical beginnings of the end of racial exclusion are very visible in the repeal of the Chinese exclusion laws in 1943. China was a key ally in the Pacific war against Japan, and the repeal was meant to be a boost to its morale. Japanese war propaganda had hammered the point that "the Chinese are rigidly excluded from attaining American citizenship by naturalization, a right which is accorded to the lowliest immigrant from Europe."[48] Accordingly, a Texan congressman characterized the bill to repeal Chinese exclusion as "not an immigration bill" but "a war measure and a peace measure" (quoted in Divine, 1957:151). Even the Citizens Committee to Repeal Chinese Exclusion, composed of New York business, intellectual, and religious elites who had started the campaign in 1942, avoided any reference to racial equality as a "boomerang argument."[49] There was no need to use it. Alongside the foreign policy reasoning of the State Department, the Immigration and Naturalization Service (INS) pointed out that the 1924 Immigration Act itself had made the Chinese exclusion laws superfluous (Riggs, 1950:37). Because the 1924 act was not touched by the repeal, all the Chinese would win from making them eligible for naturalization was a token quota of 100 persons annually. This was a costless way of doing "justice to our Chinese Allies" (ibid., p.129). Interestingly, a Chinese quota of 100 already existed under the 1924 law, but only people of non-Chinese ancestry could use it. The 1943 repeal added a Chinese ancestry quota to the already existing place-of-birth quota. Within the quota system, this constituted an anomaly: Europeans were admitted on the basis of their place of birth, whereas Chinese (and soon other Asians too) were admitted on the basis of their ancestry. The removal of racial exclusion thus entailed another racial discrimination: Asians, wherever they were born or whatever citizenship they held, were charged against the small minimum quota of "their" titular country, even if they were factually attached to a different country whose quota was high or that was exempt from any quota at all.

The admission of European refugees constituted a second foreign policy–related wedge on racial exclusion. This became an issue especially in the emergent Cold War confrontation, when every refugee from Communism was proof of the superiority of the West. Throughout the immediate postwar period, displaced persons and refugees were the subject of constant wrangle between presidents, who wanted to maximize their intake in the pursuit of foreign policy objectives, and a restrictionist Congress, which was seeking to minimize that intake. Because the majority of these refugees originated from southern and eastern Europe, the national-origin quotas were a major obstacle to their admittance. Part of the compromise struck in the 1948 Displaced Persons Act was to charge displaced persons against the future quota of their country of birth if these quotas were currently oversubscribed. They all were oversubscribed indeed. Although some 400,000 displaced persons could be admitted this way until 1953, they hopelessly clogged the national quotas into the far future—for instance, 50 percent of Estonia's and Latvia's small annual quotas (116 and 236 according to the 1924 law) had to be reserved for absorbing these refugee intakes until the years 2146 and 2274, respectively (Auerbach, 1955:52–53). Further refugee legislation in the 1950s wisely exempted the new intakes from the quotas, but this action made the latter even more an anachronism that eventually stood to be removed. As President Truman characterized the blatant gap between the original purpose of the quota law and current foreign policy needs, "[t]he countries of Eastern Europe have fallen under the Communist yoke . . .We do not need to be protected against immigrants from these countries—on the contrary, we want to stretch out a helping hand, . . . to succor those who are brave enough to escape from barbarism . . ." (quoted in President's Commission on Immigration and Naturalization, [1952] 1971:279).

However, the period's packaging of immigration reform as in the interest of winning the Cold War could cut both ways, for or against liberalization. This ambivalence became the signature of the 1952 Immigration and Nationality (McCarran-Walter) Act. Vetoed by President Truman, it marks the high point of the "liberal-presidential" versus "conservative-congressional" fault line in postwar U.S. immigration (and civil rights) politics,[50] and the conservatives prevailed over the liberals on the premise that "opening the floodgates of unlimited immigration (would destroy) . . . the national security of the United States."[51] The act retained the national-origin quotas, but avowedly "[w]ithout giving credence to any theory of Nordic superiority." Instead, the quotas were presented as "a rational and logical method of . . . preserv[ing] the socio-logical and cultural balance in the population of the United States."[52] If one considers only the official statements of Congressional committee leaders, this was not so different from those in 1924—except for the avoidance of racial terminology. Epitomizing the conservative implica-tions of the national security imperative, the law was fashioned as a pro-tective measure "in times . . . too perilous for us to tinker with our national institutions," as Senator McCarran put it (quoted in Gerstle, 2001:260). On the liberal side, the McCarran-Walter Act erased all racial restrictions to naturalization, which had been in force for more than 160 years. In principle, this removed the main obstacle to Asian immigration. In reality, new hurdles were erected against it. The ancestry quota for-mula first used in the 1943 repeal of Chinese exclusion was extended to all Asian countries, defined as the "Asia-Pacific Triangle." This was to make sure that the one million Asians living in Latin America and the 16 million Chinese living outside China would not enter under the nonquota provisions of Western Hemisphere countries or under the larger-quota pro-visions of some Eastern Hemisphere countries (such as Britain).[53]

Interestingly, the ancestry formula that had gone uncriticized by liberal reformers in 1943 was now widely perceived as a "new element of racial discrimination."[54] This shows the rapid normative evolution in the per-ception of race discrimination. In addition, the 1952 act introduced a "subquota" of 100 each for colonies or dependent territories, which had previously been charged against the larger quota of the governing coun-try (mostly imperial Britain). This subquota was based on immigrants' place of birth rather than their ancestry. However, it was still racially motivated, targeting the increasing number of black immigrants from the West Indies, most notably Jamaica (whose annual entries were thus cut from 1000 to 100). The eight British colonies in the Caribbean were now the only part of the Western Hemisphere subject to quotas, and obviously because their immigration-prone populace was overwhelmingly black. For the first time, "the Negro question" was raised in the context of immigration, and "race" came to be interpreted through the prism of the black-white civil rights struggle of the time. Witness that liberal critics attacked the law for its "bias against Negro immigrants" and for its set-ting up of a "Cape Town–Washington D.C. axis."[55]

Before it was formally abolished in 1965, the national-origin quota sys-tem was overcome by events. Only 34 percent of the 2.6 million legal immigrants entering between 1953 and 1962 were quota immigrants.[56]

One reason is that refugees now entered quota-free, as did the beneficiaries of numerous special legislations for family immigrants, orphans, victims of disasters, and other classes of immigrants.[57] Furthermore, the growing number of Western Hemisphere immigrants, especially from Mexico, had been quota-free all along.[58] Finally, two-thirds of the existing national quotas could not be filled, because the traditional European source countries with large quotas, most importantly Britain, were no longer sending immigrants in large enough numbers. In light of these facts, a liberal proponent of scrapping the national-origin quota system could minimize the action as "updat[ing] our basic statute to conform more with our actual practice since 1952."[59]

The civil rights revolution, and the pressure by ethnic groups disadvantaged by the existing law, provided further impetus for repeal. The case for reform was not at first in terms of the "human rights" of immigrants but of the "civil rights" of Americans who were harmed by the old policy—harmed symbolically because their ethnic origins were slighted by the policy, or harmed materially because their requests for family unification were shattered by small and oversubscribed quotas. Chinese, Polish, and Italian ethnic organizations, especially, lobbied for reform. During the congressional hearings in 1964, a representative of the American Committee for Italian Migration addressed the plight of families divided by the quota law: "A married son or daughter born in England or Germany can join his or her American citizen parent almost immediately. The son or daughter of an American citizen may not be able to join his or her parent in this country for many, many years if he were born in Greece or Italy."[60] This unequal treatment of "American citizens" bothered even some nativists opposed to reform, such as the director of the notorious Liberty Lobby: "Apparently the quota system is not an insult to foreigners as such as it is to Americans of foreign parentage of identifiable racial strains such as the Italian-Americans and Chinese-Americans, who feel that the quotas make them less valuable . . . as American citizens than others, and I can understand their feelings" (quoted in Chin, 1996:303, n. 121).

Not just the dominant discourse of civil rights but demographic changes gave the losers of the old policy more weight. The 1960 census showed that 65 percent of the U.S. population was of non–Anglo-Saxon origins (Bennett, 1966:134, fn. 9). Since Franklin D. Roosevelt had embraced them in the 1930s and 1940s, the southern and eastern European ethnics, especially Jews, were overwhelmingly voting for the Democratic

Party (see Gerstle, 2001:129). Immigration reform, though bipartisan in the early 1960s, had to appeal especially to these ethnic voters. Exactly as in the 1924 debate over instituting national-origin quotas, the antirestrictionists in the 1965 debate over abolishing the quotas were mostly from the immigrant-receiving states in the Northeast and the industrial areas in the Midwest; now, however, they were in the majority, particularly after the landslide victory of the Democratic Party in the 1964 presidential elections. Representatives from ethnic urban districts, such as the chair of the House Judiciary Committee and sponsor of the 1965 Immigration Act, Edmund Cellar (a Democrat from Brooklyn, New York), set the tenor of the debate.[61]

In the debate surrounding the 1965 Immigration Act, foreign policy considerations were still prominent. Twice, in 1964 and 1965, Secretary of State Dean Rusk stated in House Committee hearings that "discrimination in our hospitality to different nationalities" was at odds with America's ambition to provide "critical leadership in a troubled and constantly changing world."[62] However, as Skrentny (2002:52–57) admits, the theme of equality was increasingly decoupled from foreign policy and national-security concerns. The temporal coincidence (as well as discursive linkage)[63] of immigration reform with the Civil Rights Act of 1964 and the Voting Rights Act of 1965 is too obvious to be missed in this respect.

Under the impact of the civil rights movement, racial equality was no longer the "boomerang argument" that it had been twenty years earlier; it now was a matter of principle not to be undercut by pragmatic considerations. While the biggest direct pressure originated from the (predominantly European) ethnic vote and lobbying, there is no evidence that the plight of "Europeans" was in any way put above that of "Asians" in the debate surrounding the 1965 reform. "Perhaps the most discriminatory aspect of the present law is the so-called Asia-Pacific triangle . . . It represents an overt statutory discrimination against more than one-half of the world's population," said Secretary Rusk during the 1964 House committee hearings.[64] Even "Europeans" presented their case in universalistic terms, as did this representative of the Committee for an Increase in the Spanish Immigration Quota: "[T]his [national-origin quota] law violates our basic national philosophy because it judges individuals, not on their worth, but solely on their place of birth."[65] Whatever their particular motivations, all participants in this debate were locked into a universalistic idiom that, in contrast to the idiom of 1924, could not be one for "Europeans" only. In fact, not a single proponent for change failed to draw the linkage between a universalistic immigration policy and America's "traditional ideals,"[66] which became encapsulated in John F. Kennedy's (1964) programmatic statement that America was, or rather had to be again, a "nation of immigrants." The metaphor of "return" to an allegedly universalistic founding myth may have been blind to America's racial origins as a white settler state, but it shows that immigration reform was a matter of principle, not just of (group or sectoral) interest.

Having said this, the 1965 (Hart-Cellar) Immigration Act, which established a country-neutral quota system selecting according to family ties and skills, still contained some concessions to restrictionists, most importantly an overwhelming emphasis given to family unification (which was meant to minimize the possibility of ethnic change)[67] and a ceiling on Western Hemisphere immigration. Particularly the latter is of interest here, because it was preceded by a debate on whether exempting Western Hemisphere countries from any quota restriction (as the President and State Department desired) would not constitute an impermissible positive discrimination. Since the 1924 Immigration Act, the Western Hemisphere countries[68] had been exempt from quota restrictions. This had bothered restrictionists from the start, because especially Mexican immigrants were racially despised as "illiterate, unclean, peonized masses," stemming from a "a mixture of Mediterranean-blooded Spanish peasants with low-grade Indians."[69] However, in this case the foreign-policy objective of maintaining a "special relationship" with the American "sister republics," plus southwestern growers' interest in cheap Mexican farm labor, prevailed over the restrictionist desires (see Pastor, 1984). This does not mean that Western Hemisphere immigration was unregulated; on the contrary, the negative individual screening on the basis of literacy, public-charge, contract-labor, and other individual-level administrative provisions fully applied to Western Hemisphere immigrants, and these provisions made it possible to keep the numbers effectively down, especially of Mexican immigrants.[70] In addition, an initial loophole of transit migration by people originating elsewhere was closed by making only native-born Western Hemisphere immigrants eligible for quota exemption (see Hutchinson, 1981:486).

The novelty of the 1965 debate was that the restrictionist case against the Western Hemisphere exemption could now be recast as one for non-discrimination, because this was the undisputable idiom of the day. This allowed the camouflaging of other interests, such as the fear of cheap-labor competition or the traditional ethnic animus against Mexican immigration. Consider this exchange between House Immigration Subcommittee chair Michael Feighan, a moderately restrictionist Ohio Democrat closely allied with labor unions, and Attorney General Nicholas Katzenbach. If the purpose of the present bill was "to remove a discrimination based upon where a person was born," Feighan argued, it was inconsistent not to apply this to the Western Hemisphere as well: "[B]y what logic do you distinguish between a privilege which favors some people because of where they were born and a penalty which disfavors other persons because of where they were born?"[71] Feighan's own "logic" obviously flattened the distinction between a positive and a negative discrimination, which the Attorney General sought to resurrect in turn: "I have not heard any of the Polish groups complain about this or suggest that a ceiling should be put on Western Hemisphere immigration . . . [T]he nonquota status of the Western Hemisphere people was never intended to be discriminatory against anyone."[72]

This exchange reveals two important things about ethnically selective immigration policies. First, not every particularism in which one national-origin group is favored over another is an ethnic particularism. When opposing the imposition of a Western Hemisphere ceiling, the government argued that the Western Hemisphere exemption of 1924 "was not based on race, religion, ancestry, or ethnic origin. It was simply recognition of Western Hemisphere solidarity."[73] Second, a positive discrimination becomes problematic only if there is a credible loser who openly finds fault with it. "I know of no dissatisfaction from other countries on this score. I know of no people who think this is discriminating or object to it. So why create a problem?" argued the Attorney General.[74] From a foreign-policy point of view, a Western Hemisphere ceiling *would* create a problem because the bulk of immigration from the Americas originated from the two neighboring countries, Canada to the north and Mexico to the south, with which the government "maintain(ed) very close relations" that it did not want to see harmed.[75]

Examples abound in which neighboring states, for the sake of friendly relations and the facilitation of economic exchanges, have created special migration regimes for their respective citizens, from the Nordic Passport Union between the Scandinavian countries to the Trans-Tasman Travel Arrangement between Australia and New Zealand, both of which allow free entry, residence, and work rights for their respective citizens. Interestingly, the United States chose not to establish such a special regime with its immediate neighbors. The 1965 Western Hemisphere ceiling, which limited the number of immigrants from the Americas to 120,000 per year, was only a first step toward folding the Western Hemisphere countries into the general quota regime, according to which every country had the same quota limit of 20,000 immigrants per year. If one asks why a positive derogation for neighboring countries—briefly supported by the Nixon administration in 1973–74 (see Gimpel and Edwards, 1999:114)—did not come, part of the answer is a syndrome of "guilt by association": the association of a positive discrimination with the negative discriminations that had been the hallmark of the national-origin quota system.

This syndrome is visible in the rejection of a higher quota for "contiguous countries" by the House Judiciary Committee: "The decision by this Committee to limit all countries to 20,000 has been based primarily on the desire that this legislation mark the final end of an immigration quota system based on nationality, whether the rationale behind it be the alleged national origins of our citizenry, as it was in the past, or geographical proximity—the argument previously advanced for preferential treatment of Canada and Mexico. The proposed legislation rejects the concept of a 'special relationship' between this country and certain other countries as a basis for our immigration law, in favor of a uniform treatment for all countries."[76]

Australia

Whereas postwar Americans would look back at the prewar legacy of racial exclusion as an extraneous and rapidly anachronistic violation of their democratic creed,[77] White Australia retained its prewar status as a "national dogma" (Elkin, 1945:6), the "indispensable condition of every other Australian policy," as one historian put it.[78] White Australia even met the ultimate test of a national creed, to provide for continuity across generations: "We inherited the White Australia policy from our fathers and grandfathers. We have in large measure been saved by it during the war. It is our responsibility to see that it is there to be handed down by the great-grand-children of our great-grand-children," said a government minister in 1945 (ibid., p. 7). Because of its intrinsic alignment with national self-definition, the White Australia policy persisted considerably longer than the racially exclusive immigration policy of most other new settler states.

Australian elite reasoning in 1945 is well captured in anthropologist A. P. Elkin's influential statement, "Re-Thinking the White Australia Policy" (1945). It takes the continuation of White Australia for granted, and suggests ways to make it "compatible with the dignity of such nations as India and China" (p. 9). After all, the latter had proved to be worthy and reliable allies in the Pacific war against Japan, so that their continued racial exclusion would amount to an inexcusable affront. The first thing to do was to change the justification of the policy so as to make it one motivated by a concern about "cultural difference, not colour" (p. 20). While the "colour" component was, in effect, difficult to eradicate, the relevant move was to shift from a claim of superiority to one of mere difference. Second, even better than dwelling in justifications, was to deny that any "White Australia" policy existed at all. As Elkin cunningly suggested, "Why not refer to the policy in Acts and speech simply as the Australian Immigration Policy?" (p. 24). Third, Elkin suggested that the goal of "limiting quite severely the numbers of oriental persons who can settle in Australia" (Elkin, 1945:31) was much better achieved by a "positive method" such as increasing nonpermanent entries or granting a "small annual quota" for permanent settlers from India and China.

With the exception of the quota proposal, which marked him as a far-out liberal at the time, Elkin anticipated almost point for point the changes that the White Australia policy would undergo after World War II.[79] What Elkin did not foresee is that the adjustments made to save the policy ultimately militated against it. In fact, one can reconstruct the end of White Australia as the unintended consequence of the government's attempts to save the policy. The most obvious example is the large-scale recruitment of European immigrants after World War II. The novelty of this was to put the "pulling" of certain (European) immigrants into the service of more effectively "blocking" the entry of other (Asian) immigrants and thus to combine policies that had so far proceeded on separate tracks. The reasoning was that Australia's vast continent had to be filled in order to forestall international (especially regional Asian) pressures on the restrictive policy. "[W]e cannot continue to hold our island continent for ourselves and our descendants unless we greatly increase our numbers," said Immigration Minister Arthur Calwell in his announcement of the Labor Government's massive postwar policy of "populate or perish."[80] The ambitious goal was to achieve 2 percent population growth per year, half of it from immigration, which would amount to 75,000 new immigrants per year. Naturally, Britons were targeted first, in an envisaged (and never achieved) ratio of 10:1, but other Europeans were proactively recruited also, "displaced persons" and refugees first (some 170,000 between 1947 and 1954), and regular immigrants later on, on the basis of bilateral agreements with several European governments.[81] This policy was remarkably successful on its own terms: already by 1953, 750,000 new European immigrants could be recruited, increasing the Australian population by over 10 percent in less than ten years (Holt, 1953:3). However, an unintended consequence of successively opening Australia to all Europeans was to make the continued exclusion of Asians more blatantly visible and thus less acceptable.

A second policy, which was likewise meant to shore up White Australia but eventually came to undermine it, was the "good neighbour policy" with the surrounding Asian countries. "We can help the people of Asia to raise their own standards of living, and indeed this is an obligation which we are eager to meet," said Immigration Minister Calwell in early 1949 (quoted in Brawley, 1995a:231–232). The manifold foreign aid programmes, participation in regional pacts and alliances (such as ANZUS and SEATO), bilateral trade agreements, and increased diplomatic exchanges on which Australia now embarked had the one purpose of making her restrictive immigration policy more acceptable to her Asian neighbors. However, in reality they helped create the regional ties, obligations, and involvements that had to militate against the policy itself. For instance, as a partial result of the 1950 Colombo Plan, which was meant to "buy Asia's acceptance of the White Australia policy" (ibid., p. 254), a large presence of Asian exchange students evolved at Australia's universities— by the late 1950s, one-tenth of all University of Sydney students were non-European (Jordens, 1997:16). Their presence fed the first wave of domestic student and academic activism against the White Australia policy in the early 1960s (see London, 1970:123). Even more dysfunctional for White Australia were the economic ties and interests that resulted from the good-neighbor policy. The paradigmatic case is Japan, which transmuted from Australia's main enemy to main trading partner, not just within Asia.

The foreign policy imperative of good neighborliness was the main immediate factor behind a tacit liberalization of the restrictive immigration policy. It had to be a tacit liberalization, proceeding within the closed doors of the Department of Immigration and the Cabinet, because public opinion[82] and most political parties[83] continued to stand solidly behind "the established immigration policy." A first set of liberalized entry, residence, and family unification rules for non-Europeans was passed in October 1956.[84] One key provision, which had been pushed for by the Department of Exterior Affairs, allowed the "entry for extended stay" of "highly qualified Asians." In combination with another provision that, for the first time in federated Australia, made permanent residence and naturalization available to Asians after fifteen years of stay, this measure meant that the veil of White Australia had in principle been lifted, because certain Asians were now allowed to enter for de facto settlement. Finally, the new rules relaxed what one author had called "perhaps the cruelest aspect of the [White Australia] policy" (Jordens, 1997:137), the absolute ban on nonwhite family immigration that had previously afflicted even Australian citizens.

However, the tacit, de facto liberalization of the White Australia policy was hidden behind new rhetorical devices to beef up racial exclusion. One new justification was to avoid the frictions that pluriracial societies, both in the West and in the decolonizing East, were undergoing at the time. This was, indeed, an old theme that had underlain the anticipatory thrust of the original White Australia policy in 1901. But it was lent new relevance by contemporary race conflicts, such as the civil rights struggle in the United States. "The experience of countries where racial intermixtures have been tried is not encouraging," said Immigration Minister Downer in July 1960 (quoted in Rivett, 1962:159). Australia's very success at keeping nonwhites out offered her the unique opportunity to exclude from the start the possibility of U.S.-style race conflict. Even domestic critics of the White Australia policy underlined the qualitative difference between a racially restrictive entry policy and a policy, such as South African apartheid, that oppressed a domestic racial group. "No such charge can be laid fairly against the White Australia policy. The people we exclude are not thereby deprived of possessing the same control over their own affairs as we exercise over ours," conceded an influential critique of the White Australia policy in 1962 (Rivett, 1962:93).

Immigration reform for the sake of Asian regional integration received an unprecedented boost when a career diplomat from the Department of External Affairs, Peter Heydon, became the new secretary of the Department of Immigration in 1961 (see Brawley, 1995b). Heydon embodied the foreign-policy material from which the protracted death of White Australia was made, although for domestic public consumption the façade of continuity was stubbornly maintained. Heydon's main cause was to put Asian immigrants on a par with European immigrants with respect to permanent residence and naturalization rights. According to the 1956 rules, Asians had to wait fifteen years before they qualified for both, whereas most Europeans had to wait only five years, some even less. Evidently, the standard of reference had silently shifted—what had constituted a blow to the blanket exclusion of Asians in 1956 appeared as a discrimination only a few years later.[85] A second inequity was that "highly qualified" Asians according to the 1956 rules were initially admitted for nonpermanent residence only, which entailed sharply reduced family rights. Heydon's proposal was to accept "well qualified" Asians (note the change from "highly" to "well") as settlers from the start, which would allow them to bring their families immediately. This became policy in 1966. It was by now a ritual that any reform, even one that subsequently was hailed as the de facto end of White Australia, was presented as a basic continuation of the "established immigration policy." Accordingly, Immigration Minister Opperman declared in Parliament that the new policy was "not departing from the fundamental principles of our immigration policy . . . and the basic aim of preserving a homogeneous population will be maintained."[86] At least, there was no denying what had motivated the reform: foreign-policy and regional integration concerns. As Prime Minister Holt put it before Parliament, "Australia's increasing involvement in Asian developments, the rapid growth of our trade with Asian countries . . . the expansion of our military effort and the scale of diplomatic contact, the growth of tourism to and from the countries of Asia combine to make such a review desirable in our eyes" (quoted in Brawley, 1995a:310).

Unlike the American case, where the emphasis shifted over time from foreign policy to domestic equality concerns, the Australian liberalization of immigration policy remained fixed on the foreign-policy dimension. It could not be otherwise, because, as a result of the very success of White Australia, there were no significant domestic groups around who were harmed by the policy. The opposition to White Australia was mostly intellectual opposition, in terms of the Immigration Reform Group (IRG), which formed in the early 1960s at the University of Melbourne.[87]

The IRG's widely read manifesto, *Immigration: Control or Colour Bar* (Rivett, 1962), is striking in several respects. First, it purportedly did "not seek a change in the present law, but in the policy administered under that law" (ibid., p. 28). Indeed, after the removal of the notorious dictation test in the Migration Act of 1958, there was little to find fault with in the letter of the law, which was perfectly neutral and, in giving near absolute discretion to the Immigration Minister in the granting or refusal of entry permits, could be implemented in either direction—liberal or illiberal. Second, whereas it presented the "immorality" of the color bar as the first and foremost reason for change, IRG strangely conceded that in certain situations there could be "differential treatment" on the basis of race (ibid., p.87). IRG advocated a regime of "occupationally balanced" intakes on the basis of bilateral agreements with Asian states, so that nationality clearly had to be a factor in selecting Asian immigrants. The leap from nationality to race would occur through deciding how many to admit from a particular Asian country; here, as the Nestor of the group, Kenneth Rivett (1992b:16), bluntly admitted, "race and colour could be taken into account if public attitudes in Australia made this advisable." Such pragmatism on race, which at that time was no longer conceivable in the United States, shows that the White Australia legacy cast its long shadow over its opponents too.[88]

Foreign policy concerns were again dominant when the symbolic rupture with the "established immigration policy" finally occurred under a Labor government in 1973. Gough Whitlam, whose election victory in December 1972 marked the end of 23 years of liberal-conservative rule,[89] was singularly concerned about Australia's image abroad, and he tellingly took on the portfolio of Foreign Minister in addition to that of Prime Minister. Under his leadership in the opposition, the Labor Party had shed its classic role as White Australia's watchdog, becoming in June 1971 the first party to commit itself explicitly to a nondiscriminatory immigration policy. For a short but significant moment, this put to an end the traditional bipartisanship in immigration policy; in this sense, the end of White Australia was simply the result of Labor's election victory in 1972. Party differences continued to be secondary, however, because upon its quick return to power in 1975 the Liberal-Country Party did not dare to turn the clock back. The one constant shared by all parties was immigration policy in the interest of foreign relations. Tellingly, the official abdication of White Australia occurred within a "ministerial statement on international affairs," made by Whitlam in his capacity as Foreign Minister: "One of the crucial ways in which we must improve our global reputation is to apply our aspirations for equality at home to our relations with the peoples of the world as a whole . . . [W]e have an obligation to remove methodically from Australia's laws and practices all racially discriminatory provisions . . . As an island nation of predominantly European inhabitants situated on the edge of Asia, we cannot afford the stigma of racialism."[90]

The Whitlam government flanked the end of White Australia with two additional measures: the end of (some) positive discriminations for British immigrants and the launching of "multiculturalism" as a new national self-description. Regarding the first, there is no necessary link between ending the negative discrimination of nonwhite immigrants and removing a positive discrimination for British immigrants. This is because the reference point for the latter was not the excluded Asians but European immigrants, who had never been excluded but formed the baseline of "alien" immigrants, from which positive derogations were made for British immigrants. One can observe here the same syndrome of guilt by association that had driven the United States to eradicate all discriminations, negative *and* positive, from its immigration laws after 1965. Before 1973, British immigration to Australia was "like walking from one room to another," as a Labor deputy put it in the 1950s (quoted in Jordens, 1997:192). Much as in Britain itself, important rights, such as the (active and passive) franchise or the right to enter the public services, were invested in the status of "British subject" and not in that of "Australian citizen." Accordingly, there were few incentives for British immigrants to acquire Australian citizenship, few of them actually did, and nobody on the Australian side bothered (see Zappala and Castles, 2000:38–39). In fact, British immigrants were not even "aliens" as that status was defined (until 1984) as not having the status of British subject, Irish citizen, or protected person. If British immigrants nevertheless wanted to become Australians, they did not have to "naturalize" after five years of minimum residence, as "alien" immigrants had to; instead, they could "register" as Australian citizen after only one year of residence, and this without attending a public citizenship ceremony. Under Whitlam, a crucial first move in assimilating British to "alien" immigrants was to subject all of them to a uniform naturalization regime, with a (shortened) minimum residence period of three (instead five) years.[91] Interestingly, Whitlam later misrepresented this reform as one that benefited non-Europeans, even though its main thrust had been to remove the distinction between British and "alien" immigrants (which at that point could be either European or non-European).[92] This shows the tendency in new settler states to short-circuit the removal of negative discriminations with that of positive discriminations also, even though both were not necessarily related.

The thrust of removing positive discriminations for British immigrants is clear: Australia was to be no longer British. That this became an issue just when White Australia was officially buried confirms that White Australia itself had previously stood, however subterranean and incompletely, for the non-Britishness of Australia. Now that White Australia was gone, the non-Britishness of Australia had to be achieved and reaffirmed by other means—negatively, through the removal of privileges for British immigrants; positively, through a new national self-description in terms of "multiculturalism." Like the approximation of British to other immigrants, multiculturalism was born in the very moment that White Australia was put to rest. Its meteoric rise as national self-description, immediately shared across party lines and not seriously questioned until the mid-1980s, shows by implication the previous centrality of White Australia for national self-description, even in its anonymous postwar version. Whitlam's immigration minister, Al Grassby, who is credited with the invention of Australian multiculturalism, interestingly preferred the notion of "family of the nation" to that of multiculturalism proper, thus conveying the nation-building function of the new creed.[93] More than in any other country in the world (including Canada, from which the concept was borrowed),[94] multiculturalism in Australia represents a "new idea of the nation" (Meaney, 1995:185), though not necessarily one that ever came to be clearly defined. "What it was into which all 'ethnic' groups should integrate or what 'the common values' were with which all Australians should identify remained unclear and elusive," argues one Australian observer (ibid.), particularly with respect to the ambiguous British element in Australian self-definition.[95] A closely related new self-description, which had been cautiously ventured already before Whitlam's symbolic break with White Australia, was that of Australia as an American-style "nation of immigrants."[96] In contrast to the American case, however, where the "nation of immigrants" formula was linked to a return to an allegedly untainted past, there could at least be no presumption that Australia had ever been a "nation of immigrants" in any meaningful sense before.

Challenges to Source-Country Universalism

Once they are put in place, nondiscriminatory immigration policies are typically subject to two opposite pressures: "liberal" and "restrictive." On the liberal side, the claim is that not enough has been achieved. Other admissions policies, such as asylum and refugee policy, may still be discriminatory and thus in need of adjustment; or, as some American "critical race" theorists have argued, "facially race-neutral" immigration policies may be clouded by "unmistakably disparate impacts on immigrants of color" (Johnson, 2000:532).[97] On the restrictive side, there is the opposite claim that too much has been achieved. As one notorious critic of U.S. policy put it, "[t]he racial and ethnic balance of America is being radically altered through public policy . . . *Is it what Americans want?*" (Brimelow, 1995:xvii).

The turn to source-country universalism in the mid-1960s to early 1970s has indeed radically altered the ethnic and racial composition of immigration flows and with it the texture of the American and Australian societies. The most dramatic change is with respect to the once excluded Asians, who now represent well above one-third of the annual immigrant intakes in both countries. Conversely, the share of the once favored European immigrants has significantly decreased, in the United States from one-third in the 1960s to just 16 percent by 2000 (Schuck, 2003:89), and in Australia from 70 percent in 1972 (the last year of the White Australia policy) to under 30 percent already by 1988 (Jayasuriya and Sang, 1992:42). Three decades of diversified flows have left a significant imprint on the population balance. The Anglo-Celtic component of the Australian population dropped from nearly 90 percent in 1946 to 70 percent in 1998, while the Asian and North African component increased from under 1 percent to over 8 percent (Price, 1998:127–128; 1999:12). In the United States, characterized by far more diverse immigrant flows from the start, the post-1965 "third-worldization" of immigration has increased the population share of Hispanics from 3.5 percent in 1960 to 13.4 percent in 2000 and of Asians from 0.6 to 4.2 percent in the same period. In Peter Brimelow's (1995:62) paranoid imagery, American whites are "pincered" by the rapid growth of Hispanics, blacks, and Asians, and they are likely to "becom[e] a minority by 2050."

Given the magnitude of the population changes brought about by nondiscriminatory immigration policies, there has been surprisingly little opposition to the new settler states' radical departure from their European origins. For this precise context Gary Freeman (1995a:884) has coined the term "antipopulist norm," which prohibits political elites from "argument over the ethnic composition of migrant streams." This norm is in a circular way backed by settler states' memory of their own racist past. Now universally condemned across the political spectrum, this racist past is mobilized whenever it seems to reappear in the present, and thus it functions as a guarantee that it will not be repeated. The antipopulist elite norm has certainly not prevented mass publics from taking an opposite stance, creating a gap that is occasionally exploited by populist entrepreneurs.[98] However, as particularly the Australian case will show, such critical moments have usually been occasions for elites to solemnly reconfirm their commitment to the principle of nondiscrimination.

Under the reign of the antipopulist norm, concerns about ethnically skewed immigration flows can be expressed only indirectly. The legitimate idiom of immigration policy has moved away from the open favoring or disfavoring of certain "races" or nationalities to the ethnically anonymous balancing of skill-based, family-based, and humanitarian flows. However, because these ethnically anonymous selection categories tend to be disproportionately used by specific nationality groups, there is the persistent suspicion that favoring one over the other category is ethnic or racial discrimination in disguise. The call for skill-based immigration, raised in Australia and the United States alike since the onset of perceived "globalization" in the late 1980s, is then denounced as a preference for European immigrants. Conversely, parallel attempts to restrict (usually low-skilled and heavily non-European) family migration are denounced as proxies for opposing non-European immigrants.

Such reasoning is inherently polemical and reserved to the critics of government policy. Governments usually deny that ethnic considerations shape their immigration policies. Accordingly, it is most often impossible to know whether the statistical correlation between ethnic group and selection category is also a causal "mechanism" (Elster, 1989) that motivates government practices. To be sure, on the side of ethnic immigrant groups and their advocates, there is a clear awareness of which selection criteria suit them best. Ethnic groups have usually rallied in defense of large family quotas as well as expansive definitions of what constitutes a family. An example is Asian-American and Hispanic ethnic organizations in the United States, which helped avert a (skill-oriented) attack on the existing large family quota in the 1990 Legal Immigration Act. This is not to say that the ethnic groups who mobilize for large family quotas are necessarily those who eventually profit from these quotas. In Australia, for instance, southern European immigrant groups helped institute generous family provisions in the early 1980s, which were then mostly used by Asian immigrants instead.

The matching of ethnic groups with nonethnic selection criteria is evidently a tricky affair. This holds true not only for family-based but also for skill-based selection. Quotas for skilled immigrants, which used to be taken as a subterfuge for preferring European immigrants, are now heavily used by non-European immigrants also. In Australia, for instance, 44 percent of the skill-based intakes in 1997 were of Asian-origin (Winkelmann, 2001:28). The increasingly equal distribution of non-European immigrants over family- *and* skill-based selection categories is removing the basis for the racism-by-subterfuge charge, which used to be raised whenever governments were trying to restrict family immigration and increase skill-based immigration instead.

The following discussion of contemporary challenges to source-country universalism in the United States and Australia will show two things. First, the principle of nondiscriminatory immigration policies has proved resilient to its occasional challenges. This supports Freeman's claim that the underlying "antipopulist norm" has come to correspond to the very "ethos" of liberal democracy, irrespective of "historically specific" conjunctures, which was Rogers Brubaker's counterclaim (1995:905). However, there are indirect possibilities for states to shape the ethnic composition of migrant streams through manipulating the facially nonethnic selection criteria for skill-based, family-based, and humanitarian immigration. Whether this shaping is only in the eye of the critic or is intended policy, cannot be judged beforehand; it depends. This is also because (with the curious exception of so-called "diversity" immigration in the United States) the involved governments have mostly denied that ethnic concerns are influencing their immigration policies. Short of resorting to a conspiracy theory, it is difficult to prove intent if intent is denied.

Second, source-country universalism is generically incomplete. Even facially nonethnic immigration policies will always have disparate impacts on different ethnic groups. As Hiroshi Motomura (1996:1941) put it with respect to the United States, "[e]qual protection does not necessarily lead to equal outcomes." Accordingly, a charge that ethnic favoritism or racism is driving facially universalistic immigration policies can always be made. If even the uniform country quotas in U.S. legal immigration policy constitute "discrimination" against would-be immigrants from populous (non-European) states such as Mexico or the Philippines, as some critics have argued (most lucidly, Ting, 1995), the very possibility of source-country universalism and nondiscrimination is indeed in question. A truly impartial immigration policy is an impossibility because in including some, all others have to be excluded, and an ethnic pattern in this can always be found. This guarantees that the immigration policies of new settler states will remain tainted by the charge of ethnic favoritism or racism in the years to come.

Unrepealed Plenary Power, Discriminatory Asylum, and Diversity Immigration in the United States

After the scrapping of racial exclusion and national-origin quotas in 1965, U.S. immigration policies have been subjected to the opposite critiques of "not enough" and "too much" nondiscrimination and source-country universalism (with the caveat that the latter could be raised only indirectly, in universalistic justice terms). The most prominent example of an incompletely discarded, racially discriminatory past is the legal doctrine of plenary power, which largely exempts immigration law and policy from judicial scrutiny. Formulated in the context of the 1880s Chinese exclusion cases, plenary power remains unrepealed today, and well into the 1980s courts have affirmed that on its grounds Congress was in principle free to exclude immigrants on the basis of race, if it so wished (Chin, 1998:3, n. 5 and 6). Immigration law thus constitutes the only branch of American law that is exempted from judicial suspicion of racial classifications. A return to racial exclusion may be politically unthinkable; however, it would be a return for which no constitutional remedy exists, as long as plenary power invests Congress and the federal executive with near-absolute immigration powers. Throughout the past decades, there has been an impressive list of legal arguments against this anomaly in public law (most recently Aleinikoff, 2002). Among them, Gabriel Chin (1998) has given the most compelling reason why plenary power has become anachronistic and thus should be rescinded. Not enumerated anywhere in the Constitution, plenary power was derived from international law, which in the 1890s enshrined the absolute power of sovereign states.[99] However, in the meantime international law has changed, endowing individuals with the status of legal subjects and adopting the principle of racial nondiscrimination. Accordingly, Chin concludes, there is no longer any substantive justification to retain plenary power, and courts have incidentally retained it in the thin terms of *stare decisis* only.

Moving from law to policy, refugee and asylum admission is that aspect of U.S. immigration policy in which source-country universalism has remained notoriously incomplete. The same 1965 Immigration Act that abolished the national-origin quotas also established an ideologically and geographically skewed system of refugee admission in which only refugees from Communism or from the Middle East formally qualified.[100] In retrospect, it is astonishing that this obvious inconsistency between universalistic legal immigrant and particularistic refugee admission went unnoticed and unopposed at the time—at the height of the Cold War it was probably not thinkable that refugees could be from other than Communist regimes. However, once this equation mellowed, and other-than-Communist regimes turned out to be refugee-generating (especially in Latin America), the pressures for a nondiscriminatory refugee policy mounted. The result was the Refugee Act of 1980, which incorporated the spirit of the international refugee regime, as well as the source-country universalism of the domestic immigration regime, in putting refugee admission on a universalistic basis. According to a House Judiciary Committee report, the purpose of the new law was that "the plight of the refugees themselves as opposed to national-origin or political considerations should be paramount in determining which refugees are to be admitted to the United States" (quoted in Zucker and Zucker, 1992:63).

This promise remained unfulfilled. While the letter of the law was now universalistic, in its administrative implementation U.S. refugee and asylum policy continued to be dominated by foreign policy considerations, especially the Cold War confrontation with Communism. Note that this is a case in which foreign policy imperatives did not push for a universalistic but a particularistic admissions policy, simply because admitting refugees from "friendly" (if nondemocratic) regimes would delegitimize the latter and undermine the common cause against Communism.

In assessing the consequences of this violation of the nondiscrimination principle, one first has to distinguish clearly between the separate domains of refugee resettlement and asylum. Though both were covered jointly by the 1980 Refugee Act, their operations (as well as conflict potentials) are rather different. Refugee policy proper consists of resettling predesignated groups, in numbers and modalities determined by the refuge-offering state. Given the high number and spread of refugees worldwide, such proactive refugee admission cannot but be particularistic and be influenced by foreign-policy considerations and particular obligations of the receiving state to particular refugee groups. In legal terms also, predesignated refugee intakes are discretionary, determined by the executive, and nonjudiciable, to be remedied only by legislation in Congress. Thus it was occasionally deplored, but not really contested, that refugee resettlement remained ideologically and geographically skewed.

Between 1987 and 1991, 89 percent of predesignated refugee allotments went to Communist areas in Asia (especially Indochina) and Europe, while fewer than 4 percent each went to Africa—the world's most refugee-ridden continent—and to Latin America, including the Caribbean (Lennox, 1993:711).

The matter is altogether different with respect to asylum adjudication, which deals with would-be refugees presenting themselves at the U.S. borders or already inside the United States. In this situation there are not only beneficiaries but like-situated losers from positive discrimination, stirring the minimum charge of morally and legally impermissible national-origin discrimination. When the era of mass asylum seeking suddenly opened in the early 1980s with "boat people" from Cuba and Haiti and "feet people" from civil war–ravaged Central America, the federal government indeed prolonged its discretionary approach in refugee policy to the new asylum seekers. Only Cubans and Nicaraguans were welcome, without even being subjected to much of an individual procedure of refugee recognition, because they originated from Communist regimes. By contrast, Haitians, Salvadorans, and Guatemalans were branded as "economic" migrants subject to deportation because they originated from regimes that were certainly nondemocratic yet anti-Communist. In contrast to refugee resettlement, which produces only winners, an equally ideologically and geographically skewed asylum policy produced concrete losers, in terms of those asylum seekers who were denied a fair procedure and detained or deported only because they originated from "friendly" regimes. Their plight was taken up throughout the 1980s and 1990s by courts and protest movements, such as the church-led sanctuary movement.

It is important to see that the national-origin discrimination inherent in U.S. asylum policy were not ethnic but ideological discriminations; they judged an individual's entry bid not on the basis of her ascriptive group membership but on that of the political orientation of the regime that she was seeking to escape. In this sense, the migration engendered (or prevented) by this policy is not "ethnic migration" and falls outside the purview of this study.

The only possible exception to this is Haitian asylum seekers, who—in the view of some critics[101]—were singled out for exclusion because they were black. There is no doubt that Haitian asylum seekers, mostly seeking to enter illicitly by boat, received a singularly harsh treatment, in terms of accelerated deportation, detention, and interdiction at sea.[102] Between 1981 and 1990, peak years of Haitian asylum seeking, only 28 of 24,000 Haitian asylum applications were accepted (Little, 1998:722). However, the claim that race was motivating this policy, and not the Haitians' origins from a ruthless yet "friendly" regime, is difficult to prove. The celebrated district court rule, *Haitian Refugee Center v. Civiletti* (1980), outlawed as "impermissible discrimination on the basis of national origin" the INS's so-called "Haitian Program" of accelerated deportation and denial of due process to Haitian asylum seekers. In addition, the court vaguely suggested that the fact that "[a]ll of the plaintiffs are black" could be a "possible underlying reason" of this national-origin discrimination, especially if one compared their harsh treatment with the warm welcome bestowed at the same time on Cuban boat people, few of whom "are black."[103] No court ever went further to suggest that "race" was driving the incriminated asylum policy. There is simply no good evidence for such a claim. For instance, if Haitian exclusion was a race policy, why were Salvadoran and Guatemalan asylum seekers who entered illicitly across the southern land border treated little better than the Haitians? The biggest plausibility of the race claim derives from a counterfactual. In the words of New York Democratic representative Charles Rangel, "[i]s there any question in your mind that if the people on these boats came from Ireland that we would exercise the same policy? Do you think for one minute that the United States would return these people to Ireland?" (quoted in Lennox, 1993:717, n. 234). Like all counterfactuals, this one is impossible to disprove. However, against the race claim speaks the fact that other nonwhite asylum seekers fared much better than the Haitians, as long as they originated from Communist or nonfriendly regimes.[104]

Its implausibility did not make the claim of race discrimination any less effective as a weapon in domestic politics. Here the Congressional Black Caucus and other civil-rights organizations drew an analogy between the exclusion of Haitians and the oppression of domestic blacks. Such pressure moved the Clinton administration to end the policy of the wholesale high-sea repatriation of Haitian boat people in 1994 (see Ortiz Miranda, 1995:724–727). This was only a small step in the gradual (and still incomplete) move toward source-country universalism in U.S. asylum policy. However, contrary to the claim of race discrimination against Haitians, one could as well argue that their blackness was a resource for them, securing them domestic allies that equally disadvantaged asylum-seeking groups did not have.

In contrast to asylum- and refugee policy, whose national-origin distinctions appeared only in the administrative implementation of a facially neutral refugee law, a feature of "diversity" immigration is to inscribe national-origin distinctions into the letter of immigration law itself. In principle (though not in reality) this makes diversity immigration a more serious affront to source-country universalism. Critics usually include diversity immigration in their list of discriminatory features prevailing in current U.S. immigration law and policy. However, diversity immigration differs from other discriminations, such as past racial legacies or admissions policies "not yet" seized by the norm of nondiscrimination, in having arisen as a response to the nondiscriminatory immigration policy established in 1965. At heart, it is a backlash to the 1965 Immigration Act, articulating a sense of "too much" source-country universalism after 1965. In the words of Daniel P. Moynihan, one of the early supporters of a "diversity" quota in the U.S. Senate: "The effort to limit immigration in 1924 to some groups, to prefer some groups over others, was not well received . . . *Now, we seem to have moved too far in the other direction,* and I think a mid-course correction is in order."[105] However, the smallish scale of diversity immigration, as well as the gentle and camouflaged tone in which it was brought forward, attest to the resilience of source-country universalism. Diversity immigration shows that the only legitimate opposition to source-country universalism is one that claims to perfect it.

At the origin of diversity immigration is ethnic politics. The 1980s witnessed a massive wave of Irish immigration, which was caused by a severe economic crisis in Ireland. In the New York area alone, some 150,000 Irish newcomers arrived between 1982 and 1988, mostly entering as students or tourists and then overstaying.[106] Their precarious status revealed some shortcomings of the present immigration system. Lacking the requisite family ties, the Irish newcomers could not profit from the large family quotas that dominated U.S. legal immigration since 1965; and there were too many of them (and insufficiently skilled at that) to profit from the small occupational quotas. Finally, as illegal immigrants the Irish were not covered by the (Hispanic-oriented) amnesty provision under the 1986 Immigration Reform and Control Act (IRCA) either, because they had arrived after its cutoff date in 1982. At the same time the most mythologized of all European immigrant groups in America, the Irish quickly came to symbolize a sense that Europeans were the losers of the 1965 immigration reform and its sequels.

The first success of Irish lobbying, primarily by a newly formed organization called the Irish Immigration Reform Movement (IIRM),[107] was a last-minute addition to IRCA, the so-called "NP-5" visa program, which allotted 5,000 extra visas for 1987 and 1988 to citizens of 36 countries that were deemed "adversely affected" by the 1965 Act.[108] Twenty-seven of these countries were European, two Asian, two African, four North and South American, and one Oceanian. Interestingly, a measure that had a clear national and regional focus—Ireland and Western Europe—still could not present itself as such explicitly, but had to camouflage its intention in neutral language, thus allowing the entry of other countries and regions not primarily "meant" by the measure. That indirection did not matter much. 40 percent of NP-5 visas according to IRCA's section 314 were reaped by Irish applicants, not least because they were better informed and organized than any other nationality group. In 1988 the NP-5 program was extended for two more years, now with the triple amount of 30,000 visas to be handed out. Because there was concern about the Eurocentric bias of the program, Congress also passed an additional "OP-1" program in 1988, which consisted of 20,000 visas over a two-year period for natives of "underrepresented countries." Both formulas, "adversely affected" and "underrepresented," were regional formulas. Yet they differed in important ways. "Adversely affected" made the 1965 Immigration Act the touchstone: Only natives from countries that sent fewer immigrants after the act than before the act qualified. By contrast, "underrepresented" referred to any country that, at the time, used less than 25 percent of its annually allotted maximum visas. This included many African and Asian states that could not have been "adversely affected" by the 1965 act because they had been barred from sending *any* immigrants up to that point. Accordingly, it was mostly immigrants from non-European states who would profit from the OP-1 program— Bangladesh, Pakistan, Egypt, or Peru.

The interesting further development is that, within the umbrella of diversity immigration, the "adversely affected country" component was gradually eliminated, whereas the "underrepresented country" formula was rendered permanent. This must be read as a concession to the principle of source-country universalism, which was more blatantly violated by the (Eurocentric) "adversely affected" formula than by the "underrepresented" formula. As a result, the Europeans who originally were to profit from diversity immigration were eventually pushed to the margins. Diversity immigration took this final form in the 1990 Legal Immigration Act. The

NP-5 program for "adversely affected" countries was prolonged for only three more years (yet with a significantly increased visa total of 120,000). Curiously, 40 percent of these visas were to go to "natives of the foreign state the natives of which received the greatest number of visas issued under section 314 of I.R.C.A." (quoted in Jacob, 1992:300, fn. 15). The state meant by this contorted circumlocution was Ireland. An Irish lobbyist explains: "The Senate didn't want to be country-specific. The attitude was, 'We'll do this for you guys, but let's not talk about it'" (ibid., p. 334). From 1994 the permanent diversity visa program, modeled on the "underrepresented country" formula, was to take the place of the temporary program that was modeled on the "adversely affected" formula (and that had become known as the "Irish lottery"). Using a complex mathematical formula that divides the world into "high-admission" and "low-admission" states and regions, the permanent program provides 55,000 visas per years to natives of states from which immigration had been lower than 50,000 in the past five years. Epitomizing the drift away from its European origins, in 1990 this permanent diversity program excluded only those twelve states in the world that had monopolized legal immigration to the United States at this point.[109] In the late 1990s, in a further concession to the charge of Eurocentrism and Irish favoritism that continued to cloud diversity immigration, Congress introduced a self-correcting formula that excluded from the program those countries that had used almost all of their allotted diversity visas during the preceding five years. Accordingly, the leading sending countries in 2002 included Ghana, Nigeria, Sierra Leone, Ukraine, Bangladesh, and Ethiopia.[110] Ireland, whose late-1980s (and long-finished) immigration emergency had started the whole program, is now far down the list (Schuck, 2003:128).

Besides its increasingly extra-European focus, diversity immigration underwent a second interesting transmutation. Initially, the call for more European immigrants was fused with the call for reorienting the selection focus from family unification to skills. The massive third-worldization of post-1965 immigration occurred predominantly through the large family quotas. For instance, by the mid-1980s Mexico and the Philippines alone accounted for almost 40 percent of the two million registered would-be family migrants waiting "in the pipeline."[111] Studies showed that this Asian- and Hispanic-dominated family immigration went along with a decrease in the human capital of migrants (e.g., Borjas, 1990). Conversely, in the early debate preceding the 1990 Legal Immigration Act, there was an automatic equation of "more skilled" with "more European" immigrants. This equation was most obvious in the category of "independent immigrant," which was proposed by Senators Kennedy and Simpson in 1987. They were to be selected on the basis of a points system stressing origins in "any country adversely affected" by the 1965 law, education, needed skills, and English-language competence. This Senate proposal married two agendas: Kennedy's interest in helping out the Irish, which was presented as strengthening "the 'old seed' sources of our heritage;"[112] and Simpson's interest in more skill-based immigrants, characterized by him as "the 'new seed' immigrant, 'classic immigrant,' if you will, [who] . . . represents now only five percent of our total immigration."[113] Crucially, the space for "independent immigrants" was to be created by cutting the second and fifth preferences for family immigrants, which were jealously guarded by the Asian and Hispanic lobbies. Their opposition helped crush this proposal in the House, where it was perceived as "racially-biased" (in Tichenor, 2002:269). The Irish lobby was not happy either, because they feared to be outskilled by English-speaking Asians[114] and because this proposal did little to help those who were currently illegal.

The further development, culminating in the 1990 Legal Immigration Act, was to turn the negative-sum into a positive-sum game, so that the (ethnic) wins in one category would not occur at the cost of (ethnic) losses in another.[115] And, crucially for our purposes, the trend was to differentiate more clearly between skill-based and diversity immigration. The 1990 Legal Immigration Act, which increased legal immigration by 40 percent, could thus be hailed as a simultaneous "triumph for 'cultural diversity,' 'family unity,' and 'job creation.'"[116] This meant that the skill-component in diversity immigration had now practically disappeared; a high-school diploma or two-year work experience sufficed on the skill side to qualify for a diversity visa. Because of the differentiation between skill-based and diversity immigration, the United States now has four modes of selecting immigrants instead of the usual three: humanitarian, family, skills, and—diversity.

With respect to the debate surrounding diversity immigration, its proponents tried to set it apart from the maligned national-origin quotas, whereas its opponents did everything to identify the two. On the proponents' side, the dominant move was to present the case for diversity immigration as a matter of justice. This is encapsulated in the very notion of "diversity," which was pirated by European ethnics from non-European minority groups in the U.S. "We need to restore fairness and balance to our immigration laws to ensure that certain individuals are not penalized because of their long heritage in this country," Senator Moynihan underscored the justice motif.[117] In this sense, diversity immigration was not a violation of a nondiscriminatory immigration policy but a matter of "fine tuning" the latter.[118] Strictly speaking, however, this was not so different from the justification of the old national-origin quotas, which were also presented as a matter of justice for old-stock (northwestern European) immigrants. There were even slippages into the long-discarded notion that new immigrants should somehow "mirror" the ethnic makeup of the domestic population. Moynihan spoke of "sort of a principle of representation": "[P]eople who arrive in the future ought to in some sense reflect those who have arrived in the past."[119] From here it was not far to the notion that more European immigration was good for social integration, which had been the most important justification for the national-origin quotas: "[W]hen native-born Americans see the lands of their forefathers more justly represented in today's immigrant pool, they are reminded that we are indeed a 'nation of immigrants.'"[120] This was a barely concealed hint that diversity immigration would help ease social tensions and distemper inspired among European-origin groups by non-European immigration.

A more compelling way of setting diversity immigration apart from national-origin immigration was not in terms of their justifications, but of their different scales. Whereas the national-origin quotas constituted the totality of legal immigration between 1924 and 1965, diversity immigration constituted less than 10 percent of legal immigration after 1990, and—as its proponents busily pointed out—it did not substitute for but was added on to the family quotas (which were considered by all, even the Europeans, as the legitimate turf of the non-European immigrant lobby). Diversity immigration was thus utterly devoid of the negative discriminations that had been the driving intent of the only facially positive discriminations enunciated in the national-origin quotas. "Our proposals do not take any number away from any other countries. If our proposals are implemented, the vast majority of visas will continue to go to countries which currently dominate the immigrant stream," said the leader of the IIRM.[121] This explains why the opposition by the non-European ethnic groups was more ceremonial than acidic—the two camps fished in different waters.

On the critics' side, there was every attempt to identify diversity immigration with the discarded national-origin quotas. In one critic's words, a preference for immigrants from "adversely affected countries" comes "very, very close to a national origins concept, which we worked very, very hard to get out of our laws for many years."[122] For the Organization of Chinese Americans, the "adversely affected country" criterion was "discriminatory *per se* against most Asian, Hispanic and Third World countries," simply because it left out most of them.[123] This complaint overlooked the fact that this exclusion was de facto, not de jure, and that the European ethnics could make precisely the same argument with respect to their de facto exclusion from the family quotas. A more effective critique was to point to the faulty baseline of the "discrimination" charge made by the European lobby. In the latter's view, the sharp drop of European immigrants after 1965 constituted "discrimination in reverse."[124] This objection, however, ignores the fact that the privileged position of (some) Europeans before 1965 was itself premised on an explicit and intended discrimination, in part against southern and eastern Europeans but first and foremost against Asians and Africans, who were not even included in the national-origin calculations. It is astonishing that the proponents of the "discrimination against Europeans" charge, many of whom had impeccably liberal credentials,[125] could close their eyes on this. As Stephen Legomsky (1993:334) correctly pointed out, their claim was equivalent to asking to be compensated for the abolition of slavery.

The critics of diversity immigration identified a second flaw in its justification: the assumption that "justice" was to be dispensed to countries, rather than to individuals. Consider this statement by the chief pro-Irish House member, Brian Donnelly (D-Mass.), who had helped to forge all "diversity" schemes since 1986: "By correcting imbalances in our current system, we will once again open our doors to those who no longer have immediate family ties in the United States and are therefore unable to use the annual ceiling of 20,000 available per country."[126] In this statement there is a slippage with respect to its referent, from individual ("no family ties") to country ("unable to use the annual ceiling"). Lawrence Fuchs has powerfully argued against this that "countries do not immigrate; persons immigrate."[127] Would-be-immigrants without family ties, from the Philippines or from Ireland, are "very much in the same pickle" when lining up to apply for a visa under the small occupational quotas.[128] Even worse, the Filipino or Filipina without family ties was worse off than the Irish, because he or she originated from a far more populous and poorer country with a far higher demand for emigration. Accordingly, if justice was for individuals and not for countries, not the large family quotas but the uniform country ceilings under the 1965 law were the culprit. As Fuchs concludes, true to the spirit of the 1965 reform, immigrants should be selected "because they are desirable for their attributes as persons and not because of their national or ethnic backgrounds."[129] In this minimal sense, diversity immigration is indeed a violation of the principles of non-discrimination and source-country universalism to which post-1965 U.S. immigration policy has notionally subscribed.

"Too Many Asians" in Australia

The Australian case is marked by the near-absence of a liberal critique of "not enough" source-country universalism and more virulent and period-ically raised restrictive charges of "too much" source-country universal-ism after 1973, as a result of which Australia was allegedly losing its European roots and becoming "Asianized." It has to be said up front that these restrictive challenges have at no point amounted to a serious threat to the principle of nondiscrimination. On the contrary, they have all been occasions for ceremonially renewing the consensus around a nondiscrimi-natory immigration policy—so much so that one author deemed Austra-lian immigration policy in the clutches of a "new class" of liberal opinion-makers and political elites who systematically discarded the different wishes of the majority population (Betts, 1988; 1999). Although the antipopulist norm thus appears equally well established in the United States and Australia, the more frequent grumblings in Australia about "too many Asians" still stand out in comparison. They reflect Australia's geographic proximity to Asia, which became all the more relevant after the abolishment of the assisted passage scheme in 1982 (Jupp, 2001:77). But more profoundly still, these restrictive grumblings reflect the continued absence of a universalistic "nation of immigrants" mythology à l'américaine. As one observer put it, "Australia's immigra-tion mythology is redolent with fear, with anxieties about the size, the composition or the profile of the immigration program" (Cronin, 1993:87), which sets Australia apart from the more relaxed attitude pre-vailing in other settler states such as the United States or Canada.

In comparison to the United States, contemporary Australian immigra-tion policy is marked by two features: a more robust and effective "will to control" (Birrell, 1992:24–25), according to which the selection of immi-grants was to occur on the Australian government's and nobody else's terms; and, partially as a result of this, a much greater fluctuation in the absolute size of immigrant intakes and in the relative prominence of family-based versus skill-based selection categories. With regard to the first feature, the Fitzgerald Report of 1988, which has become the blueprint for successive government policies ever since, stated as the first of its "ten guiding principles for immigration policies": "The Australian Government alone will determine who will be admitted to Australia consistent with laws enacted by the Federal Parliament to regulate immigration" (Fitzgerald, 1988:21). At one level, this resolute stance arose in the context of reorienting Australian immigration policy from family-based to skill-based selection, because at this point immigration policy was seen as "unduly hostage" to sectional "family reunion interests" (ibid., p. 29). However, it also expresses the "will to control" (Birrell) that distinguishes the Australian approach to immigration more generally and that had found its fullest realization in the rigorous offshore selection under the pre-1982 assisted-passage schemes. Even Australia's humanitarian obligations are subordinate to the will to control, as is evident in the peculiar coexistence of one of the world's most generous (but controlled) refugee resettlement programs with one of the Western world's harshest regimes for unsolicited (and thus uncontrollable) asylum-seeking (Nicholls, 1998). It is important to see that the will to control per se is not discriminatory, even if aliens of particular nationalities may be explicitly targeted under some measures.[130] On the contrary, the harsh persecution of disorderly "queue jumping" is generally presented as the best defense of the "orderly migration programme" under the sign of non-discrimination,[131] particularly against the backdrop of a mass public that has become increasingly hostile to (predominantly non-European) immigration in the past two decades.[132]

A second, closely related feature of contemporary Australian immigration policy is a great fluctuation in the absolute size and internal composition of immigrant intakes. What in the United States is fixed by law, and thus relatively inert, is at the discretion of the government of the day in Australia. Whereas the U.S. Legal Immigration Act of 1990 has committed successive governments to continuously high intakes well above the 700,000 mark per year, the Australian annual intakes have fluctuated greatly in the 1990s, between a peak of 121,688 new permanent arrivals in 1990–91 and a low of 69,768 in 1993–94.[133] A comparison of the "divergent paths" of U.S. and Australian immigration politics in the 1990s found that, because of its more centralized yet publicly accountable government structures, only Australia was able to (or had to, depending on the view taken) respond to a similar populist challenge to high immigration flows by decreasing annual intakes and turning to a tighter control of legal and illegal immigration alike (Freeman and Birrell, 2002).

However, more relevant for our purposes than the Australian government's capacity to control the *size* is its unique capacity to control the internal *composition* of the immigrant intake, according to economic need and perceived public tolerance levels. In the 1965 Legal Immigration Act, the United States made a long-term commitment in favor of family reunification over skill-based selection, which was only marginally modified in the 1990 Legal Immigration Act. By contrast, family-based selection never enjoyed the same level of sustained public support in Australia; or, rather, the so-called ethnic lobby's hold on immigration policy was never taken there with the same indifference.[134] Conversely, there is a much stronger sense that immigrant selection should express "a commitment to Australia"[135] and not be under the sway of sectional interests.

The frequent back-and-forth between skill-focused and family-focused immigrant selections raises the question of whether the driving force has been ethnic selectivity by subterfuge. Because of the discussed difficulties of establishing intent when intent is denied, the best answer is: initially "perhaps," but over time increasingly "no." Until about the late 1980s, with the Fitzgerald Report as the critical turning point, there was indeed a close association, among all involved political actors, of skill-based selection with Anglo-European immigration and, conversely, of family-based selection with non-European (especially Asian) immigration. The "Numerically Weighted Migrant Assessment System" (NUMAS), a skill-based, English language–focused selection system in place between 1979 and 1981, was fiercely criticized by ethnic groups and the oppositional Labor Party for its "British bias" (Betts, 1999:277), and some even saw it as "a return, to some extent, to the White Australia policy" (Hawkins, 1991:143). Ironically, the southeastern European immigrant groups who achieved the scrapping of NUMAS under the late Liberal Frazer government, and who were further rewarded by the "highest priority" granted to extended family migration under the incoming Labor government of Bob Hawke in 1983 (Betts, 1988:157), were the least to profit from this change. Instead, (southeast) Asians, who had first entered in greater numbers as resettled refugees in the late 1970s, became the major users of the expanded family categories. This was also the moment of the first major debate on "too many Asians," and it was tellingly followed by a gradual reduction of the extended family categories and a reorientation to skill-based selection. Of course, government and opposition parties alike denied that in their preferences for either family-based or skill-based immigration any ethnic preferences were involved. For Immigration Minister West, the unexpected near-doubling of projected skilled and business migration in the 1984–85 immigration program did "not represent a response to any perceived need for 'balance' in the intake on racial grounds," even though its timing clearly suggested the opposite.[136] Conversely, a conservative opposition spokesman claimed to be in favor of a "balance of categories" rather than a "balance of race."[137] This was sitting oddly with his parallel invective against a Labor government that was "without doubt, anti-British and anti-European in their bias."[138]

The fact that Asian immigrants more and more entered through the skill angle as well eventually removed the ground for all charges of ethnic selectivity by subterfuge. Accordingly, already in the 1980s the Asian shares were increasing in *all* selection categories. With regard to skill-based selection, the Asian share increased from 12.9 percent in 1982–83 to 21.3 percent in 1985–86 and 34.4 percent in 1988–89 (Jayasuriya and Sang, 1992:48); the separate "business" category became even almost completely monopolized by ethnic Chinese entrepreneurs (Jupp, 2001:78). By 1988, when the Fitzgerald Report opted for "young, skilled and entrepreneurial people with language skills" (p.56), the preference for skilled immigrants was tantamount to the welcoming of "Asians filling this bill" (Birrell and Betts, 1988:264). One commentator aptly summarized the new situation: "Those who are opposed to any pronounced increase in an Asian presence must renounce the principles of skill, language and youth and quite frankly accept a quota system based on race, color and creed."[139]

This trend further increased in the 1990s. Within the shifting balance from family-based to skill-based immigration, Asians now increasingly came to dominate the skill categories also. Of an average skill-based intake of 34,500 per year between 1990–91 and 1999–2000, Asians (excluding Middle-Easterners) accounted for an annual average of about 17,500, clearly dwarfing the European and CIS (former Soviet Union) annual average of only some 10,400.[140] When the attack on extended (and fraudulent nuclear) family migration and the parallel turn to highly skilled immigration took high gear under the conservative Howard government entering in 1996, no one could seriously argue that this was ethnic selectivity by subterfuge. After all, the new stress on courting foreign information technology (IT) and business specialists, as well as the new practice of allowing fee-paying foreign students to remain in the country after the end of their studies, was known to address a predominantly Asian clientele (Birrell, 1999, 2001).

There were three moments when the increasing Asian share in Australia's immigrant intake stirred major political debate. When the enigmatic historian Geoffrey Blainey launched the first debate in March 1984, the disestablishment of the White Australia policy had already "successfully passed" its "first real test" (Viviani, 1984:115): By 1984, Australia had accepted almost 100,000 Indochinese refugees, which made it the world's major refugee-receiving country in per capita terms. Interestingly, Whitlam's Labor Party, champion of the end of White Australia, at first was unwilling to accept Vietnamese refugees in larger numbers (though for political rather than ethnic reasons),[141] and the resettlement started in earnest only under the Liberal Party government of Frazer, which had less scruples against accepting "anti-Communist" refugees. The refugee entry coincided with the parallel (but entirely unrelated) turn from skill-based to family-based immigrant selection, which peaked under a new Labor government entering in 1983.[142] This meant that the Asian refugees could immediately sponsor their extended-family members. When Blainey entered the scene in March 1984, this was the moment in which Australian immigration policy was maximally decoupled from economic need and tied instead to political concessions (in terms of family reunion) and humanitarian considerations (Birrell and Birrell, 1987:277–278). As a result, the Asian proportion of the permanent settler intake jumped from 25 percent in 1982 to 38 percent in 1983 (Betts, 1988:159), while Asians constituted only about 2 percent of the Australian population at the time. This disproportion inflamed the first restrictive attack on "too much" source-country universalism after 1973.

Blainey's momentous address to the Rotary Club in the provincial town of Warrnambool on March 18, 1984, which was quickly expanded into a bestselling book (Blainey, 1984), contains a right and a wrong. Factually true was his charge that the "pace of Asian immigration to Australia is now well ahead of public opinion."[143] A Gallup poll taken at the height of the controversy in May 1984 found that 62 percent of the public "disapproved" that "[a]n increasing proportion of migrants are coming from Asia compared with the United Kingdom and Europe," with only 30 percent "approving" this trend.[144] In fact, whenever the political and media elites, now or in the future, would debate whether "too many Asians" were entering Australia, there was no doubt where sizeable portions of the public stood on this. Interestingly, the persistent animus against Asians could go along with a professed support for a "nondiscriminatory" selection policy. For instance, a poll taken in 1996 found that 77 percent of respondents were in support of such a policy; at the same time, 51 percent also found that "too many" were coming from a particular region—with 88 percent of those listing "Asia" as that region (Betts, 1996:12–13).

However, Blainey also propagated a clear wrong, and one that injected particular venom into this first Australian immigration debate after 1973: the claim that an "Asian preference," shared across party lines, had been driving government policy at least since the late 1970s (Blainey, 1984:10–12). In other words, the turn to Asian immigration was not (as the current Labor government claimed) the unintended consequence of a nondiscriminatory selection process but of intended ethnic selectivity. He couched this suspicion in the metaphor of the "secret room" in which "the government, for political and ethnic reasons, bends its rules to encourage immigrants from Vietnam" (ibid., p. 103), and he even claimed that the Asian immigrant share of 38 percent in the past year was the result of a deliberate "Asian quota": "[T]hey were probably the percentage that . . . the government aimed for" (ibid., p. 116). This was conspiracy reasoning for which no evidence existed.

In response, Prime Minister Hawke and Immigration Minister West credibly dissected the causes of the Asian immigration hike—the "priority (given) to family reunion and refugees," which had commenced under the previous government,[145] plus the "lessening of interest" from the traditional source countries, most notably the United Kingdom.[146] To his defense, Hawke even presented figures that showed a continued pro-British bias in admissions practice: whereas over two-thirds of British and Irish applications to migrate were accepted, only one-third of Asian applications were accepted; in the contested family category, even nine out of ten British and Irish applications were accepted, as against only one of two Asian applications.[147] Interestingly, what in the United States surely would have spurred a liberal campaign against "not enough" source-country universalism was used in Australia only to deflect a restrictive attack on "too much" source-country universalism.

Reviewing the conservative opposition's attempt to capitalize on the Blainey attack, one notices the difficulty this opposition faced in refracting into partisan terms what it too had done when still in power—accept Indochinese refugees and prioritize family-based over skill-based selection. The opposition's continued support for both[148] was hardly reconcilable with its charge that the Labor government had "adopted the most anti-British stance which we have ever seen in this country."[149] In the words of a prominent commentator (Kelly, 1992:126), the opposition danced around the dilemma that "the only alternative to a non-discriminatory policy was a discriminatory policy." For Blainey this was no dilemma: all immigration policy was inherently "discriminatory," and accordingly it was best to place a "ceiling" on Asian immigration "open[ly] and honestly" (Blainey, 1984:162). That far (back to White Australia), no mainstream political actor was willing to go. In fact, the opposition did not openly charge the government of being "pro-Asian" and mocked "the twisted logic of those . . . who say that if one asks a question about British or European migration one is being racist."[150] Instead of a cap on Asian immigration, the opposition proposed the notion of "balancing": not reducing the Asian intake but "increasing the European element."[151] However, this notion was quickly dropped, because it would require an explicit ethnic quota and an increased total intake, to which the public was opposed.[152] After a brief internal debate over the rivaling objectives "nondiscrimination" versus "social cohesion," the Liberal Shadow Cabinet committed itself to nondiscrimination, thus "retreat[ing] to the orthodox" (Kelly, 1992:133). This outcome incidentally revealed the truth of the initial government response to the Blainey speech, which had done much to inflame the entire "debate" surrounding it—that the "increasing Asianisation of Australia was inevitable," at least as long as Australia remained committed to a nondiscriminatory immigration policy.[153]

If the Blainey debate was a blast, the two following debates on "too many Asians" were ripples, with a fixed script of reaffirming the nondiscriminatory immigration policy and marginalizing its challengers. In August 1988, opposition leader John Howard said in a radio interview that it would be "supportive of social cohesion if [the Asian intake] were slowed down a little" (quoted in Morita, 1999:114).[154] Howard's temporary loss of leadership of the Liberal Party in May 1989 is generally attributed to this statement (see Betts, 1999:299), and six senior Liberal Party members (including former Prime Minister Frazer and Howard's own later Immigration Minister Ruddock) supported Prime Minister Hawke's symbolic motion in parliament for an "unambiguous and unqualified commitment" to a nondiscriminatory immigration policy (Rubenstein, 1993:153).[155]

Though in terms of "debate" this was it, its context deserves further attention. Howard felt emboldened by the Fitzgerald Report's critique of multiculturalism and plea for an immigration policy with "a sharper economic focus" (Fitzgerald, 1988:xi). Although the Hawke government had responded to the Blainey debate by tightening the contested extended-family migration criteria and increasing the skill component,[156] about two-third of the total intake was still through the family (and refugee) categories. Because of sheer demand, sibling migration represented the biggest growth point within the entire immigration program, increasing from 12,464 in 1983–84 to 32,349 in 1987–88 (Birrell, 1990:3). Despite their marginal population share, six of the eight top sending countries in the sibling category were Asian, the Philippines topping the list in 1987–98 with 5,519 migrants (ibid., p. 16).[157] The situation with respect to the spouse/fiancé(e) and parent categories was similar (ibid., chs. 4 and 5). Accordingly, not only did Australian immigration remain family-dominated; the Asian share of family immigrants also continued to increase, from about 50 percent in 1983–84 to 60 percent in 1988–89 (ibid., p. 43). This is why Howard's incriminated statement could invoke the old association of functional selection category and ethnic group: "[I]f you have less family reunions, you have less coming from Asia" (quoted in Morita, 1999:114).

Although the Fitzgerald Report tapped into the same critique of an immigration program unduly dominated by low-skilled family immigration, its whole point was to transcend the association between selection category and ethnic group. Authored by a prominent Asian scholar and diplomat, Stephen Fitzgerald, who was certainly not known to be fearful of "too many Asians," the report started from the premise that "[r]acism is by no means excised from Australia"—a claim that soon would be powerfully affirmed by the overwhelming popular support for Howard's anti-Asian invective.[158] However, the report's answer to this was precisely "not to halt immigration from Asian countries or abandon the principle of non-discrimination" but to give the program a "sharper economic focus." This was in the hope that the public legitimacy of a large immigration program could be recovered by presenting it as good "for the whole of Australia" and not just for ethnic groups (Fitzgerald, 1988:8–9). What Howard's anti-Asian statement and concurrent "One Australia" campaign had ignored was that, even after the cutting of the extended-family categories, Asians would continue to arrive in the skill categories. The linking of an Asian immigration that had to continue, under a skill-focused as much as under a family-focused policy, with Australia's own national interest was appositely the key in Prime Minister Hawke's rebuttal of Howard: "An interesting consequence of a sharper economic focus—as also proposed by the Opposition—could be to increase the number and proportion of Asian migrants. The reason is that Asia is our fastest growing source of business and skilled migrants. To reduce Asian immigration would therefore mean reducing the skill level of the migrant intake . . . The Opposition simply does not appreciate the extent to which Australia's economic livelihood is now enmeshed with that of Asia."[159]

Epitomizing its progressively diminishing scale, the third challenge to "too many Asians" was no longer raised from within the political mainstream but by a populist right-winger. After her surprise capture of what had been deemed a "safe" Labor seat in the federal elections of 1996, the partyless Pauline Hanson said in her infamous parliamentary "maiden speech": "I believe we are in danger of being swamped by Asians. Between 1984 and 1995, 40 percent of all migrants into this country were of Asian origin. They have their own culture and religion, form ghettos and do not assimilate" (quoted in Deutchman and Ellison, 1999:36). Stripped of her Liberal Party membership just before the elections for insensitive remarks about Aborigines, Hanson spoke to an empty chamber, and some have explained her success in terms of a self-produced media phenomenon (ibid.). This claim ignores her resonance with large sections of the populace. A 1996 poll showed 53 percent of the public endorsing her call for a reduction of Asian immigration (see Perera and Pugliese, 1997:18, n. 21). Nevertheless, by October 1998 the Hanson phenomenon had run its course, her recently founded "One Nation" party dissolving after having fared badly in the next federal elections.

More relevant for our purposes, Hanson's meteoric rise on the political scene only reconfirmed the bipartisan commitment to a nondiscriminatory immigration policy. Now as the Prime Minister, John Howard declared in parliament that he would "always defend the non-discriminatory character of Australia's immigration policy,"[160] and in a Joint Parliamentary Statement of 30 October 1996 the entire House of Representatives "reaffirm[ed] its commitment to maintaining an immigration policy wholly non-discriminatory on grounds of race, colour, creed or origin."[161] This time round there was no bickering about a more "balanced" immigrant intake, and Howard's Immigration Minister, Philip Ruddock (1999a:6), declared that "the whole idea of playing around with immigration policy to deliver some particular ethnic composition is to me totally repugnant."

Although short-lived and without major effect on Australian immigration policy,[162] the Hanson phenomenon still expressed a "deeper problem," which a commentator aptly identified as the final "dismantling of the post-federation Australian Settlement" (Kelly, 1998:96). This settlement had consisted of the White Australia policy, trade protection, centralized wage arbitration, a paternalistic welfare state, and linkage to the British

Empire. Since the onset of perceived "globalization" in the late 1980s, even the political-economic dimension of this settlement fell apart, giving way to a commitment to free trade and a general retreat of the state. Moreover, in the hour of the Asian economic miracle, when the Japan-led Pacific emerged as the world's third major economic bloc,[163] and reflecting a continued trend toward dependence on regional trade,[164] "enmeshment" with Asia became the order of the day. A sarcastic observer even found that political conflict had shrunk to a question of "product differentiation . . . on the question of 'enmeshment'" (Higgott, 1994:50). Under the Labor government of Paul Keating (1993–96), an Irish Catholic who had sworn himself to close down the Australian "branch office of empire," "enmeshment" with Asia went to almost comical extremes, as Australian "mateship" was reinterpreted as one of those fabled "Asian values."[165] Just when Pauline Hanson was declaring "that the most downtrodden person in this country is the white Anglo-Saxon male" (quoted in C. Johnson, 1998:217), Australia figured as a lunatic "torn country" in Samuel Huntington's epic of the "clash of civilizations" (1996:151–157). A "torn country," according to Huntington, was one that had a "single predominant culture" yet "its leaders want to shift it to another civilization"—to the West in the case of Russia or Turkey, but to Asia in the case of Australia.

At the level of political rhetoric, Prime Minister John Howard, not unlike Hanson, threw himself against the Asian-*cum*-Republican drift, defending the cause of the marginalized "Aussie battler" against the cosmopolitan elites. However, in terms of actual policies he only continued the dismantling of the old "Australian settlement." Although two academics think that under Howard "White Australia . . . is being effectively reconstituted in the present" (Perera and Pugliese, 1997:5), there is no sign of this in immigration policy. In fact, Howard's immigration policy is the most consequent realization yet of the Fitzgerald Report's demand for a "sharper economic focus." In 1995–96, the last year of the old Labor government, the family component within the (nonhumanitarian) migration program had still accounted for 68.7 percent of new immigrants, whereas the skill component amounted to only 29.2 percent. In 2000–01 this order had reversed, with 55.5 percent of visas in the various skill categories and 41.5 percent family-related.[166] To the degree that extended family reunion still exists, it is now rigorously subordinated to skill factors, as in the new "Skilled Australian Linked" category of 1997 ("Skilled-Australian Sponsored" since 1999). At the same time, widespread fraud in spouse and fiancé(e) migration has been countered by imposing waiting periods and enhanced *bona fides* tests.[167] Finally, and obviously influenced by the parallel welfare cuts for legal immigrants in the United States, the Howard government imposed bonds on Australian residents or citizens sponsoring their relatives abroad, and newcomers were excluded from most welfare and social benefits during the first two years after entry.

There is no denying that these measures hit hardest on Asian immigrants, and some even farther-reaching proposals were blocked on this note in the Senate (Birrell, 1996). However, there still was a remarkable absence of charges of ethnic selectivity by subterfuge, simply because Asians were also the major winners in the parallel expansion of skilled immigration. This is especially visible in the inclusive approach toward foreign students graduating at Australian universities, who are in the majority Asian.[168] Throughout the 1980s, Australian governments had subsidized Asian overseas students as a foreign-aid measure. This changed in 1989, when full fee–paying foreign students came to be considered as a "market to be exploited" (Birrell, 1999:55). Responding to a worldwide competition for the "best and brightest," a rule change in 1999 released foreign students who graduated at an Australian university from a twelve-month occupational experience requirement and allowed them to apply directly for an immigrant visa. This is just a facet in a broad campaign for highly skilled immigration, which recently has also focused on accommodating a growing trend toward *temporary* skilled migration (Ruddock, 1999b).[169] In a minimalist reading, the perceived need to master the challenge of "globalization" has chased away old ethnic sentimentalities. More than that, Immigration Minister Ruddock (1999a:6) now views "our cultural diversity" as "one of our strengths as we move into the twenty-first century."

Conclusion

The comparison of the rise and demise of ethnoracial immigration policies in the United States and Australia showed that particular national self-definitions (in terms of race and ethnic European origins) were a driving moment in setting up these policies. However, their demise has to be understood as a differentiation between national self-definition of whatever color and immigration policy. Otherwise Australia, an unambiguously ethnic nation from the start, and still in 1973 reluctant to see itself as a universalistic "nation of immigrants," would not have given up its White

Australia policy. A liberal norm of racial nondiscrimination, born in the aftermath of World War II and slowly consolidating from pragmatic foreign policy consideration to moral principle, accounts for the turn to universalistic immigration policies in the United States and Australia alike. In the United States, the general nature of this constraint could be hidden by the existence of a domestic legacy of civic nationhood, as whose glorious recovery the turn to source-country universalism in 1965 came to be understood. Daniel Tichenor's (2002:289) observation is certainly correct: "Americans are perhaps unusual to the degree that they have woven immigration narratives and iconography into their collective cultural identity." However, the case of Australia shows that a particular national "narrative" cannot be the gist of the turn from an ethnoracial to a universalistic immigration policy. This was a general turn, not specific to the United States but commanded by the exigencies of liberal stateness as such.

By the same token, it would be misleading to argue that America's "multiple traditions" (Smith, 1993) could at any time tilt the movement back to an ethnoracial policy. Not just domestic "path dependence," as suggested by Tichenor (2002:292–296), makes this an unlikely outcome. What the Fitzgerald Report cautiously observed for the case of Australia is true more generally: "[R]acism in many forms pervades our society. It seems, however, that its open institutional articulation in an immigration context is for some reason inhibited, and is perhaps felt to be unacceptable" (Fitzgerald, 1988:7). Gary Freeman (1995a) captured this with the notion of the "antipopulist norm." The fact that restrictive challenges in the 1980s and the 1990s could not derail nondiscriminatory immigration policies in Australia and the United States confirms Freeman's (1995b) claim that the underlying principle of nondiscrimination has come to be part and parcel of the "ethos" of liberal democracy itself. Although the turn to nondiscrimination is of course a "historically specific" (Brubaker, 1995:905) event, occurring in different moments and with different connotations in each state, like a ratchet it is subsequently immune to revision. Retreating from it would immediately be branded as a violation of fundamental liberal-democratic norms and be tantamount to a civilization break, which may always be possible but then could not be limited to immigration policy.

As we have seen, one additional mechanism shoring up nondiscriminatory policies is the instantly available memory of the settler states' own racist past. Diversity immigration in the United States, a smallish measure of positive discrimination for Irish and other European immigrant groups who had lost out after 1965, became immediately couched by its critics as a rebirth of the maligned national-origin quotas, even though the thrust of the latter had been the opposite of negative racial discrimination. In fact, diversity immigration became tolerable only once its European tilt had been eradicated, within the "underrepresented country" formula.

This shows a more general characteristic of settler states' contemporary immigration policies: the removal of positive along with negative discriminations, even though both are made from different moral cloth and often had coexisted as separate policies with their own legal infrastructures. I characterized this nexus as "guilt by association." The examples abound. Just when Asian exclusion was laid to rest in Australia, positive derogations for British immigrants were abolished too. The Western Hemisphere was subjected to the general quota regime in the United States, even though good, nonethnic reasons existed to keep it exempt from quotas. In all these cases, positive discrimination has been tainted by the historical legacy of negative discrimination, even in the absence of an identifiable loser.

We saw that restrictive challenges to source-country universalism have been relatively more repeated and severe in Australia. But only in the United States did they find institutional sedimentation in the form of diversity immigration. Diversity immigration is ethnic migration, and thus it deviates from the usual triad of selecting on the basis of skills, family connections, or human need. However, the important matter is that diversity immigration purports to be not a violation but a realization of a nondiscriminatory immigration policy. Perhaps not in practice, but in theory, diversity immigration is a reaffirmation of the nondiscrimination principle. Being structurally similar to affirmative action, in which a temporary violation of equal treatment is justified with respect to bringing about terminal equality, diversity immigration privileges immigrants from currently "underrepresented" countries for the sake of a more even balance of immigrants from all countries, thus realizing the promise of the 1965 Immigration Act.

In this sense, the notion of "restrictive" challenge to source-country universalism has to be qualified. A truly "restrictive" challenge that would reject the very principle of nondiscrimination has remained the exception, such as, in the United States, Brimelow (1995), or in Australia, Blainey (1984). Most restrictive challenges have defended their claims in terms of justice and nondiscrimination, however, intent on undoing a predominantly non-European immigration after the introduction of nonethnic selection criteria. Only with respect to this intended effect, not to its usually egalitarian rhetoric, can one speak of a "restrictive" challenge to source-country universalism at all.

3

Europe's Postcolonial Constellations, Northwestern and Southwestern

Empires can be defined as "relationships of political control imposed by some political societies over the effective sovereignty of other political societies" (Doyle, 1986:19). Empires thus imply political boundaries drawn wider than those of nation-states, creating space for movement of, and ethnic mixing between, the members of the respective political societies. Such movement and mixing occurred in two directions: at first, and predominantly, from the imperial states to the colonies in terms of conquest, settlement, and trade; later, and in much smaller numbers, from the colonies to the imperial states, mostly in terms of labor migration of colonial natives, who exploited equal-citizenship provisions that imperial states introduced after World War II to "democratize" their besieged colonial possessions.[1]

Decolonization after World War II entailed an "ethnic unmixing" that is everywhere the "aftermath of empire" (Brubaker, 1996:166). In particular, two opposite movements had to be regulated by devolving empires: the return of former settlers and their descendants, and the increasing entry of (post)colonial natives in search of work and a better life.[2]

The postcolonial constellation is thus one in which ethnicity and national origin had to become more or less explicitly deployed criteria of the involved European states' immigration policies, and this precisely in the moment that such categorizations had fallen into disrepute. This deployment was further vitiated by the fact that European colonialism had mostly been the "rule over peoples of different race" (Emerson, 1968:1), creating the suspicion that racial discrimination was inherent in increasingly restrictive postcolonial immigration policies. This charge was especially made by British authors with respect to Britain: "While the United Kingdom had been strengthening racial discrimination in its immigration controls, the countries which had imposed racial restrictions in the early years of the century were getting rid of them" (Dummett and Nicol, 1990:231).

This polemic obscures a decisive difference between the postcolonial and settler-state constellations. Postwar European states such as Britain first established and then revoked regimes that had exempted migrating natives of their former colonies from the restrictions on entry and settlement that "other" aliens already faced. The removing of positive derogations, in a process that equated formerly privileged postcolonial migrants with "normal" migrants, is difficult to class as "racism" if we conceive of the latter as a negative discrimination that puts the respective group *apart from* and *below* like-situated groups. To the degree that hostility to non-white immigrants has been driving the removal of derogatory postcolonial regimes, it had the paradoxical (because nondiscriminatory) effect of establishing the norm of source-country universalism in the respective European states as well. Accordingly, while the restriction of postcolonial immigration may have been racially motivated in some instances, it did not appear this way; on the contrary, European states' immigration laws and policies became increasingly universalistic in the process.

With respect to immigration, the postcolonial constellation in Europe is a continuum with two opposite ends. On the one end, the ethnic impulse is negative: postcolonial immigration is ethnically or racially unwanted immigration, but for a while it was tolerated by receiving states for the sake of other (political or economic) interests, such as the maintenance of imperial power status or the meeting of shortages on war-ravaged labor markets. On the other end, the ethnic impulse is positive in one of at least two possible forms: selective schemes for former settlers and their descendants (creating the delicate problem of how to distinguish them from nonprivileged colonial natives) or general preference schemes for indiscriminate migrants (as "citizens") from the newly independent states, who are construed as belonging to a state-transcending, panethnic community.

What I shall call in the following discussion "northwestern" and "southwestern" postcolonial constellations represent the opposite ends of this continuum. In Britain and France, examples of the northwestern constellation, there has been a *disjunction* of ethnic and political preferences: postcolonial immigrants were mostly perceived as not "belonging," but they were tolerated in the pursuit of other (geopolitical or economic) interests. By contrast, in Spain and Portugal, protagonists of the much lesser known southwestern constellation, there has been an *overlapping* of ethnic and political preferences: indiscriminate migrants from the former colonial realms were construed as members of a panethnic "historical and cultural" community[3] to whom were due privileged access to the territory and citizenry of the receiving state.[4] In short, in the northwestern constellation, at best some (carefully carved out) fragments of postcolonial migration constituted ethnic migration, whereas in the southwestern constellation postcolonial migration *tout court* is ethnic migration.

The Northwestern Constellation: Britain and France

Although the northwestern constellation shares the disjunction of ethnic and political preferences, Britain and France took different directions in resolving the underlying tension. Britain, which generally rejected immigration as an economic asset (or disposed of the "shadow" army of Irish migrant workers for this purpose), went toward screening within the pool of postcolonial immigrants between wanted return settlers ("patrials") and unwanted colonial natives, who were gradually adjusted to the status of "normal" aliens. Introduced in the 1971 Immigration Act, "patriality" was a mechanism that in effect divided the devolving empire into a white settler (Old Commonwealth) and nonwhite colonial (New Commonwealth) part, keeping the door open for the former but closing it on the latter. While functioning as a proxy for citizenship (which Britain did not have until 1981), and notionally an innocent device to retain "family connections,"[5] patriality created a storm of domestic criticism because of its racially discriminatory implications. It thus figured as a positive discrimination tainted by a negatively discriminatory effect.

Postwar France differed from Britain in being in desperate need of immigrants for economic and demographic needs. Accordingly, postcolonial immigration, especially from Algeria, was at first tolerated for economic reasons. France's main strategy for resolving the disjunction of ethnic and political preferences was to counterbalance ethnically unwanted postcolonial immigration with ethnically wanted European immigration, in the context of an ethnically neutral immigration law passed in November 1945.[6] There was no attempt to screen among postcolonial immigrants between privileged return settlers and nonprivileged natives, because— with the important exception of Algeria (and, no longer relevant, Quebec)—the French empire had never been one of settlement. France was greatly helped in separating cleanly from its former colonies by disposing of an externally exclusive national citizenship, which had only temporarily been roofed by an imperial citizenship during the Fourth Republic. There was only one postcolonial immigration problem in France: Algeria, once considered an integral part of France, cut loose in a bloody and traumatic independence war, then the sending state of France's biggest immigrant colony, and subsequently targeted for restrictive measures.

Struggle over "Patrials": Britain

Three parameters shaped British postcolonial immigration policy: the absence of a perceived economic or demographic need for immigrants; the nonexistence of a national citizenship that would allow clean distinctions to be made between citizens and aliens; and the existence of British settlements overseas (the so-called Old Commonwealth or "Dominions": Australia, New Zealand, and Canada), toward which primordial ties of "belonging" existed that called for statutory expression. All three parameters converged on an immigration policy that sought to make the cuts where the pressure was: immigrants from the New Commonwealth—that is, Britain's former possessions in East Africa, the Caribbean West Indies, and the Indian subcontinent. That most of these immigrants happened to be nonwhite has spurred the accusation that this policy was "racist" (e.g., Dummett and Nicol, 1990; Paul, 1997).

Having turned its back on labor migration from early on,[7] Britain faced the problem of containing postcolonial immigration, put on the map by alarming societal disapproval since the late 1950s. Containing this mostly unwanted immigration was aggravated by the lack of an exclusive citizenship scheme, which also might have allowed "filtering in" the trickle of wanted postcolonial immigration from the Old Commonwealth. From the passing of the British Nationality Act in 1948 until 1981, Britain disposed only of an overinclusive, quasi-imperial "United Kingdom and Colonies citizenship," which did not distinguish the natives and residents of Britain itself from those of its vast possessions around the globe. United Kingdom and Colonies citizenship was complemented by a second status of "citizens of independent Commonwealth countries," who had broadly identical rights, including free entry to the United Kingdom. The 1948 British Nationality Act, the first explicit citizenship scheme in British history, had a backward-looking purpose: to retain the uniform status of British subject throughout the empire, which had become threatened by Canada's introduction of a national citizenship in 1946. It was certainly not meant to allow immigration from the New Commonwealth; the only free movement intended at the time was that of Old Dominion citizens, with that of colonial subjects tolerated at best, if it occurred temporarily and in limited numbers (see Hansen, 2000, ch. 2).

One has to realize the anachronism as well as immense self-confidence expressed in the 1948 citizenship scheme. At a time when all other Commonwealth states, most notably Canada and Australia, busily controlled the immigration of British subjects, especially those not wanted for racial reasons, Britain was deliberately abstaining from all such controls, including the racially mischievous ones, in its quest to "maintain our great metropolitan tradition of hospitality to everyone from every part of our Empire."[8] The result was free entry rights for some six hundred million British subjects around the globe, which proved most difficult to correct because of the path-dependent inertia of the underlying citizenship scheme.

If more than one decade of unsolicited and socially contested New Commonwealth immigration passed by without the introduction of controls, this is because the wish not to erect a "colour bar," shared by Labour and Conservative Party elites alike, put before the government the uncomfortable choice either to control all immigration from the Commonwealth, including the Old, or not to have any controls at all. Only in 1962, against the backdrop of rising numbers and increasing social tensions, did a Tory government opt for controls, in terms of the first Commonwealth Immigrants Act. This act pioneered the peculiar approach of "legislating by exception,"[9] which was necessitated by the absence of a metropolitan citizenship, and in which all "Commonwealth citizens" (another word for "British subjects" after 1948) were made subject to controls except a privileged subclass of primordial "belongers."[10] In 1962, these "belongers" were defined as people either born in the United Kingdom or having passports issued by the United Kingdom government. This mechanism was meant to distinguish within the overinclusive 1948 "United Kingdom and Colonies citizenship" category between the natives and residents of Britain proper and the colonial rest. Crucially, this narrow definition of "belonging" did not allow distinguishing between Old and New Commonwealth immigrants, thus accepting the control of the former as a price for controlling the latter, under the overarching imperative of avoiding a "colour bar."[11]

The distinction between privileged Old Commonwealth and nonprivileged New Commonwealth immigrants became possible only with the "patrial" category, introduced in the 1971 Immigration Act. Technically, this act completed the gradual move toward a uniform immigration regime, in which (most) Commonwealth immigrants were equated with "normal" immigrant aliens. Politically, it was forced on a reluctant Tory government by "Powellism"—that is, Enoch Powell's immensely popular anti-immigrant crusade at the time. At one level, the notion of patrial is the functional equivalent to citizenship for an immigration policy that could not be based on citizenship—"a quasi-nationality for immigration purposes" (Dummett and Nicol, 1990:217).

Who were the patrials? In the words of Home Secretary Maudling, "patrial" was a word for "[p]eople who have a right of abode."[12] Controversy arose for including in it not only certain United Kingdom and Colonies citizens (those who either were residents in or one of whose parents or grandparents was born in the United Kingdom), but, in the original bill brought to Parliament in March 1971, "any Commonwealth citizen who had a father or mother or grandparent born in the UK."[13] Though formally neutral vis à vis the race or geographic origins of the respective (Old or New) Commonwealth immigrant, this provision factually favored the descendants of white Old Dominion settlers, in recognition of "special ties of blood and kinship,"[14] while excluding many of the British passport–holding Asians stranded in the nationalizing states of West Africa. This "racial contrast"[15] would incense the liberal conscience.

The storm unleashed over the patrials nevertheless took the Tory government by complete surprise. While the word was new, the underlying concept "has been evolved in principle by succeeding Governments," as Home Secretary Maudling put it at the second reading of the 1971 Immigration Bill.[16] Every independence act since the 1950s had included a special citizenship provision for ex-colonials with at least a grandparental connection with the United Kingdom; more recently, the Labour government, when passing the second Commonwealth Immigrants Act of 1968, had widened the original circle of "belongers" to United Kingdom and Colonies citizens with a grandparental connection, then intent on excluding Asian British-passport holders in Kenya (see Hansen, 1999). Considering these precedents, the patrial category was indeed more a culmination of past practice than the fundamental conceptual innovation as which it was attacked.

There were two ways of defending patriality. The official government version was that patriality was not a "racial" category but one that simply recognized a "family connection."[17] Indeed, the line between patriality as an individual right recognizing family ties and an ethnic concept is exceedingly thin. Every state grants citizenship rights to first-generation descendants born abroad, and extending this to second-generation descendants makes for a difference that is one "of degree rather than kind" (Hansen, 2000:195). However, there was a second, more dubious defense of patriality, advanced only by some Tory backbenchers but picked up by the liberal critics as indicative of the "true" government intention. According to this version, the intention of the Immigration Act was to cut "coloured" immigration because this was the source of all troubles, and there was no point, in an act of "bogus uniformity" (Tory MP Kenneth Clarke), to exclude also white immigrants from the Old Commonwealth, who after all faced no problem of acceptance in society: "It is intellectually dishonest for liberal opinion . . . to pretend that the debate about immigration control . . . centres on anything other than the racial problems which the country faces . . . [I]t is desirable to restrict the number of coloured immigrants into this country . . . [W]hy should a system which faces up to that regrettable necessity impose hardship on groups of people, in particular those who are the descendants of fairly recent emigrants from this country to Australia, New Zealand and British South Africa?"[18]

Liberal critics of patriality focused on the dual aspect of patriality to include people who were citizens of other Commonwealth countries, while excluding some whose only citizenship was that of the "United Kingdom and Colonies." It was thus attacked as a positive discrimination that entailed an easily identifiable loser, who in addition was marked by race. David Steel of the Liberal Party put it this way: "[O]ne gets into a situation where a one-year-old female child who emigrated with [her] parents . . . 150 years ago, could be the grandmother of somebody today claiming entry under the patrial clause . . . If we contrast that . . . with somebody who . . . holds a United Kingdom passport but who lives with no other citizenship, say, in East Africa, we realize the racial contrast which exists under this legislation."[19] Only this second, exclusionary aspect made patriality suspicious, which in its inclusive dimension was analogous to return provisions that can be found in all emigrant or settler-sending states.[20]

However, there was in addition a nonliberal, restrictive critique of grandparental patriality. It was formulated above all by flamboyant Tory outsider Enoch Powell. He branded grandparental patriality as a reversed "Grossmutter nicht in Ordnung" rule, by means of which the Nazis had exorcised Jews from the German nation: "We, conversely, are saying that such is the magic of birth within this country that one quarter of such descent is sufficient to mark a man out from the rest of humanity and to make him one of us."[21] Revealing his true intention, he continued that "hundreds of thousands" of "Anglo-Indian" persons—that is, people of mixed race—would qualify for entry under grandparental patriality. Later he would add to this the open-ended scenario of (nonwhite) New Commonwealth immigrants with children born in the United Kingdom returning to their home countries, and these children being "patrials" for two generations of New Commonwealth immigrants in the future.[22]

The synergetic confluence of liberal and restrictive critiques of grandparental patriality forced the government into a retreat. In committee stage, a small majority supported a motion by Enoch Powell to limit patriality for Commonwealth citizens to people with a parental (rather than grandparental) connection with the United Kingdom. Powell was joined by liberal Tories and Labour and Liberal Party critics, most notably David Steel, many of whom opposed patriality as such and for altogether different reasons.[23] Interestingly, when cut down to the parental connection, Commonwealth patriality suddenly appeared as a measure of sex equality. Already under existing law, Commonwealth citizens (as any other alien for that matter) whose *fathers* were born in the United Kingdom enjoyed automatic entry and residence rights in the United Kingdom. Commonwealth patriality only extended this right to Commonwealth citizens whose *mothers* were born in the United Kingdom, thus removing an obvious case of sex discrimination.[24] The "racism" charge now lost every basis: "It has always been the law that someone born in this country or the child of a father born in this country had a special position. We are now extending it to mothers."[25] Thus converted into a "progressive" equality measure, patriality proved to be the kind of bird whose feathers could take on many a color.

Had that been the end of the matter, patriality could hardly have been the ethnically, or even racially, flavored concept as which it would become known. When the Immigration Rules implementing the 1971 Immigration Act were put before Parliament in late October 1972, they also included the free movement provisions for European Community (EC) nationals that were required for Britain's pending entry into the European Economic Community in January 1973. Now an altogether different contrast opened up: that between privileged EC nationals and nonprivileged nonpatrial Commonwealth citizens, who were downgraded to "aliens" in the new Immigration Act. This was the historic moment in which Britain finally "turned away from the open seas,"[26] toward a Europe that was perceived more as economic necessity than affective allegiance. And it was a historic moment in which even for liberal Labourites the "open seas" was above all the Old Commonwealth. Labour front-bencher Peter Shore pointed out that "no other country in Europe or in the world has had this experience of its people forming separate yet linked states in other continents as we have done in Australia, New Zealand and Canada," and he even compared the links between them to those of "people . . . divided by war between countries or civil war"—such as the two Germanies, the two Koreas, and the two Vietnams. To be downgraded to "third countries" had to be a "deep and unforgivable offence" to the Old Commonwealth states, "which share with us the same Head of State, operate a substantially open door for our own citizens, and are peopled predominantly with British people."[27] The reality of Old Commonwealth ties came alive in Parliament when an Australian Labor MP exchanged "the cap I normally wear as the Member of Feltham" for his "Australian cap," reminding his peers that Australia had not only always provided "good and cheap food" to Britain but had also fought on its side during World War II against a European enemy: "[M]y first experience of this country was . . . flying Lancasters over Germany with, be it noted, a mixed Commonwealth aircrew."[28]

However, the tempestuous debate over the immigration rules was above all a field day for a heady backbench alliance of Old Commonwealth loyalists and Euroskeptics within the ruling Conservative Party, which eventually would bring about "the most important Government defeat in post-war Parliamentary history" (Norton, 1976:413). Like the liberal critics of patriality during the debate over the Immigrant Act, the conservative advocates of nonpatrial Commonwealthers used invidious contrasts to bring out apparent injustice. One Tory cited his relatives "who went from Connecticut to New Brunswick in 1776 . . . because they . . . want[ed] to be subjects of her Majesty the Queen," whose offspring were now downgraded to aliens, whereas (via membership in the EC) the Frenchmen living just off the coast on a small island that is still a department of metropolitan France "will be perfectly entitled to enter Britain with no conditions," even though they "have done nothing for us."[29]

Home Secretary Carr sought to assure the Old Commonwealth loyalists that, with the new immigration rules, "patrial Commonwealth citizens will be more favorably treated than EEC citizens, and non-patrial

Commonwealth citizens will be more favorably treated than non-EEC aliens."[30] However, this fourfold hierarchy of citizens and aliens dodged the main point of contention: nonpatrial Commonwealth citizens were put below the status of EC citizens. Even when assuring, now more to the point, that nonpatrial Commonwealthers, once admitted, enjoyed all the rights of British subjects that EC nationals did not enjoy (such as the rights to vote and stand for Parliament),[31] the government sidestepped the fact that those rights were without value if not accompanied by the right of entry and residence. The oddity of reversely privileged EC citizens and nonpatrial Commonwealthers before and after entry was aptly captured by Enoch Powell: "We have said to one set of people 'You cannot come in except under certain pretty stringent controls. But, once you are in, you belong to us' . . . To another set of people we have said 'You can all come in for work . . . However, once you are in, you are an alien' . . . That is an absurdity."[32]

After its defeat on the immigration rules, the government had to win back the Old Commonwealth loyalists within its own Conservative Party. This is how the old concept of grandparental patriality for Commonwealth citizens, dead for two years, was resurrected, within redrafted Immigration Rules presented to Parliament in January 1973. Interestingly, the leaders of the Tory rebels had long been in favor of an alternative solution to affirm the special ties with Old Commonwealth countries, and one of its advocates (the moderate Tory G. Sinclair) had actually participated in knocking down grandparental Commonwealth patriality in 1971. This alternative to patriality was "reciprocity." It would have meant that all "citizens" (and not just the "patrial" subclass of them) of contracting countries would enjoy free entry and residence privileges in Britain, provided these countries granted the same privileges to Britons. As even Home Secretary Carr had to admit, "patriality" was not at all liked by the Old Commonwealth governments.[33] It was dividing their citizenries between those of French and British origin in Canada, between those of European and British origin in Australia, and between those of Maori and British origin in New Zealand, and, of course, patriality divided British-origin citizens themselves along the random generational marker—and all this in a moment when these states were desperately struggling for post-British national unity. However, according to the Home Secretary, initial negotiations with these governments over reciprocal immigration rights had turned out unsuccessful.[34] This is why the ball eventually rolled back to reinstating grandparental patriality for Commonwealth citizens.[35]

The larger irony of this final outcome of the struggle over the patrials should not be overlooked: an Immigration Act that was notionally committed to bringing down overseas immigration to the "inescapable minimum"[36] opened Britain's doors to an estimated eight million Old Commonwealth patrials (though only a trickle would act on this; see Twaddle, 1994:45–48). And patriality was not all. To win back the rebellious Old Commonwealth loyalists, the redrafted, and eventually approved, Immigration Rules of February 1973 also extended from a three-year to a five-year maximum the "working holiday-maker" scheme, which was formally open to all Commonwealth citizens but was factually used mostly by young people from the Old Commonwealth. This meant that these "visitors" could make their stay permanent by registering as citizens with a right of abode after four years. When made aware by the Labour frontbencher Shirley Williams of this "very wide loophole," Home Secretary Carr responded that under the new immigration rules this citizenship acquisition was no longer as of right but discretionary— omitting the fact that such "discretion" was only in the rarest of cases used against Old Commonwealth citizens.[37]

Moreover, the "racial contrast" that had provoked the first row over patriality in 1971 came full circle. When announcing the revised Immigration Rules, whose purpose was to "give the freest possible access to Commonwealth citizens whose close family ties are with this country," Home Secretary Carr also pointed out, in the same breath, that there would be no further "generosity" for the 70,000 to 80,000 Asian holders of British passports still stranded in East Africa, who were thus left de facto stateless.[38] "The door opens to the whites, but closes on the Asians"[39]—this remained the quintessence of patriality.

After its contested birth, patriality for (Old) Commonwealth citizens remained alive for only ten years, succumbing to an almost unnoticed death in the British Nationality Act of 1981. This act "redeployed" patriality as "British citizenship" (Fransman, 1983). All living Commonwealth patrials before the enactment of the new law on 1 January 1983 retained their privileged status. However, the crucial novelty was that no Commonwealth citizen born after the new act could claim patrial status; Commonwealth patriality was thus made to disappear after one generation. Although it was criticized for topping "the larger postwar discourse of blood, family, and kith and kin" (Paul, 1997:183)[40], the 1981 Nationality Act had the exact opposite effect, at least with respect to the reviled concept of Commonwealth patriality.

*Ethnic Selectivity in an Ethnically Neutral Immigration
Regime: France*

French postcolonial immigration policy largely escaped the "racism"
charge that was routinely thrown at the British policy. In fact, instead of
"a policy" in the singular we are dealing in the French case with multiple
country- and region-specific policies, based on international treaties with
newly independent states. Subsaharan Africans, for example, continued to
enjoy certain postcolonial privileges well into the early 1990s, most notably eased access to French citizenship, which had been long denied to the
citizens of independent Algeria (see Marot, 1995). Such discrepant treatment, and the obvious absence of a color line in it, cannot possibly be
classed as "racist." If, from the narrow point of view of immigration policy, decolonization proceeded more smoothly in France than in Britain,
this is in paradoxical contrast to the opposite domestic impact of decolonization in both states, which was traumatic and fiercely contested in
France yet largely unproblematic in Britain.

Several factors are responsible for the comparatively lesser degree of
politicization surrounding French postcolonial immigration policies.
First, the European and native portions of postcolonial "repatriate-
expatriates" (Etemad, 1998) were inversely distributed in France and
Britain: in Britain there were vastly more native than European-origin
postcolonials moving to Britain proper in the wake of decolonization,
whereas in France the distribution was the opposite.[41] Second, there was,
until 1974, no zero-immigration imperative as in Britain. On the contrary, parallel to postcolonial immigration France had large-scale, state-
sponsored labor migration, solicited by bilateral agreements, partially
even with states that had once been under the purview of the French
empire (Morocco and Tunisia). France's huge appetite for immigrants
easily "assimilated" the postcolonial portion, even though European and
(the non-European portion of) postcolonial immigrants were accorded
sharply differential treatment. As we shall see, a distinct feature of the
French case is that its postcolonial immigration always has to be seen in the
context of European immigration, which was specifically solicited to counterbalance the (ethnically less desired but tolerated) postcolonial intakes.

Furthermore, there could not be a French parallel to the British patriality debate because of the different structures of both empires and the
different citizenship regimes in both states. With respect to the structure
of empire, the second French empire of the late 1800s that was subject
to devolution after World War II[42] had never consisted of "colonies de

peuplement" (Betts, 1961, ch. 2), except Algeria. There was nothing akin in France to the British Old Dominions that would call for preferential treatment in immigration policy. Even in the "jewel" of the second empire, Indochina, there were never more than 5,000 French settlers, and they were not occupying (presumably) empty space to be filled out in their image but meeting fully developed civilizations (Heffernan, 1995:35). In Algeria, the one instance of massive French settlement, less than half of the ruling *colons* were of French origin, the majority being from Italy, Spain, Switzerland, and other European states (all of whom, of course, were recruited with the promise of French citizenship). Reciprocity concerns for French settlers were one major motivation for allowing the immigration of former colonial subjects, including Algerians. However, pointing to the different citizenship regimes in the two states, the French policies framing this immigration could rest on the firm basis of national citizenship. Under the Fourth Republic, all residents of the colonies were granted French citizenship[43] and—in addition—a superimposed "French Union" citizenship.[44] These concessions were easily revocable at independence, particularly because most postindependence states showed little interest in maintaining colonialism-reminding ties with the *métropole*. There was no parallel in France to imperial "subjectship" in Britain, which was antecedent to (rather than superimposed on) state citizenship and which, as the revolving axis of residence and participation rights, could get into the way of controlling immigration from the outer reaches of empire (see Vanel, 1951).

There are also strong ideological reasons that speak against selecting among postcolonial (and any other) immigrants along ethnic or racial lines. In Britain, the animus against ethnic selectivity was a liberal one, addressing the inequities resulting from such a policy; it coexisted, somewhat uneasily, with a robust sense of the "kith and kin" who were to be preferred over others. By contrast, the French aversion to ethnic selectivity stems from a (not always liberal) national self-understanding along Jacobin-Republican lines, according to which France is the home of the universal citizen, where no intermediate structures or group allegiances were to stand in between the abstract individual and the state. In the almost comical pathos of a contemporary Republican intellectual, France's "main contribution to the history of humankind is to have liberated democracy from its original ethnic stranglehold, and to define the citizenry without reference to any notion of race or blood" (Todd, 1994:14). Indeed, even in the face of an ethnically and racially diversified society, where there is an obvious need for group-specific information as basis for targeted intervention, the French state has steadfastly refused to use ethnicity or race as official statistical categories and benchmarks of public policy making.[45] From a Republican point of view, the only group distinction allowed to be drawn by the state is the one between citizens and foreigners, with their difference not measured in ethnic but political terms—"the only foreigners in France are the bad citizens," a man of 1789 famously said. This national self-understanding sets high hurdles for distinguishing between different categories of foreigners according to their ethnic fit with the domestic population.

It is therefore no small irony that in the very moment that the Republic was resurrected from Vichy and the German occupation, France came precariously close to institute an ethnoracial immigration regime that strongly resembled the national-origin system then in place in the United States. This is because some of the leading figures in the *Haut Comité de la population et de la famille*, created by De Gaulle in April 1945 to prepare a new immigration policy for a country desperately short of manpower and population, were steeped in the eugenic and racist discourse of prewar demography (see Schneider, 1990). There was an astonishing consensus in the *Haut Comité* for ethnic preferences (see Weil, 1995b). However, it was only one member, Georges Mauco, the *Haut Comité*'s general secretary, who thought exclusively in ethnoracial terms. In his monumental prewar doctorate on the situation of foreigners in France, Mauco had considered Asians, Africans, and Levantines (Eastern Mediterranean Jews) as "absolutely unassimilable" (Mauco, 1932:523), and for the acceptable Europeans he favored an intake according to their spatial and cultural proximity. According to Mauco's 1945 blueprint, which initially had the support of De Gaulle's transition government and was crossed out only at the last minute by the *Conseil d'État*,[46] France would have selected her postwar immigrants according to an ethnic quota system, in which 50 percent were reserved to "Nordics" (which included the defeated Germans), 30 percent to "Mediterraneans," and only 20 percent to the least-favored "Slavs."

Two considerations dominated the deliberations of the *Haut Comité:* Does the quality of a population depend more on their size or on their inherent characteristics, and is "assimilability" more a function of the ethnic origins or of the individual characteristics of the immigrant (see Weil, 1995b)? In both respects, Alfred Sauvy, the second demographer on the *Haut Comité*, took opposite positions from Mauco, favoring a huge and less discriminate over a small and more selective intake, as well as prioritizing individual over ethnic-group screening. To be sure, Sauvy shared with Mauco an astonishing penchant for ethnoracial categorizing and stereotyping. In his demographic treatise *Des Français pour la France,* cowritten with Robert Debré (Debré and Sauvy, 1946), Asians and black Africans were quickly excluded from further discussion, simply because their recruitment was anyway "not envisaged" (ibid., 227). This meant that, even for a moderate voice, France's own colonies were deemed irrelevant for meeting the country's demographic needs. Not unlike Mauco, in Sauvy's view ethnic-origin selection was to occur only from within the pool of "people of white color." Among the latter there were some problematic groups, such as Germans, whose character deficits (such as "collective cruelty" or "passive obedience") called for their "sufficient dispersion" and "attentive surveillance" (ibid., 228). Overall, however, Sauvy favored individual over generic ethnic screening: "[E]n matière d'assimilation et de françisation, l'élément individuel doit l'emporter sur tout autre. Ce sont les caractères de chaque immigrant qu'il faut examiner . . . chaque individu soit en quelque sorte mis en observation pendant un certain temps" (ibid., 230).

This was the position that prevailed within the ethnically neutral *Ordonnance* of 2 November 1945, which is still today the legal basis of France's immigration policy. It represented a victory of the "Republican Resistance jurists" (Weil, 1995b:100) on the *Haut Comité,* most notably Alexandre Parodi, who also served on the *Conseil d'État* that eventually suppressed Mauco's plan of ethnic-origin selections.

However, this was not the end of ethnic considerations in French postwar immigration policy. Having been formally erased from the letter of the law, the pressure for ethnic selectivity survived informally. This was already guaranteed by personal continuities—Mauco continued serving as general secretary of the *Haut Comité* until 1970, and Sauvy would hold leading positions in the Ministry of Public Health and Population as well as France's state demographic institute, INED, well into the 1970s. One can interpret much of the dynamics of postwar French immigration policy as a perennial struggle between "economists," who argued for ethnicity-blind, flexible intakes according to labor market needs, and "populationists," who wanted permanent and thus "assimilable" and ethnically select immigrants as a remedy to population decline (see Tapinos, 1975).

The most striking aspect of the deliberations surrounding the 1945 *Ordonnance* was the complete absence of, even active opposition to, consideration of the colonies for meeting the country's manpower and demographic needs. When the colonial governor of Algeria, in April 1945, offered to transfer 100,000 native workers to France, the French authorities rejected this, arguing—with Georges Mauco—that the "sanitary, social, and moral risks" were too high (Weil, 1995a:93). The struggle between "economists" and "populationists" over the direction of French postwar immigration policy thus occurred against the backdrop of discarding the colonial option. While the populationists (whose stronghold was the Ministry of Public Health and Population) eventually lost against the economists (based in the Ministry of Work), they still scored some partial victories. Initially, bilateral treaties were made only with, and state recruitment offices opened only in, places that ranked high on Mauco's ethnic hierarchy: Italy, Germany, Spain, and Portugal. Italy, especially, the single most courted immigrant source in the early postwar period, was granted unique privileges that even came to be resented by other European immigrant-sending states. Italian migrants received family allowances, even if their families did not reside in France, in a breach of the territoriality principle of the French welfare state; they could remit a bigger portion of their monthly wages (60 instead 50 percent); they were granted preferential work permit renewals and freedom of profession and movement; and, ahead of all other nationalities, they were relocated from the shabby bidonvilles to HLM housing (Viet, 1998:265–267).

A major site for playing out informal ethnic preferences was family reunification. The 1945 *Ordonnance,* which was a law on labor migration, not permanent settlement,[47] was silent on the issue. However, as early as 1948 there was a stress on family reunification, and a reformed *Office national d'immigration (ONI)*[48] was instructed to "apply the rules fixed by the Ministry for Public Health and Population regarding the selection of immigrants," which included consideration of their "national origins" (quoted in Tapinos, 1975:32). In principle, the family reunification of European immigrants was favored, that of Algerians was not. There was a formal legal basis for this discrimination, because Algerian immigration occurred outside the *Ordonnance,* and in countries without an ONI office, migrants simply had to fend for themselves. However, there was additional targeted discrimination, both negative and positive. Ministerial circulars show that in the case of Algerians family reunification in "predominantly Maghrebinian milieus" was to be prevented (see Rodier, 1995; Spire, 2001:14), and that from early on this immigration was considered "as a simple economic necessity and not as an enterprise of populating [France] *(entreprise de peuplement)*" (quoted in Viet, 1998:159, n.1). At the same time, financial help from the Public Health Ministry was reserved to reuniting Italian, German, Polish, and Yugoslav families. Note that the growing imperative of counterbalancing unsolicited Algerian inflows with solicited European inflows led, from 1951 on, to the granting of family allowances to workers of *all* European nationalities, thus undermining the intra-European ethnic hierarchy wanted by Mauco and other populationists (Viet, 1995).

Informal ethnic selectivity was never more visible than in 1968, when a revision of the Evian Accord put an end to the free circulation of Algerians, and also the established practice of "regularizing" after the fact non–state-channeled "wild" migration was cut down. Deliberately exempted from the ban on ex-post regularization were the Portuguese, simply because after the drying out of the Italian and Spanish sources the Portuguese represented the last pool of ethnically wanted European immigrants. For a leading ONI administrator, the Portuguese were "exceptionally useful in economic regard and also of very great demographic interest," because they represented "the last immigration that is easily assimilable on our territory."[49] While the percentage of "regularized" immigrants declined from a peak of 82 percent in 1968 to just 44 percent in 1972 (Tapinos, 1975:99), almost all of the Portuguese who massively entered after 1968 were still granted a regularization—90 percent in 1969, and 94 percent in 1971 (ibid., p. 107).[50] In 1971, the year that the Algerian annual quota was further reduced from 35,000 to 25,000, an accord was reached with the Portuguese junta over a 65,000 annual quota. These discrepant figures show "the constant intention of drawing as much as possible from European labor reserves in order to counterbalance the immigration originating from developing countries" (Viet, 1998:273–274). As a result, the Portuguese quickly became the second-largest immigrant group in France, with 660,000 members in 1972 clearly ahead of the stagnating or even shrinking Spanish and Italian contingents (600,000 and 560,000 in the same year, respectively), and second only to the Algerians (720,000), whose inflows continued at high level, now mostly due to family reunification.

While the ethnic concerns of populationists obviously had an impact, they were nested within a larger economic frame that ultimately determined policies and flows. This is evidenced by the very practice of "regularization," which stands for the primacy of the market over the state in controlling immigration flows. Due to an increasingly tough intra-European competition for migrant labor, France was forced to tap ever more remote source countries via bilateral agreements—Yugoslavia, Tunisia, Morocco,[51] and Turkey.[52] Considering only state-sponsored ONI immigration, this led to a striking ethnic-origin reversal: whereas 96 percent of new entries in 1957 had originated from Italy, Spain, or Portugal, their share was down to 46 percent in 1972; in the same period, the combined share of Moroccans, Tunisians, Yugoslavs, and Turks increased from just 4 percent to 45 percent (Tapinos, 1975:106).

There was a second reason why populationist concerns withered: since 1945, France was undergoing the biggest population growth in its history. After having stagnated around the 40 million mark since 1850, the French population grew by an unprecedented 52.4 percent between 1945 and 1990 (Le Bras, 1991:68). While this may not have put to an end the traditional French "obsession with demography" (Le Bras), the latter was no longer directed at immigration.

Striking about France's deliberate expansion of source countries is the inclusion of Morocco and Tunisia, two former protectorates. This occurred under the overarching imperative of "minimizing Algerian immigration" (Weil, 1995a:100). Turning to other Maghreb countries in order to minimize Algerian intakes demonstrates the negative centrality of this former colony to the French politics of immigration. This politics largely revolved around the "Algerian problem" (ibid., 93).

Why was Algeria different? A general animus against a Muslim country will not do, given France's parallel recruitment of Moroccan and Tunisian labor migrants. Instead, an explanation has to be looked for in colonial history. Nowhere was the clash between colonial ideology and reality more extreme: against the colonial ideology of France and Algeria as indissolubly one (divided only geographically "as Paris was divided by the Seine")[53] stood the reality of two closed societies on France's putative "Left Bank," Algeria. In an early work, Pierre Bourdieu (1974:115–116) had characterized the colonial society in Algeria as a "caste system," composed of "two juxtaposed and distinct communities" whose contact was reduced to the "indispensable minimum." The European-French elite's total rejection of the natives found expression in assigning to them a separate legal status, which allowed them to follow Islamic rules in their personal affairs and family lives but also excluded them from the full rights of citizenship, particularly in the political sphere, even after their nominal award of French citizenship in 1946 (see Barrière, 1995). This institutional separation was sealed by the complete nonexistence of intermarriage. After the contradiction between assimilationist ideology and differentialist practice exploded in the "national folly of the Algerian war" (Todd, 1994:297), Algerian immigrants were chronically suspected of a loyalty deficit toward France. Indeed, the Algerian FLN (Front de Libération National) was heartily supported by the Algerian immigrant colony in France. In 1957, the year of the ferocious battle of Algier, some 40,000 Algerian immigrants (which is almost one-fifth of all Algerian immigrants in France according to the 1954 census) had to pay for this support with their temporary imprisonment (Gillette and Sayad, 1984:67).

More than any other immigrant group, Algerians epitomize the disjunction between ethnic and political preferences that is characteristic for the northwestern postcolonial constellation in Europe. If, in the Evian Accords of 1962, Algerians were granted free movement and all the other rights that French citizens enjoyed (except political rights), the main reason was the reciprocity concern for the 1 million French *colons (pieds-noirs)* then residing in Algeria—which became famously irrelevant with their near-total exodus in the same year. Formally the most privileged, while informally the most despised postcolonial immigrants, Algerians were henceforth subjected to unique measures of restriction (see Hauteville, 1995). Singling out Algerians was possible because of their exemption from the common regime of the (ethnicity- and national-origin blind) *Ordonnance* and their special treatment according to international agreement, which in the French hierarchy of laws precedes domestic law.[54] This special legal situation allowed the French state to reduce privileges for Algerians either through modifying the underlying international agreement or through not applying the immigrant-friendly reforms occurring meanwhile within the common immigration regime. As a result of both measures, the status of Algerians slipped below that of ordinary immigrants, without the open appearance of discrimination.[55]

The Southwestern Constellation: Spain and Portugal

At the summit at Tampere, Finland, in October 1999, European Union leaders conceded that a future EU immigration policy would have to respect not just the limited "reception capacity" of member states but also "their historical and cultural links with the countries of origin."[56] Among the fifteen (pre-Enlargement) member states of the European Union, only Spain and Portugal have noteworthy immigration (and nationality) laws and policies that take into account such "historical and cultural links." As the Tampere statement indicates, these links have come on a collision course with the pending Europeanization of the immigration function, which requires the construction of a standardized Euro-foreigner (or "third-state national"). As in the case of Britain or France, these "links" refer to a colonial past. However, in contrast to those countries, in Spain and Portugal the links transcend the narrow political and economic dimensions and have taken on cultural and panethnic contours, pointing to the existence of a state-transcending community that calls for privileged treatment of its members in immigration and nationality law and policy.

Spain and Portugal are alike in giving preferential access to territory, labor market, and citizenship to undifferentiated immigrants from the former imperial realms of both countries. Besides being characterized by an overlap (rather than disjunction) between political and ethnic preferences, the southwestern postcolonial constellation differs from the northwestern constellation in two further respects. First, its central legal principle and justification is "reciprocity." That is, immigrants from the respective states are granted privileged treatment, if and insofar as Portuguese or Spanish emigrants are granted the same privileges by these states in turn, as laid down in bilateral treaties and conventions. This reflects the significant emigration traditions in both countries, which as such are without parallel in Britain or France. "Emigration," as against intra-imperial "settlement," implies a change of political jurisdiction, after which the emigrant becomes subject to the whims of a different sovereign—and thus remains dependent upon protection by his or her country of origin. Consider that one-third of all Portuguese live abroad, 1.2 million of them (which is about 10 percent of the entire Portuguese population) in Brazil alone. In the context of massive emigration, reciprocal immigration and citizenship privileges between Portugal and Brazil are as much the expression of a "Lusophone" identity as in the pragmatic interest of protecting the sizeable Portuguese emigrant colony abroad.

Second, the southwestern postcolonial constellation involves, on the European side, states of greatly reduced, even marginal status. Both the Spanish and Portuguese preference schemes originated under authoritarian regimes (Franco and Salazar, respectively), which made both states pariahs in a democratic postwar Western Europe and consequently looking for alternative spheres of influence and standing. This meant, in the case of Francoist Spain, the rebuilding of postcolonial ties that had been ruptured more than half a century ago. This is rather different from the standard postcolonial *problématique* of regulating the transition from empire to nation-state. After the fall of Franco and Salazar in the mid-1970s, postcolonial ties were re-evaluated under the new democratic regimes as assets to upgrade the marginal status of both countries within Europe, often with a "third-worldist" tinge of Portugal and Spain serving as bridgeheads between the poor South and the rich North.

Next to these communalities, there are interesting internal variations between Spain and Portugal. The Portuguese preference regime makes the status of Portuguese as official state language the essential criterion of granting immigration and citizenship privileges, whereas the Spanish regime's interpretation of "historical-cultural links" is wider than language and, as we shall see, potentially transcends the postcolonial context. This difference shows in the curious fact that Portugal (as well as Portuguese-speaking Brazil) is included in Spain's preference regime (as being part of the Ibero-American nexus), whereas Spain is not part of Portugal's preference regime (of course, this distinction has become meaningless in the context of European Community law). Second, at least in immigration law, the Spanish preference regime has successively been cut down since 1985 (the year of the first Spanish immigration law passed under the imperative of European integration), and it has silently disappeared in new immigration laws passed in 2000. By contrast, the Portuguese preference regime has even gained impetus and expanded through the 1990s, the initiative for this (among other factors) coming from Brazilian and Cape Verdean attempts to forge a "Community of Lusophone Countries."

For our purposes, more important than these internal variations is one central feature shared by both southwestern preference regimes: there has been little domestic opposition to them. Instead, the pressure on these schemes has been mostly external, originating from the emergent European Union immigration regime. Why has there been so little domestic opposition? First, these schemes have remained invisible.[57] They are marginal aspects of belatedly introduced immigration laws and policies that themselves—until most recently—have not stirred much public discussion. Second, these schemes are "politically correct" because they do not distinguish between ethnic or racial subcategories of postcolonial immigrants and thus prominently include nonwhites. Moreover, in progressive discourse they are justifiable as redemption of historical injustice (i.e., colonialism) and as expressing solidarity with the poor South. The preference regimes are embedded within the general posture of southern

European states to take a more generous and humane approach to immigration than the petty restrictionism prevailing in northern European states. Third, to the degree that most immigration has occurred on the preference ticket, as in the case in Portugal, there are no disadvantaged groups to raise equity concerns; or, where such groups exist, as in the case of Moroccans in Spain, they have lacked the resources and leadership to make themselves heard (see Danese, 2001). Fourth, the legal preferences correspond to popular sentiments—Latin Americans in Spain and Brazilians in Portugal are favorably perceived as ethnically and culturally close, even more than the fellow Europeans.

Spain and the Comunidad Hispánica

In the case of Spain it is not easy to pin down precisely the boundaries of the state-transcending community that has found expression in preferential immigration and citizenship rules. There is not even a shared word for it, and a variety of labels have been used—"historical community of Hispanic nations," *comunidad hispánica,* Ibero-America (a notion that allows the inclusion of non-Hispanic Portugal and Brazil), with *Hispanidad, Hispanismo,* or nondescriptive "historical-cultural ties" as the shared features of this community. Whatever the label, it corresponds roughly to the space carved out by the Spanish colonization of Latin America.[58] Language is one element of it, but not exclusively, because Portugal and Portuguese-speaking Brazil have from the start been included. In fact, while rarely explicitly stated, one must surmise that the Catholic religion is—next to language—the *comunidad hispánica*'s basic cement.

The preferred notion under Franco, the period of forging the dual-nationality treaties that have remained this community's legal backbone, was *Hispanidad*. It blends the ethnic elements of a common Hispanic heritage and *raza* (race) with a heavy dose of political ideology, depicting a traditionalist, antidemocratic, Catholic Spain as *madre patria* and leader of the Hispanic world, posed against the twin forces of liberalism and Marxism that allegedly prevailed in the Anglo-Saxon world (see Pike, 1986:83). Constitutive of *Hispanidad* is also a strange dichotomy of "materialism" versus "spiritualism," with *Hispanidad* claiming to be on the "spiritual" side. This motif originated in the traumatic loss of the last Spanish colonies (Cuba, Puerto Rico, and the Philippines) in the war of 1898 against the United States. Now that Spain no longer had material power, it had to compensate for this with "spiritual" power. *Hispanidad*'s stress on "spiritual" values is in this sense "surrogate imperialism" or "ideology of sublimation" (Hennessy, 2000:106).[59]

Whatever its contents, *Hispanidad* never had much resonance outside Spain. With the exception of Peronist Argentina, the predominantly liberal regimes in Latin America frowned upon Francoist Spain, accepting instead a good part of its Republican refugees. The post–Spanish Civil War exodus of intellectuals, writers, professors, and scientists, in fact, opened up an alternative and more enduring way of building a Hispanic community around a shared language and culture. In the words of Spanish philosopher José Gaos, the Spanish exiles in Latin America felt *trasterrados* (removed) but not *desterrados* (uprooted) (Torregrosa, 1996:116). The mutual refugee experience of, first, Spanish and, later, Latin American intellectuals (who escaped Latin America's authoritarian turn just when Spain turned democratic in 1975) has always helped Hispanism to be more than a Francoist ploy.

Hispanidad fell into disrepute after Franco, when the emphasis shifted toward more mundane and pragmatic "historical and cultural links" (see Pollack, 1987:89–90). Now Spain figured less as "leader" than equal "partner" of Ibero-American states, even though her leadership aspirations were indirectly reinforced by holding her successful transition to democracy as the model to follow in postauthoritarian Latin America.[60] However, especially for writers and intellectuals, the existence of a state-transcending, Hispanic cultural community has remained as vital as ever. Recently touring Mexico and the Hispanic immigrant communities in the United States, former Socialist Prime Minister Filipe Gonzales stressed that on the basis of a shared language all Hispanics also held the same "cultural citizenship"—and this in contrast to England and America, which were "separated by the same language."[61] When Spain recently acquiesced to a new EU visa requirement for Colombians, Nobel Prize winner Gabriel García Márquez, supported by leading Colombian and Spanish intellectuals, protested that Spanish Americans "cannot be treated just like any other group of foreigners" because they were the "great-grandchildren of Spain," who had "never considered [Spain] as something foreign to ourselves."[62]

The first legal articulation of the *comunidad hispánica* can be found in the short-lived Republican constitution of 1931, whose Article 24.2 allows dual nationality for the "citizens [*naturales*] of Portugal and the Hispanic countries of America, including Brazil," provided there is reciprocity. This provision, which was never implemented, responded to the forced attribution of nationality by some Latin American states in the late nineteenth and early twentieth centuries (Virgós Soriano, 1990:239), and it was meant to protect the two million Spaniards (equaling 10 percent of the total Spanish population) then living in Latin America, mostly in Argentina, Cuba, Mexico, and Brazil (Pike, 1980:190–191).

The dual-nationality regime of the Spanish Republic, which ran contrary to the international ban on dual nationality in the Hague Convention of 1930, was retained, even reinforced, under Franco. In 1951, at the *Congreso hispano-luso-americano* in Madrid, the influential law professor Federico de Castro suggested a system of dual-nationality treaties with Spanish-American states, which would give legal expression to a state-transcending "Hispanic community" based on shared "origin, culture, and belief" (de Castro y Bravo, 1948:104). The idea was quickly picked up by Franco, who sought in the revival of the long-severed ties with Spain's former colonies in Latin America a compensation for his near-total isolation in early postwar Europe. Article 22 of a new nationality law passed in 1954 opened the door for twelve bilateral dual-nationality treaties with Latin America (and, though never realized, the Philippines), the first of which was signed with Chile in 1958 and the last (under Franco) with Argentina in 1969.[63] As the Preamble of the 1954 Nationality Law outlines the thrust of this policy, Spain shared a "spiritual mission [with countries with which] for well known reasons, and superior to all kind of contingencies, it is inextinguishably linked."[64] Clearly invoking an ethnic theme, the preamble to the treaty with Chile states that Spaniards and Chileans belonged to a community of "tradition, culture and language," so that they would not feel like foreigners when staying in the other country (see Hailbronner and Renner, 2001:137).

The dual-nationality regime established under Franco was constitutionally sanctioned, even further expanded, in the democratic post-Franco era. Article 11.3 of the 1978 Constitution says: "The state can negotiate dual-nationality treaties with Ibero-American countries or with those that have had or have a particular tie with Spain. In these countries, even if they do not recognize the reciprocal right of their own citizens, Spaniards of birth can naturalize without losing their Spanish citizenship."[65] This article adds an important novelty to the dual-nationality regime by expanding the range of privileged countries beyond the Ibero-American nexus to any country with a past or present "particular tie" with Spain. Accordingly, there have been proposals to enter into dual-nationality agreements with France (on behalf of the Basques inhabiting both sides of the border) or Germany (on behalf of the Spanish guestworkers residing there). In fact, the new Spanish constitution, reflecting the guestworker experience since the late 1950s, also contains a new commitment to protect the rights of Spanish workers abroad, even to induce their return.[66] One could argue that potentially enlarging the pool of privileged countries reflects this new commitment, which is different from the original purpose of the dual-nationality regime to "juridically vest a cultural identity" (Virgós Soriano, 1990:244). However, the only additional dual-nationality treaty to come after Franco was with Colombia in 1978, which obviously corresponds to the original purpose of the underlying regime to build a Hispanic community. More plausible is an alternative interpretation of expanding the range of privileged countries in the new constitution: the new formulation allows Spain's former colonies in Africa and Asia (Equatorial Guinea and the Philippines) to be included in the preference regime.[67]

For our purposes it is important that only Spaniards by birth can invoke the dual-nationality privileges of Article 11.3 of the 1978 constitution. This fact reveals the ethnic thrust of the *comunidad hispánica* to be expressed by the dual nationality regime. In fact, this was no novelty, because all dual-nationality treaties passed since 1958 had included this ethnic restriction.[68] By contrast, when the purpose of dual nationality was to protect Spanish emigrants abroad, dual nationality was also available to naturalized Spaniards. Accordingly, the former Article 23 I(2) of the Civil Code, which prescribed the loss of Spanish nationality in the case of naturalization elsewhere, exempted from this all individuals who had emigrated, and who declared at the consulate that they wished to retain their Spanish nationality.[69] This exemption, whose purpose was not to build the *comunidad hispánica* but to protect the individual, applied to "all kind of nationals, natives and naturalized, and in relation to any foreign state" (Virgós Soriano, 1990:245), its constitutional basis being Article 42, which obliges the state to protect Spaniards abroad, not Article 11.3, which lays out the dual-nationality regime.

While the legal backbone of the *comunidad hispánica* has always been nationality law, it has also found some—though limited and legally contested—expression in immigration law and policy. A critical juncture in this respect was the passing of the 1985 Foreigner Law *(Ley Orgánica 7/1985)*, the first Spanish legislation on foreigners in more then 130 years. Passed at a time of insignificant immigration pressures, and without any major debate, the heavily restrictive thrust of *Ley Orgánica 7/1985* is generally attributed to Spain's joining of the European Community at the time. Interestingly, though, the "police approach" (Arango, 2000:267) taken in the new law was not at all visible in its high-minded title: "Law on the Rights and Liberties of Foreigners in Spain." This rhetoric echoed Spain's post-Francoist liberal-democratic commitments; it was also legally commanded by Article 13.1 of the new constitution, which stipulates that "foreigners will enjoy the public freedoms guaranteed in Title I" (covering fundamental rights and freedoms). According to the Preamble of *Ley Orgánica 7/1985*, "[t]his constitutional mandate is the primary reason for the [new law]."[70] However, the real thrust of the law was restrictionist, granting far-reaching deportation and detention powers to the state and imposing a new system of employer sanctions. Most notably, the law established a complicated system of separate (and mutually dependent) work and residence permits, mostly of only short duration; exceedingly difficult to comply with, it amounted to the legal creation of illegality, forcing most immigrants to shuttle back and forth between periods of legality and illegality (for details, see Calavita, 1998).

The restrictive thrust of the new law, which practically closed down all legal immigration into Spain,[71] has to be considered if one wants to assess the system of national-origin privileges that is also built into it. Overall, it made all (non-EU) immigrants worse off, with the privileged foreigners just a little less worse off than the rest. The preamble to *Ley Orgánica 7/1985* reiterates Spain's special commitment to the *comunidad hispánica*. After presenting the securing of "maximum" rights and liberties for foreigners and the (EU-imposed) fight against illegal immigration as the strangely dual mission of the law, the preamble closes with a somewhat cryptic reference to the acquisition of nationality, in light of which also immigration law and policy should preference those categories of individuals who show "a larger degree of adaptation to Spanish life." The enumerated privileged categories are people born in Spain, people linked to Spaniards through family ties, long-term residents, and, last but not least, the *comunidad hispánica:* "In this line, the law also foresees a preferential treatment for Ibero-Americans, Portuguese, Filipinos, Andorrans, Equatorial Guineans, Sephardic Jews, and Gibraltarians; because all these involve cases of identity or cultural affinity, they are entitled to this consideration." The law thus establishes a link between cultural affinity and better adaptability of some immigrants, on the one hand, and their preferred admission, on the other. This is structurally equivalent to the pre-

1965 national-origins regime in the United States, which had made the same link between cultural affinity, assimilability, and the preferred admission of some (that is, northwestern European) immigrants. In its instrumental concern about integrating immigrants, this justification is notably weaker than giving expression to the *comunidad hispánica*, which had been the rhetoric surrounding the dual-nationality regime. The privileged groups are still the same in both, including, in an act of historical reparation, also Sephardic Jews, who had been driven out of Spain in 1492.

For Ibero-Americans and Filipinos, the sober effect of the 1985 law was to suppress the privileged immigration status they had enjoyed since the *Ley de 30 diciembre de 1969,* which had exempted them from the need to hold a work permit[72] and had guaranteed them equal social rights. Reminiscent of the noninstrumental *comunidad hispánica* rhetoric of old, the purpose of the 1969 law had been to acknowledge the "singularity of the ties that bind Spain with the peoples that are members of the Ibero-American and Filipino community," and to complement the dual-nationality regime with the creation of "an effective social community."[73] Certainly, the provisions of the 1969 law presupposed rather than created legal residence rights. However, the combination of the 1969 law with bilateral agreements on the suppression of visas and on the recognition of diplomas and professional titles (on the latter, see Espósito, 1991) amounted to a free movement and residence space for the members of the *comunidad hispánica* that equaled, and increasingly clashed with, the emergent European free-movement regime.

Despite the (weak because assimilationist) rhetoric of the 1985 preamble, not many of these privileges are left in the letter, not to mention the implementation, of the 1985 *Ley Orgánica* (see Alvarez Rodriguez, 1994). Article 18 of the 1985 law only states that the privileged groups mentioned in the Preamble, among them the members of the *comunidad hispánica,* are to be preferred in the distribution of work permits, without specifying the precise content of these preferences. Article 23 further exempts the national-origin groups (but strangely not the other preferred groups of the preamble) from the payment of work-permit taxes.

The 1986 Regulation to implement the law *(Real Decreto 1119/1986)* further cuts down and, de facto, nullifies the privileged treatment promised in the preamble of the foreigner law. Article 21 of the regulation grants a special ten-year residence permit to the privileged groups of the preamble. However, this is contingent on a prior two-year legal residence minimum, which is equally difficult to obtain for anyone. The highly precious type C work permit of Article 39, which is valid for five years and allows the free choice of employer and unhindered geographical mobility, is available for the privileged national-origin and ethnic groups after only two (instead of five as for all others) years of holding a lower-degree work permit in the past. However, this "privilege" is nullified by not allowing these groups preferential access to a lower-order B work permit (valid for one year and renewable), which would exempt them from the "national employment situation" proviso (which gives priority to Spanish and other EU citizens). Such preferential access to the type B work permit is granted in Article 38 to all the other privileged groups mentioned in the 1985 preamble (as well as some additional groups, such as refugees and asylum seekers) but, capriciously and inexplicably, not to the ethnic and national-origin groups. Several Spanish legal scholars have pointed out that the only meaningful "privilege" granted by the 1986 regulation was the exemption from the national-employment-situation proviso according to Article 38, so that not granting this privilege to the Ibero-Americans and other members of the *comunidad hispánica* had de facto nullified their privileged treatment regarding immigration.[74]

However, the Spanish Supreme Court has found an alternative source of retaining a privileged regime for some Ibero-Americans: the dual-nationality conventions. Article 7 of the conventions with Chile and Peru (Article 8 in the case of Ecuador) stipulates that also those who do not wish to benefit from the provisions of the respective treaty (that is, opt for dual nationality) enjoy the "rights and advantages" granted by domestic legislation. Unique to the mentioned conventions, the same article further specifies the content of these rights (Art. 7.2): "[To] travel and reside in the respective territories, settle down wherever they may wish, acquire and possess all sorts of goods, exercise all types of dependent or independent work, enjoy labor protection and social security, and have access to authority and justice, all on the same conditions as nationals."[75] Article 7 closes with a relativizing clause (7.3) that subjects the "exercise of these rights" to domestic legislation. The Spanish administration has invoked this last relativizing clause to invalidate the earlier enumerated work and residence rights, thus folding back the respective Ibero-Americans into the general, restrictive aliens regime.

Interestingly, Spanish courts have not followed this restrictive line. Lower courts in Mallorca and Asturias interpreted Article 7.2 of the Convention with Chile as exempting the Chilean plaintiffs even from the need to hold a Spanish residence permit.[76] Although subsequent decisions of the Supreme Court did not uphold this maximalist line of lower courts, the Supreme Court still held that Article 7.2 contained substantive rights that could not be invalidated by domestic immigration law. In doing so, the Supreme Court could invoke Article 3 of the 1985 *Ley Orgánica* itself, which stipulates that its provisions do not impair established international treaty rights. In a variety of decisions on Chileans and Peruvians in the early 1990s, the Supreme Court developed the doctrine that Article 7 had a mixed content—partly autonomous and partly subjected to domestic norms. More concretely, the court held that Peruvians and Chileans had the right to a work permit, irrespective of the national-employment situation—thus including them de facto in the list of privileged aliens according to Article 38 of the 1986 *Real Decreto*. However, in contrast to the maximalism of some lower courts, the Supreme Court did not exempt these Ibero-Americans from the (long-term) visa requirement, arguing that the regulation of entry and stay was the subject of separate bilateral agreements on the suppression of visas, which moreover pertained only to short-term tourism, not work-related stays exceeding three months (thus indicating that long-term immigration was never intended by them). In addition, the court held that Chileans and Peruvians were still required to obtain a residence permit as prescribed by domestic immigration law, while simply avoiding a debate on the rather opposite wording to be found in Article 7.2 of the Dual-Nationality Conventions.

In sum, judicial activism allowed some Ibero-Americans access to a privileged work permit according to Article 38 of the 1986 *Real Decreto;* however, this privilege remained contingent upon the discretionary concession of visa and residence permits by the state (see Viñas Farre, 1998). The juridical strategy of splitting up the ample rights catalog provided by Article 7 of some dual-nationality conventions into work-related rights, on the one hand, and entry and residence rights, on the other, and reaffirming only the former while remaining silent on the latter, reflects a typical balancing act of courts that have everywhere sought to maximize immigrant rights without openly challenging essential state authority on immigration (see Joppke and Marzal, 2004).

Over time, the trend for the *comunidad hispánica* has been to retain, even to strengthen, its legal foothold in nationality law, while losing out in immigration law. While it is difficult to establish a causality in this, it corresponds exactly to the exigencies of Europeanization, which (so far) touches only upon immigration, not citizenship and nationality issues. On the side of nationality law, the 1990 reform of the Civil Code provided the possibility of unilateral dual citizenship not just for Spaniards (as was the result of the 1982 reform) but also for Ibero-Americans. Moreover, this was a stronger dual nationality than the one granted by the dual-nationality conventions, because it allowed the enjoyment of two fully efficient nationalities at the same time (rather than relegating one to dormant status, as required by the conventions). Of course, these advances on the side of nationality law are on paper only, if they are not backed by corresponding immigration privileges to take advantage of them.

Regarding immigration, the Spanish state has taken a contradictory line, sticking to the rhetoric of special commitments to the *comunidad hispánica* but not living up to it in practice. In the early 1990s, when a Socialist government shifted the focus from restrictionism toward facilitating the social integration of immigrants, there was some renewed rhetorical emphasis on "special consideration" for Ibero-Americans.[77] The 1990 government report on the "Situation of Foreigners in Spain: Basic Lines of Spanish Foreigner Policy," which launched this liberalizing trend, invoked the formula of "historical and cultural ties with third states" (p. 27), which has since been reiterated at the European level.[78] Regarding the countries of "Hispanoamerica," the 1990 report reaffirms the government intention to "maintain its policy of visa exemption for the citizens of these countries" (p. 14). However, when it came into conflict with the short-term visa list set up by the Schengen partners and high immigration pressures from particular countries, this intention did not prevent the Socialist government from introducing a new tourist visa requirement for Cubans, Peruvians, and Dominicans in 1992, thus, for the first time, splitting the *comunidad hispánica* apart.[79] The 1996 *Real Decreto 115/1996,* which derogated the 1986 regulation and realized the post-1990 liberalizing impulse by introducing the long-awaited possibility of a permanent residence permit, still retained the marginally privileged position of Ibero-Americans in immigration law. By the same token, the new regulation prolonged the capricious bifurcation of the privileged groups in the 1985 *Ley Orgánica* preamble, with its Article 77 conceding to Ibero-Americans a preferential treatment in the initial concession of a work permit without, however, exempting them from consideration of the national employment situation.

The passing of the new *Ley Orgánica 4/2000* of January 11, 2000, and its swift replacement by *Ley Orgánica 8/2000* of December 22, 2000, caught public attention for first demolishing and then reinstating the rigid distinction between legal and illegal immigrants that had already characterized the 1985 law. Invisible in this imbroglio, in which, for the first time in Spain, immigration became a highly charged political issue that sharply divided left and right, has been the true historical rupture brought about by both laws: there is almost no (even symbolic) reference in them to the *comunidad hispánica*.[80] Reflecting the exigencies of Europeanization, the only special regime recognized in the new acts is regarding nationals of other EU states and regarding diplomats (both of whom are exempted from their reach). More importantly still, the new acts suppress Article 3 of the 1985 law, whose prioritization of international treaty law had allowed the courts to resurrect immigration privileges for some Ibero-Americans through the angle of dual-nationality conventions. Even this extra-domestic judicial remedy is no longer available for Ibero-Americans.

The silent disappearance of the *comunidad hispánica* in immigration law is counter-pointed by its occasional reappearance in public discourse, though in rather opposite shades and stances. For political elites, particularly those associated with the conservative Popular Party (which held the government between 1996 and 2004), a sometimes open, more often subdued preference for Hispanic immigrants is couched in terms of their better adaptability to Spanish society, especially because of their Catholicism (read: non-Muslim origins). In this vein the Secretary of State for Immigration, Fernández-Miranda, expressed his preference for Catholic Hispanic immigrants: "Aside from having a common language and a common culture, practicing the Catholic religion is an element that facilitates the integration of foreigners in Spain."[81] Interestingly, although this linkage of cultural affinity and better immigrant integration does little more than reiterate the preamble of the 1985 *Ley Orgánica* (which, notably, had been passed by a Socialist government), it now came to be identified with "cultural racism" and the political right.[82] A columnist in *El País*, the country's leading liberal newspaper, even likened Miranda's statement to Francoism: "There is a substrate of continuity between the national-Catholic discourse of Franco and the nationalist-Hispanicist discourse which the PP government is spreading, although the tone is less pompous."[83]

More closely than before associated with the political right, the preference for Hispanic immigrants still shapes formal state policies and informal administrative practices, particularly under a conservative government.[84] Regarding formal policies, the Minister of Defense, Federico Trillo, announced in March 2001 that the government was considering "very seriously" the recruitment of foreigners into the professionalized army—but only "citizens of Spanish American countries," whose "language and religion" would guarantee that "there should not be any significant problems regarding their cultural integration."[85] Regarding administrative practice, the latest round of regularizing illegal immigrants, which increased the legal immigrant population in Spain from 801,329 in 1999 to 938,783 in 2000, has clearly favored Ibero-American over all other applicants (89 percent of Brazilian, 80 percent of Argentine, 77 percent of Colombian, and 77 percent of Ecuadorian applications for a residence permit were successful; by contrast, the rates of success for Poles, Chinese, Moroccans, and Nigerians were only 64 percent, 60 percent, 51 percent, and 32 percent, respectively).[86]

Among intellectuals and writers, but also among Hispanic immigrant groups and their home governments, one finds an opposite discourse of moral obligations and ethnocultural identity, which is quite different from the utilitarian stance on better immigrant integration taken by the Spanish government and is more reminiscent of the original notion of *comunidad hispánica*. Its most powerful expression to date has been the angry response by García Márquez and other Colombian artists and intellectuals to Spain's failure to oppose the inclusion of Colombia in the EU visa blacklist. Their open letter to Prime Minister Aznar invoked the notion of Spain as *madre patria* (a phrase tainted in Spain through its association with Francoism), "which we have never considered as something foreign to ourselves." Reflecting the intellectuals' interest in retaining their recurrent and unhindered moves within the Spanish-speaking world, the authors of the protest note likened themselves to "traveling sons who once in a while return home, inverting the footsteps which were once taken by their real or invented ancestors"—though vowing not to set foot in Spain as long as the inflammatory visa obligation existed. With a sarcastic eye on Spain's tendency to boast of the international successes of Spanish-speaking (but non–Spanish citizen) writers and artists, the protest note goes right to the heart of the matter: "We cannot be occasionally accepted when it comes to emphasizing the importance of our language and our culture, only to be rejected when this is convenient to Europe. You must explain to your European partners that you have a historical obligation and a commitment toward us on which you cannot turn your back."[87]

A similar chord of particularistic ties to be honored as a matter of principle tends to be struck by Hispanic immigrant groups and their home governments. In a recent episode involving the regularization of Ecuadorian illegal immigrant workers in Spain, their representatives insisted that "[t]he *madre patria* has a historic duty toward us and must consider the problem of Spanish-speaking immigrants with a special affection."[88] The same motif of a "special relationship" was invoked by the Ecuadorian government when it reached an agreement with Spain that included a generous annual legal immigration quota for Ecuadorians (in return for readmitting illegal Ecuadorians deported from Spain): "Spain closes its doors to the world, but it opens others, selectively, and a wide and exclusive one for Ecuadorians."[89] This particularistic discourse can also be found in the opening paragraphs of the bilateral treaty itself, which expresses "the common desire [of the Spanish and Ecuadorian governments] of reaffirming their special historic and cultural links through the fluid and permanent contact of their populations."[90] Even when criticizing the accord for doing nothing to help the 150,000 illegal Ecuadorians on Spanish soil, an all-party delegation of Ecuadorian parliamentarians visiting a Spain rocked by proimmigrant activism at the time, couched its admiration for this in particularistic terms: "The Spanish people have demonstrated that they are a people united in brotherhood with Ecuador (*un pueblo hermano del Ecuador*), but we want their government to demonstrate this as well."[91]

However, the stress on particular obligations toward Hispanic immigrants is increasingly at odds with Spain's highly diversified immigrant population, which is subjected to the same ordeal of clandestinity, exploitation, and permanent insecurity, irrespective of their nationality. When a recent police raid on a strawberry *finca* in the Andalusian region of Huelva revealed that on its premises some 100 "*inmigrantes sin papeles*" (illegal immigrants) were held "like slaves," they came from four countries and three continents—Morocco, Ecuador, Lithuania, and Romania.[92] Although Hispanic immigrants were obviously involved in this, it would be a strange response to put their lot above that of the others; instead, the obvious way to address this situation would be in terms of fundamental human rights and the dignity of human beings that are being violated or not respected. Accordingly, an editorial in the (conservative) newspaper *El Mundo* phrases its indignation in universalistic terms: "The mere suspicion that there could be more hidden cases of such treatment to *human beings* in the fields of Andalusia should spur the public authorities to redouble their vigilance" (emphasis supplied).[93] The Catholic Church also, a deeply conservative force in Spain and still regarded as tainted by its close alliance with the Franco regime, employed a human-rights discourse in a much-noted pastoral letter from the Archbishop of Madrid, which urged the government to legalize the status of all *sin pape-les,* irrespective of their ethnic, cultural, or religious origins.[94]

The shift to a human rights discourse, while functionally adequate to the nationality-blind ordeal of the *sin papeles,* is also convenient because it provides a remedy for the most blatant omission in the "historical and cultural links" construct: Moroccans, with some 200,000 legal residents alone, by far the biggest immigrant group in Spain today. Morocco, as Spain's last colony and homeland of *los moros* who had been expelled from Spain for their Muslim faith some four hundred years ago, had a claim no less than that of other Hispanic countries and Sephardic Jews to be included in the *comunidad hispánica* (see Peres, 1999:10–12). How-ever, the Moroccans' Islamic creed also stood in the way of Spain's Cath-olic national identity, which had been formed precisely in the struggle against the Arab invaders of the Iberian peninsula. Even today, Moroccan immigrants are disparagingly referred to as *los moros,* and they consistently rank lowest on the public sympathy scale. In contrast, Latin American immigrants, along with West Europeans, are consistently ranked as most favored immigrants in public opinion. A recent survey by CIS (Center for Sociological Investigations), which asked respondents to rank immigrants according to their national origins on a sympathy scale from 0 ("no sym-pathy") to 10 ("much sympathy"), found "North Africans" (including Moroccans) at the bottom (with a median of 5.9), but Latin Americans (along with West Europeans and EU citizens) at the top (with a median of 7.1).[95] The exclusion of Moroccans from Spain's ethnic preference regime obviously corresponds closely to the pulse of the public.

However, when asked whether immigration policies should be the same for all immigrants, or whether there should be differential treatment according to national origins, the overwhelming majority of respondents (86.7 percent) also argued in favor of "the same policies for everybody."[96] Accordingly, Spanish immigration policy has to operate within the con-text of a strong public preference for impartiality. Any deviation from this, even if it addresses parts of the *comunidad hispánica,* must now appear as "ethnic favoritism."

This trend is visible in a recent episode involving the regularization of illegal Ecuadorians. Being both Ibero-American and *sin papeles,* this group lies at the intersection of two competing discourses, one stressing par-ticular "historical and cultural links" and the other stressing universalistic human rights obligations and impartiality. Interestingly, on the Spanish side there has been a stress on universalism and impartiality, while only on the Ecuadorian side has there been a stress on particular links. The Ecuadorian episode was kicked off by the tragic death of twelve illegal Ecuadorian immigrant workers near Lorca in the southern agricultural province of Murcia, when their crammed old Fiat van crushed into a train in the early morning hours of January 3, 2001. Since the late 1990s, when Ecuador was hit by a severe economic crisis, Ecuadorians had become Spain's third-largest immigrant group (after Moroccans and Chinese), most of them entering as tourists and then overstaying. Already in 1995 the Spanish government had wisely pushed for a modification of the 1964 Dual Nationality Convention with Ecuador, whose Paragraph 8 (identical with Paragraph 7 of the Chilean and Peruvian conventions discussed above) had guaranteed Ecuadorians automatic access to work permits and equal social benefits. Finally signed on August 16, 2000, this modification forced all newly arriving Ecuadorians into illegal employment (because they were no longer exempted from the national-employment proviso), just like all the other *sin papeles*. And this is how their dismal situation came to be perceived on the Spanish side in the wake of the tragic accident: as epitomizing the dismal lot of all *sin papeles*. "First it was the Moroccans, and now it is the turn of the Ecuadorians," wrote Spain's major newspaper.[97]

The Ecuadorian tragedy happened just when the second *Ley Orgánica* of 2000, which included harsh new measures against illegal immigrants and their employers, was going into force. This coincidence inflamed an unprecedented public debate and social protest in favor of the rightless *sin papeles*. Because the accident had directed attention to the so-far relatively unnoticed Ecuadorians, 150,000 of whom were estimated to live illegally in Spain, and because the situation was especially tense in the province of Murcia, where most of these Ecuadorians lived and worked, the government sought to calm the situation by making the Ecuadorians a unique offer—they should first return to Ecuador, ask for a regular visa there, and then return to Spain with the promise of a legal employment contract, their travel costs carried by the government.[98] As a chorus of critics shouted, this was an absurd undertaking, incurring huge costs to the state, especially when an unexpected number of Ecuadorians (25,000) rushed to take advantage of it, and it was eventually aborted in favor of in situ regularization.

However, noteworthy is the immediate charge of "ethnic favoritism" brought against the government, and the latter's strenuous attempts to deflect this charge. When he announced this offer on January 12, 2001, just nine days after the Lorca tragedy, the state secretary for immigration, Fernández-Miranda, quickly added that the offer was not limited to Ecuadorians, mentioning explicitly that it was applicable to illegal immigrants from Colombia, Morocco, and Romania also. However, because the first logistic arrangements were made for Ecuadorians, there was an immediate outcry of ethnic favoritism among other immigrant organizations. A spokesman of the Association for Moroccan Immigrants in Spain (AITME) declared, on the very day of Miranda's announcement, that "all immigrants, independently of their country of origin, should have the same opportunities and should have access to everything in conditions of equality."[99] If "ethnic favoritism" at all, it was one of a peculiar sort, because the whole operation was from the start rejected by the Hispano-Ecuadorian association Ruminahui and other proimmigrant forces on the left, denouncing it as a "friendly expulsion" and "a trap."[100]

Although the paid repatriation offer was initially open to all,[101] the unexpected rush of Ecuadorians to accept it forced the government to retract, now calling this repatriation "an exceptional operation."[102] When, at the close of the Ecuadorian epic, this limitation was made official, Moroccan and Colombian immigrant associations denounced the advantages bestowed on Ecuadorians as "discrimination" against their respective compatriots, also blaming their home governments for not pressing the Spanish government hard enough to concede similar advantages to their conationals.[103]

Rather than constituting "ethnic favoritism" for (some) Latin Americans, the regularization of Ecuadorians is really an expression of muddling through on the part of the Spanish government, intervening where the noise is loudest and limiting the regularization to this particular group more for logistic and cost-related reasons than for "ethnic" ones.[104] This view is supported by the overarching posture of impartiality taken by the government. The attempt to appear impartial is especially visible in the equal geographic spread of Spain's recent bilateral migration treaties with countries of high emigration pressure. Their logic is to exchange privileged access to Spain's annual legal immigration quota against these countries' readmission of their illegal immigrants who are expelled by Spain. After first pursuing such an agreement with Ecuador, obviously incited by the epic of the Ecuadorian workers, the government quickly reached similar agreements with Morocco, Poland, and Colombia, a further round of expansion being envisioned with the Dominican Republic and Romania.

In this way, as the Spanish state secretary for immigration explained the logic of these treaties, "we will have covered practically 90 percent of the immigrant nationalities in Spain."[105] Already, the legal immigration quotas that had been first introduced in 1993 had served mainly to regularize Spain's sizeable illegal immigrant population (particularly Moroccans). The obvious purpose of the new migration treaties is to transform this ex post policy into an ex ante policy. This novel way of tying legal immigrant admissions to national-origin selection, which can be observed also in other Southern European countries such as Italy, is not in recognition of "historical and cultural links" but in the pragmatic interest of controlling immigration, especially the illegal kind, more effectively.

Portugal and the Lusophone Community

As Europe's first and last colonial power, ceding its African colonies only after a prolonged war and a domestic revolution in 1974, Portugal has been more closely and more enduringly associated with its colonial empire than any other European state. More than that, a half-millennial legacy of overseas exploration, colonial settlement, and emigration has become constitutive of Portuguese national identity—which may be a misnomer, because Portuguese self-descriptions have always lacked the requisite territorial fixity and boundedness. Regarding the lack of boundedness, the Portuguese were, in historian Charles Boxer's emphatic formulation, the ones who first "linked up, for better and for worse, the widely sundered branches of the great human family," making the latter aware "of its essential unity" (in Maxwell, 1995:8). Regarding the lack of territorial fixity, in one government official's view the Portuguese were "*um povo peregrino*" (a pilgrim people),[106] and thus defined by movement rather than sedentariness. As Trenz (1999:44) put it succinctly, "[n]ot the sovereignty over a demarcated territory but the 'sovereign importance of movement' constitute[s] the Portuguese community."[107]

Closely linked to the self-conception of moving is that of mixing. According to this, the colonizing Portuguese, instead of closing themselves off in disdain for nonwhite colonial natives, have readily intermixed with them, thus "never allow[ing] . . . the separation of men between masters and slaves" (Freyre, 1940:41) that had been the essence of colonialism elsewhere. Brazil's most famous anthropologist-cum-intellectual, Gilberto Freyre, celebrated the "world that the Portuguese created" (ibid.) as one of "racial intermixing," in which the Portuguese colonizers' "taste for the fleshly things of life" (Freyre, 1986:226), in combination with the inclusive thrust of missionary Catholicism, overcame the racial barriers that separated colonizers, natives, and imported slaves in the other European empires, except the Spanish.[108] Interestingly, Freyre refers the Portuguese colonizers' unique "miscibility" (ibid., p. 11) to Portugal's "indecisive position between Europe and Africa," in which centuries of Moorish occupation and contact with Africa had made for "Moorish or Negro blood running throughout a great light-skinned mulatto population" (p. 4).

In short, the Portuguese embraced racial mixing in the colonies because they were racially mixed already. Although this notion is more myth than reality,[109] Freyre correctly points to the peculiar flip side of Portuguese colonialism—Portugal's own peripheral position in Europe. As Sousa Santos (1994:58) put it, Portugal was a "colonizing and a colonized country at the same time," annexed by the Spanish monarchy between 1580 and 1640, thereafter a quasi-colony of Britain, and for a short moment in the early 1800s even ruled from Brazil, in a curious and unique inversion of center and periphery in colonial relations. Paraphrasing Bourdieu, Portugal belongs to the "dominated" fraction of the "dominant class" of European powers, which narrowed the gap between colonizers and colonized and may account for her "progressive" stance in North-South relations and on immigration issues in the European Union today.

The notion of a "Portuguese exception" (Ferro, 1997:138–142) in colonial relations was cultivated under the Salazar dictatorship, in order to justify its resistance to decolonization after World War II.[110] Curiously, a nondemocratic regime that was, like Franco's in Spain, equidistant from "the excesses of liberalism and socialism"[111] also became the torchbearer of "racial equality" and "multiracialism" long before such vocabulary became standard in the liberal democracies of the West. As Salazar's Foreign Minister put it in 1967 (against the backdrop of anti-Portuguese guerrilla operations raging in the African colonies), "[b]efore all others we alone have brought to Africa the idea of the rights of man and of racial equality. We are the only ones to have practiced 'multiracialism,' the perfect expression of the brotherhood of peoples" (Ferro, 1997:138). Already before World War II, Salazar's propaganda machine was aware of Gilberto Freyre's eulogy of "luso-brasilianism," and in 1951 Freyre was officially invited to visit Portugal and the African colonies in order to expand this notion beyond Brazil (Leonard, 1997).

The result was "luso-tropicalism." It had in fact been expounded *avant la lettre* in Freyre's earlier work *O Mundo que o Português Criou*

[The World the Portuguese Created] (1940). Already here the Brazilian anthropologist attested that Portuguese colonization—not only in America, but in Africa and Asia as well—had led to a "unity of sentiment and culture" (Freyre, 1940:30), based on the uniquely Portuguese penchant for "racial intermixing" and "hybridization" (p. 52). In strikingly contemporary language, *O Mundo* depicts all Lusos, colonizers and colonized, as "transnational individuals" eager to move back and forth within the European and non-European parts of their *"patria maior"* [greater fatherland] (p. 54). Interestingly, on the part of the Portuguese the price for this is seen as "los[ing] themselves in foreign races and cultures"— that is, ethnic self-abdication (pp. 180–181).[112] Conversely (and here the political potential of this Franz Boas–style attack[113] on the "ideal of racial purity" was shining through), this "splendid adventure of dissolution" (p. 181) could be turned into a defense of Portuguese "anthropocentric imperialism" as being different in kind from the "ethnocentric" imperialisms of the other European powers, Japan, and North America (p. 189).

After World War II, when of all European powers only Portugal resisted the United Nations doctrine of colonial self-determination, thus creating the need to stress Portuguese exceptionalism, Freyre's "lusotropicalism" was readily embraced. Old and new colonial ideologies still uneasily coexist in Marcelo Caetano's pamphlet "Colonizing Traditions, Principles and Methods of the Portuguese" (1951). Reflecting the very different African experience, it draws an un-Freyrian distinction between "civilized" and "uncivilized people," yet it insists that "no colour bar" had ever existed in Portugal's colonies and that "even if the natives are at the most backward stages of civilization, they are thought of as men" (ibid., pp. 43–44). Admittedly, this was the standard line of all European colonialisms, and a French or British colonist would not have put it differently at the time.[114] Only when the United Nations (UN) critique of racism and colonialism shifted to high gear in the 1950s, and Portugal became increasingly isolated in its opposition to decolonization,[115] was there a more urgent need to stress Portuguese exceptionalism. Antonio de Andrade's *Many Races—One Nation* (1961) epitomizes the ensuing return to Freyre's theme. This pamphlet, a propaganda tract like Caetano's, claims that "racial non-discrimination" has always been the "cornerstone" of Portugal's overseas policy, starting with the solicitation of interracial marriage in early sixteenth-century India (p. 6): "[T]his brotherly attitude to natives of distant lands, even to savages, is not found in the colonizing methods of other civilizing nations, apart from certain periods of Spanish history" (p. 7). And, in a rather wishful view of why Portugal had relabeled its colonies "overseas provinces" in 1951, this was "to remove any suggestion of superiority toward the peoples whom we have assembled under one flag" (p. 24).

While the notion of a Portuguese exception has been qualified, if not debunked, by many students of colonial history and comparative race relations (see, for example, Boxer, 1963; Degler, 1971; Bender, 1978; most recently Marx, 1998), it still has come to inform public and elite perceptions in Portugal. Bender (1978:3) even argues that "for the over-whelming majority of the Portuguese people prior to the military coup of April 1974, lusotropicalism truly represented Portuguese politics, practices and goals" and that "[i]t is doubtful whether any other ideology has been more widely and fervently believed by the Portuguese or has generated as much written attention within Portugal." Its most prevalent expression today is the "myth of the gentle customs" (*mito de los brandos costumes*), the "firm conviction that (the Portuguese) are neither xeno-phobic nor racist; indeed that they cannot be."[116] Note that the term "myth" already indicates a certain distancing from the imagery of "gentle customs." However, whenever reality does not correspond to it, this "myth" provides a source of evaluating and critiquing a reality found wanting. When, in early 1993, the Portuguese ambassador in Brazil dis-paraged as "mulattos" and "vagabonds" a group of Brazilians who had been denied entry at Lisbon's Portela airport, an editorial in Portugal's most widely read newspaper retorted: "[T]he world which has been cre-ated by the Portuguese is a world of racial mixture . . . There is only one diplomat in the whole world who cannot be allowed to offend mulattos: the Portuguese diplomat."[117]

Since the late Portuguese empire had fashioned itself as a French-style unitary state with one nationality status for those who were Portuguese by origin and colonial natives alike,[118] one might expect nationality law to be the privileged site to express the existence of a state-transcending Lusophone community. However, this is not the case. Instead, the post-colonial development of nationality law has occurred under the divergent or even opposite imperatives of, first, containing immigration, especially from the former colonies, and, second, retaining links with Portugal's huge emigrant diaspora abroad. The Decolonization Statute (*Decreto-lei* no. 308-A/75) of June 24, 1975 (abrogated in 1988), foresaw the loss of Portuguese nationality for the vast majority of colonial natives. Portugal's most eminent nationality lawyer interprets this as a preventive measure against "a flood of migration to Portugal" (Moura Ramos, 2001:217). Only colonials of Portuguese descent and colonial natives residing in Portugal for five years preceding 1975 retained their Portuguese nationality. Interestingly, the descent-criterion extended into the third generation— Portugal had its grandparental "patrials" *à l'anglaise,* but they never sparked any debate. Article 5 of the 1975 statute allows the discretionary concession of Portuguese citizenship to "special cases" such as colonial functionaries or ex-combatants in the Portuguese army, but it enumerates (and thus limits) these exceptions in a very precise way. Of all colonial natives, only those born in the old State of India could keep their Portuguese nationality as of right, if they asked for it. One might argue that this entailed an indirect discrimination against Africans in the colonies, whose only chance to retain Portuguese citizenship was its discretionary concession according to Article 5. However, the privileging of Indians paid tribute to their precarious status of commercially successful "middlemen minorities" in the African colonies (especially Mozambique), who were subject to discrimination and exclusion by the ethnic citizenship laws in the new African states. Overall, the 1975 decolonization statute amounted to a rather brusque cutting of ties with Portugal's former colonies, in marked contrast to the more generous *reconnaissance* procedure provided by postcolonial France.[119]

The Nationality Law of 1981 even goes one step further in the severance of colonial ties, through removing the unconditional *jus soli* provision that had helped to integrate colonies and mother country under the 1959 Nationality Law. Now the attribution of Portuguese citizenship to the children born in Portugal to noncitizens was made contingent upon a (vicarious) declaration of will and a six-year minimum residence of one parent. According to one author, this change also was "due à la peur d'assister a un exode des natifs des anciennes colonies portugaises" (Jalles, 1985:179). Indeed, the foreign population had increased between 1960 and 1981 by a staggering 313 percent, from 29,579 to 122,195 (Moura Ramos, 2001:218). The stressing of *volonté* and prolonged residence in the attribution of citizenship were deemed more adequate to the new reality of immigration than the random attribution of citizenship through unconditional *jus soli*. Incidentally, Europe's other country with an unconditional *jus soli* tradition, Britain, moved toward a similar (and similarly justified) restriction of *jus soli* in the very same year.

However, the main purpose of the 1981 Nationality Act was not so much to respond to a new immigration reality—although the numbers were up, immigration was hardly a concern at the time. Instead, the main thrust of the new law was to strengthen the ties with Portugal's emigrants abroad. According to the Interior Minister's presentation of the bill, "territorial" principles of citizenship attribution were to be replaced by "blood-based" principles, because this was more "in accordance with a new world of emigration, where the personal element is more important than the territorial one. In reality, we are more a people than a territory."[120] In the 1960s the number of Portuguese emigrants had more than doubled, from an already high annual average of 33,000 in the 1950s (with Brazil as main destination) to an annual average of almost 80.000 (now predominantly to France).[121] Between the outbreak of the colonial wars in Africa in 1961 and the fall of the dictatorship in 1974, 1.3 million Portuguese emigrated (many of them illegal because of exit restrictions), which is over 10 percent of the total population.[122] The *emigrante* came to take the place that had previously been reserved to the *navegador* and *colonizador* in public imagination; the new democratic regime promptly dedicated the tenth of July, the traditional national holiday, to the Portuguese "diaspora."[123] Furthermore, Article 14 of the new constitution of 1976 stipulated that "Portuguese citizens temporarily or habitually resident abroad shall enjoy the protection of the State in the exercise of their right."[124] To fulfill this mandate, a plethora of new state agencies and programs were created to assist the Portuguese abroad as well as to facilitate their integration after returning. Even the political representation of the Portuguese abroad was ensured, by means of two extra-territorial parliamentary districts: one for the Portuguese in Europe, the other for those outside Europe. No European state went as far as Portugal in supporting and binding itself to its emigrants, but there is also no European state one-third of whose population lives outside its borders.[125]

The 1981 Nationality Act inscribed this turn toward emigrant protection into Portuguese nationality law. According to the 1959 law, a Portuguese naturalizing elsewhere automatically lost his or her Portuguese nationality. In the interest of protecting the Portuguese abroad, the new law introduced the toleration of dual nationality.[126] However, the most striking aspect of the new law is to be found in its section on naturalization (Article 6.2), which exempts certain Portuguese-origin people from a new six-year residence requirement and knowledge of Portuguese language. The privileged categories mentioned are ex-holders of Portuguese nationality, the descendants of Portuguese, the members of "Portuguese ancestry communities," and foreigners who have rendered "relevant services" to the Portuguese state.[127] An observer likened this provision to "a veritable Law of Return" similar to the one in Israel (Poinard, 1988:198). It indeed amounted to an open-ended entry ticket for anyone in the world who could claim, however remotely, Portuguese ancestry. However, its polemical (because discriminatory) potential was greatly diminished by including ex-holders of Portuguese nationality as well. This was a belated redemption for the colonial natives who had been abruptly deprived of their Portuguese nationality in 1975.[128]

Within the ambit of nationality law, the first explicit preferences for citizens of Portuguese-speaking countries appeared only in the 1994 reform of the 1981 Nationality Act. Against the backdrop of increasing numbers of illegal immigrants in Portugal,[129] the single purpose of this reform was restrictionist—that is, to make it more difficult for immigrants to acquire Portuguese nationality. Accordingly, both the parental legal residence requirement for *jus soli* citizenship and the residence requirement for naturalizing were increased from six to ten years. Exempted from this restriction were the citizens of Portuguese-speaking countries (the former African colonies plus Brazil), for whom the old six-year rule remained in place.

In contrast to Spain, where a dual-nationality regime has been the main legal expression of the Hispanic community, the Portuguese solution for its Lusophone community has been bilateral treaties that guarantee an equality of rights to "privileged foreigners" on the basis of reciprocity. This is sanctioned by Article 15.3 of the 1976 Constitution: "Citizens of Portuguese-speaking countries may, by international convention and under the condition of reciprocity, be granted rights not otherwise conferred on foreigners, except membership in the organs of supreme or regional authority, service in the armed forces, and a diplomatic career." In contrast to Spain, the boundaries of the state-transcending "historical community" (Moura Ramos, 1990–93:583) are more precisely demarcated, in terms of Portuguese being the official state language, the latter standing for "a common stock of concepts and a shared past" (ibid., p. 584). However, the members of this community are still accorded sharply differential treatment, depending on their state of origin and the corresponding treaty provisions.

Here one must distinguish between the treaty with Brazil, whose uniquely strong provisions go well beyond the usual ambit of interstate relations, and the "second-generation" treaties with the Portuguese-speaking states of Africa, which are more modest in scope and barely lift Lusophone Africans above the status of ordinary foreigners.[130] This difference is already visible in their respective preambles. The 1971 Convention on the Equality of Rights and Duties between Brazilians and Portuguese invokes the "historical, moral, cultural, linguistic and ethnic values" that unite both peoples into a "Luso-Brazilian community" that is further cemented by a "brotherly and indestructible friendship."[131] By contrast, the 1979 General Cooperation Treaty between Portugal and Angola, until 1975 Portugal's largest and most important African colony, does not invoke a similar panethnic community; it only wishes to consolidate the "friendship and solidarity" between both peoples, while respecting each other's "national sovereignty" and "territorial integrity."[132] This cautious wording, which in the similar 1975 Cooperation Treaty with Mozambique is spiked with a "militant" commitment to "the struggle against colonialism and imperialism,"[133] pays tribute to sovereignty concerns on the African side; however, on the Portuguese side it is surely indicative of a lesser sense of "community" with their former African colonies.

To the (limited) degree that different justifications for the privileged treatment of Brazilians and Lusophone Africans have emerged, the former are clearly more perceived as culturally and ethnically close, while the latter tend to be addressed within a more typically postcolonial discourse of historical "responsibilities." "Our love of Brazil is immense," said President Mario Soares with respect to emergent tensions between Portugal's Lusophone and European orientations, "for us, Brazil is something different."[134] A rhetoric of "brother countries," "united by the most sacred bonds in eternal alliance," has accompanied the Luso-Brazilian relationship since the 1825 Treaty of Rio, in which Portugal acknowledged Brazil's independence.[135] Epitomized by the popular notion of *Brasileiro*, the Portuguese who returns rich and successful from his sojourn overseas (see Brettell, 1993:58), Brazil has been the mythical land of plenty, attracting millions of Portuguese emigrants over the centuries (some 250,000 as late as in the revolutionary period 1974–75). More than this, the former colony, vastly bigger and more resourceful than the mother country, has eclipsed the latter in economic, political, and cultural standing at least since the early 1800s, starting with the brief moment in which the Portuguese empire was ruled from Rio de Janeiro (1807–22). At the same time, although during most of the nineteenth and twentieth centuries there have been more non-Portuguese than Portuguese immigrants in Brazil,[136] this has still remained a country entirely shaped by Portuguese language and culture, now even supplying Portugal with the icons and products of Lusophone popular culture, such as pop music and television shows. Finally, if one compares the massive presence of 1.2 million Portuguese in Brazil to the rather smallish (but proportionally significant) contingent of 20,000 Brazilian immigrants in Portugal,[137] one realizes the import of the reciprocity formula that frames the privileged regime for Luso-foreigners in general, but only in the Brazilian case makes the Portuguese side profit more from it than the other side.

The 1971 Luso-Brazilian treaty effectively assimilates the status of Brazilian residents in Portugal to that of Portuguese nationals (and vice versa). A Brazilian observer even argued that the treaty buried the "classic concept of nationality as a necessary condition for citizenship," because now "an individual [could] possess the rights of citizenship in the other [country]" without changing his or her nationality (Resek, 1978:5). As Article 1 of the treaty declares, "Portuguese in Brazil and Brazilians in Portugal will enjoy equality of rights and duties with the respective nationals." It distinguishes itself from even the stronger of the "cooperation" treaties with the African PALOP states in covering, next to civil and social rights,[138] political rights also—including the national franchise and the right to become a member of parliament, secretary of state, prefect, or judge (Resek, 1978:8).[139] In this respect, the Luso-Brazilian treaty provides even more rights than the European Community treaty, whose "citizens" enjoy some political rights at the local level only and certainly cannot become high civil servants or judges in other member states.[140] In addition, Brazilians in Portugal and Portuguese in Brazil cannot be deported or expelled, unless their state of origin asks for this. Finally, the respective nonnationals are entitled to ID cards identical to those of nationals.

However, there is one condition for enjoying equal rights that is presupposed, and thus not provided, by the Luso-Brazilian (or any other Lusophone "cooperation") treaty: permanent residence. This folds the "privileged foreigners" back to the general immigration regime, which—in contrast to the Spanish regime until 2000—has mostly been ethnically neutral, providing at best some indirect privileges.[141] However, a separate agreement with Brazil on the suppression of visas, dating back to 1960 and reaffirmed in 1996, concedes free entry for (tourism or work-related) stays up to six months,[142] then leaving the case to the (usually generous) discretion of the authorities. Demonstrating the special position of Brazil within the Lusophone community, Portugal insisted on retaining this uniquely generous visa regime even after joining the Schengen convention, whereas she did not oppose the inclusion of Lusophone Africa on the "blacklist" of states whose citizens require a visa even for short stays or transits. The price for this is a special clause in the 1992 Schengen Convention that obliges Portugal to readmit Brazilians found without visas in other convention states after the three-month period for stays without visa allowed at the European level.

The special position of Brazilians within the Lusophone community is further enhanced by their social profile in Portugal. Much like the sizeable contingent of other Europeans in Portugal,[143] Brazilians are peculiarly invisible immigrants, because of their geographic dispersal and elevated socioeconomic status and skill levels, which exceed those of the average Portuguese (see Baganha, Marques, and Fonseca, 2000:66). A 1995 survey measuring the "feelings" of Portuguese toward selected "social groups" revealed "Brazilians" on top of the sympathy scale, even ahead of "other Europeans."[144] The nonperception of Brazilians as "immigrants" is evident in an episode in the early 1990s that involved the large number of Brazilian dentists practicing in Portugal. According to the 1971 Luso-Brazilian treaty, academic and professional titles of one country are automatically recognized in the other, and no special work permit is required for Brazilian professionals to practice in Portugal (and vice versa). This led to a conflict with the Portuguese dentists' association, which had kept the number of domestic graduates artificially low over the years. It lobbied the Portuguese government to deny professional licenses to the growing number of Brazilians who rushed in to fill the void. Interestingly, in the ensuing confrontation, which on the Brazilian side involved the government itself and a high-level parliamentary delegation to Portugal, neither the Portuguese government nor any political party sided with the Portuguese dentists. Moreover, a media analysis showed the complete absence of the notion of "immigrants" to denote the Brazilian dentists in Portugal—instead, they were variously referred to as "Brazilian citizens," "Brazilian professionals in Portugal," "Brazilian residents," "Brazilian colleagues," or simply "professionals from our brother country" (Trenz, 1999:89).

Brazilians were first associated with the exigencies of immigration control in 1993, when eight Brazilians were denied entry at Lisbon airport, apparently despite possessing orderly travel documents and sufficient cash reserves.[145] By that time, Portugal had become the main European point of entry for Brazilian prostitutes and transvestites, and, as intimated in the epithets "vagabond" and "mulatto"[146] that the Portuguese ambassador in Brazil threw at the denied entrants, the latter were—justified or not—

suspected of being so. This episode, which became publicly known only through the Brazilian media and a threat of the Brazilian government to retaliate against the Portuguese community in Brazil, happened just when the Portuguese government was about to pass two new immigration acts in early 1993: one that opened the doors for EU citizens and a second that closed the doors for the "extracommunitarian" rest, including Brazilians.[147]

Accordingly, this was the moment in which Portugal's Lusophone and European vocations finally collided. Among the many critical responses in the Portuguese print media one can distinguish three motifs that have shaped the Portuguese attitude toward the Lusophone community more generally: first, the imperative of nondiscrimination, which in Portuguese self-perception stems from her legacy of "racial mixture" that prohibits the usage of "mulatto" in a pejorative sense;[148] second, Portugal's emigration legacy, in which "Brazil has always been a country of shelter and asylum for the Portuguese" and therefore now was owed reciprocal favors.[149] But perhaps the dominant and most striking motif is Brazil as an object of allegiance and identification, held against a Europe downgraded to external imposition and matter of interest only. "Europe is an accumulation of very important interests . . . The great solidarities, on the other hand, are elsewhere," wrote *O Independente*.[150] In a similar vein, another weekly opined that "the European Union may finish, but our bonds to Brazil are eternal."[151]

Indeed, not unlike Britain's qualms over cutting her ties with the Old Commonwealth in the early 1970s, Europeanization is perceived in Portugal today as in direct conflict with her traditional Lusophone orientation.[152] However, in contrast to Britain, this Lusophone orientation includes not only Portugal's equivalent to the British Old Commonwealth—Brazil—but her former African colonies as well. This is a striking reversal, because the "African orientation" had once been associated with colonialism and the old authoritarian regime and had fallen in disrepute because of this association after 1974. By contrast, already before 1974 the "European option" had been a "symbol of democracy and freedom" and was enthusiastically embraced by the post-1974 democratic regime (see Barreto, 1994). Interestingly, the only exceptions to this were the Marxist left, centered on the PCP (Portuguese Communist Party), which preached "anti-imperialist" North-South solidarity and remained cool to the "capitalist" European Community; and the moderate right,[153] centered on the Christian Democratic Party (CDS), an initially pro-European party that turned pro-Luso (and especially pro-African) in the late 1970s

and has since served as reservoir for the smallish conservative and nationalist currents in Portuguese society (Trenz, 1999:57).

In the wake of Schengen, which was widely perceived as the final act in
Portugal's turn from the "open seas" to Europe, the long-repressed identification with the former colonies went mainstream and became a cross-
party consensus (see Marques et al., 1999). Euroenthusiast Mario Soares
(PS) did much to steer his Socialist Party into this direction: "Portugal
should not forget that its space is not simply European but transcontinental:
the language of Camoes is spoken on all the continents constituting a
very strong tie in the *community of affection and of language* which we
form together with Brazil, with the African Lusophone community and
with all the other communities that speak Portuguese in the world"
(emphasis supplied).[154]

This inclusive sense of the Lusophone community, along with the
cross-party consensus to protect it from the onslaught of Europeanized
immigration control, is strikingly visible in the 1992 parliamentary debate
on the Schengen Convention and its prospective impact on Portugal. Its
minutes read like a cross-party contest for being the most committed
Lusophone.[155] As compensation for a tight forthcoming immigration law
that would largely close Portugal for "extracommunitarians," the Minister of the Interior, Dias Loureiro (Social-Democratic Party, PSD),
announced on this occasion an "extraordinary regularization of illegal
immigrants." Strikingly, it would be "principally [for illegal immigrants]
from Lusophone countries." The minister gave three reasons for this preference. Interestingly, the first-mentioned reason is the better assimilation
of Lusophones—"their knowledge of the national language would facilitate their insertion in Portuguese society."[156] Second, and more in line
with the general tenor of this debate, the privileging of Lusos was "indis-
putable proof of the solidarity of our national community with this enormous group of citizens, the majority of which are linked to us through
indelible ties of history and civilization."[157] Finally, as always closely connected to the communitarian justification of Lusophone privileges, the
minister raised a reciprocity concern: as "the children of men and women
who once had to leave their native land in search of a more dignified life,"
the Portuguese were now obliged to welcome "those immigrants who
choose Portugal as their country of refuge."[158]

Indeed, two regularization campaigns in 1992–93 and 1996 treated
illegal immigrants from Portuguese-speaking countries preferentially, and
to date this stands as the main expression of a Lusophone preference in

Portugal's immigration policies. The first regularization law of October 12, 1992 (*Decreto-lei* no. 212/92) states in its preamble that a "special treatment for citizens of Portuguese-speaking countries [is advised] for historical reasons and fundamental principles."[159] According to this law, Lusophones who had entered Portugal before June 1, 1986, were dispensed from the requirement to be employed or possess sufficient economic means. The second regularization law of May 24, 1996 (*Lei* no. 16/96), went even farther. According to its Article 1.1, "the present law establishes a process of extraordinary regularization for citizens of Portuguese-speaking countries"; only the second paragraph introduced the possibility to regularize "non-communitarian foreigners" also.[160] Although the exemption from the employment and economic-means requirement for Lusophones having entered before June 1, 1986, remained the same, there are in addition more generous conditions for more recent Lusophone entrants; Lusophones had to reside in Portugal only since December 31, 1995, whereas non-Lusophones had to be in Portugal six months longer in order to qualify for legalization. Finally, Article 17 limits the all-important government "support measures," by means of which information is spread to potential candidates of legalization, to Lusophone migrant associations. No wonder that under these uneven conditions the great majority of regularized immigrants were from Portuguese-speaking countries: 86.1 percent of a total of 39,000 in 1992–93, and 73.3 percent of a total of 35,100 in 1996 (Malheiros, 1998:175).[161]

Interestingly, both regularization laws were passed without dissent, the last under a Socialist Party government that had done much to fuel Portugal's Lusophone and pro-African drive since taking office in 1995 (and remaining there until 2002). Only the extreme left centered on SOS Racismo denounced the national-origin discrimination inherent in the 1996 regularization law as "institutional racism." As its leader José Falcão complained bitterly, "[c]learly, a small organisation like SOS would never break the national consensus, just for a few hundred blacks, Asians, or Romanian gypsies" (Falcão, 1997:425). In fact, SOS Racismo did not limit its protest to oral pronunciations but filed a constitutional complaint (see Dupraz and Vieira, 1999:45). In its view, the unilateral preference for Lusophones was not sanctioned by Article 15.3 of the Constitution, which makes such preferences contingent upon reciprocity; accordingly, the 1996 law violated Article 13.2 of the Constitution, which outlaws not only negative but also positive discrimination on the basis of sex, race, national origins, and other ascriptive markers. However, the court refused to consider the complaint, arguing that Article 7.4 of the Constitution obliges Portugal to "maintain privileged bonds of friendship and co-operation with Lusophone countries."

What brought about the 1990s cross-party consensus for privileging Lusophone immigrants, particularly from the African PALOP states? At the moral level, it was redemption for having repressed and ignored the colonial past after the revolution and decolonization in 1974–75. Moreover, in the two decades following this radical juncture, the number of postcolonial immigrants from Africa sharply increased, most of them living in precarious legal and socioeconomic conditions. For instance, 70 percent of the estimated 70,000 illegal immigrants residing in Portugal in the early 1990s were from PALOP states (Rocha-Trindade and Oliveira, 1999:286). While many of them were filling important jobs in Portugal's booming construction and public works sectors, they were increasingly pushed to the margins by tightened citizenship and immigration laws in the early 1980s and 1990s, respectively. There was an obvious case for displaying postcolonial "responsibility" toward PALOP immigrants (Dupraz and Vieira, 1999:43).

Second, demographic factors mattered. The 1990s consensus was also enabled by the fact that the large majority of Portugal's immigrant population (not considering Europeans) is of Lusophone origin. This trend even increased between 1986 and 1996 (see Machado, 1997). In 1986, only two of the five most numerous immigrant groups were Lusophone; by contrast, four were Lusophone in 1996. In the same period, the Brazilian share of Latin American immigrants increased from 60 percent to 78 percent. Furthermore, 95 percent of African immigrants in 1996 were from PALOP states. Striking is the near-complete absence of Moroccan and other North African immigrants, who are among the most populous immigrant groups in Spain and Italy. At the same time, the large contingent of PALOP immigrants (74,000 out of 178,000 legal immigrants in 1998)[162] still makes Portugal the country with the highest proportion of African immigrants in Europe. Whereas other Southern European countries are characterized by the high diversity of their immigrant populations, Portugal stands out through the relative homogeneity of her immigrants, most being from Lusophone countries (94,000 out of 129,600 non-EU immigrants in 1998).[163] This helps explain the low degree of conflict surrounding "Third-World" immigration in Portugal: most of her immigrants are already immersed beforehand in Portuguese language and culture (see Corkill and Eaton, 1998). Conversely, in the face of a predominantly Lusophone illegal immigrant population, there are no clear-cut, organizable losers to put pressure on the Lusophone preference policies.

Finally, external developments helped forge the 1990s consensus for privileging Lusophone immigrants: the creation, at the initiative of Brazil, of the Community of Portuguese-Speaking Countries (CPLP) in 1996, followed by the introduction of a "Lusophone citizenship" by Cape Verde in 1997. To be sure, the CPLP is mostly "cultural affirmation" of the 200 million people in the world who speak Portuguese (Brigagão, 1996:13),[164] and its seven African, European, and American member states are divided among various regional alliances (such as the European Union or Mercosur). However, one of the CPLP's declared goals is still "to facilitate the circulation of member state citizens within the space of CPLP."[165] To this was added, one year later, the "Lusophone citizenship" construct of Cape Verde, which (among other things) grants visa exemptions, a facilitated access to Cape Verdean citizenship, and the active and passive local franchise to CPLP citizens residing in Cape Verde.[166] The concept was quickly promulgated not just by the Portuguese High Commissioner for Immigration and Ethnic Minorities but the Prime Minister himself (Leitão, 1998:41).

In light of these external developments, it is not far-fetched to speak of an increasing "double allegiance" of Portuguese authorities between the EU and the Lusophone community (Marques et al., 1999:3). Interestingly, whenever the compatibility between both commitments is ceremonially invoked, the Lusophone orientation is one of "identity," whereas the European is one of "interest" only. Comparing the CPLP and the EU, Manuela Aguiar, a prominent member of parliament representing the (non-European) Portuguese abroad, finds that the EU is entirely a "political" creation and thus could not survive without the states organizing it, whereas the CPLP is carried by a prepolitical "Lusophone community" that could also live on otherwise (Aguiar, 1998:99). Striking a similar chord of a merely political Europe against an ethnocultural Lusophone community, one Portuguese observer (Pires, 1997) argues that the Lusophone citizenship, in contrast to the European one, is a "prelegal" and "prepolitical," "natural citizenship," containing "an element of the concept of people (*povo*)—the language" (p. 37), and he consequently refers to the CPLP as a "linguistic nation" (*nação lingüística*) (p. 47). This is not just an "isolated stance" of intellectuals but "echoes a very influential position in all four major political parties—ranging from the right to the left," writes a group of Portuguese sociologists (Marques et al., 1999:5).

However, to the degree that Portugal cannot indefinitely shield herself from the increasing diversification of contemporary immigration flows, particularly the irregular ones, the Lusophone preference will be difficult to maintain. Indeed, Portugal's immigration law of January 10, 2001 (*Decreto-lei* no. 4/2001), which created a new type of temporary work permit for illegal immigrants with a formal employment offer (the so-called "authorization of permanence"),[167] took shape in the context of an increasing number of illegal immigrant workers from Eastern Europe, such as Ukraine and Romania.[168] Tellingly, in the parliamentary debate surrounding the law, which launched Portugal's third large-scale regularization since 1992, there was almost no reference to Lusophone preferences.[169] Instead, the bill was presented by the Interior Minister as a general measure to combat "slave labor"; and in his countercharge that the bill would enshrine just that, a Communist deputy characterized the underlying issue as one of "the fundamental rights of all human beings, independently of their race, color, nationality, or ethnic origin."[170]

Discussion

The rejection of Algerian immigrants in France and the embrace of Brazilian immigrants in Portugal mark the extreme ends in European states' handling of postcolonial immigration. I tried to capture this divergence with the distinction between "northwestern" and "southwestern" postcolonial constellations, the ethnic impulse being mostly negative in the first and positive in the second. As I would like to argue in the following, there is an affinity between these responses and different approaches to colonialism, particularly a penchant for racial mixing in the southwestern constellation, and its rejection in the northwestern constellation.

This raises the question of whether our four cases can be meaningfully grouped in this way. Is it not more reasonable to say that there are as many postcolonial constellations as there are decolonizing states; moreover, that there is internal variation depending on which particular part of empire is being devolved, and at what particular time? Furthermore, the joint grouping of Britain and France under a "northwestern" constellation runs counter to a widespread tendency to take them as cases apart. For instance, in the comparative colonialism literature the classic distinction is between Britain's "indirect rule" and France's policy of "assimila-tion" (see, for example, Emerson, 1968:4). A similar contrast between Britain and France can be found in the literature on citizenship and immigration, according to which both are paragons of opposite "multi-cultural" and "assimilationist" approaches to immigrant integration (see, for example, Favell, 1998).

Let me begin to render plausible my suggested classification by juxta-posing the English and Spanish colonialisms as "sharply antithetical," as Samuel Finer (1997:1375) put it. In interesting ways, these two arche-types of European colonialism have been re-evaluated over time. Until it abruptly ended in the 1820s, the extracting and conquering Spanish colo-nialism in the Americas,[171] killing off or indenturing the indigenous popu-lations, was perceived as a negative model of what an empire should not be, an "inflexible, illiberal and ultimately corrupting tyranny" (Pagden, 1995:116), put on a par by Montesquieu with the despised empire of the Turks. By contrast, Montesquieu celebrated the English settlement colo-nies, which were "mixing their labour with the soil" (in John Locke's words) and self-governing, as shifting the European colonial project from medieval "conquest" to modern "commerce" (ibid., 68). For contempo-raneous observers this transition from conquest to commerce reached a new level in British India, where no notable settlement occurred at all and, instead of being killed off, the natives were engaged as "willing, if lowly paid" laborers and even participated in what later came to be called "indirect" colonial rule (ibid., 8). Indeed, the second European empires built from the early nineteenth century on in Asia and Africa largely avoided the carnage that had marred the conquest and settlement of the Americas: "India and Africa today are, very largely, populated by Indians and Africans, whereas in America the autochthonous people . . . are a largely disenfranchised minority . . . in a predominantly Creole commu-nity" (ibid.).[172] If contemporary Spain and Portugal can look at their long-lost empires in Latin America in terms of panethnic communities, this is also because most indigenous structures were destroyed there and they are facing societies lastingly remade in their image.

However, the negative evaluation of a "conquering" Spain as against a positively valued "commercial" Britain, which had been the dominant view since Montesquieu, becomes reversed once the "strikingly different" (Finer, 1997:1380) race relations in both empires move into the picture. Once the indigenous population in the heart of "New Spain" (encom-passing what is now Mexico and Central America) had shrunk from 30 million to just 3 million, there was a need to preserve them, for the sake of labor and reproduction. Because only one-third of Spanish emigrants were female, and "not colour-conscious like the English," a "huge miscegenation took place," officially encouraged as early as 1503 (ibid., p. 1381). This was accompanied by the evangelization of the Catholic Church, on whose behalf the Spanish colonizing effort was officially taking place. The Spanish, during the domestic *reconquista* that had preceded their American conquests, had certainly advocated *limpieza de sangre* (purity of blood), but it was directed only against heretic Jews and Moors, and was compatible with including Christianized people of other races (see Hoetink, 1967:5). By contrast, no comparable intermarriage or evangelization took place in the British colonization of North America. As Anthony Pagden (1995:36) put it, the Calvinist settlers "had little interest in converting Native Americans": "The Puritan 'Cities on the Hill' were to be their cities. They were to contain no aliens" (p.37).

Beginning with Tannenbaum (1946), and peaking with Hartz (1964), U.S. students of comparative race relations contrasted the more inclusive and benign race relations of Latin America with the exclusionist and segregationist United States, focusing on the differential legacies of black slavery in both societies. For Tannenbaum (1946:97–98), the Spanish and Portuguese legal traditions, which were continued in the New World, had always invested a nonracially defined slave with "a juridicial and a moral personality" and prevented him or her from being considered "a mere chattel." In combination with the missionary Catholic Church, which had condemned the slave trade as early as 1462, "the social milieu in the Spanish and Portuguese colonies made easy room for the Negroes passing from slavery to freedom" (ibid., 88–89).[173] The crypto-Marxist account of Hartz (1964) adds to these historical legacies of law and church the different "ideologies" of the respective "fragments" transported into (and subsequently frozen in) the Americas, hierarchical "feudalism" in the Iberian cases, "bourgeois" egalitarianism in the English case, the former ironically entailing more benign and inclusive race relations than the latter. Entirely uninfluenced by Hartz, the same theme is invoked by the ideologically inconspicuous Michael Mann (1999:27): "Since the imperial authorities (of Spain or Portugal) were not committed to rule 'by the people', they were less likely to develop theories emphasizing the racial (or other) commonality of all settlers."

In these (half-mythical, half-explanatory)[174] accounts of comparative colonialism and race relations the British and Spanish are clearly set as cases apart. What about our other two cases? The Portuguese case is easily accommodated—this is Spanish "racial cosmopolitanism" writ large, because untainted by the brutish conquest.[175] By contrast, the French case is more difficult to classify. For Hartz, France was part of the "feudal" fragment, as it, much like Spain, sought to "[project] into the New World [an] authoritarian society at the zenith of its power" (McRae, 1964:221). In fact, confirming the Hartzian race implications of the feudal fragment, Anthony Pagden (1995:150)—no myth maker but a myth scrutinizer—attests that "[o]f all the European powers only the French had attempted to replicate their society in America with a mixed population," epitomized by Colbert's plan of a miscegenated-cum-Frenchified society in Canada. Although that may have been true for *ancien régime* France, the different logic of the (potentially) racially exclusive "bourgeois" fragment would be expected to apply to postrevolutionary France, at least if one follows Hartz. However, in French self-descriptions, which emphatically eschew ethnic and racial "differentialism," France unambiguously inherits and perfects the line of "Latin universalism," which (at least in Emmanuel Todd's optimistic account) had started with Roman imperial citizenship, continued with Iberian racial mixing in the Americas, and was crowned by the French invention of "l'homme universel absolu" (Todd, 1994:15).

Indeed, one could argue that the strong emphasis on "assimilation" in French colonial ideology and practice is a reflection of this, because it counts on the universal assimilability of other peoples and races. The doctrine of assimilation, while never uncontested and chronically violated on its own terms (see Betts, 1961), offered a solution to the obvious contradiction between a Republican self-definition and colonial rule. Following Condorcet's diction that "a good law is good for all men," assimilation meant the "complete identification between the inhabitants of the colonies and the French of the *métropole*" (Brunschwig, 1986:49). However, the very commitment to ethnicity-blind, universalistic assimilation also confirms the lack of any particularistic, identity-forging ties binding metropolis and colonies that would grant the latter a preferential status for immigration purposes. On the contrary, as Algerian-born Albert Camus formulated with great psychological insight, the focus on *l'homme abstrait* may lead to the disregard for *l'homme concret;* in Algeria at least it factually implied the complete separation between *colons* and natives. With an eye on the exclusive race relations in the French Antilles, even Todd (1984:340) admits that the French *colons* never had the same "reputation of racial indifference" as the Spanish or Portuguese, and he assigns to the former a "middle position" between the "absolutely catholic Latins and the Anglo-Dutch Calvinists."[176] This is a euphemism, particularly if one contrasts the polarized race relations in French Haiti (the site of modern history's most famous slave revolt and where the racially mixed "coloureds" were strenuously kept apart from the ruling—and eventually evicted—white segment) with the "racial mingling" prevailing in the neighboring Spanish Dominican Republic; for Hoetink (1967:181), French Haiti was no less than "the dramatic expression" of the "North-West European Caribbean variant."

The unclear positioning of the French case shows the limits of classification. However, due to France's notorious population shortage, the French is distinguished from the other European empires by the much lesser degree of settlement and emigration throughout its various phases. This limited the possible rise of a state-transcending community and, for our purposes, justifies its grouping under the "northwestern" postcolonial constellation. Even in French Canada, due to an "almost morbid reluctance of the French authorities to depopulate France," total immigration during the entire French rule in the seventeenth and eighteenth centuries did not exceed 10,000 persons (McRae, 1964:226); and Quebec is, to date, the one example of a settlement colony thoroughly created in the French image. The second attempt, in Algeria, though on a much more massive scale, turned out a colossal failure because it became stuck in "two populations coexisting without exchanging spouses" (Todd, 1994:297).

The dividing line between the northwestern and southwestern postcolonial constellations is the existence of a perceived "community" that transcends the boundaries of nation-states and that becomes expressed in privileged immigration and citizenship rules for its members. This is a case of "transnationalism" *après la lettre,* because scholarly attention has been fixed on migrant ties across borders while neglecting the no less interesting case in which entire state collectivities perceive themselves as linked across borders.

However, one might object, are not "Francophonie" and Old Commonwealth "patriality" examples of a trans-state community, so that the distinction between the northwestern and southwestern constellations collapses? Beginning with the former, privileges for "francophone" immigrants, which French nationality law has granted since 1973,[177] are little more than anomalous afterthought within a policy toward the ex-colonies that has generally been led in the spirit of pragmatic "cooperation",[178] not of cultural affinity. Francophone privileges are an "afterthought," because they were introduced at the tail end of a postwar immigration policy that had explicitly discarded the colonial option to meet France's economic and demographic needs; and they are "anomalous" because its ethnic touch sits oddly with the nonethnic, "Republican" understanding of French nationhood that numerous government *statements* on immigration and citizenship have extolled as the official line. Interestingly, when the introduction of facilitated naturalization for francophone immigrants was debated in 1972, reference was made to "analogous rules" already existing in "Hispanic" and "Portuguese-speaking countries," as well as Britain (presumably with respect to the Old Commonwealth), all preferring "citizens close to them in language and culture."[179] Perhaps sensing the ethnicizing potential of what became known as *la Francophonie,* there have been strenuous attempts on part of the French state to fashion it in a nonethnic light. For instance, with respect to preferential naturalization the quasiethnic "mother tongue" requirement of 1973 was complemented in 1993 (upon recommendation of the 1988 Long Commission) by a five-year French-schooling requirement. Moreover, the Francophone network of states, forged since the mid-1980s, has come to include states such as Poland, Bulgaria, Albania, and (Spanish-speaking) Equatorial Guinea, which are all outside France's colonial ambit and in which French is obviously not the official language.[180] This openness is a deliberate continuation of France's "*vocation universelle.*"[181] In a superb irony, the content of this vocation is now defined as the "promotion of linguistic and cultural diversity," and any country subscribing it can join the club. Watered down to a label for cultural diversity and opposition to the global dominance of Anglo-American language and culture, *Francophonie* is a mere vessel for many a cultural content, and it is as much (or as little) a "community" as non-Anglo humankind is a "community."

Regarding Old Commonwealth "patrials," they are the exception within a postcolonial immigration policy whose rationale has been to cut down, rather than to enable, such immigration. This instance of ethnic migration still merits further attention, particularly if one contrasts it with the rather different Spanish and Portuguese mode of prioritizing their postcolonial immigrants. First, patriality is not the result of an explicit and principled commitment, which is even endowed with constitutional status in Spain and Portugal. Officially referred to as acknowledging not an ethnic or national-origin tie but a "family connection," patriality was only indirectly (though fully intentionally) an ethnic concept. This raises the interesting question of when a kinship concept turns into an ethnic concept. In the British debate, the turning-point was second-generation as against third-generation ties—though the (initially successful) opponents of third-generation patriality did not provide a theory why the abhorred ethnic or even racial dimension of patriality was linked up with third- (and not second-) generation ties. Second, patriality was only the result of a highly contingent concatenation of events and pressures. Stated in terms of a counterfactual, if, in late 1972, the Tory government had not tabled the new rules resulting from EC accession together with the new Immigration Rules implementing the 1971 Immigration Act, which suddenly opened up the invidious contrast of privileged EU foreigners and non-privileged Commonwealth citizens, there would not have been the (Euroskeptical cum Old-Commonwealth-loyal) Tory backbench rebellion; and without that rebellion there would have been no need for the Tory government to pacify its rebels by upgrading parental to grandparental patriality, thus reviving the ethnically or even racially flavored concept that had been knocked down earlier by an odd liberal-cum-restrictive coalition of friends and foes of nonwhite immigration.

However, the most interesting contrast between Britain's patrials, on the one hand, and Portugal and Spain's privileging of Hispanic and Lusophone immigrants, on the other, is the legal mechanism chosen to express the underlying preference: unilateral recognition of individually checked kinship ties versus bilateral "reciprocity," on the basis of generic and formal state membership. This difference should not be overstated, because the "reciprocity" alternative was evidently considered for a moment in Britain also. However, there is a striking affinity between these solutions and deep-sitting differences in the colonial experiences. Patriality, because of its essence as a kinship category, allows to slice the postcolonial populations into those who are of British origins and all others who are not. To be sure, this slicing is never perfect, because it has to honor acquired (spousal) family ties—whence the Powellite opposition to patriality as a Trojan horse for mixed-race immigration into Britain. By contrast, on the basis of reciprocity there is no possibility for the receiving state to ensure even a minimum of shared national origins, because the simple holding of the formal citizenship of the sending state suffices.

These different solutions to postcolonial migration mirror fundamental differences of the colonial societies built by Britain, on the one hand, and by the Iberian states, on the other. In his study of the Caribbean colonies, Hoetink (1967) has captured this in his distinction between the "North-West European" and "Iberian" variants. In the Iberian variant, "homogenization through mingling" (p. 175), particularly between whites and the mixed-race population, has taken place, producing a society thoroughly shaped by Spanish or Portuguese language and culture, up to a point that national-origin identifications become irrelevant. By contrast, in the "North-West European" variant, "the native white group shuts itself off from the coloureds" (p. 161), giving rise to heterogeneous societies without a shared (European) language and culture and in which national-origin (and racial) distinctions thus remain important.[182] There is an obvious affinity between British colonial societies, which overall have remained racially divided, and the concept of "patriality," and an affinity between the less racially divided Iberian colonial societies and the "reciprocity" solution to postcolonial migration.

Whatever the affinities between colonial experience and postcolonial immigrant reception, it is not my claim that they alone have shaped the northwestern and southwestern constellations. In an excellent discussion of "colonization" legacies and postcolonial immigrant "integration" in Britain and France, Bleich (2001a) found very little direct connections between both, but instead the prevalence of situational, "hodge-podge policymaking" in combination with the borrowing of solutions from domestic (and not colonial) history and from abroad. Although our focus is on postcolonial immigrant "selection" rather than "integration," there is no reason not to heed this word of caution, especially because in the case of Spain and Portugal (the latter with respect to Brazil) we are dealing with "postcolonial" immigrants in a very weak and remote sense, originating from former "colonies" that turned independent almost two centuries ago. Next to the colonial experience, there are of course additional, more contemporary factors that have shaped the southwestern constellation.

One such factor is readily visible in the "reciprocity" formula: the protection of emigrants abroad. Whereas in one respect reciprocity is the legal mechanism for expressing the existence of a state-transcending community, there is also a utilitarian dimension to it, quite separate from its communitarian dimension. As poor and underdeveloped states at Europe's periphery, Spain and Portugal have traditionally been emigrant-sending states, first "immigrants" to the Americas, and after World War II "guest workers" to northwestern Europe. Since the mid-1970s the protection of these emigrants abroad became a major concern of the postauthoritarian regimes. In the case of Spain, this went as far as (potentially) severing the reciprocity-based dual-nationality regime from its postcolonial nexus. The utilitarian dimension of reciprocity—to protect emigrants abroad—is particularly visible in the case of Portugal, 10 percent of whose entire population resides in Brazil alone. In the course of Spain and Portugal's entering of the European Community and their ensuing prosperity, we have become used to looking at them as immigrant-receiving states, much like France or Britain. However, when the reciprocity regimes were constitutionally enshrined in the mid-1970s, this was not a consideration, and the prevalent concern was emigration, not immigration. Interestingly, once immigration concerns became predominant, one can observe an erosion of postcolonial preferences, particularly in Spain, where these preferences are at the point of disappearing.[183]

Turning from selection mechanisms to the justification of postcolonial ethnic migration in the southwestern states, one notices the coexistence of a variety of motifs, along with an astonishing neglect on the part of the state and its elites to explicate them or show their interconnections. Clearly dominant in de Castro's first formulation of Spain's dual nationality regime, as well as in Moura Ramos's authoritative account of the Portuguese equal-rights conventions, is the notion of a state-transcending, historical and cultural "community," from whose presupposed existence certain nationality and other "equal rights" privileges are derived for its members in the state of which they are not formerly citizens.[184] However, in contrast to the diaspora constellation discussed in the next chapter, the constitutive units of this community are not individuals but states. This follows from the fact that formal membership in a designated state triggers the adherence to that community and that the individual-rights component has generally remained subdued.

Closely connected with (and insufficiently distinguished from) the communitarian justification is the "reciprocity" justification. At the formal level, the latter merely denotes the legal mechanism for expressing the state-transcending community and thus is not a justification. In this sense, reciprocity is little more than an (in fact, *the*) international-law principle, which reflects the international-law status of the preference regimes. Reciprocity in substantive respect does, however, carry the utilitarian meaning of protecting emigrants abroad, because reciprocal rights are granted also to Spaniards and Portuguese in the Ibero-American states.

Finally, and most recently, the "assimilability" of culturally close Hispanic and Lusophone immigrants has appeared as a third justification for postcolonial preferences in the southwestern constellation. This reflects a decay of their communitarian origins and a new "Europeanized" context in which immigration control, not emigrant protection, is the key concern. Although the communitarian and reciprocity motifs cut across party lines, the Spanish case showed that the assimilation motif does not, as it violates "multicultural" sensibilities on the left-liberal side. This minimizes its effectiveness and is a safe indicator of an ethnic preference regime in decline.

Interestingly, a major justification of postcolonial migration in the northwestern states—the "responsibility" of a former colonial power toward its former colonial subjects—is nearly absent in the southwestern states. It flared up briefly in the two Portuguese regularizations in the 1990s, even though the African PALOP immigrants mainly addressed by it were quickly absorbed by the Lusophone "identity" discourse that became dominant in that decade. Addressing PALOP immigrants, however briefly, in terms of moral responsibility was not accidental, because they are the only truly postcolonial immigrants in any of the two southwestern states, their presence in Portugal being more or less directly linked to the pre-1975 colonial presence of Portugal in Africa. However, next to the generally huge temporal gap between colonialism and postcolonial immigration in the southwestern states, there are additional reasons for the relative absence of a responsibility discourse there. First, the latter is antithetical to the ethnocultural community discourse, in which the distinction between colonizer and colonized tends to be dissolved. Second, "responsibility" is premised on a position of power and superiority. This was—and is—the case for Britain or France in Europe's center, but not for Portugal and Spain at Europe's periphery. For instance, the rhetoric of "solidarity" with the impoverished South, which one finds in postauthoritarian Spain and Portugal alike,[185] configures the latter as part of the South, if perhaps in a better position to press its concerns on the privileged North.

This is not to say that immigrant reception in the southwestern states has been devoid of a sense of moral responsibility. On the contrary, the latter fares prominently in the southwestern states' self-perceived "friendlier" response to recent immigration, if compared with the "restrictionism" prevailing in the northwestern states. However, this obligation derives from the southwestern's emigrant, not its colonial past, and it accordingly applies to all immigrants, irrespective of their origins. Interestingly, this obligation rests on a reciprocity consideration: not to deny to immigrants today the friendly reception that Spanish and Portuguese (and Italian) emigrants have enjoyed elsewhere in the past.

Finally, what have we learned about the pressures on ethnic migration in both postcolonial constellations? A major dividing line is between the predominantly domestic pressures in the northwestern constellation and the predominantly external, "Europeanization" pressures in the southwestern constellation. This reflects the different timing of both migrations, the northwestern migration preceding the southwestern migration by at least two decades and occurring in a context when "Europe" was not yet on the map. However, this has to be immediately qualified. "Europe" was very much present when "patriality" was forged in Britain, and one could even argue that patriality (to the degree that it became a device for privileged Old Commonwealth immigration) is entirely the product of the rejection of Europe by certain Tory backbenchers. Interestingly, the latest round of the British patriality debate, which stood under the sign "Old Commonwealth versus Europe," prefigured the Portuguese constellation two decades later, in which Europe likewise was a matter of interest only, whereas the Lusophone community was one of identity.

If "Europe" thus ironically resurrected Old Commonwealth patriality, it logically could not be part of the forces that put pressure on it. Instead, this pressure was entirely domestic, resulting mostly (though not exclusively) from a liberal challenge to ethnic migration that addressed the racially flavored inequity between excluded, nonwhite UK and Colonies citizens and included, white Old Commonwealth citizens. The persistent scruples that this inequity had caused even for Conservative governments before 1971, which until then had opted either for no controls or for the same controls for all, suggest that they had a hand at phasing out Old Commonwealth patriality in 1981.

Domestic pressures were also predominant in the French case, even though the ethnic-preference constellation was entirely different here. The original scheme crossed out with the stroke of a pen by a "Republican"-minded *Conseil d'État* in 1945 resembled more the American model of selecting immigrants according to an ethnoracial hierarchy that was informed by prewar eugenics; it had nothing to do with postcolonial immigration. After the 1945 verdict, ethnic-preference considerations could be raised only informally, though we saw their long-standing influence on administrative practices. This involved postcolonial immigration only indirectly, as the attempt by "populationists" to counterbalance demographically unwanted postcolonial with wanted European immigration. Over time, this counterbalancing effort simply petered out, due to dwindling European immigration, accelerating domestic birth rates, and the all-dominant and ethnicity-blind economic need for labor. One could of course argue that the free movement provisions of European Community law eventually "consecrated the cultural preference for intra-European immigration" (Viet, 1998:275), even though they had only negligible impact on actual flows and became notionally decoupled from "immigration" rules at all.

Regarding the external European pressures on the southwestern preference regimes, one should not overlook an element of pretense in the response of political elites, which an observer of the Portuguese case aptly characterized as "anticipating obedience" (Santos, 1995:277). Technically, European Union constraints on immigration exist only in the form of harmonized rules for short-term visa (or visa exemptions); they do not yet touch on long-term stays of third-state nationals, that is, "immigration" proper. There is thus ample room for respecting the "historical and cultural ties" that Portugal and Spain have ceremonially insisted on at European level. Though the 1985 foreigner law was "almost entirely the result of external pressure associated with Spain's entry into the European Community" (Cornelius, 1994:345), no "external pressure" forced the (Socialist) government to neutralize, through Byzantine implementation rules, a preference for Hispanic immigrants that had been written by it itself into the law's preamble. Similarly, no Schengen rule forced the Portuguese border guards in 1993 to reject Brazilian "vagabonds and mulattos" at Lisbon's airport, which for the first time visibly subjected citizens of the "brother country" to the clutches of immigration control. More to the point, increasing prosperity in Europe's southwestern corner, as well as their vulnerable geographic position as entry posts to an internally borderless Europe, have made Portugal and Spain magnets of new immigration that would call for a restrictive response even without the (so far negligible) legal constraints of EU membership in this domain. Eager to demonstrate their commitment to a Europe that symbolizes for them prosperity and democracy, southwestern political elites quickly adopted the restrictionist mindset as the dominant game in town, with occasional (and self-serving) protestations against a demonized "new European order" (Leitão, 1997). In sum, the impact of Europe has been more atmospheric than legal-political, which of course does not make it any less "real."

Although the nature of external European pressures thus has to be qualified, we could also witness the stirrings of domestic pressure on the southwestern preference regimes. This trend was particularly pronounced in Spain, which not only faces a highly diverse immigrant population, but whose biggest immigrant group—Moroccans—have never been part of its postcolonial preference regime (which incidentally proves its ethnic texture). In the recent imbroglio over regularizing illegal immigrants, we observed a peculiar asymmetry between a (conservative) government eager to avoid the image of "ethnic favoritism" and certain South American immigrant groups invoking the opposite rhetoric of "particular" ties. The public neutrality and equity mandates of a liberal state are fully visible here, as well as the rational strategy of aggrieved groups to present their claims in particularistic terms as more worthy of redress than those of other groups. The heavily Lusophone character of its immigrant population has so far protected Portugal from this liberal state dynamic. However, if the current trend toward diversified immigration flows persists, this is likely to come to an end soon.

4

Resilience versus Demise in the Diaspora Constellation: Israel and Germany

With the diaspora constellation, we finally reach the most persistent form of ethnic migration.[1] The *Oxford English Dictionary* defines *Diaspora* as "The Dispersion," which refers to "the whole body of Jews living dispersed among the Gentiles after the Captivity." In contemporary migration and "transnationalism" studies, the notion of diaspora not only has been decoupled from the Jewish experience but has come to denote any ethnic minority group seeking to retain their cultural difference and ties to a homeland (see, for example, Lie, 1995). This use is an overextension, because it omits the involuntary and forced quality, and concomitant "return" disposition, that are constitutive of the original Diaspora experience. I therefore define the "diaspora constellation" more narrowly as any case in which ethnic minorities are lastingly stranded under foreign jurisdictions, they are subject to (however implicit or only imagined) repression for their ethnic difference, and there is a homeland state that actively pursues the return of these groups, who are perceived as repressed coethnics.[2]

The centrality of persecution against coethnics is one element in which the diaspora differs from the postcolonial constellation. In the latter, similar (though weaker) return or privileged entry provisions were coded in terms of extended family ties, cultural affinity, or the moral responsibilities of a former colonial power, but never in terms of averting harm to coethnics. A second difference is the strict avoidance of "migration" rhetoric in the diaspora constellation. Jewish immigration to Israel is called *aliyah* (which means "ascension"), ethnic German immigration is referred to as *Aussiedlung* (which means "resettlement"), and both are dealt with separately from ordinary immigration or foreigner laws. Perhaps to avoid invidious comparisons with less privileged migrant groups, diaspora migration is everywhere fashioned as a form of repatriation to which the liberal-state norms of nondiscrimination and impartial treatment do not apply.[3] Not only are the diaspora migrants not "immigrants"; neither are they "emigrants" who voluntarily left their homelands and thus in principle could not count on their continued protection by their state of origin. As in the British "patriality" category, such emigrant ties usually do not reach beyond the third (or second foreign-born) generation, and it is not clear whether the extended emigrants' privileged return recognizes a family or an ethnic connection (see Chapter 5). Indeed, from the point of view of the homeland state, diaspora migration does not at all fall under the usually peripheral and interest-driven "migration" rubric but under the far more central and principled rubric of unfinished nation-building. Its purpose is to redress a perceived noncongruence of national and state boundaries.[4]

Diaspora migration still consists of the more-than-temporary move of noncitizens (or "aliens") across state borders, which in everyday perception, as well as in international migration law (Plender, 1988), constitutes "immigration." In fact, folding back the diaspora migrants semantically into ordinary "migrants" is part and parcel of the opposition to this type of ethnic migration, which allows the liberal variant of this opposition to uncover the discrimination that is involved in privileging these migrants over other migrants, and which allows the restrictive variant to oppose this kind of immigration like any other kind.

Compared to the settler state constellation, in which the main discriminatory impulse was negative, the diaspora constellation stands under the sign of positive discrimination: specific groups are designated for preferential treatment. While clearly less pernicious than negative discrimination, the range of positive discrimination is still limited in a liberal state. As in the prototype of U.S. "affirmative action," positive discrimination is usually to improve the situation of a disadvantaged group, and it is to stop once the disadvantage has been removed. Article 1(4) of the UN Convention on the Elimination of All Forms of Racial Discrimination allows "special measures" for "certain racial or ethnic groups" only as long as "equal enjoyment or exercise of human rights and fundamental freedoms" has not yet been achieved.[5] This is why the notion of persecution becomes central to the legitimation of ethnic diaspora migration: it justifies the underlying positive discrimination on the part of the receiving state.[6]

One has to realize that this type of ethnically selective immigration policy came into existence just when the whole principle of ethnic selectivity had fallen in disrepute, after World War II. Therefore a special legitimizing effort was necessary to make it happen.[7] In Israel, this takes the extreme form of the entire Jewish collectivity conceiving of itself as entitled to an act of restitution, for which the Law of Return stands. An Israeli jurist defended the latter in such terms: "[T]he Jews, having been excluded from their homeland in the Land of Israel for much of the past 2,000 years, are entitled to the benefits of reverse discrimination and affirmative action in resettling the land" (Steinberg, 2000:17).[8] Of course, this is to ward off the charge on part of the Arab losers of Israeli nation building that Zionism is just a variant of European white settler colonialism and thus incurably "racist."[9] In Germany, the persecution rationale is weaker, applying not to the entire national collectivity throughout its history but only to the so-called expellees *(Vertriebene)* in the eastern territories who vicariously suffered retaliation for the German aggression in World War II.

A logical consequence of the positive discrimination rationale is that the migration engendered by it must come to an end when the disadvantage has been remedied and "equality" has been achieved. In Germany, ethnic migration has indeed stopped in principle (though not yet in reality), in the very moment when the "consequences of the war" were officially declared "settled" (*bereinigt*), that is, in the early 1990s. In Israel, where the very definition of Jewishness is fused with the motif of dispersal and persecution and whose entire history has been "martyrology" (Smith, 1995:14), no such endpoint is in sight.[10]

Ethnic diaspora migration is usually seen as grounded in an "ethnic" (as against a "civic") self-understanding of the receiving state.[11] This is correct in the sense that diaspora migration presupposes an ethno-nation that is pre-existing and larger than the state and that conceives of the latter as "*of* and *for*" it (Brubaker, 1996:103). By the same token, from the point of view of the receiving state, the reference point is not "other states" (and individuals only by virtue of state membership), as *grosso modo* in the postcolonial constellation, but coethnics proper in other states. An ethnic state in this sense is one that is owned by a nonterritorial nation. The purest expression of this is Israel, which perceives of itself as the state of the entire Jewish people, the nonresident and noncitizen Diaspora included. In the words of Anton Shammas (1989:9), "[t]he Jewish concept of identity has always been and still is a correlative of time, not of territory or place." Flowing from the pen of a Palestinian writer, this statement is not just profoundly ironical but bitingly polemical, if one considers the centrality of "returning" to the Holy Land in Zionist discourse.[12]

However, a state *qua* state is necessarily a territorial organization. If minimal liberal-democratic precepts are in place (such as the rule of law, individual rights, and representative democracy), and if there are competing ethnic groups residing in the same territory, this territorial logic will challenge an ethnonational self-conception and the policies flowing from it. Israel is again a prime example of this. The opposition to the Law of Return (and other laws and institutions ensuring the dominance of the Jewish majority) has been led under the notion that Israel should be the "state of all of its citizens" and not just of the Jewish majority. This call is paradoxical, because "Israel" is surely just another word for "the Jewish State" (as one can read in Israel's Declaration of Independence), and it asks for nothing less than a complete redefinition of the state. As we shall see, the case of Israel is riddled with paradoxes, which stem from its dual character of deeply divided society and ethnoreligious self-definition of the titular nation.

Israel shows *ex negativo* that a liberal, nonethnic state would be one in which there is no unfinished nation building, and national and state boundaries have come to overlap. This is incidentally demonstrated by the case of Germany, Israel's sister "ethnic state": its ethnic imprints were significantly cut down just when reunification had resolved the "national question." Overall, we shall see that ethnic stateness is certainly a starting point of ethnic diaspora migration, but it rarely goes uncontested. This is because a liberal-*cum*-territorial logic, articulated by the losers of ethnically selective policies in a multiethnic society, is working against it.

Comparing Israel and Germany as instances of the diaspora constellation is interesting in several respects.[13] Though fatefully entangled as victim and perpetrator in the twentieth century's darkest hour, both ended up with strikingly similar ethnic return provisions, accepting for permanent settlement only migrants who already were considered members of the titular nation. Of course, the vastly different scale of the two policies stretches the limits of a meaningful comparison: Israel is entirely the result of Jewish immigration, whereas ethnic German immigration has at best played a peripheral role in German nation building after World War II. Indeed, one could even classify Israel as a settler state, along with the United States or Australia,[14] and then investigate why the latter eventually shifted to a universalistic immigration policy, while Israel did not. Against such an alternative pairing speaks the fact that Israeli actors themselves have been keenly aware of Israel's greater affinities with other diaspora migrations, especially—and almost compulsively—the Germans' (see, for example, Klein,

1987:4–5). Israeli defenders of the Law of Return have frequently pointed to the existence of a parallel law in Germany, with the implication that if "they" (the perpetrators) may have it, "we" (the victims) certainly are entitled to it too. As Amnon Rubinstein (2000:199) put it, "Germany has never been called upon to annul its own 'Law of Return' on grounds that it harms the universal principles of equality, which is the argument adopted by those wishing to repeal Israel's Law of Return."

As we shall see, the days of *this* defense of Israel's Law of Return are numbered. In the early 1990s, Germany has drastically reduced, even phased out in principle, its ethnic-return migration. Along with the mutual references, even implicatedness, of ethnic migration in both cases, this divergence of outcomes is an obvious invitation to comparison. Why does Jewish immigration in Israel persist, while ethnic German immigration in Germany is on the way out? At one level, this outcome corresponds precisely to the different designs of both policies: a temporary remedy to the consequences of World War II in Germany, as against a permanent nation-building device in Israel. However, as a story of intended consequences this would be too boring to tell. More interestingly, we shall see that the Israeli Law of Return, much like its German counterpart, has become the subject of significant opposition too, which—among other forces and factors—articulates a liberal and territorial logic of treating all migrant and domestic ethnic groups equally. Then the question becomes why this opposition has not been equally successful, which is empirical and open-ended.

In the first section of this chapter I map out some communalities and differences in the justifications and functions of ethnic diaspora migration in Israel and Germany. The second section shows some of the difficulties of selecting ethnic immigrants on the basis of their ethnicity proper. Far from being obvious or static, the definitions of "who is a Jew" and "who is an ethnic German" have been extremely malleable and fluctuating over time, as a result of clashing ideologies and shifting political interests, respectively. In the third section, I compare the "liberal" and "restrictive" challenges to ethnic migration in both countries, which turned out to be successful in Germany and unsuccessful in Israel.

Diaspora Migration and Ethnic Statehood

Any comparison of ethnic migration in Israel and Germany must at first realize its vastly differing scope and relevance for nation building.

Whereas Israel is entirely the result of Jewish immigration and settlement after World War II, there surely would be a "Germany" without ethnic German immigration, and the latter has only been a temporary and peripheral aspect of nation building. The formal setting is still the same: an ethnonation larger than the state, and the latter furthering (or at least permitting) the "return" of coethnics dispersed abroad. Underneath this communality, the German return policy was spatially and temporarily specific (to remedy the consequences of World War II in the Communist east), whereas the parallel Israeli policy had no such built-in limitations and cutoff points and came to be identified with the purpose of the state itself (to "ingather the exiles"). In addition to being grounded in the ethnoreligious definition of the state-constituting nation, Jewish immigration also fulfills material state-building functions, in the context of the Jewish-Arab nationality conflict. Due to both factors, the Israeli state was bound to be an ethnic state in a much stronger sense than the German state ever was, despite the existence of civic-territorial elements to counteract the ethnic tilt in both. This provides a starting-point for understanding the different longevity of ethnic migration in both countries.

"Ingathering of the Exiles" in Israel

Israel's Declaration of Independence stipulates that "[t]he State of Israel will be open for Jewish immigration and for the Ingathering of the Exiles." This mandate was realized in the Law of Return of 1950, whose first article explicates, as the "right of *aliyah*," that "[e]very Jew has the right to come to this country as an *oleh*." This right is conceived of as a natural right preceding the very existence of the state, and the latter figures only as its "trustee" (Shachar, 1999:241).[15] As David Ben-Gurion put it when submitting the draft law to the Second Knesset, "the state is not granting the Jews of the Diaspora the right to return; this right preceded the State of Israel, and was instrumental in building it . . . The Law of Return has nothing to do with immigration legislation: it is a law perpetuating Israel's history."[16] Strictly speaking, the Law of Return incapacitates the Israeli state from restricting Jewish immigration and thus reveals this state to be the property of all Jews in the world, and not of the state's citizens. To quote Ben-Gurion again, the Law of Return is a "bill of rights . . . guaranteed to all Jews in the diaspora," and Israel was subsequently "a state for Jews everywhere" (quoted in Hazony, 2000:56). Until a 1980 amendment of the nationality law, even a Jew who was born in Israel was deemed to have entered Israel "as an *oleh*," and he or she acquired citizenship through the Law of Return.[17] This "somewhat strange" provision (Rubinstein, 1976:161), which reverses the usual priority of natives over immigrants, epitomizes the state-defining quality of Jewish immigration.

The Law of Return is one of the few laws in Israel that grant an explicit privilege to Jews *qua* Jews. There has been from the start a strenuous attempt on the part of the Israeli state to be impartial to all of its citizens, the 20 percent minority of Arab Israeli citizens included. Already the Declaration of Independence included a commitment to the "complete equality of social and political rights to all its inhabitants irrespective of religion, race or sex." Here one sees the logic of liberal-territorial stateness working against the opposite logic of ethnic stateness. Two quasiconstitutional "Basic Laws" in 1992 enshrined this dual commitment in the notion that Israel is a "Jewish and democratic state." This is a puzzling formulation, because it seems to suggest that in being Jewish the state was not democratic and that in being democratic it was not Jewish—otherwise there would be no point to list both adjectives separately. The extreme ends on the political spectrum have indeed claimed just that. According to Ariel Sharon, now the Prime Minister of Israel, "[o]ur forefathers and parents . . . did not come here to establish democracy . . . but they came here to create a Jewish state."[18] And on the Arab minority side, their claim that Israel should become a "state of all of its citizens" has always been a shorthand for demanding that Israel should stop being Jewish.

Of course, the official line is that there is no contradiction between Israel's Jewish and democratic convictions. Accordingly, a 1985 amendment to "Basic Law: the Knesset" prohibits parties that deny the existence of Israel as the state of the Jewish people from participating in Knesset elections, but it also prohibits parties that deny the democratic nature of the state or incite to racism. This amendment turned into an "incontrovertible constitutional fact" (Kretzmer, 1990:29) that Israel is a Jewish state. But when the anti-Arab Kach party of Rabbi Meir Kahane, which advocated the expulsion even of Arab Israeli citizens, insisted that the state's being Jewish contradicted its being democratic, the Supreme Court did not follow: "The existence of State [*sic*] of Israel as the state of the Jewish people does not deny its democratic nature, just as the Frenchness of France does not deny its democratic nature" (ibid., p. 31).

The claim that Israel is a normal nation-state, like France, deserves further attention. When considering in 1988, simultaneously with the Kach case, whether the Arab Progressive List for Peace (PLP) also should be disqualified on the basis of the 1985 amendment, the Supreme Court explicated the minimal definition of a "Jewish state" that no Knesset list or party was allowed to question or work against: first, there was to be a majority of Jews in the country; second, there should be a preference for Jews, over other groups, to immigrate to Israel; and, third, there was a reciprocal relationship between the state and Diaspora Jews. This sits oddly with the court's parallel claim that the Jewishness of Israel was just like the "Frenchness of France." As Kretzmer (1990:31) retorted, "[w]ould a French political party that objected to a French law granting immigration privileges to persons of French origins be denied the right to run for election on the grounds that it denied the Frenchness of France?"

In scrutinizing the difference between the Jewishness of Israel and the Frenchness of France, one must at first realize that the Zionist founding movement of Israel was at heart a secular movement that tried to "normalize" the Jewish existence by giving the Jews (who were also to be transformed from religious group to secular nation) a state, much as the French and other Europeans already had one. In Zionist leader Theodor Herzl's vision, this state would not just be part of "Europe" but would "serve as the outpost of civilization against barbarism" (Herzl, 1997:149). This secular-political project implied a conscious rupture with the mystical-religious Judaism of the Diaspora: the former was about a new beginning and the pragmatic exigencies of the day, whereas the latter was about genealogy and the principled following of the religious commandments. Tellingly, the Zionist pioneers often referred to themselves as "Hebrews" rather than "Jews," Hebrew and not Yiddish became the official language of the new state, and in the literary imagination the worldly, Israeli-born *sabra* was held against the despised ghetto Jew: "He [the sabra] is a Hebrew and not a Jew and he is destined to bring an end to the humiliation of his parents. All that the Jews lack is in him: strength, health, physical labor . . . rootedness."[19]

However, this rupture with the past, which is commanded by the very act of founding something new,[20] could not obliterate the fact that "Jews" and not "Ruritanians" were doing it. When she defined herself in the Declaration of Independence, Israel was of course the "Jewish state," and the official state symbols, from flag to national anthem and day of rest, were all Jewish symbols. Despite all attempts to secularize the meaning of "Jewish," this was an irremediably religious condition, and one that militated against the very project of building a "normal" nation-state. The core of the Jewish existence is the idea of a Covenant between God and his "chosen people," which bestows His holiness on them, but with the consequence of severing ties with all other people: "Ye shall be holy unto me, for I the LORD am holy and have severed you from other people that ye should be mine" (Leviticus 20:26). Here lies the root of Jewish exclusivism, of its peculiar coincidence of religion and ethnicity, which militates against the project of "becom[ing] a nation like every other nation" (Rubinstein 2000:38). In the dry words of Sammy Smooha: "Unlike other world religions, Judaism has remained a single-religion ethnicity (or a mono-ethnic religion) in which nationality and faith are intimately intertwined and proselytizing zeal is absent" (1978:26). The logic of this is tribal: one cannot become a member unless one already is one. As the Israeli historian Zeev Sternhell (1998:344) put it appositely, Israel is "a tribe that has won a state for itself."[21] If elevated into the nation-defining component of a state, Judaism makes for a "nation" that is inaccessible to an outsider. Surely, all ethnic nationalisms (the German, for instance) had this exclusivist and genealogical thrust. However, because Judaism is also a religion, with a script and explicit rules whose violation would be sacrilege, and with official gatekeepers to sanction it, this exclusivism is more zealously guarded and complete than that of a merely ethnic group.

This is not to say that Israel is a theocratic state. As envisioned by Herzl (1997:196), the rabbis have been kept "in their temples," at least most of the time. However, certain compromises were necessary to accomplish this. They are laid out in Ben-Gurion's famous "status quo letter" to the anti-Zionist, religious Agudat Yisrael party in 1947: the Jewish sabbath was to be the day of rest; Jewish dietary laws were to be observed in government kitchens; religious courts were to maintain exclusive jurisdiction in personal status matters—most importantly, marriage and divorce; and the autonomy of existing religious educational systems was to be preserved (see Rubinstein, 1967:113–114). The most serious of these religious encroachments on civic life is surely the religious supremacy in family law. As a result of it, there is no civil marriage in Israel, marriage between Jews and non-Jews is prohibited, divorce is prohibited, and women are systematically discriminated against. Interestingly, however, this most serious instance in which the rabbis could not be kept in their temples did not taint the neutral image of the state because—in prolongation of the Ottoman *millet* system—the other major religions were granted similar prerogatives.[22] In this respect, a more serious violation of the neutrality principle was the religious-Jewish symbolism framing the new state, which told all non-Jews that this was not and never could become their state.

Overall, throughout Israel's fifty-year history there has been a constant struggle over a secular versus religious definition of Jewishness, which incidentally is not captured in the "Jewish" versus "democratic state" dichotomy that structures the standard accounts of Israeli state development (for example, Cohen, 1983, 1989).[23] This struggle could not be won by the secular Zionists, because it turned out to be impossible to define Jewishness in nonreligious terms. As Baruch Kimmerling (2001:125) put it, the "essential difficulty in separating religion and nationality . . . [made] [t]he secular coating of Zionist nationalism . . . very thin and fragile from the start." Nonreligious Jewishness certainly could not take hold in Israeli society. A survey done in the early 1980s found that 80 percent of Jews in Israel disapproved of the classic Labor Zionists' "dissociating" of Judaism from the religious tradition (Liebman and Don-Yehiya, 1983:22).

Accordingly, a first respect in which the Jewishness of Israel differs from the Frenchness of France is the ethnoreligious exclusivity of the state-defining nation.[24] By the same token, the minimal requirement of liberal statehood—the differentiation of state and religion—is not fulfilled in Israel. To quote again Zeev Sternhell (1998:xiii): "Those who wish Israel to be a truly liberal state . . . must recognize the fact that liberalism derives from the initial attempt, in the seventeenth century, to separate religion from politics."

There is a second respect in which the Jewishness of Israel differs from the Frenchness of France: the Frenchness of France is not perennially whipped up and challenged by the existence of non-French groups that consider the same territory their national homeland. Israel is a deeply divided society, in which formally equal citizenship rights for the so-called "minorities" are accompanied by a host of overt but mostly covert discriminations that taint Israel's self-image as a liberal democracy.[25] Next to the Law of Return, a major overt discrimination is the official status granted to the National Institutions: the World Zionist Organization, the Jewish Agency, and the Jewish National Fund. All of them originated in the pre-State phase, are owned and funded by world Jewry, and thus are not accountable to the Israeli state. Although they notionally serve the Jewish sector only, the extraterritorial National Institutions are still endowed with major public functions, most notably immigration, settlement, and land development. The most important consequence of this is that about 80 percent of Israel's land, which is owned by the state but whose development has been entrusted to the National Institutions, cannot be bought, leased, or used by Arab Israeli citizens. In the words of one Arab Israeli author, the National Institutions are like "a 'black hole' . . . into which Arab land enters but cannot be retrieved" (Yiftachel, 1999:373).

However, most discriminations against the Arab minorities have not been overt but covert. Perhaps the best-known example is making a variety of welfare entitlements and other state benefits contingent on service in the Israeli Defense Forces (IDF). Although by law all Israeli residents are obliged to serve in the military, Arabs are not drafted for "security" reasons—which makes them ineligible for these entitlements and benefits, such as child allowances (see Rosenhek, 1999). The euphemisms in state statutes that exclude Arab Israeli citizens without naming them are manifold and longwinded: "demobilized soldiers," "a person to whom the Law of Return would apply if this person did not already have Israeli citizenship," and so on (see Dayan, 1993:99).

At the same time, the very fact that most discriminations against the "minorities" are forced underground shows the operation of civic-territorial principles in the Israeli state—as it were, its structural desire to be like France. A small but revealing expression of this was the overwhelming rejection in 1997 of a Knesset bill under which only Jews (indirectly referred to as "someone who, if they weren't a citizen, would be entitled to citizenship under Clause A of the Law of Return") would be able to run for the premiership of the state.[26] Oddly, the Likud proponent of the bill compared the proposed restriction to one in the United States that limits the presidency to US-born citizens. A more adequate analogue would have been an Anglo-Saxon origin restriction. Even the Likud leadership disparaged the proposal as marred by the "stench of racism," and a Likud-dominated parliament barred it from further consideration.[27] A non-Jew at the helm of the Jewish state is surely the most inconceivable of all things, and yet an apparently operative civic norm prevents it from being stated openly, not to mention being put into law. An editorial in the *Jerusalem Post* even likened the situation of Israeli minorities to those in the United States, where John F. Kennedy had proved that a Catholic also could become president: "If the Jewishness of the state is seen to prevent the possibility, however unlikely, of a member of the Israeli-Arab minority from becoming prime minister, then the ideal of the Jewish state takes on a chauvinist hue."[28]

The difference between the American (or any other "normal" nation-state) and Israeli minority *problématiques* is captured in the notion that Israel is an "ethnic democracy." Sammy Smooha defined it, in opposition to liberal, consociational, or *Herrenvolk* democracies, as a combination of "viable democratic institutions with institutionalized ethnic dominance" (Smooha, 1990:389; see also Smooha, 1997; Peled, 1992; Shafir and Peled, 1998). Smooha insists that, in contrast to *Herrenvolk* democracy, where minorities are denied citizenship status, ethnic democracy is still *democracy*, and one that is "viable" in the long run (Smooha, 1990:410–411). A number of Arab Israeli authors have argued against this that Israel was really an "ethnic state" or "ethnocracy" and thus not democratic.[29] As Nadim Rouhana (1998) put it, "[e]thnic states cannot be democratic for all citizens. It is possible to maintain democracy in an ethnic state only if democracy is limited to one ethnic group." Alan Dowty (1999) retorted that all depends on how democracy is defined, and according to the "less unforgiving" comparative standard accounts, from Dahl to Lijphart, Israel was certainly a democracy. Granted this, what the Arab Israeli authors really found fault with is the apologetic tinge in the notion of ethnic democracy, in which a profoundly contested reality is endowed with the dignity of a legitimate and "viable" political form. Even if Israel was an "ethnic democracy," speculates Oren Yiftachel (1992), it could be "viable" only if moving toward a "consociational" direction in which the Arab minorities were proportionally included in the structures of government.[30] The "ethnic state" authors rightly address the anomaly that ethnic affiliation, not citizenship, makes one a full member of the Israeli state. This conspires against the "normal" nation-state that Israel wants to be. As Yiftachel (1999:337) put it, because of the combination of diaspora inclusion and minority exclusion there is no identifiable "demos" in Israel, so that in this sense there can not be "democracy."

In sum, two antiliberal rifts separate Israel from a "normal" nation-state: the anomaly of an ethnoreligiously closed and extraterritorially located Jewish nation, and the deep division of society. Both obstacles to liberal stateness reinforce one another: there is no notional possibility for the Arab minority ever to become part of the Jewish majority nation, and this reinforces the imperative of keeping the minority down through constant and exclusively Jewish immigration. Differently phrased, Israel cannot be a liberal state, with a nondiscriminatory immigration policy, unless it ceases to be Jewish. Its definitional Jewishness prevents Israel from ever coming to rest within its territory, and from becoming a "state of all of its citizens."

In light of this, ethnic diaspora migration is both an expression of Israel's ethnoreligious self-definition *and* a material state-building device in a hostile Arab environment. Yet the matter is more complicated still. With respect to the material state-building function of Jewish immigration an altogether different vista on ethnicity opens up, one in which a perplexing variety of ethnic and national-origin groups were to be precisely robbed of their original ethnicity and cast into an Israeli standard-mold. From this angle, the Israeli state violated the liberal neutrality norm not because of its Jewish exclusivism or its discrimination of the Arab minority, but because it sought to "dissolve the Oriental culture in the European melting pot" (Cohen-Almagor, 1995:473). This is the origin of the (European) Ashkenazi versus (African-Asian) Sephardi conflict, which is one more cleavage line that is not captured by the "Jewish" versus "democratic" contrast. From this intra-Jewish perspective, the Zionist state builders appeared as Western modernizers who sought to eradicate the religious traditionalism of African-Asian Jews (who formed about half of the approximately one million Jewish immigrants between 1948 and 1960). This is the topic of the classic "immigrant absorption" account of Eisenstadt (1955), in which Israel figures as a new-nation-building project quite like the United States. More recently, it has become the topic of Israel's "new historians" (such as Segev, 1986; 1993), according to whom Jewish immigration was not a noble "ingathering of the exiles" but the "human material" that was needed for material state building.

From an intra-Jewish perspective, the problem of Jewish immigration was that it was nonselective. Among Zionist leaders there was uneasiness about this from the start, and there were serious discussions to sort out the "less desirable" elements, such as invalids, potential welfare cases, or certain ethnic groups, most notably the least wanted "African Arabs" (Segev, 1986:146). When the latter started arriving in 1948, the Foreign Office warned that the "preservation of the country's cultural level demands a flow of immigration from the West, and not only from the backward Levantine countries" (ibid., 156). Under the Jewish umbrella, Israel was finally a "normal" nation-state, worried about the economic and cultural effects of immigration.

Unlike any other nation-state, however, Israel could not practice a selective immigration policy, not only because of ideology but also because of material state interests. The mostly untold side story to unselected Jewish immigration (to which from the 1990s was even added a significant number of religious non-Jews) was the demographic competition with the Arab Israelis. Interestingly, whereas the mass flight and expulsion of Arab Palestinians in the 1948 War reduced their presence in the state of Israel from an estimated million to just about 156,000, their proportion within the Israeli population would remain constant in the following years, at 20 percent.[31] The enormous number of 2.7 million, naturally unselected Jewish immigrants between 1948 and 1998 (almost five times the amount of the entire Jewish population in Palestine at state-founding) was required to keep the majority-minority ratio stable. In demographic respect, the Jewish state was a "non-Arab state" (Lustick, 1999), in which even the Jewish credentials of newcomers came to be subordinated to their not being Arab.

Mastering the Consequences of World War II in Germany

In contrast to Israel, ethnic migration in Germany has not been central but peripheral to state and society. In addition, despite its limited role in nation building, ethnic German immigration has never been as unambiguous and consensual as Jewish immigration in Israel. Even when, in the 1950s, the fate of some 12 million ethnic Germans expelled from their homelands after World War II figured prominently in public policy and debate, there were considerable tensions between newcomers and natives. The (Catholic) Bayern Partei, for instance, rejected the Equalization of Burdens Act (*Lastenausgleichsgesetz*)[32] of 1952 because "Prussian" (that is, Protestant) refugees would mostly profit from it (Levy, 1999:64). In the debate surrounding the Federal Expellee Law of 1953, a leader of the Bayern Partei dismissed the expellees (whom he referred to as "in-migrated" [*Zugewanderte*]) as "queen-bees (*Drohnen*) for whom the domestic people (*Einheimische*) have to work."[33] To repudiate such claims, the Federal Minister for Expellees, Hans Lukaschek (an expellee himself), stressed that the Federal Expellee Law, which originally was more contested for its redistributive aspects than for the ethnic recognition procedures laid out in it, aimed only at "parity with the *Einheimische*" and thus was not meant to create "special rights for a specific group of citizens."[34] Even when the war-related sufferings of coethnics were most obvious, and when their coethnicity was not at all in doubt,[35] the very fact that a "community of destiny" had to be conjured up by the expellee minister showed that it did not really exist.[36]

Accordingly, the linkage between ethnic migration and the ethnocul-tural tradition of German nationhood is less straightforward and direct than conventional wisdom would have it (as, for example, Brubaker, 1992). In the past there were certainly no precedents for the ethnic-return policy. Moreover, during the crafting of the Federal Expellee Law, one can observe a certain distancing from the ethnocultural tradition. When the definition of who is an ethnic German entitled to return was debated, a member of the Liberal Party (FDP) proposed that ethnicity should be based on self-definition alone and thus be devoid of any objective genealogical dimension. "The belonging to a people should derive from the free decision of each individual alone," and German leg-islation should "provide a model for the future of other states" in this respect.[37] The Federal Minister for Expellees in principle agreed: "The tendency of your proposal is absolutely shared by the Federal Govern-ment . . . You know, my name is Lukaschek, and this is a Polish name. In any case, these are difficult moments."[38] The only justification brought forward in this moment for a definition of *Volkszugehörigkeit* that also comprised an objective dimension was that it was easier for a state agency to classify people "on the basis of specific tangible markers."[39] Except in the negative, there was no reference at all in this exchange to the German ethnocultural tradition.

However, one sees the workings of an ethnic sense of stateness in the fact that postwar Germany, like Israel, has always denied that its ethnic migration is "immigration" at all, but the "return" (*Rückführung*) of coethnics to their homeland.[40] In both cases, this points to an ethnic con-nection between people and "their" states: not states building citzenries in their image, and thus the former preceding the latter, but preconsti-tuted people forming states for their self-representation and protection (which are thus "owned" by them).

Is then Germany the "state of the Germans," as Israel is the "state of the Jews"? A crucial difference between the two is that as a very result of the fateful entanglement between Germans and Jews under Nazism the German ethnocultural idiom of nationhood has in principle been delegit-imized, whereas the idea of Israel as a Jewish state has been powerfully reaffirmed as a safe haven from persecution. German ethnic statehood certainly had institutional grounding in an ethnic citizenship law and in the ethnic German clause of the Basic Law (Article 116). But it was not openly articulated or, if it was,[41] it was immediately rebutted by the charge of "exalted nationalism."[42] In fact, the ethnic dimension of the

(West) German state became internally invisible, as it was transferred into the future (as the mandate of national reunification) and extraterritorialized (as the commitment to admit coethnics). To the degree that there was an "other" that defined the identity of the West German state, it was its East German twin state. And this "other" did not whip up German ethnicity, as Jewish ethnicity was constantly whipped up by the Arab minority within the state; instead, Germany's doubling invited an identification of each half in terms of its sociopolitical regime form, as capitalist democracy versus Communist dictatorship. Peter Brückner (1978:150) has perceptively argued that in postwar Germany "the one nation became decoupled into society and its counter-society." The "nation" disappeared in the contest between "capitalism" and "socialism," which was convenient because of its delegitimization by Nazism. In its understated self-presentation, the West German state was a postnational state, which sought identity in Europe rather than in the outmoded rituals of the nation-state. The underlying mindset was crisply articulated by Karl Jaspers (1960:53), Jürgen Habermas's precursor as West Germany's First Intellectual: "The history of the nation-state has come to an end. What we, as a great nation, can teach to ourselves and to the world is the deep insight into the world situation today: that the principle of the nation-state is the disaster of Europe and of all continents." Whereas Jewish immigration is Israel's proudly exhibited nation builder, ethnic German immigration occurred through the back door of a culturally postnational state.

On the other hand, Daniel Levy (1999:22) has sensitively argued that in the 1950s the ethnic German expellees allowed the "rehabilitation" of Germany's otherwise delegitimized ethnocultural self-understanding: through reference to the "victimhood" of expellees, ethnocultural nationhood could be "dissociated from Nazism" (p. 49). Was (West) Germany at least in this indirect and minimal way a state of Germans, as Israel is a state of Jews? Turning to West Germany's founding document, the Basic Law, one can observe a tension between ethnic and liberal elements. The ethnic elements are tellingly tied to the temporariness and incompleteness of the West German state, suggesting that they were only skin-deep. Accordingly, the preamble of the Basic Law states that it was to apply only for a "transition period" (*Übergangszeit*), until the "unity and liberty of Germany" were completed. Moreover, the "German people," in crafting this constitution, had "acted also for those Germans who were denied participation"—the German division obviously reactivated the traditional noncongruence between state and people. On the liberal side, the Basic Law's preamble commits the new state to a "united Europe" and "to serve peace in the world," and the constitution's first seven articles protect universal human rights independently of citizenship. In contrast to the ethnic provisions in the Basic Law, these human-rights guarantees were formally invested with an *Ewigkeitsgarantie* [guarantee of perpetuity], that is, immunity from future revision or amendment.[43] Interestingly, these liberal commitments all transcend the nation-state. They point to the peculiar fact that in preunity Germany the liberal opposition to ethnic stateness was generally not conducted from the point of view of a "civic" nation-state alternative but from a "postnational" position according to which the entire nation-state construct was found fault with (see Joppke, 1999, ch. 5).

In addition to the Basic Law's preamble, a second cornerstone of postwar Germany's ethnic orientation, and the constitutional foundation of its ethnic migration, is Basic Law Article 116(1), which defines who is a German. It contains a liberal element in simply stating that a "German" is someone who "owns German citizenship," leaving the determination of citizenship to the political process. Accordingly, the German Basic Law never prescribed an ethnic citizenship law, like the one that was in force until 1999. However, Article 116(1) contains an ethnic element in adding that a "German" is also who "as refugee or expellee of German origin [*Volkszugehörigkeit*] or as his spouse or descendant has found reception in the territory of the German Reich according to its borders of 31 December 1937." This meant that (West) Germany was not only the state of its citizens but of certain noncitizens also, if they qualified as coethnics. However, as in the preamble, this ethnic commitment was again to be temporary only. This is expressed in the facts that Article 116 was put under a statutory proviso, and that it appears only in the last section of the Basic Law, dealing with "Transitory and Concluding Regulations."

Next to their different temporal scopes, Article 116 points to a categorical difference between Jewish and ethnic German immigration: whereas the former was an invitation to every Jew in the world, the latter applied only to those ethnic Germans who were "refugee or expellee." From Article 116 alone one might conclude that the pool of potential claimants was both wider and narrower conceived than the actual ethnic migration that would occur under its name: "wider," because there was no geographical specification attached, so that, say, ethnic German refugees from

Pinochet's Chile would qualify as well; "narrower," because in common understanding "refugee or expellee" is someone who is actually forced to leave one's homeland by a persecuting power. The Federal Expellee Law (FEL) of 1953, which spells out the statutory framework for Germany's ethnic migration, reversed this pattern. It was authorized to do so by Article 116 itself, which had been put under a statutory proviso (*"vorbehaltlich andersweitiger gesetzlicher Regelung"*). Accordingly, Article 1(2)(3) of the Federal Expellee Law stipulates: "An expellee is also [one] who as German citizen or as a German ethnic [*Volkszugehöriger*] . . . *after the end of the general expulsion measures* has left or leaves the former eastern territories, Danzig, [the Baltic States], the Soviet Union, Poland, Czechoslovakia, Hungary, Romania, Bulgaria, Yugoslavia, Albania, or China" (emphasis supplied).

This peculiar expellee, who was not actually expelled, but who had to originate from a Communist country, was labeled a "resettler" *(Aussiedler)*. Resettlers, some of whose ancestors had left the "German" lands as far back as eight hundred years ago,[44] and thus before there was anything akin to a German national consciousness, let alone a German nation-state, formed the bulk of German ethnic immigration after World War II. Accordingly, what had started as a temporary measure to integrate the millions of ethnic Germans who were actually expelled from their homeland after World War II was expanded by the *Aussiedler* clause of the Federal Expellee Law and its—rather lax—administrative implementation into an open-door policy for anyone from Eastern Europe and the Soviet Union who could claim, however remotely, German origin.

Selecting Jews and Ethnic Germans

If ethnic diaspora migration is grounded in an ethnic self-conception of the receiving state, one would think that straightforward criteria are available to define a coethnic qualifying for return. This is not so. First, there is a huge gap between the lofty self-descriptions of the state and the need for detailed and explicit selection criteria that allow low-level agencies to sort out qualifiers from nonqualifiers. The first are given by political leaders and intellectuals, the latter are written (and constantly rewritten) by jurists, especially courts who, willy-nilly, had to become involved in adjudicating doubtful and contested claims. The problem of selection is compounded by the fact that in the diaspora constellation no generic selection criteria are available, such as citizenship or place of birth. Much as in asylum adjudication, a case-by-case examination of the truthfulness of an individual claim must be made, often requiring the state agency to reconstruct complicated family histories on the basis of dubious and spotty documents. Furthermore, the implementation of selection rules stands in the crossfire of differently minded state agencies, courts generally taking a lenient and rights-oriented approach, whereas executives tend to take a more restrictive, cost-oriented approach.

The most profound source of uncertainty and disagreement, of course, is about the definition of selection rules themselves. One element of this is the balancing of subjective and objective criteria of ethnicity. In Max Weber's classic account, ethnicity is an essentially subjective, self-defined phenomenon. However, for the purposes of a state's ethnic immigration policies, which require the identification of legitimate ethnic claimants, a purely subjective definition of ethnicity would cast the net too wide and invite the fabrication of ethnicity, particularly when, as in Israel and Germany, ethnic status entails significant benefits and privileges. Accordingly, objective, other-defined tests of ethnicity came to complement, or even to replace, subjective recognition criteria.

The development of this has been very different in Israel and Germany. At the behest of religious groups, Israel shifted from an initially purely subjective, bona fide approach in determining Jewishness to an objective definition, as prescribed by religious law (*halacha*). However, it pulled the restrictive sting out of this narrow definition of Jewishness by allowing the non-Jewish extended-family members of Jews to enter also under the Law of Return, thus corresponding to the material state-building imperative behind Jewish immigration. Germany, by contrast, from the start combined subjective and objective tests of ethnic Germanness. Interestingly, however, the overarching idea was Germanness as essentially a matter of subjective "confession to German peoplehood" (*Bekenntnis zum deutschen Volkstum*), with objective markers only as "affirmation" (*Bestätigung*) of subjective Germanness. This conception contradicts the stereotypical view of Germanness as constituted by objective blood ties (see, for example, Hampton, 1995). However, the subjective confession test had from the start a rather objective tilt, epitomized by the strange legal construction that a confession could be inherited across generations. Moreover, as a result of court intervention, the weight shifted over time from subjective to objective criteria, whereby the latter were taken as "indicative" for the existence of subjective Germanness. In a delicate twist, this was in order to redress discrimination against Jewish claimants for ethnic German status, for whom the subjective confession test was more difficult to meet. Ironically, the definition of ethnic Germanness became more blood-oriented in order to accommodate the victims of a blood-based definition of Germanness under Nazism.

Sometimes overlapping with, sometimes differing from the oscillation between subjective and objective ethnicity criteria, the struggle over selection rules has also been linked to clashing ideologies or political interests. In Israel, the question of "who is a Jew" for the purposes of the Law of Return has been the central battleground over a religious versus secular definition of Jewishness, and it was won by the religious forces. In Germany, a most obviously political determinant in answering the question "who is an ethnic German" has been revealed in a recent change in the status of German-language competence: at first a subordinate aspect of the recognition practice, language moved to center stage in the 1990s, when the state took a double interest in restricting the number of ethnic claimants and in ensuring their acceptance by domestic society.

Who Is a Jew?

The Law of Return originally did not define who is a Jew entitled to return (see Rosenne, 1954:25–26). This was a deliberate omission, to avoid a clash between secular and religious forces over the crucial question of identity, not just of immigrants but of the State of Israel. According to tradition, it was clear that Jewishness, grounded in the Covenant idea, was an indissolubly ethnic *and* religious condition. However, after the establishment of the state the matter became more complicated. This was meant to be a secular state that derived its authority from the people and not from God. Moreover, as a liberal state Israel was committed to the principle of freedom of conscience and religion. A Jew therefore had the right to be either religious or nonreligious.[45] How could Jewishness then still be defined in religious terms? If the question of "who is a Jew" was eventually settled in favor of a religious definition, it was also because the advocates of a secular definition had no better alternative than to suggest that everyone who declared herself a Jew should be considered by the state as a Jew. This meant that the whole world was potentially Jewish—clearly, no state could ever give in to such an overinclusive definition of who belonged to it. The nonfeasibility of the secular alternative tilted the outcome toward the religious solution.

The legislature's initial refusal to deal with the question of who is a Jew naturally could not make it disappear. It only shifted to other arenas, most notably the Supreme Court. The Supreme Court's two central interventions in the "who is a Jew" question show the impossibility of a nonreligious definition of Jewishness, either by virtue of intrinsic argument, as in the famous *Rufeisen* case, or by virtue of political implication, as in the no less famous *Shalit* case.[46]

In the *Rufeisen* case of 1962, the question was whether a Jew who had converted to Catholicism could still be considered a Jew entitled to the right of return. This was no prankish case; it concerned someone who— by the court's own admittance—had "rescued hundreds of his fellow Jews from the Gestapo in legendary feats of daring" (quoted in Galanter, 1963:10), and whose deep and lifelong commitment to the Zionist cause was not in question despite his life as a Carmelite monk. The arguments on both sides of this case were full of twists and paradoxes. Whereas in substance this was a case for Jewishness as a subjective, spiritual commitment to the Jewish people and the Zionist cause, Rufeisen's lawyers still built their defense around the formal argument that Rufeisen was born to a Jewish mother, and thus had to be considered a Jew according to halachic religious law.[47] Conversely, the Supreme Court, in its rejection of Rufeisen's claim, argued that for the purposes of a secular law, such as the Law of Return, a secular definition of Jewishness had to be given, one "as it is usually understood by the man in the street."[48] However, this meant that "[a] Jew who has become a Christian is not called a Jew."[49] In other words, a secular definition of Jewishness in terms of "national sentiments,"[50] as suggested by the Supreme Court, was one that had a religious content, in the sense that one could not be a Christian and a Jew at the same time. While at heart confirming the traditional view that one could be a Jew only through pertaining to the Jewish religious faith, this decision still could be presented as affirming the supremacy of civil over religious law: "Israel is not a theocratic state because, as the present case demonstrates, the life of the citizens is regulated by the law and not by religion . . . [I]f the religious categories of Jewish law applied, the petitioner would indeed be regarded as a Jew."[51] However, the more profound implication of this rule was to define Jewishness in terms of tradition and heritage (which were inevitably religious), and not in terms of a historic break and secular nation building, as envisioned by the Zionists. The *Rufeisen* case was the first admission that the Zionist project had failed. In the words of the court: "Only a simpleton believes or thinks that we are creating a *new* culture here. It is too late for that! . . . Our new culture in Israel will, even in the most extreme case, be no more than a new edition of the culture of our past" (quoted in Galanter, 1963:15).

Whereas the *Rufeisen* case dealt with the marginal question of how one *exited* from Jewry (or rather whether one could exit at all), the Supreme Court's second central intervention, in the *Shalit* case of 1970, dealt with the more important question of how one *became* a Jew, at least for the purposes of state law (the Law of Return included). In contrast to the *Rufeisen* case, in which the rift between religious and secular understandings of Jewishness could be concealed,[52] the *Shalit* case brought it into the open, with far-reaching political consequences, particularly for the Law of Return and the future of Jewish immigration. The origins of this case date back to the late 1950s, when Orthodox religious groups (present in every government coalition since 1948 in the form of the National Religious Party, NRP) became worried about the missing Jewish credentials of recent mixed-marriage immigrants, especially from Communist Eastern Europe (see Samet, 1985:88–89). Up to that point a subjective, bona fide declaration had sufficed to enter under the Law of Return and to be registered as a Jew in the domestic population registry (which in turn determined the "nationality" and "religion" entries on a person's domestic ID card).[53] When a tacit attempt by the NRP head of the population registry department within the Interior Ministry to move the registration practice toward a religious definition of Jewishness was thwarted, Israel had its first political crisis over the "who is a Jew" question. This sequence of events is often misconstrued, and a March 1958 administrative order under a fiercely secular Interior Minister that decreed a subjective definition of Jewishness[54] is taken as the jolt out of the blue that sparked the religious opposition. Instead, the March 1958 order only rendered explicit and reinstated the status quo ante that had been obstructed by the religious forces in the coalition government.

Although it had long been practiced implicitly, this was the first time that a subjective, bona fide definition of Jewishness was explicitly decreed, and in opposition to it the National Religious Party resigned from the government. To resolve the coalition crisis, Prime Minister Ben-Gurion wrote a famous letter to forty-five eminent Jewish scholars in Israel and abroad, the "Sages of Israel" (*Hachmei Israel*), who should advise the government on this matter.[55] The fact that the "Sages of Israel" included a U.S. Supreme Court judge shows the peculiarly nonterritorial nature of Israel as the state of the Jewish people, wherever they resided in the world. As the letter outlined, the thorniest issue in the "who is a Jew" debate was not immigrants seeking entry on the basis of false Jewishness but how to register the children of mixed marriages. "Four considerations" were to guide the Sages' evaluation, two tilting toward an objective-religious definition (that is, to preserve the unity of Jews in Israel and with Diaspora Jews), two tilting toward a subjective-secular definition (that is, freedom of religion and trust in the assimilatory forces of Israeli society). Strikingly, thirty-seven of the forty-five Sages who replied to the letter argued in favor of a religious definition of Jewishness and thus slapped the government's current handling of the issue.[56] Following this recommendation, the government gave out new directives to the population registry department, according to which only a person born of a Jewish mother or properly converted could be registered as a Jew. This was the status quo when the famous *Shalit* case came to the consideration of the Supreme Court.

The *Shalit* case was the ultimate test case of whether there could be a secular-national, as opposed to a religious, definition of Jewishness. It concerned Benjamin Shalit, a secular Jew married to a non-Jewish woman (like her husband an atheist), who wanted his two children registered as "Jewish" in terms of nationality and as "none" in terms of religion. Following the 1960 directives that had been passed upon the Sages' recommendations and that had helped resolve the 1958 coalition crisis, Shalit's children were duely registered as "no registration" for nationality and as "father Jewish, mother non-Jewish" for religion (see Nesis, 1970:54). The children obviously were not registered as of Jewish nationality because they were not born to a Jewish mother. In his plea before the Supreme Court, Shalit brought out the paradox inherent in the refusal to recognize his children as Jews: "Kamal Mimri, an Al-Fatah member . . . is entitled to call himself a Jew; and I, a native of country, and my wife who considers herself a Jewess in all respects, may not register our children as Jews?"[57] And in a foreboding of what would become one of Israel's key problems that this very case helped bring about: "What will happen when the day comes and Jews start arriving from Russia? . . . In Russia, one's identity is registered in accord with one's own choice. Are you going to tell such a person he is not a Jew?" (quoted in Abramov, 1976:300). A slim five-to-four majority of the Supreme Court ruled in Shalit's favor, ordering the population registrar to register his children as of Jewish "nationality."

However, this decision was reached on procedural grounds; it did not decree a secular definition of Jewishness. First, the 1960 directives invalidated in this decision neither had the status of law nor were they based on any law, so that they were deemed in principle unenforceable. Second, it was considered beyond the authority of registration officers to reject information that was furnished to them in good faith. However, while notionally refusing to answer the "who is a Jew" question, the majority judges still implicitly favored a secular definition, if only because they held that a secular law could not decree a religious content. As Justice Berenzon opined, the Law of Return and Population Registry Law were both secular laws, so that they had to apply equally to all citizens of the state, irrespective of race or religion.[58] However, as Justice Silberg pointed out for the minority on the court, this secular posture dodged the problem that Jewishness was at heart a religious matter, and a purely secular definition opened up the bizarre possibility of Christians or Muslims demanding to be registered as ethnically Jewish (Jewish Agency for Israel, 1998).

Much as in 1958, the Orthodox religious groups were furious about this secular affront, and the National Religious Party threatened to leave the government coalition. To avoid this in a moment of national crisis,[59] a hasty compromise was reached that would shape modern Israel as no other political decision has in the last thirty years. An amendment of the Law of Return for the first time defined who is a Jew, and this in accordance with the wishes of the NRP: "For the purposes of this Law, 'Jew' means a person who was born of a Jewish mother or has become converted to Judaism and who is not a member of another religion."[60] Except excluding converts (in consideration of the *Rufeisen* case), this was *grosso modo* the halachic-religious definition of Jewishness. However, responding to the concern of secularists that a narrowly religious definition of Jewishness would deter mixed couples from immigrating to Israel, and thus be in violation of material state-building interests, a second section was added to the Law of Return that invested also the grandchildren of Jews and their immediate family with the right of return, whether their Jewish ancestor was still alive and accompanying them or not.[61] Not foreseen at the moment, this section (4A) would become the inroad for a massive immigration of non-Jewish Russians twenty years later.

While offering a bit for everyone, the religionists as much as the secularists, the 1970 amendment to the Law of Return really satisfied no one. The secularists were bothered by the fact that biological descent, and not spiritual identification, came to define one's main link with Judaism. "[C]onversion being at best exceptional, the normal link to Judaism derives by heredity . . . ad infinitum in an unending chain of pedigree research," wrote a disgruntled jurist (Ginossar, 1970:266). And a Mapam (then part of the Labour Party) leader opined that the act of *aliyah* itself should contain the roots of a secular Jewishness, a possibility that was undermined by the religious-*cum*-biological thrust of the 1970 amendment: "[*Aliyah*] is the supreme act of identification, although of a secular character, an identification that recognizes no limits with the destiny of the Jewish people. If you wish, *Aliyah* is the most profound act of conversion for everyone who wishes to join the Jewish people and become attached to it" (quoted in Abramov, 1976:307). On the opposite side, the Orthodox religious forces were not happy either, because their request to add "according to the Halacha" to the conversion clause in Section 4B of the amendment was not granted. This request was refused because it threatened to antagonize the Diaspora Jewry, whose predominantly Conservative and Reform branches adhered to more lenient, nonhalachic conversion practices. Conversely, Orthodox leaders threatened that the specter of mingling with impure Jews would force them to withdraw from society: "We shall be constrained to grow apart, to destroy the existing bridges and social contacts, and to erect fences" (quoted ibid., p. 306).

The definition of Jewishness that was finally institutionalized in the amended Law of Return was peculiarly asymmetric, religious with respect to the acquisition of Jewishness, secular-national with respect to the possibility of exiting from Judaism. While the Law of Return always figured centrally in the protracted "who is a Jew" debate between 1958 and 1970, this was still a debate in which immigration concerns were peripheral; instead it was a debate about the definition of the Jewish state. Both *Rufeisen* and *Shalit* were no hard immigration cases in which an entry would have been denied because of lack of Jewish credentials. Rufeisen was admitted on the basis of the 1952 Entrance to Israel Law, which regulates non-Jewish immigration, and he died as an honored naturalized citizen of Israel; Shalit's children were Israeli citizens already, *jure sanguinis*. Even for people with questionable Jewish credentials, there was always a different way to enter or reside in Israel. The fact that a subjective definition of Jewishness could be in place for a while in the 1950s shows that either "too many" or the "wrong" people entering was simply no issue at the time. This would change only in the 1990s, when the cornerstone of the Jewish state, the Law of Return, became the inroad for massive non-Jewish immigration.

Who Is an Ethnic German?

As laid out by the Federal Expellee Law, there are two criteria for being acknowledged as an ethnic German qualifying for return. First, one had to be a *Vertriebener* (expellee) "in connection with the events of World War II" (Article 1.1). Second, one had to be either a German citizen or of German origin (*Volkszugehörigkeit*). The link between both is that one had to have suffered "expulsion pressure" (*Vertreibungsdruck*) for one's Germanness. Regarding the first criterion, one could be a *Vertriebener* as someone who was expelled and persecuted by a foreign power, or as someone who had to flee Germany after 1933 because he or she was persecuted by the Nazis for political, racial, or religious reasons. Accordingly, this was a law for the victims of Nazism as much as for those who suffered retaliation by a different state for the deeds of Nazism. In addition, there was a disjunction in the territorial scope of the law between those who already had been expelled and others who were only nominally expelled and would leave on their own demand, "after the end of the general expulsion measures." [62]

With regard to the actual expellees, it did not matter where the expulsion had taken place and which had been the expelling state—east or west. The bill report by the Parliamentary Committee on Expellees *(Heimatvertriebene)* stated that Article 1 covered "not only the collective expulsions . . . in central and eastern Europe, but also . . . individual measures . . . for example, in western Europe and in any other country."[63] An earlier version of the bill that had not yet included a clause for the nominal expellees *(Aussiedler)* listed some of the countries where an expulsion was presumed to be "in connection with the events of World War II"—Italy, Belgium, France, Luxembourg, the Netherlands, and Austria, among others.[64] Such delicate references to violence against Germans committed by a western state were eradicated from the final version of the bill. Moreover, the latter came to include a clause for the nominal expellees, and this was territorially limited to Communist states, among which are China and Albania, not known for harboring any German minority groups. This reveals, as the administrative Expulsion Pressure Guidelines of 1986 put it, the "regime- and ideology-reference" of the notion of resettler *(Aussiedler)*.[65] In other words, only ethnic Germans under Communism qualified for resettler status. By the same token, one could forfeit one's claim by "special tie[s] to the political regime of the state of origin."[66] Communists could not become resettlers. The resettlers' status was obviously not only ethnic but political also, betraying the pivotal role of the Cold War in shaping ethnic German immigration.

During the parliamentary debates surrounding the expellee bill, the Communist Party was keenly aware of this Cold War dimension of ethnic-return migration, and it naturally objected to it. One of its members argued that the Adenauer government's new notion of "expellee," which had replaced the earlier, more neutral notion of "refugee" in 1949, was "revanchist" and a weapon in a new "crusade toward the east."[67] Moreover, he suggested that the territorial scope of *Aussiedler* admission should include Western states and regions too—Italy, Austria, France, the Saar region, the Benelux states, Spain, England, even overseas.[68] This was a provocation against the Allied Powers that stood no chance to be realized.

While without expulsion pressure one could not be a resettler, administrative practice, sanctioned by decisions of the Federal Administrative Court (FAC), came to define it in the widest possible sense. This was formalized in the Expulsion Pressure Guidelines of 1986, which state that "the oppression [*Bedrückung*] of Germans in the resettlement territories continues to exist [and] is generally presumed to be the essential cause for leaving . . . and not to be individually examined."[69] It thus applied also to someone who worked and lived in privileged position in one of the eastern states, simply because "the assumption [of persecution pressure] is valid independently of its probability in the concrete case."[70] According to FAC's case law, *Bedrückung* was already constituted by the "solitarization (*Vereinsamung*) of those who were left behind in the expulsion territories after the latter became largely depopulated of Germans."[71] This made "expulsion pressure" meaningless as a selection criterion, because "solitarization" could also be seen as a result of ethnic migration itself.

Expulsion pressure thus being effectively neutralized as a selection criterion (no one from the listed eastern states and regions could fail in this regard), all the weight came to last on determining the "Germanness" of the applicant. This was easy for those who were German according to the 1913 Nationality Law—that is, the inhabitants of the former German eastern territories or their descendants (even if they were ethnically Slav, and subsequently Polonized via so-called "verification procedures" between 1945 and 1951).[72] It was more difficult for noncitizens, whose Germanness had to be established through the ethnic route of *Volkszugehörigkeit*. Article 6 of the Expellee Law lists two conditions for being ethnically German: the subjective component of a "confession" (*Bekenntnis*) to German peoplehood (*Volkstum*) and the existence of objective marks to "affirm" (*bestätigen*) this confession, such as descent, language, education, and culture. As the critics of ethnic migration never failed to mention (see, for example, Otto, 1990:25), this definition of ethnic Germanness was copied almost verbatim from a 1939 Nazi ordinance, by means of which parts of the populations in the conquered eastern territories had been "Germanized."[73] However, the interesting part of this definition of ethnic Germanness was less its ignoble origins than the reduced role of descent in it. It was in principle possible to be ethnic German without being of German descent, *if* other affirmation marks (such as language or education) existed to corroborate one's "confession" to Germanness.

There was nothing in the German case like the extreme oscillation between subjective and objective identification criteria in the (early years of the) Israeli case. The 1980 administrative Guidelines to Implement Article 6 of the Expellee Law (henceforth referred to as Ethnicity Guidelines) state that subjective and objective components were "two separate and independent legal presuppositions," both of which had to be fulfilled by a person to be recognized as ethnic German (quoted in Liesner, 1988:78). The Ethnicity Guidelines further explicate, in great detail, what counts as "confession" and what are "affirmation marks." However, this explicitness doesn't make either of the two criteria any less muddled. "Confession" is not self-identification, relying on the claimants' *bona fides,* as in the Israeli case, but depends on their verifiable perception by third parties before the end of the war (after May 8, 1945, the beginning of the official mass expulsions, confessions were deemed to be too demanding on the applicant). In fact, the function of "confession" in the recognition procedure was to make sure that the respective applicant had been persecuted for his or her other-perceived Germanness, whereby "confession" took on a rather objective dimension. A confession could be given either as "explicit declaration" (as in the census, passport applications, school enrollment, or the military draft) or in terms of "conclusive behavior." Regarding the second route, Article 2.3.2 of the Ethnicity Guidelines states that "the public use of the German language and the tie to German culture point to a confession to German peoplehood" (quoted in Liesner, 1988:81). Strictly speaking, this rendered the distinction between subjective and objective recognition criteria moot, because objective criteria were used to determine subjective ethnic Germanness.

A second curiosity of "confession" is that it could be inherited, de facto (though not de jure) into the third generation. This is patently against the common-sense meaning of what a "confession" is. Accordingly, the expellee authorities and courts in the 1980s had to evaluate the subjective Germanness of an applicant by evaluating the subjective Germanness of his or her parents or grandparents in or before 1945. An administrative judge called this "beyond the limits of justiciability," and the subjective part of the recognition procedure was in effect reduced to the "non-verifiable claims" of the would-be ethnic migrant (Alexy, 1989:2858).

Particularly delicate was the handling of Jewish applications for ethnic German status. After all, the Nazi model for the Expellee Law's ethnic German clause (Article 6) had stated that "persons of species-alien *(art-fremden)* blood, especially Jews, are never German *Volkszugehörige,* even if they have so far considered themselves as such" (quoted in Otto, 1990:25). Accordingly, the 1980 Ethnicity Guidelines contain a section on how to determine the "confession of Jewish applicants." It states that membership of a religious community is "neutral vis à vis peoplehood" *(volkstumsneutral).* This means that Jews also could have been confessing Germans.[74] For obvious reasons, their confession "deadline" was moved back from May 8, 1945, to January 30, 1933, the day when Hitler was elected *Reichskanzler.* Asking Jews also for a "confession" was, of course, commanded by the Expellee Law. However, it created special difficulties, not only because a Jewish confession was even further back in time—and thus more difficult to prove—than a "normal" one. The more difficult matter was that in the multinational territories of southeastern Europe, from which many Jewish applicants for ethnic German status originated, Jews were themselves considered a national minority, and—as in Romania—one that was an official census category. According to the Ethnicity Guidelines, a Jewish as against a German census entry obliterated one's German confession claim. Because of the separate existence of Jewish and German minorities in Romania, the expellee offices and administrative courts seemed to have put more exacting confession standards on Jews than on non-Jews. In one case, a court even considered the enrollment in a Jewish theological school as an indicator against confession.[75] Furthermore, many of the German homeland *(Heimat)* associations in these territories, participation in which counted as a confession, were anti-Semitic and Nazi-oriented, and it is a strange thing to ask Jews to have been part of that. All this indicated that for Jews it was not just more difficult but *made* more difficult by the administrative state to prove that they were confessing Germans.

In 1981 the Federal Constitutional Court ruled on a number of Jewish applications for expellee status that had been rejected by administrative courts because of unsatisfactory "confessions."[76] This ruling, which reinstated the Jewish claims, wiped out the previous strict separation between subjective and objective recognition criteria. Referring to the intentions behind the making of the Expellee Law, the Court established that ethnic Germanness was at heart a matter of subjective confession. The objective "affirmation marks" had only a "complementary" function in establishing this confession. This meant that the existence of objective marks could be seen as "evidence" (*Indizwirkung*) for a subjective confession. This evidential nexus applied especially to applicants from the multinational states of southeastern Europe and to Jews, for whom "the threshold for proving the confession to peoplehood must not be set too high" because of the larger time gap.[77] This landmark rule changed the balance between subjective and objective components in the determination of ethnic Germanness in deeply ironic ways: in the name of establishing ethnic Germanness as essentially a matter of subjective confession, it upgraded the role of the objective "affirmation marks" (including descent) as "indicative" of this confession, while downplaying the role of the subjective confession test.

Although the tension between subjective and objective ethnicity tests was mildly reminiscent of the Israeli case, a unique feature of the German case is a differentiation within the recognition procedure according to the generation of expellees. This points to a fundamental difference between the two ethnic migrations: in the Israeli case, it is recurrent migration, permanently renewed by intergenerational reproduction; in the German case, it is a one-time migration that revolves around a unique historical event, the expulsion of Germans after World War II. This was clarified in a landmark decision of the Federal Administrative Court of 1976: "The Federal Expellee Law is no resettler but an expellee law, which considers even the resettlers . . . only as the rearguard [*Nachzügler*] of the general expulsion in a specific historical situation."[78] Contradictory to its restrictive thrust, the court established in this decision that someone born *after* the "general expulsion measures" could be a nominal expellee, but for maximally one generation—a condition that was chronically violated by administrative agencies before and after this rule. The expellee law itself was mute on subsequent generations because it was originally meant to apply only to people who actually had been expelled, and one obviously had to have been born to undergo this experience. However, the law's nominal expellee (or resettler) clause opened up the possibility of expellee status for subsequent generations as well. This raised the problem of how to determine the "confession" of someone either too young at the moment of the "general expulsion measures" (the "early born" [*Frühgeborene*]) or born after these measures (the "late born" [*Spätgeborene*]). For both groups the Federal Administrative Court stipulated that "the family association mediates the confession context."[79] This meant that the confession of the claimants' parents was attributed to the youngsters, yielding the strange construct of inheritable confessions.

The general tendency was to tighten the recognition procedure for later-generation expellees, while treating the primary generation (*Erlebnisgeneration*) as leniently as possible. Accordingly, a reform of the expellee law in 1992 introduced an entirely new recognition procedure for ethnic claimants born after 1923, who by now constituted the vast majority of applicants. Their ethnic Germanness was made contingent on the cumulative fulfillment of three recognition criteria—descent from a German parent (only now this was listed separately!); objective affirmation marks such as language, education, or culture; and a subjective confession that could no longer be inherited but had to be present in the applicant herself. Accordingly, while for certain (Jewish) applicants of the primary generation the recognition criteria were de facto reduced from two to one, for all latecomers they were expanded from two to three criteria, all of which had to be fulfilled.

In this differentiated recognition procedure one can discern the interest of the state in reducing ethnic migration and to make sure that those who were accepted would not create an acceptance problem in society. As in Israel, ethnicity was not a primordial given that would yield a clear and stable blueprint for state agencies. However, in Germany the definition of ethnicity was shaped more by political interests of the state than by competing visions of the nation.

This is especially visible in the changing status of German-language competence in the recognition of later-generation expellees. Originally the very absence of German language skills had been taken as a sign of oppression and forced assimilation and thus was held in favor of the ethnic claimant. The 1992 reform of the Federal Expellee Law turned this around, elevating "language" to the key objective affirmation mark, prior to "education" and "culture." The new centrality of language was affirmed in a 1996 ruling of the Federal Administrative Court.[80] The court argued that there is a "close internal connection" between language, on the one hand, and education and culture, on the other hand; someone whose mother tongue was Russian "normally belongs to Russian culture" and thus could not qualify as ethnic German. This important ruling, which came to legitimize the introduction of very tight language tests in the admission procedure, implied a redefinition of ethnic Germanness. In this case, the Russian plaintiff, who descended from an ethnic German mother (who already lived as resettler in Germany) and whose "confession" to German peoplehood was likewise not in question, still did not qualify as ethnic German because he was "incapable of conducting a simple conversation in German language."[81]

The new centrality of language is less the result of a new vision of ethnic Germanness than of the pragmatic need to better "integrate" ethnic migrants. This became explicit in the government response to the Federal Administrative Court's revision of its 1996 decision in the year 2000. In this new ruling the court argued that it was sufficient if the German language had been mediated by parents in the past; the actual mastery of German at the moment of the application was not required.[82] The government immediately warned that the eased recognition procedure would have "detrimental consequences for the social acceptability of this migration," because without German-language competence the resettlers would "no longer be publicly perceived as . . . ethnic Germans."[83] In order to reinstate the administrative status quo ante, in which the language test had held a central role in the "steering" of ethnic migration,[84] the government legislated a new wording of the ethnicity clause in the Federal Expellee Law. Language was now made the *only* objective affirmation mark, which was established if in the moment of resettlement the applicant could "conduct a simple conversation in German." The government argued that this new wording was internally consistent with the meaning of the 1992 reform of the Federal Expellee Law, which had asked later-generation expellees for a credible "confession" at the moment of actual resettlement. "From this necessarily follows," two government lawyers argue cleverly, "that the affirmation mark also must be present at this moment" (Kind and Niemeier, 2002:189).[85] However, such lawyerly consistency was clearly secondary to the overarching imperative of cutting numbers and ensuring the social acceptance of ethnic migrants. In fact, the upgraded status of language in the recognition procedure revealed ethnic German immigration as unmistakably in demise.

Liberal and Restrictive Challenges

Since the late 1980s both Jewish and ethnic German immigration have faced serious social and political challenges. The external cause of this is the same: the removal of exit restrictions in the declining Communist states of Eastern Europe and the Soviet Union. This greatly increased the number of ethnic migrants, many of whose claims to be either Jewish or ethnic German appeared rather dubious. In response, a dual liberal and restrictive challenge to ethnic migration emerged in Israel and Germany alike. Mobilizing the civic-territorial against the ethnic commitment of the state, the liberal challenge addresses the discrimination that is inherent in preferring one ethnic group (even if it coincides with the majority nation) over other migrant and minority groups. In Israel the losers by or on behalf of whom the liberal challenge has been raised are the Palestinians, who were never granted a similar right of return. In Germany, the losers have been asylum seekers and the descendants of Turkish guest workers, whose persecution and membership claims, respectively, were not taken as seriously as those of the ethnic migrants.

The fact that the liberal challenge was raised just when there seemed to be a dilution of the ethnic features of the Jewish and German ethnomigrants points to a subterranean relationship with the restrictive challenge to ethnic migration. Instead of deriving from a tension between ethnic and civic statehood, the restrictive challenge takes ethnic statehood for granted and attacks an overly extensive implementation, or even a misguided direction, of the preference policy that allows the entry of "false" coethnics. In doing so, the restrictive challenge articulates the point of view of usually underprivileged segments of the titular nation, which see themselves threatened by the cultural and economic consequences of unrestricted immigration. As in the liberal challenge, there is a semantic folding back of "returning" coethnics into ordinary migrants, yet with the intention of keeping them out rather than treating all migrant groups equally.

Although the duality of liberal and restrictive challenges has been the same in Israel and in Germany, their scope, content, and outcomes have sharply differed in the two cases. With respect to *scope*, the liberal challenge in Israel has been a maximalist challenge of transcending the Jewish-Zionist character of the state, whereas in Germany it consisted of a more moderate campaign for making the ethnic return policy a subordinate aspect of a comprehensive and explicit "immigration policy." With respect to *content*, the restrictive challenge in Israel was largely (though not exclusively) religious, seeking to limit the entrants under the Law of Return to halachic Jews. By contrast, the restrictive challenge in Germany was populist, incensed by the material benefits and privileges bestowed by the state on newcomers whose ethnic credentials were deemed vacuous across the board. Finally, the liberal and restrictive challenges have yielded opposite *outcomes:* Jewish immigration survived unscathed, while ethnic German immigration has been drastically reduced.

Resilience in Israel

Current diagnoses of Israeli society stand under the sign of fragmentation and the withering of the Zionist center.[86] Labour Zionism had maintained, however uneasily, a synthesis between Jewish particularism and the universalistic precepts of a liberal democracy. After the watershed event of the 1967 Six-Day War, the Zionist synthesis fell apart, and one can observe a polarization between "liberal" and "ethnonational" forces and developments (Shafir and Peled, 2002). Formal state institutions became in important respects less discriminatory and more civic, especially under the growing influence of the judiciary, whereas society and identity became "less civic and more 'Judaic' and religious" (Kimmerling, 2001:111).

In striking contrast to most other Western societies, Israel did not become less but more religious over time. The 1967 War was a catalyst for this, as it brought the religious heartland under Israeli control. As Defense Minister Moshe Dayan expressed the messianic sentiment unleashed by the war, "[w]e have returned to Shilo and Anatot in order never to leave" (Kimmerling, 2001:109). Along with the Holy Sites came 1.5 million additional Palestinians in the West Bank and Gaza Strip. Their incorporation placed before the Israeli state the stark choice of either turning into a binational state by making the new subjects citizens or becoming a nondemocratic state when the citizenship option was denied. To avoid both, the territories were never formally annexed, and the state opted for a "permanently-temporary policy of 'enlightened occupation'" (Cohen, 1983:114), while tolerating or even supporting the religious-nationalist settlement movement that rammed the Jewish Fact into the occupied territories, in open violation of international law. If pre-1967 Israel had been on its way to become a "normal" state with settled borders, a manageable minority *problématique,* and the religious forces kept at bay, post-1967 Israel turned ever further away from this prospect.

At the same time, the liberal forces of a highly developed and globally integrated economy, an educated and Western-oriented society, and a "constitutional revolution" that held the state accountable to elementary rights and freedoms were working against the religious-nationalist fervor unleashed by the 1967 War. If there ever was a society that is simultaneously traditional and modern, religious and secular, mobilized and settled, contemporary Israel is it.

The liberal and restrictive challenges to Jewish immigration have to be seen against the backdrop of a society torn between liberal and religious-nationalist principles and forces. Accordingly, there has been a breathtaking range of objections to the Law of Return in its present form, from the religious-Orthodox standard request to let in only halachic Jews to the post-Zionist call for abolishing the "racist" law in toto. However, there are also other positions that fudge the liberal-restrictive dualism, such as Orthodox groups muting their halachic campaign because "non-Arabs" were needed for settling the West Bank, and Labour Zionists, even some Arab circles, favoring a halachic restriction of the Law of Return because then there would be fewer Jews around and more hope for the peace process with the Palestinians. From whatever angle one approached the Law of Return, any attempted change to it opened up all sorts of unwanted concatenations and consequences, so that, in the end, it was not touched at all.

The Liberal Challenge In his indictment of the Law of Return as a "racist law," Anton Shammas (1989:9) attributes a "perfect cabalistic duality" to it: "It does not declare that a *non*-Jew is *not* entitled to claim an immediate Israeli citizenship and residency." The implicit suggestion is that the Law of Return, in its camouflaging of a negative as a positive discrimination, is structurally equivalent to the White Australia policy. Are the Palestinians the targeted losers of the Law of Return in the same way that Chinese and other Asian immigrants were the targeted losers of White Australia? Among the many differences one stands out: The Law of Return was not passed to ward off an unwanted migration but to solicit a wanted migration. Despite its name, the White Australia policy followed an opposite lexical order, to keep out certain "races" first (by means of crude physical screening) and then to have an open-door policy for the rest, with positive incentives for the most desired national-origin groups. Those who denounce the Law of Return as "racist" seem to be unaware what a "racist" immigration policy *really* looks like.[87]

In one respect, however, the discrimination inherent in the Law of Return is more serious than the one inherent in White Australia: the former goes against people who may consider the same territory their national homeland (the Palestinians), whereas Asian immigrants could not claim a similar right of place in Australia. The exclusion of the Asians was precisely justified as an anticipatory act to ward off such claims in the future. Accordingly, the discrimination inherent in both policies is one with respect to different reference groups. The main reference group in White Australia is external to domestic society, in terms of like-situated would-be migrants who are differently treated on the basis of the "race" attributed to them; in the Law of Return, the main reference group is inside domestic society, in terms of its Jewish and non-Jewish parts being accorded sharply different immigration privileges. Accordingly, the opposition to the two policies has been led in different terms—in abstract human-rights terms in the case of White Australia, addressing the impropriety of judging individuals (whatever their origins) on the basis of their "race"; and in communitarian membership terms in the case of the Law of Return, invoking a historical right of place that has been denied to a concrete group.

The main charge against the Law of Return has always been that the Palestinians who had been expelled or fled in the 1948 war between Israel and the Arab states were never accorded a similar right of return. As the Knesset member of the United Arab List put it: "If the Jewish people have the right, according to the Law of Return, to come to the State of Israel, and this on the basis of a historical claim from 2,000 years ago, why is this right denied to those Palestinians who were forced to leave their towns and villages, not 2,000 years ago, not 1,000 years ago and not 100 years ago, but only 51 years ago?" (quoted in Joppke and Rosenhek, 2002:317–318). At the most general level, this is a classic national (and not "racial") conflict situation, where the presumed "right" of one collectivity clashes with that of another. It is undoubtedly true that Israel's citizenship law of 1952 capriciously excluded from Israeli citizenship the many Palestinians who had temporarily fled from their homes in 1948 and returned shortly thereafter, which left them stateless and without legal residence rights for almost three decades.[88]

However, one could equally argue that these returning refugees were surely not flocking back to "Israel," the Jewish state, and that their exclusion was a condition for the viability of the Israeli state. At least this is how Israeli Foreign Minister Sharett put it before the Knesset in 1949: "[A]llowing the refugees to return without a peace settlement with the neighboring countries would be suicide for the State of Israel, it would be like stabbing ourselves in the chest, no other state in our situation would even consider such a step" (quoted in Shachar, 1999:250 n. 102). This sense of threat is confirmed by the fact that the Palestinians emerged as a national collectivity precisely around the idea of a "return" to their "ancestral homeland" (Khalidi, 1992:29), and emphatically not within an Israeli framework. Until the mid-1970s, the "return" to Palestine was meant to be the end of Israel. As the Egyptian foreign minister put it in 1949, the Arabs intended to return "as the masters of their homeland, and not as slaves. More explicitly, they intend to annihilate the State of Israel" (quoted in Weiner, 1996:31). In this geopolitical context, the Law of Return's implicit discrimination against Palestinians may well have been the price to pay for Israel's existence. As if it were recognizing this, the Palestinian national movement shifted the territorial focus of its claimed right of return from Israel proper to a future Palestinian state that would presumably mirror the Israeli state in its ethnic orientation.[89] From this angle, the question is not how the Law of Return could so blatantly exclude the Palestinian refugees, as claimed by the Arab party member quoted earlier, but why the neighboring Arab states that took in those refugees would do so little to integrate them in their societies (with the notable exception of Jordan), using them instead as a pawn in their confrontation with Israel (see Weiner, 1996:44).

When moving from the macrocontext of clashing nation-building projects to concrete discriminations against Israeli citizens entailed by it, the Law of Return has interestingly proved more vulnerable to revision, at least in its administrative implementation. One of its most concretely felt discriminations was with respect to different family rights for Jewish and non-Jewish Israeli citizens. Until 1996, the foreign spouses of Jewish Israeli citizens were allowed to enter under Section 4A of the Law of Return, which extends the benefits granted to a Jewish immigrant to his or her spouse. By contrast, the foreign spouses of non-Jewish Israeli citizens had to enter under the far more arduous path laid out by the ordinary immigration and naturalization laws, which denies them elementary benefits such as health insurance. When justifying its eventual retreat from privileging the spouses of Jewish citizens, the Interior Ministry argued: "Should the rights of a foreigner who marries a Jewish citizen . . . be any greater than those of a foreigner marrying a citizen who is not Jewish?"[90] This was hypocritical, because equal treatment could as easily have been achieved by upgrading the family rights of non-Jewish Israelis. The downgrading of the rights of Jewish Israelis betrays the true motivation for this equal treatment, which was to fight against "marriages of convenience" that had become an issue after the influx of foreign workers in the late 1990s.[91] Moreover, this unfriendly measure against Jews—originating, *nota bene,* under a nationalist-religious coalition government—reinforced a traditional Jewish norm against outgroup marriage. Whatever the true motivation of the measure, it reveals (and in turn strengthens) a civic norm of equality operating in the immigration domain, which so far had been a stronghold of Jewish particularism.

To be sure, this equalization concerned only the administrative implementation, not the content of the Law of Return itself. A liberalization of the law itself, which would really be equivalent to its transformation into a universalistic immigration policy and thus to its abolition, depends on the prospect of the "normalization" of Israeli state and society. Not by accident, the first stirrings of a liberal challenge to the Law of Return emerged just when the peace process with the Palestinians seemed to be nearing its completion, after the Oslo Agreement of 1993. This is an ironic coincidence, because normatively it could be (and has been) argued that only after the existence of a Palestinian state with its own Law of Return would the parallel Israeli law become legitimate.[92] Such reasoning notwithstanding, shortly after Oslo the editor of Israel's most prestigious newspaper, *Ha'Aretz,* launched a provocative proposal to let the Law of Return expire in 2023, seventy-five years after the founding of Israel.[93] Hanoch Marmari's main justification was that the two pillars of Israel's non-normality existed no longer: peace with the Palestinians was removing the demographic, material state-building imperative of Jewish immigration, and Diaspora Jews were no longer persecuted and either stayed where they were or arrived for merely economic reasons, so that the ideological rationale of the "ingathering of the exiles" had disappeared too.[94]

"Post-Zionism," from which perspective the liberal attack on the Law of Return has mostly been conducted, comes in two versions. One version questions the very legitimacy of the Zionist project, dismissing the latter as based on the original sin of European colonialism and expelling the Palestinians from their homeland (see Pappe, 1997).[95] Another version accepts the legitimacy of Zionism but argues that its goals have been accomplished and that Israel is at the threshold of becoming a "normal," post-Zionist state (see Kelman, 1998). Whatever the accentuation, post-Zionism may be understood as Israel's liberal state movement, which seeks to transform Israel into a state of "all of its citizens" and not just of the Jewish majority. A simple definition of this project has been given by Herbert Kelman (ibid., p. 46): "In a post-Zionist Israel, the status of non-Jewish Israelis would be upgraded and the status of non-Israeli Jews downgraded." In such a state, there would be no place for laws that favor Jews over non-Jews, the Law of Return included,[96] and "the full exercise of citizen rights is unrelated to ethnicity" (p. 49). As in Marmari's scenario, this was presented as not just the wish of liberal intellectuals but as driven by objective forces—most importantly the peace process, which put a brake on Israel's need to be a constantly vigilant and mobilized society; and the diminished status of the Diaspora, which allowed the Israeli state to turn from an ethnic to a territorial orientation.

A fine line divides the so-called post-Zionists from left-liberal Zionists, and the biggest scorn against the post-Zionists has not originated from Israel's right, as one might believe, but from the liberal left. If the idea of a nonethnic "Israeli people" is taken seriously, scoffs Amnon Rubinstein, then there would be no need after all for two separate states in Palestine, and thus for the Oslo Agreement that had energized the post-Zionist drive in the first place: "What would be the ethical, political and intellectual consequence of accepting the post-Zionist concept of an 'Israeli people,' in whose name its critics attack Zionism? Nothing but empty slogans" (Rubinstein, 2000:239). Indeed, post-Zionism is mostly the vision of a small Arab Israeli elite that wants to stay put in (and identify with) Israel and that remains cool to the prospect of a Palestinian state across the so-called Green Line.[97] For them, the "struggle is within the framework called Israel."[98] This struggle is about filling "Israel" with a non-Jewish content, to make it a territorial embodiment of all "citizens" living in it. In a way, this is the project that Zionism had left unfinished. As Anton Shammas (1988:49) put it, this project is about creating an "Israeli nationality" that at present does not exist. This would imply a new flag, a new anthem, or—within the literary domain—the "un-Jew[ing of] the Hebrew language . . . , to make it more Israeli and less Jewish, thus bringing it back . . . to its Place" (Shammas, 1989:10). To which A. B. Yehoshua, a Jewish fellow writer, coolly responded: "For me, 'Israeli' is the authentic, complete and consummate word for the concept 'Jewish'" (quoted in Grossman, 1993:253).

In their fascinating dialogue (solicited and documented by Grossman, 1993, ch. 15), Shammas and Yehoshua restlessly circle around Israel's core dilemma: in order to become a nonethnic state of all of its citizens, Israel would have to undergo a "de-Judaization" and "De-Zionization" (Shammas), for which not even left-liberal Jews are prepared. As Baruch Kimmerling argued, "Jewishness" is one of the two remaining "narratives"[99] within the massive cultural pluralization that contemporary Israel is undergoing: "There are not yet even terms and concepts by means of which to characterize and question [Jewish primordialism]" (Kimmerling, 2001:173). Conversely, Yehoshua objected to Shammas that even most Palestinians "don't want to be part of the Israeli people or nationality" and instead were happy with being a protected national minority (in Grossman, 1993:267). Indeed, in a mirror image to growing Jewish primordialism, Arab Israelis' sense of Israeliness has steadily declined in recent years, from 63.2 percent in 1995 to 32.8 percent in 1999 (Shafir and Peled, 2002:120). On both sides of the Arab-Jewish divide, there is little evidence for the rise of nonethnic Israeliness.

However, more than a state of mind, as which it is negligible, post-Zionism is really an institutional development, in which the forces of liberal statehood and of a secular society are making themselves felt. From the school curriculum, in which Bible-based "Motherland Studies" have recently been replaced by a non-Jewish centered "universal history," to a new formal code of ethics adopted by the Israeli Defense Forces, in which allegiance is sworn only to the anonymous entities of "state," "citizens," and "democracy," one can observe the same retreat of Jewish particularism (see Hazony, 2000, ch. 2). Here Israel joins in a general trend across Western liberal democracies, in which only those national particularisms survive that are deemed compatible with the universal creed of liberty and equality. In Israel, of course, this is compounded by the problem that any reference to "Jewish" is per se discriminatory, and thus to be avoided within the realm of the secular citizen state.

The legal system is the institutional domain in which the post-Zionist trend has been most felt. Because of a conflict between religious and Zionist forces over the origin of state authority—whether God or the people—Israel originally did not have a constitution. After the passing in 1992 of two Basic Laws protecting "occupational freedom" and "human dignity and liberty," Supreme Court Chief Justice Aharon Barak ("the single most influential person in Israeli public life today," which was not meant as a compliment)[100] declared that Israel now had a constitution, on the basis of which the court could strike down government laws.[101] Henceforth only those laws that corresponded to the "values of the State of Israel as a Jewish and democratic state" would pass constitutional muster. This formulation, in the 1992 Basic Law: Human Dignity and Liberty, raised the question of how to define "Jewish." According to Justice Barak, "Jewish" had to be defined at a "high level of abstraction." More than that, Barak continued, "the level of abstraction should be so high, until it becomes identical to the democratic nature of the state" (quoted in Neuer, 1998:12). In a nutshell, a Jewish and democratic state is a state that is democratic. As a result of Israel's "constitutional revolution" (Justice Barak), the government was forced to import nonkosher meat, rabbinical courts were required to apply secular law when dividing property in divorce cases, and—most importantly—the government was told that in the allocation of state land there could not be any discrimination between Jews and non-Jews (for the latter, see Kedar, 2000; Steinberg, 2000).

However, the legal thinning of Jewish statehood stopped short of questioning the Law of Return. On the contrary, this has remained the last vestige of Jewish particularism in the constitutional revolution. When laying out his doctrine that "Jewish" had to be interpreted in a "democratic" way, Justice Barak conceded: "The State is Jewish not in a halachic-religious sense, but in the sense that Jews have the right to immigrate to it" (in Neuer, 1998:12). And when state-owned land was made available to non-Jews in the Supreme Court's famous *Qaadan* decision of 2000, the court struck the same note (in an opinion written by Barak): "[A] special key for the entrance to the house is given to members of the Jewish people (see the Law of Return, 1950), but when a person is present in the house as a legal citizen, he enjoys equal rights as all the other members of the house" (quoted in Kedar, 2000:10, n. 23). This is a striking metaphor, because it admits that the "members" of the Israeli "house" cannot decide who is to live in it. According to this logic, the Jewish state is indeed not a democratic state.

The Restrictive Challenge In contrast to the liberal challenge, the restrictive challenge does not question the Law of Return as such, but only the overinclusive way in which it is currently practiced. Both challenges thus find fault with the law for opposite reasons: the liberal challenge finds it too discriminatory, whereas the restrictive challenge finds it not discriminatory enough because too many non-Jews are allowed to enter under it. We thus get two radically different pictures of the law: in one the law discriminates against non-Jews (especially Palestinians), in the other it is too "liberal" and fails to discriminate against non-Jews. Accordingly, the involved parties in both challenges differ. The liberal challenge pits Israeli Arabs against Jews; the restrictive challenge pits Jews against Jews. More precisely, the restrictive challenge reopens the internal conflict over a secular versus religious definition of Jewishness, which is entirely separate from the external nationality conflict between Jews and Arabs. The restrictive challenge in essence wishes to limit the applicability of the Law of Return to halachic Jews, worried about the "creeping de-Judaization of Israel" in the wake of massive non-Jewish immigration from Russia in the 1990s: "Left unchecked and unreformed, the liberal immigration code effectively will transport to Israel the intermarriage and assimilation plague that is ravaging the Diaspora."[102] Notably, a religious definition of Jewishness was invoked not only by the Orthodox religious parties but also by forces within the "secular Israeli Zionist mainstream" that wanted to return to the original purpose of the law, which had become diluted by the unforeseen consequences of the 1970 amendment.[103]

However, before an increasing wave of non-Jewish immigration would bring the Zionist mainstream into the fold (also because this immigration threatened to undercut the peace process with the Palestinians), the restrictive challenge was entirely a matter of the Orthodox religious forces. Ever since the 1970 amendment had failed to specify that only Jews who had converted "according to the Halacha" would be allowed to enter under the Law of Return, there had been an unceasing campaign by Orthodox religious parties to insert this qualification into the law. In terms of numbers, this was a nonissue—there were at most five or six contested conversion cases per year.[104] Moreover, the Israeli Rabbinate, the sole authority for Jews in personal status matters, was not required to accept the state's definition of Jewishness for its issuing of marriage or divorce licenses, and usually it double-checked each individual for her halachic Jewishness. Many a "Jew" in the state's view was subsequently not allowed to marry in Israel because he or she had failed the halachic test that reigned in the personal status domain. Although devoid of any practical importance, the conversion issue was still of utmost symbolic importance to the Orthodox-religious forces: it signaled their will to supremacy over the Conservative and Reform branches of Judaism, which predominated in the Diaspora. "The Reform and Conservative movements are not part of Judaism," declared a leader of the ultra-

Orthodox Shas party, "They do not obey the commandments. They belong to another religion."[105]

In the Orthodox view, which predominates in the organized Judaism of Israel, the Conservative and Reform Judaisms of the Diaspora are too soft on dogmatic issues and in effect condone mixed marriage, bastardy, and—the *bête noire* of all branches of Judaism—"assimilation." The particular charge is that Reform and Conservative rabbis either dispense with or are not strict enough in following the three requirements of halachic conversion—male circumcision, immersion in a ritual bath, and strict acceptance of all of the Torah commandments. More specifically still, Orthodox Judaism does not condone conversion for extrinsic purposes, such as marriage, and insists on an intrinsic motivation that is measured by devoting one's whole life to the *mitzvot* (commandments) (Abramov, 1976:310). By contrast, especially Reform Judaism, which predominates in the American Diaspora, considers an eased conversion procedure as a last-ditch measure against assimilation in the context of epidemic outgroup-marriage, which since the early 1990s has exceeded the 50 percent mark in the United States. Accordingly, the conversion battle pitted organized Judaism in Israel against organized Diaspora Judaism, and only the dramatic intervention of the latter in 1988 would bring to a terminal halt the Orthodox campaign for excluding non-halachic converts from the ambit of the Law of Return (see Landau, 1996).

In the wake of the massive Russian immigration wave in the 1990s, the focus of the restrictive challenge shifted from the semihalachic conversion clause to the nonhalachic family clause of the Law of Return. Of the 950,000 Russian immigrants entering in the 1990s, about 25 percent are estimated to be non-Jewish according to the Halacha (Shafir and Peled, 2002, ch. 12). More importantly, the proportion of non-Jews among the Russian newcomers increased significantly toward the end of the decade. Whereas only about 5 percent of (predominantly Russian) newcomers were registered as non-Jews in 1990, the rate of registered non-Jewish newcomers hiked to 50 percent by 2000.[106] And a recent scare scenario by Interior Minister Yishai predicts that by 2010 a staggering 96 percent of immigrants entering under the Law of Return would be non-Jewish.[107] In contrast to *pre-perestroika* Russian immigrants, many of the more recent Russian immigrants were not just nonhalachic but nonpracticing Jews, driven more by economic than by ideological motivations, stubbornly sticking to their ethnic habits (such as talking

Russian and eating pork) and—a novelty in Israeli history—forming their own ethnic party, Yisrael BaAliya.

Since 1990 there have been repeated attempts to restrict the extended-family rights (Section 4A) under the Law of Return. These attempts originated from the same Orthodox religious circles that had earlier backed the halachic conversion campaign. Most of these attempts focused on abolishing or at least qualifying the so-called grandfather clause in Section 4A, which allowed the grandchildren of Jews to enter under the Law of Return (irrespectively of the Jewish grandparent's current status, dead or alive, and residence, in or outside Israel). In 1990, the chair of the Knesset Immigration and Absorption Committee, Michael Kleiner (Likud), and Interior Minister De'ri (Shas) first proposed that non-Jewish grandchildren should be allowed to enter only when actually accompanied by the Jewish grandparent.[108] In 1991, Kleiner launched a second proposal, according to which only a family with one person born of a Jewish mother among them could immigrate.[109] In 1994–95, Israel's chief rabbis wanted the entire grandfather clause deleted, so that one needed a Jewish parent in order to qualify for entry.[110] And in 2002, the old Likud-Shas duo of Knesset member Michael Kleiner and Interior Minister Eli Yishai suggested that only those grandchildren should be allowed to enter under the Law of Return who were actually persecuted for being Jewish or whose Jewish grandparent was alive and lived in (or accompanied the grandchild to) Israel.[111]

Two features of these repeated attempts by religious-nationalist forces to abolish or modify the grandfather clause of the Law of Return stand out. First, the abolition of the grandfather clause would have reduced the number of non-Jewish immigrants by only 3 percent, so that the entire campaign must be considered as merely symbolic.[112] Second, however small in scope they were, all of these attempts to restrict the Law of Return never gained majority support, even within the religious-nationalist camp, and they never even reached the Knesset floor. Two factors are responsible for this failure, one discursive, one strategic.

On the discursive side, the grandfather clause became sacralized as the Holocaust clause. This is astonishing. When the measure was passed in 1970, it was simply a concession to the secularists for the religious "who is a Jew" definition inserted into the law at that time. More precisely, it was presented as a measure to accommodate mixed marriages and provide for family unity. It was also a measure that was to make sure that immigration would remain large despite a narrowly religious definition of "who is a Jew." However, in the wake of the Holocaust revival in and outside Israel, which started only a decade later (Segev, 1993:516), the 1970 amendment was refashioned as providing a shelter for all those who were persecuted under the Nazi definition of who is a Jew (which included the grandchildren of Jews). As a *Jerusalem Post* editorial put it, "[i]t is logical that those who would have met Hitler's criteria for annihilation qualify as returnees to the Jewish State."[113] If the 1970 amendment was indeed "written as Israel's 'answer' to Nazi Nuremberg laws, which marked even 'quarter Jews' for extermination,"[114] any change to it could be attacked as an affront to the many victims who were still alive. Interestingly, the last attempt to abolish the grandfather clause, in 2002, included an explicit persecution proviso precisely to accommodate the Holocaust objection—to no avail. As a *Jerusalem Post* editorial put it, "the powerful symbolism of the grandparent clause far exceeds its practical effects,"[115] and this made it lastingly immune to revision.

However, the more important question is not why such a paltry measure of restricting non-Jewish immigration could fail, but why no furthergoing restrictive challenge was raised at all by the religious-nationalist forces. The reason is strategic: massive immigration, whatever its religious credentials, strengthened the claim to the entire land of Israel, the occupied territories included. "[B]ig immigration requires Israel to be big as well," said Likud Prime Minister Shamir at the very beginning of the Russian immigration wave in 1990 (quoted in Lustick, 1999:426). In reality, the underlying rationale was the reverse: if one wanted to keep Israel big, one needed big immigration. "Filling up Judea and Samaria with Jews would solve the political problems here," said a leader of the right-wing Kiryat-Arba settlement in the West Bank.[116] This was in reference to certain rabbis' curious search for descendants of the so-called "Lost Tribes" in Southeast Asia, who would then be converted abroad and brought to Israel as cannon fodder for the religious-nationalist settler movement. But the logic is the same: for the religious-nationalist annexationists Halachic credentials were eventually secondary to the strategic need for large "non-Arab" immigration. From a demographic point of view, the beast to beat through large non-Arab immigration was "parity date", defined as the time when as a result of low Jewish and high Arab birth rates the number of Arabs would equal the number of Jews in the land of Israel (the occupied territories included). In the early 1990s, "parity date" was estimated to be in 2019, with every 100,000 immigrants pushing it back by just one year (Richmond, 1993:264, n. 127).

While never in the open, the political debate over the occupied territories was subterraneously driving the debate over non-Jewish immigration in the 1990s. On the Palestinian side this was immediately understood, and at the very beginning of the Russian immigrant wave there was a sense that this would "constitute additional obstacles to the proposed historical compromise between the Palestinian people and the State of Israel" (Kuttab, 1990:16). While this consideration to a certain degree divided the religious-nationalist forces, it brought the secular Zionist mainstream around the Labour Party to the forefront of the restrictive challenge. "[D]ramatically increased population . . . complicates peace negotiations, and makes future war more likely," argued a Labourite who wished to "save the Zionist dream" by restricting the Law of Return.[117] However, there were also intrinsic reasons to find fault with the grandfather clause of the Law of Return. This was a blood-based concept that made the Law of Return "racial in character" precisely in its secular part (Section 4A). And from this perspective one could turn the tables against the Holocaust rationale: "This readiness to make use of the Nazi's racial theory is problematic and undesirable."[118]

Moreover, within the restrictive challenge and without questioning the legitimacy of the Law of Return as such, one could take a liberal position in attacking the discriminations that were inherent in the grandchildren clause. "[T]he hundreds of thousands of Russian non-Jews admitted under the Law of Return are not returning . . . They have far less claim to the land than Arab refugees from 1948, who can still point to their ancestral homes."[119] Whereas the reference to Arab refugees threatened to slide into a liberal challenge to the Law of Return as such, a safer way to critique it on its own premises was to point to the Jewish losers of the grandfather clause. Some such losers were the Falash Mura, Ethiopian Jews who were forced to convert to Christianity six to eight generations previously and who thus did not qualify for the grandfather clause even though they still considered themselves Jewish. Considering the inequity of accepting Russian non-Jews but rejecting Ethiopian self-identified Jews, one "secular Zionist" observer found that "not even the aegis of the law can diminish the feeling of discrimination," and he favored canceling the grandfather clause.[120]

Under the two last Labour governments of Rabin and Barak, there was also a sense that with the prospect of peace and rising prosperity Israel would attract people with sinister motives: "Now Israel is an attractive place with a prosperous economy," said a foreign ministry official under the Rabin government, "[t]his has created a situation where people who might not be Jewish are trying to get here simply to improve their economic position."[121] This raised the old Zionist desire for a "selective *aliyah*." Rabin's, Social Affairs Minister Ora Namir suggested to bar elderly immigrants unless they were joined by their families, in the assumption that young Russians who preferred to go to Canada or the United States "parked" their parents in the safer and more generous welfare net of Israel: "I cannot accept . . . children shirking a basic obligation towards their elderly parents and placing the entire responsibility for their welfare on Israel while they run off to another country. That is not how I view Zionism."[122] This welfarist rationale, which it is not unsurprising to find in a *Labour* Party, obviously struck a chord among Israelis who were resentful of housing and tax benefits for Jewish immigrants. In this moment Israel's restrictive challenge came very close to Germany's counterpart, which was populist and cost-oriented.

Under Labour's two reigns in the past decade, the scattered calls from the secular Zionist center for a more restrictive Law of Return never gained any momentum. "There is no such thing as 'selective *aliyah*,' and God help us if we get to that," retorted the late Prime Minister Rabin to his cocky social minister, and that was the end of this matter.[123] Prime Minister Barak made the leader of the Russian Jews, Natan Sharansky, his interior minister with the declared purpose of "protecting the Russian *aliyah*,"[124] and, pounding his fist, he decreed that under his rule the Law of Return "will not be discussed or changed."[125] One motive for refusing any such discussion was delivered by Sharansky: "The Law of Return belongs to the entire nation of Israel, not only to those who live in Israel, or those who live outside."[126] Interestingly, the Diaspora constraint was weighing equally on the religious-nationalist and the Zionist challengers to an overexpansive Law of Return. But only the Zionists would openly acknowledge that, simply because the secular Diaspora Jews were allies of the Labour Zionists in their internal struggle with the religious-nationalist camp.

More interesting was a new motive that put a brake on any restrictive challenge from within the Zionist center: the fear that a small change to the Law of Return, however reasonable in itself, would immediately be outflanked on the religious right by a renewed call for recognizing only halachic conversion and on the post-Zionist left by the call for abolishing the Law of Return as such. This became known in the internal Israeli debate as the "Pandora's box" argument. "Today they will stop the *aliyah* of right-wing fundamentalists and, tomorrow, people who share my views," said Jewish Agency chairman Burg in response to calls for a more security-conscious *aliyah* after the killing of Prime Minister Rabin in 1995 (which had been openly endorsed by some Orthodox rabbis in the United States). The apparent fear was that Orthodox forces might seize "well-intentioned attempts" to open discussion on the Law of Return for their own purposes of further discrediting the Reform and Conservative movements in the United States.[127] Particularly in the late 1990s, which were marked by a cacophony of post-Zionist and religious-Orthodox objections to the Law of Return, Labour Zionists were anxious not to play into the hands of their opponents on the left and on the right. This eventually muted a restrictive challenge from these quarters.

In light of the multiple (Holocaust, demographic, Diaspora, and "Pandora's Box") objections to restricting the Law of Return, one must conclude that the failure of the restrictive challenge(s) was overdetermined. The Law of Return survived one of the most turbulent decades in Israeli history without the slightest change. "This is not the time to begin a problematic debate," said Sharansky (by then Minister for Construction and Housing in a religious-nationalist coalition government under Ariel Sharon) after the rejection of the (so far) latest proposal to restrict the Law of Return in July 2002.[128] "No time is a good time," he could have said as well.

Demise in Germany

Between 1950 and 1987, about 1.4 million resettlers were admitted to the Federal Republic, which is an average annual trickle of 37,000. Low numbers kept ethnic German immigration outside the public limelight. This abruptly changed in 1988, when, due to the liberalization of Eastern Europe and the Soviet Union, the number of admitted resettlers jumped to about 220,000. Between 1988 and 1997, a total of 2.2 million resettlers arrived—which is almost double as much as in the preceding four decades (Münz and Ohliger, 1998).

As in the Israeli case, escalating numbers of ethnic migrants, many of whose "ethnic" credentials were rather doubtful, created pressures on the underlying policy. In a second parallel to the Israeli case, these pressures originated from both liberal and restrictive positions. As in Israel, the liberal challenge spoke on behalf of those migrants and minorities who were disadvantaged vis à vis ethnic migrants, in this case primarily asylum seekers and secondarily the (descendants of) guest worker immigrants. However, the restrictive challenge was different in kind. There could not be a "creedal" challenge to return to the original spirit of Germany's ethnic-return policy, because the rationale of this policy—mastery of the consequences of World War II—had irretrievably disappeared. There simply was no original spirit to recapture. Instead, Germany's restrictive challenge was a populist challenge, in which the economic and social privileges given to expellees (who in some respects even fared better than the native population) lost their public support. The populist challenge proved decisive for the center-right government's gradual retreat from ethnic migration.

However, the liberal challenge also was centrally involved in the demise of ethnic migration. At its behest, this migration increasingly took on the features of "normal" immigration—limited by quota, processed through consulates abroad, and so forth. For the liberal challenge, such refashioning of ethnic-return migration was a testing ground for a "normal" immigration policy that was to replace the outmoded foreigner policy (*Ausländerpolitik*) of the guest worker period. And, to the degree that ethnic-return migration was tolerated as a privileged form of immigration, the liberal challenge insisted that an increasingly demanding (that is, individually established rather than generally presumed) persecution test had to be applied. Finally, the introduction of a cutoff point for future ethnic-return migration was the liberal challengers' price for supporting the restriction of the constitutional asylum right, within the historical "asylum compromise" of December 1992, which the liberal left had so far adamantly opposed.

The microdynamics of mutually reinforcing liberal and restrictive challenges has to be put into the larger context of German reunification and the coming congruence of national and state boundaries. To the degree that the noncongruence of the latter had fed (West) Germany's mantra not to be a "country of immigration" and had kept its huge guest worker population outside the citizenry, this condition no longer applied after 1990. "With the realization of German unity, the ratification of the German-Polish border on the basis of international law, and the treaties with the four occupation Powers and Poland, the postwar period is considered to be over," declared a parliamentary commission dealing with *Aussiedler* matters in 1992 (quoted in Levy, 1999:178). The resolving of

Germany's national question and the stabilization of its borders led to a dual process of cutting the ethnic commitment to the dwindling diasporas abroad, and of strengthening the civic-territorial commitment to her non-citizen residents at home. Just when ethnic migration was successively reduced, the descendants of the guest workers, who were born and raised in Germany, were admitted into the citizenry, first by granting them a right to citizenship (in 1992) and later by making them automatic citizens at birth (in 1999). This was no coincidence but part of the same process. After unification, Germany was no longer destined to be an ethnic state; instead of conceiving of herself as the state of her dispersed coethnics abroad, Germany was in principle free to become "the state of all of its residents-turned-citizens," to modify the Israeli formula.

The Liberal Challenge   Just when Chancellor Helmut Kohl declared the reception of ethnic German resettlers "a national task for all,"[129] his center-right government responded to a growing number of asylum seekers by trying to renege on the constitutional asylum right. "Refugees" were both the asylum seekers and the resettlers who were officially deemed to suffer "expulsion pressure." However, how could resettlers from post-Communist Poland, Hungary, or Romania still be subject to "expulsion pressure" when—according to the new "safe country of origin" rule in asylum policy—the same states were officially labeled "persecution free," so that asylum requests from these quarters could be categorically denied? The contradictory treatment of German and non-German "refugees" was first attacked by a leading SPD politician, Oscar Lafontaine. Calling the center-right government's preference for ethnic German over other refugees "*Deutschtümelei,*" Lafontaine declared: "I have certain problems to admit German-origin people in the fourth and fifth generation, while colored people whose lives are at risk are rejected."[130] Chancellor Kohl called this statement "disgusting," and he warned that the Germans would be a "morally depraved people" if they did not stand by their "compatriots."[131]

As in Israel, this was a struggle between liberal and ethnic interpretations of the German state, the liberals rallying around the defense of the constitutional asylum right (Article 16), and the ethnics pointing to the commitments enshrined in the Basic Law's ethnic German expellee clause (Article 116). The one difference was that the commitment to asylum seekers was an abstract human-rights commitment, directed at people outside Germany's territorial and national boundaries, whereas the Israeli liberals' reference to disadvantaged Palestinians meant a group that was not only within the state's borders, but considered its territory their ancient homeland, much as Jews did. In this regard, the structural equivalent to Palestinians in Israel is the descendants of non-European guest workers (especially Turks). They were kept out of the citizenry by an ethnic citizenship law, while the resettlers were immediately made citizens even though they had no concrete ties to German society. This was a more potent comparison because it pointed to a discriminated group in, rather than outside, society. The calling of those Polish, Russian, and Romanian newcomers "Germans who want to live among Germans" (Liesner, 1988:3), while calling those who were born and raised in Germany "foreigners," showed *in extremis* the obsoleteness of the ethnocultural idiom.

Liberal challengers of ethnic migration, in fact, were drawing references both to disadvantaged asylum seekers and to guest worker immigrants. If the asylum seeker reference was more prominent, the reason at one level was that they were—next to the ethnic resettlers—the single biggest migrant group in the early 1990s,[132] singled out by the resettler-friendly center-right government for restrictive measures. However, at a deeper level this also reflected the fact that the liberal challenge was led more in a postnational than in a civic-national idiom. Accordingly, the reference point was more in terms of abstract humanity being violated by the state's unequal treatment of different migrant groups than of the policy's production of concrete losers in domestic society.

A peculiarity of the German immigration debate was that even proimmigrant advocates were slow to ask for the guest workers' civic incorporation, demanding instead that they should find their place in society *qua* foreigners, through granting them a safe residence status, minority rights, or the local franchise (see Joppke, 1999, ch. 5). From this angle it was no scandal that the ethnic Germans were granted automatic citizenship whereas ordinary migrants were denied the citizenship option, even into the second or third generation. Inviting the latter into the citizenry would have smacked of "Germanization" (*Eindeutschung*), which was despised by left and right alike. At an earlier point, when the government was still worried that not enough ethnic Germans were allowed to leave the Soviet Union, a Green deputy had attacked the "hypocrisy" of a (CDU/FDP) government that "demands respect for the minority rights of the Russia-Germans" yet "confronts the Turks in Germany with the alternative 'integration or return'"[133]—obviously implying that the Turks should stay in Germany without becoming a part of it. In this perspective the problem was less that the Turkish Germans were "out" than that the

Russian Germans were "in," and the stake of the conflict was not so much the *kind* as the presence of *any* national semantics in this matter. Accordingly, the Green deputy rejected any "special responsibility of the mother country" toward the Russian Germans, because this was assumed to be a "smokescreen for nationalist demands"; the only support that the German minority in the Soviet Union should receive was the support that was due to "national minorities in *all* countries" (emphasis supplied).[134]

The Greens were the friends of all mankind and thus deaf to any particularism, be it ethnonational or civic-territorial: "Within a politics of open borders the Greens welcome the arrival of any human being, independently of their nationality, skin color, or motivations."[135] While not going quite so far, SPD chief Oscar Lafontaine defended his preference for the "colored" refugee at risk in similarly universalistic terms: "The obligation to humanity (*Menschlichkeit*) is all-important. It is indivisible and . . . not limited by the borders of past states."[136]

At the discursive level, the liberal challenge came in two variants. One was to consider resettlers as just one of several migrant groups and to call for a comprehensive and self-declared "immigration policy" to take care of all of them. As a Green MP put it, "resettlers are immigrants and refugees, independently of their ethnic origins."[137] Another variant was to take sides, particularly with asylum seekers against resettlers, as in the Lafontaine response. Behind these responses were different images of resettlers: as what they were—a sociological minority, seeking to escape poverty and state breakdown—or as what they were made to be in official rhetoric—coethnics, and thus unloved relics of ethnic nationhood.

Reflecting these different approaches, there is a tension in the liberal challenge between wanting to stop ethnic migration and defending ethnic migrants as a discriminated minority. Overall, the first posture dominated within the SPD in opposition, whereas the second dominated among the Greens. Just two months after the fall of the Berlin Wall, the SPD in parliament proposed to abolish the Federal Expellee Law: "[A]fter the political change in the states of east and southeast Europe . . . the German minorities are no longer subject to expulsion pressure. Therefore the basic condition for acquiring expellee status has ceased to exist."[138] The SPD walked a thin line between critiquing the CDU-government's alleged *Deutschtümelei* and joining in the populist-restrictive chorus against the "fake Germans" (*Scheindeutsche*), whose reference points were not disadvantaged migrant and minority groups but disgruntled "ordinary" Germans. Along such lines, a SPD deputy welcomed the first of a series of laws that were passed since 1989 by the CDU/FDP government to restrict ethnic migration: "For a long while already we have pointed out that the privileges of the resettlers . . . vis à vis the domestic population must be removed."[139] And in 1996, eight years after his *Deutschtümelei* intervention of 1988, it was again SPD leader Lafontaine who called for a "limitation of resettler migration," but now in reference to mass unemployment and overburdened pension funds, which was altogether outside of any "liberal" discourse.[140]

Revealing a delicate schism within the political left over the *Aussiedler* question, the Greens used the SPD leader's populist intervention in 1996 to propose a parliamentary resolution "No Polemics against *Aussiedler*": "There is a risk that the late resettlers (*Spätaussiedler*) are made the scapegoats for social and economic problems in this country. Such a strategy massively threatens the social peace."[141] To the degree that the resettlers could be recast from the rearguard of ethnocultural nationhood to a discriminated minority, the Greens (as well as the PDS on the far left) took up their cause. This implied recognition of Germany's "historical obligation" to admitting resettlers, and thus a move away from the Greens' earlier "postnational" denial of any such obligation.[142] The changing social profile of the resettlers, three-quarters of whom are now believed to have no ethnic German traces left in them,[143] made it increasingly plausible to perceive them as ordinary "migrants," and as such they became acceptable to the Greens.

While there were obviously nuances within the liberal challenge between stopping ethnic migration or defending ethnic migrants from a "minority" point of view, the liberal challenge converged on the demand to embed the ethnic-return policy within a "comprehensive" immigration policy. As the Green migration spokesman Özdemir put it, "[i]n the long run all migrants (*Zuwanderer*) should be selected independently of their origins, and according to the same criteria. The resettlers . . . will play an important role in this in the future, not least because of their discrimination in the GUS states, as well as because of existing family ties."[144] However, except a vague hint that this could imply a "reduction of the quota for resettlers," Özdemir remained silent about the concrete implications of a "comprehensive" immigration policy for resettler reception.[145] The growing chorus of those who called for an "integrated program" (*integrales Gesamtkonzept*)[146] to coordinate Germany's multiple and fragmented migration policies, from asylum to ethnic resettlement and seasonal labor, ignored that ethnic migration (like asylum migration) is constitutional, "as-of-right" migration. Short of a constitutional change, this severely limits the state's discretion in this area. Tellingly, when a self-conscious immigration policy finally came, in terms of the Immigration Law (*Zuwanderungsgesetz*) passed by a SPD/Green government in 2002,[147] the only change for resettlers was a further tightening of the language test (which now was imposed on family members too), accompanied by the hope that in the course of time the reservoir of ethnic migration would become naturally depleted.

The Restrictive Challenge   In the context of a center-right coalition government in power during most of the 1990s, the restrictive challenge had to be more immediately effective than the liberal challenge to ethnic German immigration. The Federal Expellee Law of 1953, the legal basis of ethnic migration, had in the first been an integration law that provided a long list of positive discrimination measures (see Otto, 1990:193–208). Elderly resettlers, for instance, received fictionally wage- and employment-based pensions that equaled or even exceeded those of comparable native Germans, even though they had never worked in Germany and thus had not contributed to the social security fund.[148] "Who has lost his home and property because of his Germanness may well expect that the great insurance community of West Germany will compensate him for this," said the responsible minister during the crafting of the Federal Expellee Law.[149] This reasoning may have been appropriate in early 1953, when the number of resettlers was down to a trickle and, because of exit restrictions in all Communist states, was likely to decrease even further. The argument became anachronistic when masses of them arrived after 1988, with a notably smaller sense of obligation on the part of West Germany's "great insurance community."

Against the backdrop of increasing mass unemployment and slimming welfare benefits for natives, the generous benefits bestowed upon the resettlers had to stir massive resentment and social envy. By 1990, over 80 percent of the public was in favor of restricting ethnic migration, which was deemed by most economically rather than ethnically motivated (Levy, 1999:143). Pushed by the recent successes of the far-right *Republikaner* party, which was the first to scandalize the privileges for ethnic resettlers, it was again a Bavarian conservative party, the CSU, in an interesting rehash of the 1950s' constellation, that started campaigning from within the political mainstream against overly generous pensions for resettlers (Puskeppeleit, 1996:112).

In response to the collapse of public support for ethnic migration, the center-right government quickly retreated from its "national task" approach. A few months after passing an ambitious Special Program for Integrating Resettlers in 1988, the focus shifted toward keeping resettlers in their places of origins, by means of development aids and securing minority and self-government rights in eastern Europe and Russia: "The primary goal of our policy is to improve, within the framework of international relations, the living conditions of the Germans in the resettlement areas, so that they can maintain their German language and cultural traditions and identity. No German in these areas is called upon to come into the Federal Republic."[150]

For the restlessly mobile, a series of laws was passed since 1989 to make immigration more difficult. The Integration Adjustment Act of January 1990, among other things, replaced wage-based unemployment benefits by a standardized and more modest "integration money," limited to one year. The Interior Minister euphemistically defended this as in the resettlers' own interest, but admitted that he was bowing to popular pressure: "With the Integration Adjustment Act the resettlers are to be saved from the misunderstanding that they receive more benefits than comparable, long-established Germans."[151] Six months later, the Resettler Reception Law shifted the application procedure to the countries of origin. This amounted to an unofficial quota system, almost halving the number of admitted resettlers from their all-time high of 400,000 in 1990 to 220,000 in 1991.

The restrictive trend culminated in the Law on Settling the Consequences of the War *(Kriegsfolgenbereinigungsgesetz)* of 1993. This was a compromise between the ruling CDU and the oppositional SPD. The SPD had wanted to put an end to ethnic migration as such by means of a "deadline" *(Stichtag)*, after which no further applications were to be accepted, arguing that after the liberalization of Eastern Europe there was no longer any "expulsion pressure." On the other side, the CDU rejected such a "deadline," but interestingly with the defensive argument that the resulting "exit panic" would further increase ethnic migration. As the government's Commissioner for Resettler Affairs realistically envisioned the consequences of a deadline, "all German ethnics . . . in (the resettlement states) will provisionally file a claim to be admitted. They have to do this in order not to lose the chance of leaving later . . . A deadline will bring more resettlers than before."[152] This way of rejecting an end to ethnic migration implied a considerable mellowing of the earlier national-solidarity rhetoric; the wish to decrease ethnic migration had evidently become consensual at this point.

There was still particular bite to the SPD demand for phasing ethnic migration out, because the parliamentary opposition's consent was needed for the center-right government's parallel plan to curtail the constitutional asylum right. In the so-called Asylum Compromise of December 1992, the SPD gave in to the long-resisted restriction of the asylum clause, but only at the price of restricting ethnic migration too. Accordingly, the *Kriegsfolgenbereinigungsgesetz*, which (among other things) implemented the *Aussiedler* component of the Asylum Compromise, bears the mark not only of the restrictive but also of the liberal challenge to ethnic migration. In a further concession to the SPD, the Asylum Compromise contains a section that asks for a liberalized access to citizenship for guest worker immigrants, while restricting it for emigrant Germans "without ties to the state territory."[153] The Asylum Compromise thus suggests a direct connection between the German state's loosening of ties with its emigrant and diaspora communities abroad and the strengthening of ties with its noncitizen residents at home, making it a critical juncture in the transition from ethnic to civic-territorial statehood.

The crucial novelty of the new law is to deny the status of resettler to all persons born after January 1, 1993. This means that ethnic German immigration has in principle come to an end; it will expire with the natural lives of all potential claimants born before 1993. This was the compromise offered to the SPD for the government's rejection of a deadline for new claims. For those still eligible to apply, the procedure has been fundamentally reshuffled. First, an official quota of 200,000 admissions per year was established (further reduced to 100,000 a few years later). Second, except for applicants from the former Soviet Union, the existence of expulsion pressure was no longer to be presumed but had to be proved by the applicant. Third, the criteria for *Volkszugehörigkeit* have been tightened for applicants born after December 31, 1923, as previously outlined.

Next to establishing a generational cutoff point for new claims, the second important novelty of the new law is to make proven German-language competence central to the recognition procedure. As the parliamentary report accompanying the *Kriegsfolgenbereinigungsgesetz* states, "the central affirmation mark of the German *Volkszugehörigkeit* is the mastery of the German language" (quoted in Peters, 2000:1373). Motivated by the wish to better "integrate" ethnic migrants, this new emphasis is as such difficult to reconcile with the official logic of "returning" coethnics—how could true "co-ethnics" create an "integration" problem? Harsh new guidelines stipulate that the language test, which has become obligatory since the Federal Administrative Court's landmark decision of November 1996, cannot be retaken, because—as the government says—its purpose is the "determination of a status." By 2000, about half of all applicants in Russia failed the individual language test and thus, once and for all, forfeited their chances to be admitted as resettlers. At the same time, the German government generously finances German-language classes throughout Russia, which are currently attended by over 100,000 potential resettlers. This shows the "integration" concern behind the mandatory language test—the German government simply wants to make sure that resettlers are not subject to "integration" problems in Germany. Making language competence the key to admission amounts to conceding the obsoleteness of "ethnic return" migration. The new language policy is contradictory in a second respect. If its official purpose is "determination of a status," why does the government help to create this status by means of its self-proclaimed "great language offensive," offering some 128,000 extracurricular places of German language instruction throughout Russia and Kazakhstan in 1997 alone?[154]

There is an unresolved tension between the status determination and integrative dimensions of the language tests. The new ethnicity clause within the 2001 Late Resettler Status Law stipulates that the capacity to "conduct at least a simple conversation in German" has to be the result of "mediation within the family" (*familiäre Vermittlung*). From this angle, the "great language offensive" amounts to state-supported cheating. As Münz and Ohliger (1998) put it with some understatement, the language classes could have the "unintended effect" of increasing rather than decreasing the number of ethnic claimants. However, this unintended increase is bound to be short-term only, because there cannot be ethnic Germans born after 1992.

Having reviewed the liberal and restrictive challenges to ethnic German immigration, can one say that one was more important than the other in the decline of this migration? First, in terms of the central role played by the SPD in the reduction of ethnic migration, there was a significant blurring between the two challenges, as the SPD wavered between a populist questioning of the ethnic migrants' credentials and privileges and a liberal call for a more equitable treatment of all migrant groups, asylum seekers included. Second, if one assumes that of the two criteria that made one a resettler the liberal challenge centered more on the persecution criterion, whereas the restrictive challenge was more aroused by false or diluted coethnicity, one must keep in mind that the persecution criterion was lexically prior to the coethnicity criterion. Even the most committed ethnonationalists (of which there are not many today) have to concede that a claimant's German ethnicity *alone* had at no point been strong enough to justify and trigger a claim for admission, and that without the persecution rationale there could be no ethnic German immigration. This was a liberal limitation that was built into this migration from the start. Since SPD leader Lafontaine's early polemic about two kinds of (German and non-German) "refugees," a central thrust of the liberal challenge had been to put its finger on the persecution rationale that justified the positive discrimination inherent in ethnic-return migration: Was it still valid or not?

Conversely, one should not exaggerate the impact of questionable coethnicity, which might suggest that not the weakening but the very strength of ethnic nationhood conditioned the demise of ethnic German immigration. A tightened persecution proviso, desired by the SPD, essentially limited ethnic migration after 1992 to people from the Eurasian successor states of the Soviet Union. While for Eurasian claimants the existence of persecution is still automatically assumed, it is only a question of time for this to be questioned too. When SPD-led Rheinland-Pfalz launched a (still ongoing) campaign to impose a personal persecution test on Eurasian would-be ethnic migrants also, the center-right federal government of the time rebuffed it in traditional terms: "Abduction, persecution, and long-standing discrimination have destroyed the structures of the German minority so lastingly that no special proof is required in which way a concrete person has been affected by this."[155] However, there was already a more subtle, tactically motivated response at this point: if persecution was no longer presumed on part of the German state, the Russian government would lose an incentive for continuing its course of "rehabilitating" the Russia-Germans.[156] From this angle, the days of the persecution presumption are numbered with respect to the Russia-Germans too. If this presumption falls, ethnic German immigration would shrink to insignificance even before its inevitable generational depletion. *This* ending would be one that bears the exclusive imprint of the liberal challenge to ethnic migration.

In its strongly reduced form since 1992, ethnic German immigration is supported today by a cross-party consensus, according to which the inflow should be reduced as much as possible, while the state accepts the "responsibility for the German minority" in eastern Europe and Russia.[157] Whenever a new restrictive measure against the "German minority" is introduced, it is more the "minority" than the "German" component that is mobilized in protest against it, by whatever party is the parliamentary opposition at the moment. This implies many a curious reversal. When the Liberal Party (FDP) was still in power, a party deputy found no problem with a measure that tied social benefits to the resettler's mandatory residence in certain (underrepresented) *Länder*;[158] when removed from the government bench, the same deputy argued to the opposite that such a measure amounted to a "massive limitation" of the "constitutional right of free movement."[159] Strikingly absent in these wrangles is any reference to the "Germanness" of the migrants—all the Liberal Party turncoat would mention in this respect was his indignation that the SPD/Green government had not proposed a similar tying of social benefits and mandatory residence "for *all* migrants" (emphasis supplied).[160] Similarly, when an SPD/Green government tightened the ethnic recognition procedure in the 2001 Late Resettler Status Law, all that a CDU deputy would say against it was that "a specific migrant group, the resettlers, is targeted here for restrictions."[161] The fact that even former proponents of ethnonational rhetoric now refer to the resettlers as "migrants," all of whom should receive equal treatment, testifies to the greatly diminished status of ethnic German immigration.

Conclusion

This chapter had two objectives: to show some communalities of ethnic "diaspora" migration; and to account for a significant internal variation within the diaspora constellation, the resilience of ethnic migration in Israel and its demise in Germany. What have we learned in both respects?

A first shared feature of the diaspora constellation is to force the state into the difficult business of checking individual identity claims—not unlike asylum policy, in which individual biographic claims are the subject of an excruciating recognition procedure. In this the diaspora constellation differs from the postcolonial and settler state constellations, in which citizenship or place of birth functioned as generic proxies for ethnicity. A second source of uncertainty was not just the application but the very definition of recognition criteria. Answers to the "who is a Jew" and "who is an ethnic German" questions did not derive from a fixed sense of collective identity, but instead were plastic, subject to conflict, and shaped by political interest or ideology. In Israel, the "who is a Jew" question went to the heart of the definition of the state, which was contested between secular and religious forces. In Germany, political interest conditioned an upgrading of language in the definition of ethnic Germanness. In doing so, the state responded to the oddity of sociological non-Germans entering as official coethnics, which had brought up the public against the policy and found concrete manifestation in obvious integration problems (see Dietz and Hilkes, 1994). If the state still insists that the language test is determination of a status and thus cannot be repeated, it also admits that the status of ethnic German is more the result of exogenous policy considerations than of primordial ethnicity. All this is powerful affirmation of Max Weber's "constructivist" vision of ethnicity.

This leads to a second feature of ethnicity-examining migration policies: the production of ethnicity by the very policies that are meant to presuppose and to passively register this ethnicity. These policies are "performative," they help create the ethnic reality that they nominally presuppose (as argued in a slightly different thrust by Bourdieu, 1991; see also Brubaker, 2002). This paradox is also known from affirmative action policies in the United States, in which preferential race quotas in college admission or public employment provide an incentive on the part of individuals for identifying along "minority" lines (see Ford, 1994). In the German case, the state even knowingly supports strategic behavior on the part of would-be migrants, in terms of funding the language courses that produce (or at least sufficiently improve) the competence that is then deemed to be the result of "family mediation." Strategic identification on the part of would-be migrants is invited by the high material benefits connected with diaspora migration but also by some demographic features of the sending regions. The pool of applicants for ethnic German or Jewish status in eastern Europe and Eurasia is not sharply bounded but marked by high degrees of intermarriage and cultural and linguistic assimilation with their local environments (see Münz and Ohliger, 1998). Especially with respect to later-generation Russia-Germans, German authorities had to deal with individuals who repeatedly changed their officially registered nationality entries in domestic Russian passports (which were self-defined and voluntary),[162] evidently for strategic reasons;[163] and the number of resettlers from certain states (such as Poland) exceeded existing estimates of the size of the German minority there (Alexy, 1989:2856). It is therefore not far-fetched to assume that not "real" ethnicity but the "official" ethnicity of the receiving state is driving this strangely "non-Euclidean" immigration, in which "outmigrations may increase rather than decrease the reservoir of potential ethnomigrants" (Brubaker, 1998b:1053). No wonder that more recently this migration has created massive integration problems. Only 22 percent of resettlers admitted in the first nine months of 2002 were ethnic German, the rest being non-German family members; and the bulk of this small ethnic core originated itself from mixed backgrounds that allow for multiple ethnicity options.[164]

As the most persistent form of ethnic migration in the liberal state, diaspora migration has some "liberal" checks built into it. It is notionally decoupled from "immigration," which absolves the state from any non-discrimination norm in this domain. To the degree that the underlying policy discriminates, the direction of this discrimination is positive, not negative. Finally, like all positive discrimination in a liberal state, this one is also justified in reference to remedying a disadvantage for the respective group, which in this case is constituted by the presumed "persecution" that the favored group is exposed to in a foreign state. We saw that the degree of explicitness of the persecution rationale differs across cases. In a world divided into nation-states, one may presume that any group that differs from the titular nation(s) will suffer from some (however marginal) disadvantages and restrictions that may justify a positive discrimination on part of the receiving state. In the Jewish case, the entire self-description of the collectivity and of the state that represents it is couched in terms of the diaspora experience, so that being Jewish becomes equivalent to being persecuted. This creates a paradox: a corrective and thus inherently temporary measure is elevated into a state-defining (and thus more than temporary) measure. Built into the self-definition of collectivity and state, the "persecution" rationale is nowhere to be explicitly found in the Law of Return and its administrative implementation. In this the Israeli differs from the German case, where a persecution rationale was written into the law and observed in its implementation, and which allowed inflows to be delimited in geographic and temporal respects. Somnolent during the Cold War, the persecution rationale was resurrected thereafter as an effective tool to curtail ethnic migration.

Despite these liberal checks built into ethnic diaspora migration, it still provoked a "liberal challenge" in both cases examined here, in terms of this migration's domestic minority losers in Israel, and (predominantly) its extradomestic losers in Germany. While the possibility of a liberal challenge is a shared feature of all types of ethnic migration, a distinct feature of the two diaspora cases examined in this chapter is its coincidence with a significant "restrictive challenge," which addresses the economic and cultural costs of immigration in general. The restrictive challenge results from the high visibility of this migration from a certain moment on, which casts doubt on its premise, the coethnicity of migrants—full churches and mosques in Israel, Russian-speaking and foreign-mannered *Aussiedler* enclaves in Germany are the typical starting points of restrictive challenges. The two challenges are differently motivated: the liberal challenge wants to have ethnic migrants treated equally with other migrants, while the restrictive challenge (usually) wants to stop this migration altogether.[165] Although they are differently motivated, the interesting matter to observe in this chapter were "synergistic" effects between the liberal and restrictive challenges, one reinforcing the other, which could grow into a severe threat to ethnic migration. Such synergy was directly observable in the German Asylum Compromise of 1992, which led to the death in principle of ethnic German immigration. On the other hand, the specter of a liberal-*cum*-restrictive, total attack on the Law of Return motivated the Zionist mainstream in Israel not to touch this law at all.

Turning from the communalities to internal variations of both cases, the contrast of resilient Jewish immigration in Israel and declining *Aussiedler* immigration in Germany stands out. Despite all the (sociologically appealing) noise of liberal and restrictive mobilizations against both ethnic migrations in Germany *and* Israel alike, this outcome was overdetermined. In a way, we *are* dealing with two rare examples of "intended consequences" in society and history. Germany's ethnic migration was meant to accommodate a unique historical event, the expulsions and repressions that ethnic Germans suffered in retaliation for World War II. That episode is now closed, and with it the migration engendered by it. Israel's ethnic migration was never meant to be temporary only, as it came to define the central purpose and raison d'être of the Jewish state. This ideological underpinning, in combination with the Jewish state's precarious positioning in a sea of hostile Arab states and people, guarantees that Jewish-priority immigration will not stop any time soon.

Considering the design of this study, it is tempting to read this outcome as a "victory" of liberal state principles in Germany and as their "defeat" in Israel. However, such a reading omits an important point: both states ended up in their respective positions only with the "help" of the other. The coming of the liberal state in Germany was premised on the compromising of the ethnocultural tradition that was the result of the Holocaust. Conversely, decreeing a "liberal" state on Israel, Saint-Just-style, abstracts from Israel's historical roots and asks for nothing less than a different state for a different people.

5

The Liberal State between De- and Re-Ethnicization

If one compares the first national immigration policies crafted by Western states at the twentieth century's beginning with those conducted by such states at the century's end, it is obvious that "ethnicity" has come to play a greatly reduced role in them. This is as such surprising, if one considers that the function of immigration policy (shared with nationality law) is to police the (always particular) boundaries between national societies, and its persistent status in international law as prime expression of a state's sovereignty. The reduced role of ethnicity in contemporary immigration policies indicates that liberal norms have circumscribed what states can do in this area, rendering the underlying sovereignty one on paper only. One could even infer from this that the only legitimate self-descriptions of national societies are liberal self-descriptions, according to which all of them are in principle joinable in time, irrespective of an immigrant's ethnic origins. In his modernization theory, Talcott Parsons (1971:15) has argued along such lines that the "values" integrating modern societies had to become increasingly "generalized" to cope with these societies' increased complexity and centrifugal tendencies. One does not have to subscribe to the Parsonian theory of integration through values to understand that an increasing differentiation of society, which creates the "individual" as distinct and different from any particular group or stratum, renders obsolete an ethnic immigration policy that considers the individual only as the representative of a group.

To say that the role of ethnicity in the contemporary liberal state's immigration policy has shrunk is not to say that it has disappeared or that it eventually will disappear. This study has shown that the uses of ethnicity in states' migration policies were and are manifold, some more, others less compatible with liberal principles. Three distinctions are relevant for understanding why some ethnic migration policies persist while others have disappeared: the discriminatory direction of the policy (positive or negative); the relative salience of ethnicity in the selection process (dominant or subordinate); and the question of whether the policy creates a loser.

The first relevant distinction is the one between positively and negatively discriminatory policies. The English-speaking settler state constellation showed that negatively discriminatory policies, in which one or several groups are explicitly targeted for exclusion, have been extinguished root and branch. Wherever the suspicion of negative discrimination may arise today, in or outside the settler state context, the underlying policy is branded as "racist," even where no phenotypical distinctions are involved—an example being the Palestinian critique of Israel's Law of Return. In the narrower settler state context, the shadow of negative race discrimination looms so large that even positive discrimination has become impossible. When in the early 1990s more quota space was to be carved out in U.S. legal immigration policy for the Irish, a group of considerable standing in America's immigrant pantheon, no European-style "cultural affinity" or "special link" rhetoric was available for this; instead, all reference to a particular group in law and policy had to be strenuously avoided, and the Irish cause could be pursued only as a general quest for "diversity" immigration.

Beyond the settler states, the outlawing of negative "race" discrimination has grown into the strongest international regime norm in the migration domain, along with the right of asylum (Goodwin-Gill, 1978, ch. 5). This is codified in the United Nations' International Convention on the Elimination of All Forms of Racial Discrimination (1966); its Article 1(3) exempts matters of "nationality, citizenship or naturalization" (a formula that is usually taken to include immigration) from its reach, but only "provided that such provisions do not discriminate against any particular nationality."

The prohibition of negative race discrimination has set a baseline for all other ethnically selective migration policies waged by Western states after World War II, including those in the "postcolonial" and "diaspora" constellations. This prohibition notwithstanding, it is obvious that at the "northwestern" end of the postcolonial constellation a negatively discriminatory intention had been driving the closing of the respective migration. This was especially visible in the British case, where public displeasure about nonwhite New Commonwealth immigration whipped hesitant elites into restricting the latter. That "race" was involved in this restriction is proved by the fact that similarly massive but phenotypically inconspicuous Irish migration continued unabated. Although in one instance the European Court of Human Rights formally condemned this policy as "racist" (Joppke, 1999:109–110), and domestic critics did not get tired of launching this accusation across the board, the British state generally got away with restricting postcolonial immigration because of the legal-political peculiarity of the latter: it was migration enabled by a positive derogation from a generally restrictive immigration regime, and the restrictive move consisted of assimilating postcolonial to "normal" migrants, all of whom came to be treated equally under a common regime. In an ironic twist, a nondiscriminatory, universalistic immigration policy was achieved by means of a racially mischievous intention, wherever the latter may have been originally located—at the level of elites (Paul, 1997) or of the mass public (Hansen, 2000). In a similar vein, the French case showed that even within an ethnically neutral immigration regime that was conditioned more by the French Republican legacy than by contemporary liberal norms, there is ample space for informal negative discriminations, which in this case were targeting Algerian immigrants.

The matter is altogether different with respect to positive discriminations. They are expressly allowed in Article 1(4) of the UN Convention on Eliminating Racial Discrimination, if only on a remedial and temporary basis, for the sake of helping out an aggrieved "minority" (a word not used but implied in the article). All ethnically selective migration policies that still exist today are positively selective. Interestingly, however, not all of these policies are justified in remedial minority terms. In fact, minority rhetoric is limited to the strong "return" provisions that one finds in the diaspora constellation. At the "southwestern" end of the postcolonial constellation, we found a rather different justification of weaker positive discriminations in terms of "cultural affinities" and "special links." Such stubbornly maintained positive discriminations, which may appear strange to American or Australian ears that are used to the elite mantra of "nondiscriminatory" immigration policies, are premised on the absence of a legacy of race discriminations in the respective states.

At least in one instance, an international court has expressly allowed such positive discriminations. Ruling on Costa Rica's privileged treatment of Ibero-Americans and Spaniards in its naturalization procedures, the Inter-American Court of Human Rights held that this did not violate the American Convention of Human Rights, because its beneficiaries "objectively . . . share much closer historical cultural and spiritual bonds with the people of Costa Rica" (quoted in Orentlicher, 1998:324). Moreover, as the court continued, "[t]he existence of these bonds permits the assumption that these individuals will be more easily and more rapidly assimilated within the national community and identify more readily with the traditional beliefs, values and institutions of Costa Rica, which the state has the right and duty to preserve" (ibid.). Along such lines, the liberal, promigration magazine *The Economist* recently fathomed that "opening the doors" for more immigration in Europe could involve "favouring [migrants] . . . from culturally similar backgrounds," because they "seem to integrate most readily."[1] Although such a policy may be more difficult to carry through than meets the eye,[2] these examples show the vitality of positive ethnic discriminations in the real world, even though they may run counter to the normative constructions of the liberal theorist.

However, the "real-existing" positive ethnic discriminations in contemporary liberal states' immigration and nationality laws and policies are usually tied to two provisos. The first refers to the relative salience of the ethnic discrimination: Is this the only or main selection criterion, or is it nested within or tagged onto other, nonethnic selection rules? If I said earlier that the ethnic discrimination in favor of Ibero-Americans in Spain's *Ley Orgánica* of 1985 was in some respects "structurally equivalent" to the pre-1965 national-origin regime in the United States, one also has to see the fundamental difference between the two: not just the absence of a racial discrimination in the Spanish law but also the subordinate status of the ethnic discrimination within the Spanish law, compared with its dominance in the American law. Formally added in the 1952 McCarran-Walter Act, skills and family ties had the subordinate status of "other" considerations in pre-1965 American law, and they were nested within the overall ethnoracial frame of the national-origin system. By contrast, in the Spanish law, as well as in most other contemporary immigration laws, the overarching frame is nonethnic, and ethnicity is tagged on as a second-order "other" consideration, subordinate to skills or family ties—in the Spanish case, this "other" consideration was even further minimized by Byzantine implementation rules. So peripheral are the (pan)ethnic preferences in the Spanish or Portuguese cases that outside small legal and scholarly circles, and apart from affected migrants of course, no one in the larger public is really aware of them. It is obvious that the subordinate status of an ethnic discrimination within a state's immigration policy makes the latter less objectionable from a liberal point of view.

The matter is of course different in the diaspora constellation, where the presence of an ethnic qualification *alone* may trigger an as-of-right claim to be selected. However, we saw that these much stronger "return" provisions required additional justification on part of the receiving state. One is the state's denial that this is a matter of "immigration" at all, with the claim that it is one of "repatriation" or fulfillment of a "national" obligation instead. The other is the tying of the policy to a remedial "minority" rationale, and the assumption that coethnics have to be protected from "persecution" in a foreign state. An interesting implication of this is that diaspora migration, in contrast to the "special link" or "cultural affinity" migrations in the postcolonial context, is notionally geared to be temporary only. Sooner or later this constraint is bound to make itself felt even on Israel's Law of Return,[3] which is the strongest ethnic immigration policy in any state today.

Israel, of course, is different because the "persecution" rationale is not just applied to coethnics abroad, but to the entire national collectivity of Jews, those in Israel included. In terms of the Holocaust identity, and reinforced by Israel's precarious geopolitical location, "persecution" is part and parcel of the self-definition of Jews and of the state that represents them. At one level, this may help perpetuate the Law of Return. At another level, however, one may also question whether remedial "affirmative action" is an adequate metaphor at all for Jewish-preference immigration, even though the former has been widely used to justify the latter (especially Kasher, 1985). This is because this immigration is tied to a particularistic project of national self-determination, whereas the thrust of affirmative action is universalistic, to undo (rather than to establish) an ascriptive marker as distributor of certain resources (see Gans, 2003, ch. 6). In short, affirmative action addresses blacks or women *as individuals*, whereas the reverse logic of the Law of Return is to address individuals only *as Jews*. A second oddity of the affirmative-action analogy is this: whereas in affirmative action the cost of remedial discrimination is carried by the party that in the past has profited from the incriminated negative discrimination (white males), in Israel's Law of Return the cost is shouldered by an innocent third party, the Palestinians. As Chaim Gans (ibid.) rightly points out, the weakness of Asa Kasher's (1985) defense of the Law of Return in terms of a remedial "case of the founding fathers" is the assumption that this founding occurred in a *terra nullius*, thus ignoring the injustice done to those who previously occupied the land and may rightfully consider it theirs. Instead, Gans proposes an alternative defense of the Law of Return in terms of a nationalist (and thus nontemporary) "case of the continuing sons," according to which "now that the Jews constitute a majority in the state of Israel, the moral problem presented by the Law of Return in the past no longer exists" (ibid., p. 139). For Gans, the "moral problem" no longer exists because the function of the law now is to sustain rather than to create a demographic advantage of Jews. However, such a defense is at the price of abandoning a liberal framework altogether. It counts on the impermeability of a fixed group "owning" a state, which is at odds with the territorial inclusiveness and "self-limiting" nature of nation building in a liberal state (see Kymlicka, 2001). Although the "case of the continuing sons" may adequately depict the sociological reality of the Israeli state, it is tantamount to saying that Israel is not, and does not even aspire to be, a liberal state.

The Israeli case *ex negativo* points to a second proviso that usually sustains ethnic immigration policies in the liberal state: not to create losers. To create or not to create losers is often taken to be the distinguishing mark between positive and negative discriminations. Nobody is harmed by giving an advantage to a certain group, while exclusion by definition harms those who are excluded. However, at closer inspection this distinction is elusive. Affirmative action in the United States, the strongest positive discrimination to be found in a liberal state, has been attacked as "reverse discrimination" against whites who have not personally discriminated against nonwhites, but are now asked to pay for this. In the context of immigration policy, the notion of loser is admittedly a weaker one. This is because here winners and losers are not in a zero-sum relationship, in which one side wins *because* the other loses. For instance, asylum seekers or the descendants of Turkish guest workers in Germany are not worse off *because* the ethnic Germans are treated more generously by the state; rather they are worse off in the sense that a perhaps stronger persecution or citizenship claim, respectively, on their part is not adequately recognized by the state, in comparison to the more generous treatment bestowed on the ethnic Germans. To cite a second example discussed in this study: New Commonwealth immigrants are not "out" *because* Old Commonwealth immigrants are "in" through the patriality clause of the British Immigration Act of 1971; rather the liberal challenge has been one in favor of similar entry and residence privileges bestowed on New Commonwealthers too.

In his defense of ethnocultural selectivity in the liberal state's immigration policy, Joseph Carens tied its legitimacy to the condition that the positive discrimination was not "a disguised form of racial or ethnic prejudice" (1992:44). The problem is that in an ethnically pluralized society a charge of "disguised prejudice" can always be made against a policy that singles out a single group for favorable treatment—the prejudice then consists of the fact that the "others" are not included. The resilience or demise of the ethnic immigration policy then depends on the sociopolitical mobilizing capacity of those who deem themselves disadvantaged in light of this policy or who act vicariously for these "losers." In the case of Spain, we saw that with respect to an ethnically highly diverse immigrant population the state has strenuously attempted to appear neutral, even in the context of a conservative government that has not at all been hostile to a Hispanic preference discourse; by contrast, the particularistic card of "special ties" was played by certain Hispanic migrant groups who sought favored treatment by the state. By the same token, the stronger cross-elite emphasis on preferring Lusophone migrants in Portugal, which one could observe in the 1990s, was also enabled by the demographic fact that most non-European migrants at this point originated from Portugal's former colonies. As a result, this policy created only a "few hundred" losers, as an SOS Racism leader put it sarcastically. Tellingly, in the past few years, which have been marked by a significant diversification of source countries, the Lusophone preference discourse has become markedly weaker.

With respect to the reference group(s) by or on behalf of whom equality claims are raised, perhaps the most interesting distinction revealed in this study was the one between "citizens" or de facto members, on the one hand, and "other migrants" or abstract humanity, on the other. Both reference groups invoked (or were invoked within) different rhetorical strategies, in one case concrete citizen interests or identities being harmed or denigrated by an ethnic preference policy, in the other case abstract humanity being offended by the policy. In both cases, immigration policy is empirically subjected to a justice test that is notionally absent from it (if one presumes, from Rawls to Walzer, that justice is possible only within but not beyond a bounded community). With respect to nonmembers, the key constraint is articulated in Article 1(3) of the UN convention on preventing racial discrimination: while in principle not covered by the convention, the state's immigration and nationality provisions must "not discriminate against any particular nationality." In particular, White Australia was fought in this way (apart from the pragmatic foreign-policy rationale), because as a result of the very effectiveness of the policy in keeping society homogenous, there were no domestic losers. With respect to citizens and de facto members, Kasher (1985) mapped out two different ways in which they may be negatively affected by an ethnic preference policy: first, the "interests" of certain ethnic subgroups of the citizenry may be harmed by not replenishing their ranks with coethnics, driving up prices for goods that are more easily provided when the group size is high; secondly, the "self-respect" of such subgroups may be denigrated by omitting them from public policy. Both motifs were empirically effective in the demise of the U.S. national-origin system, which was very much the cause of European ethnics who saw themselves as materially and ideally slighted by this policy.

The reductio ad absurdum of the liberal opposition to ethnic migration is certainly that the state is asked to abstract from its own name and identity in its migration policy. Why should the German state not preference putative "Germans" in its migration policy? If the state could not do so, it surely would not be a state at all, embodiment of a historical collectivity with an obligation to those who somehow are or were connected with it; instead, it would be a nameless cash register for the transactions randomly occurring on its territory. However, if this study showed anything, then it was to document an empirical questioning of the innocent-sounding terms "putative," "somehow connected," and so forth. The internal diversification and individualization of contemporary Western societies have undercut the notion of The Nation as a personality writ large to be defended, completed, or replenished at the immigration front. Along with the greatly increased migration pressures from highly diverse source countries, these developments have robbed most positive discriminations of the liberal state of their former innocence. Nevertheless, coming back to the German example just cited, an ethnic preference policy that targets those who share the name of the state, while not the *only* possible ethnic preference policy, is the one that has most stubbornly refused to go away.

Instead of stating a linear decline of ethnic migration in the liberal state, it is more adequate to conceive of the state as in the crossfire of countervailing trends and forces, some pushing for its "de-ethnicization," others instead pushing for its "re-ethnicization." To understand this paradox, one must realize that states are both territorial and membership units. With respect to territory, an increasing permeability of the state's

borders to material and symbolic goods, resources, and personal movement has made their "nationalizing" control an elusive endeavor. To the
inside—that is, with respect to its territory and the domestic society situated on it—the liberal state in the age of globalization is subjected to
strong "de-ethnicization" pressures. At heart this means that, with the
increased ethnic complexity of domestic society, the self-descriptions and
identity impositions by means of which the state seeks to contain and
"integrate" this complexity have to become increasingly thin and procedural. To the outside, however, the matter is different. In this respect the
state is first and foremost a membership unit. A characteristic of the global age is increased personal mobility across borders. It is in the interest of
the state to retain ties with its members, even though these members may
no longer reside in its territory. The questions "At what point are the ties
of membership severed?" and "Are they recoverable, and by what
means?" are increasingly topical and are differently answered by different
states. In short, with respect to retaining links with its members abroad,
the state is subjected to "re-ethnicization" pressures.

The interesting matter is that often the same global processes that
force the liberal state to "de-ethnicize" to the inside also move it to "re-
ethnicize" to the outside. This alone will guarantee that ethnic migration
will not come to an end any time soon, irrespective of the "ethnic" or
"civic" self-definition of the state. The remainder of this concluding chapter further delineates the countervailing trends and forces of "de-" and
"re-ethnicization."

De-ethnicization . . .

In order to understand the meaning of "de-ethnicization," one must at
first realize that the modern nation-state is a nagging anomaly to the logic
of functional differentiation that has seized most other spheres of modern
society. Whereas one participates in the functionally differentiated and
formally organized spheres of society mostly in only specific respects, and
never exclusively, one is a member of a nation-state in a total and mutually
exclusive sense.[4] In fact, seen from the point of view of the system of
states, states are not functionally but segmentarily differentiated, self-
contained units, in each of which society reproduces itself across the totality of its functions. Membership in a state thus resembles the membership
in a premodern group, clan, or segment, which was likewise exclusive and
all-encompassing, an unmovable master status that accompanied (or

rather caged) the individual from the cradle to the grave. As Luhmann has shown most succinctly, the hallmark of modern society is the individual's expulsion from the group, and her exterior position to the differentiated subsystems that "include" her in only specific and nonexclusive respects: "The principle of inclusion replaces the solidarity that was based on belonging to one and only one group. Universal inclusion is idealized with value postulates such as freedom and equality" (Luhmann, 1980:31). Accordingly, the liberal creed of freedom and equality is an accompaniment of functional differentiation, which includes the individual in abstraction from all other characteristics (most notably those of the ascriptive kind) in the subsystems of society.

A disciple of Luhmann (Nassehi, 1990:263–264) sharply observed that there is a striking omission in the master's enumeration of modern value postulates—solidarity—and he suggests that this is the place of modern nationalism. In fact, in historical terms the simultaneous rise of individualism and nationalism, as symbolized in the French revolutionary triplet of "*liberté, égalité, fraternité*," is conspicuous. As Louis Dumont argued, "the nation is the sociopolitical group corresponding to the ideology of the individual. It is thus two things in one: a collection of individuals and, at the same time, a collective individual, an individual on the level of groups, facing other nations-individuals" (1986:130). The link between individualism and nationalism is that nationalism conceives of the people as "fundamentally homogeneous," and only "superficially divided by the lines of status, class, locality" (Greenfeld, 1992:3). The nation includes abstract individuals whose only marker—in perfect circularity—is their shared nationality. As Nassehi (1990:265) further suggests, one can interpret nationalism as a semantic figure that compensated for the individual's expulsion from the premodern group, enabling her full inclusion in society, separate from and beyond the differentiated subsystems. The "nation," after all, is not a differentiated subsystem, like economy, law, family, or polity, but a particular name for the totality of society that otherwise has moved out of reach under the reign of functional differentiation.

This raises the interesting question how durably the state is aligned with nationalist semantics. We are used to call "nation-state" the modular state that emerged in the late nineteenth century, whose key characteristic is perhaps the wholesale penetration and incorporation of society (see Mann, 1993). However, if one deploys this formula to late nineteenth- and late twentieth-century states alike, one glosses over important changes with respect to how the "nation" is aligned with and deployed by the state. What the "nation-state" was initially is explicated in detail by James Scott (1998). Reminiscent of Foucault, Scott depicts the "high modernist" state as one that aspires to "a perfectly legible population with registered, unique names and addresses keyed to grid settlements; who pursue single, identifiable occupations; and all of whose transactions are documented according to the designated formula and in the official language" (p.82). This was "society as a military parade" (ibid.), as well as one in which politics was to be replaced by rational engineering on the basis of scientific knowledge. It is precisely in this context that the United States crafted its first national immigration system, based on race and ethnicity, which in one form or another were used as selection criteria by all migrant-receiving states of the time. From Scott's perspective, the use of race and ethnicity for selecting immigrants was not archaic but in an overshooting way modern, because the state sought to recruit identical units for its serial nation-building exercise.

However, if the development of immigration policy is any measure, this was not to last. As Scott (1998:89) notes, the high modernist state could operate only on the basis of a "prostrate civil society that lacks the capacity to resist [the state's] plans," and the project of making society "legible" clashed with certain "liberal democratic ideas"—the autonomy of the private sphere, a liberal political economy, and representative institutions (pp. 101–102). In addition, as Scott's notion of "society as a military parade" suggests, the original nation-state building project was fundamentally tied to a world of interstate conflict and war. First and foremost from this external point of view, the nation had to be "one," composed of individuals as uniform equal units, because in this way wars could be waged and won. Once this condition is relaxed, and the plural forces of domestic society have space to unfold, another "state" moves into the picture, one that is distinct from and taking its hands off the other subsystems of society, and whose nation building is "qualified and self-limiting" (Kymlicka, 2001). This is the "liberal state" whose existence and operation have been both presumed *and* demonstrated in the course of this study.

Even in a context of external conflict, the nationalist trope of personalized collectivities and depersonalized individuals is no longer available in the contemporary liberal state. Compare the different responses of the United States to warlike external attacks in 1941 and 2001. After Pearl Harbor, all Japanese in the United States, about half of them Japanese-origin people who had been American citizens since their birth,[5] were summarily interned, because *qua* national (and, one must surmise, racial)[6] origins they were deemed to share certain personal characteristics that made them a security risk to the United States. After the terrorist attacks in September 2001, on the other hand, there was no mass internment of Muslims in the United States, even though the U.S. government formally declared to be in a "war" again. There was certainly a tightening of visa procedures for male applicants from Muslim countries,[7] and there was close surveillance of men from Muslim countries visiting or temporarily residing in the United States.[8] But the reasoning for targeting Muslims was in terms of the greater probability of identifying terrorists, not of presumed personal characteristics that Muslims might share *qua* being Muslim. Moreover, in contrast to 1941, a further targeting of U.S. citizens or permanent residents of suspect religious or national backgrounds was not fathomed by anyone this time around. Considering that the United States is the only Western state that continues to live in a "Hobbesian" world of anarchy and war, this was a rather subdued and differentiated response. Needless to say that in "Kantian"[9] Europe, enmeshed in dense international rules and institutions, political leaders even more abstained from any collectivistic interpretation of the terrorist attacks. The one European leader who dared interpret the attacks in such terms, as one between "our civilization" and "Muslim countries," was immediately whistled back and ostracized—for a European Union official this stance was "totally contradicting the values in which we believe."[10]

The EU official did not explicate what those "values" were, but one can read from the contemporary construction of "Europe" that these values resonate closely with the "de-ethnicization" of the liberal state. There is little space for particularistic nation-building pretensions in Europe today. As one can see from the conditions with which potential accession states to the European Union formally have to comply, the European construct itself is nonethnic. According to the 1993 Copenhagen Criteria, the three conditions that a state needs to fulfill to qualify for entry in the EU is to have "stable institutions" (including democracy, rule of law, human rights, and minority protections), a "functioning market economy," and incorporation of the EU laws and regulations (the *acquis communautaire*) into its own laws and administrative structures. Interestingly, the deliberately noncultural, nonethnic definition of "Europe" yields a problem: Turkey's long-standing, and increasingly urgent, bid for entry cannot forever be refused on these grounds. And if

Turkey can join, there is no intrinsic reason why Turkey's southeastern neighbors, Iraq, Iran, or Syria, could not one day join too. On the basis of the liberal democratic creed that Europe's leaders have chosen to define what "Europe" is, no lasting boundary can be drawn at all. "Who listens to Sibelius or Puccini . . . hears the boundary [of Europe]. On none of the possible cultural maps of Europe does one find Turkey," wrote a critic of Euro-universalism.[11] Ironically, and a telling example of what de-ethnicization is, the fact that Turkey, a Muslim society, has not historically been on the "maps of Europe" ultimately strengthens its bid for entry because—in the face of some 15 million Muslims of immigrant origins already residing in European Union states—no European leader today can afford to project an image of Europe as exclusively "Christian." Note that in the final draft of the European constitution, presented in summer 2004, there is no reference at all to "God" or "Christianity." Europe's "identity is not an exclusive one", writes Yasemin Soysal (2002:276–277), "[it] fails to create its cultural, and symbolic, other; and rightly and fortunately so."

Already before the discovery of "globalization," Daniel Bell (1975:164) had noticed that across Western states "nationalism" was at "low ebb." The reasons for this are manifold, but there is no doubt what is ultimately driving its decline: the "internationalization of world society" (Stichweh, 1988:289). The communications and transactions of most subsystems of society, such as economy, science, culture, religion, family, and, in important respects, even the state's own components such as courts or regulatory agencies (for this see Slaughter, 1997), increasingly transcend the boundaries of states. Instead of being contained by national markers, as was the "national economy" of old, these subsystems increasingly link up with their counterparts abroad, giving rise to a new transnational order that passes through states but is not encompassed by states. It is the signature of the contemporary liberal state to be increasingly self-limiting about its interventions in these autonomous subsystems of society (see Willke, 1992). This is why a policy like the French *Loi Toubon*, which prohibited the use of foreign (read: English)-language terms in a variety of public and private settings, has raised eyebrows, and it has been partially struck down by the Constitutional Council as an offense against free speech.[12] "Constitutional politics" in fact sets an increasingly felt limit to the nation-building possibilities of the state, in terms of constitutionally protected liberty and equality rights of the individual (see Stone-Sweet, 2000).

One might of course argue that with respect to foreign migrants the diminishing grip of the national marker is precisely reversed, and that the state, losing out on so many other fronts, seeks compensation here via "singl[ing] out the border and the individual as the sites for regulatory enforcement" (Sassen, 1998:56). From this viewpoint, migration control is a domain of "re-" rather than "de-nationalization" (ibid.). There is much to this analysis, as is demonstrated in the increasing salience of border control and the refashioning of migration as "security" concern across Western states (see Andreas, 2001; Koslowski, 2001; Bigo, 2001). Note, however, that in this context the meaning of "re-nationalization" is simply an increased display of state presence at the border, not the state's differentiated treatment of would-be entrants according to their ethnicity. The scope for the latter is altogether unaffected by toughness at the border and may be as restricted as ever.

Apart from migrant selection, which was the focus of this study, the de-ethnicization of the contemporary liberal state is most visible in what this state does to, and expects of, migrants once they have passed the selection hurdle. Let me illustrate this in the overlapping domains of nationality law and integration policies.[13] One could argue that in the past 200 years the citizenship laws in Western states have become increasingly "ethnic" (Boes, 1993). In this sense, ethnicity is not a premodern residual but a result of modernization, providing the boundaries only within which a universalization of rights (that is, Marshallian citizenship) could occur. The paradigmatic transition is the one from *jus domicili* to *jus sanguinis* and *jus soli*, that is, from residence to birth as the main attributive mechanism of state membership (see de Groot, 1989:312–313). Beginning with France in 1804, the quintessentially modern citizenship was ethnic citizenship *jure sanguinis*, and it became the norm in nineteenth-century Europe. Only in a few peripheral states, most notably Britain and Portugal, did citizenship *jure soli* prevail, whose roots are in feudalism and which shared with the old *jus domicili* the territorial element. Among continental European states, emigration countries such as Germany or Spain retained their ethnic citizenship laws relatively unmodified until quite recently, whereas an immigration country such as France came to complement *jus sanguinis* with relatively strong *jus soli* provisions at a relatively early point (see Weil, 2002, ch. 7).

The interesting recent phenomenon is the strengthening of territorial citizenship across the same European states that had championed ethnic citizenship at an earlier time. This went along with a revaluation of *jus soli*

as the quintessentially modern citizenship principle. Discussing international opposition to strongly "ethnocultural" citizenship laws in some
post-Communist states in eastern Europe, Diane Orentlicher (1998:312)
has argued that "increasingly . . . international law has subtly reinforced
territorial/civic conceptions of nationality." This reflects an infusion of
human-rights constraints in a domain that had classically been considered
the reserve of the sovereign state.[14] The idea behind the revaluation of
territorial citizenship is simple: "[S]tates owe human rights obligations to
individuals who are vulnerable to their exercise of sovereign power"
(ibid., p. 322, n.117). To the degree that European states have become
immigrant-receiving states after World War II, they have all added territorial elements to their previously ethnic citizenship laws (Hansen and Weil,
2001). With a few exceptions, all European Union states today grant as-
of-right citizenship to second-generation immigrants, either at birth (*jure
soli*) or optionally at a later stage. In a comparison of twenty-five European and non-European states after World War II, Patrick Weil has shown
that convergence toward increasingly territorial citizenship laws depends
on three factors: "stable borders" that include the majority of nationals,
the consolidation of "democratic values," and a legacy of "immigration"
rather than "emigration" (Weil, 2001b:32).

With the help of Weil's grid one immediately sees why Israel has stuck
to ethnic immigration and citizenship policies, while Germany has
recently moved away from both: "stable borders" were available to Germany after 1989, but they are not yet (and perhaps never will be) available in Israel. The case of Germany, until most recently a prototypical
"ethnic state," shows the full weight and implications of the turn to territorial citizenship (see Joppke, 2000). Previously German citizenship law
had required the individually examined cultural assimilation of citizenship
applicants (except those who were ethnically German according to Article
116 of the Basic Law), and even if this stiff requirement was fulfilled, the
state could still say no. With the introduction of "as of right" citizenship
for second-generation and long-settled immigrants in the early 1990s, a
less demanding, liberal logic has been instituted. The lawmaker explicitly
abstained from asking for the cultural "assimilation" of the citizenship
applicant; all that was asked for was her "integration," which was generically presumed to have happened once a threshold of residence time and
schooling was taken (Hailbronner and Renner, 2001:659). Interestingly,
the throwing out of the cultural assimilation requirement was initially so
radical that even applicants without any knowledge of the German lan-

guage could in principle be naturalized. This led to the inconsistency that the conditions for being granted permanent residence were more exacting than the acquisition of citizenship, because the former (but not the latter) required sufficient German-language competence. Accordingly, the wholesale reform of nationality law in 1999 tightened the integration requirements for as-of-right naturalization, in asking for "sufficient knowledge of German language," as well as for a written "commitment to the liberal democratic order" of the Federal Republic. This, however, was no return to cultural assimilation. As I shall demonstrate subsequently, this reform incorporated the two basic integration requirements of liberal states: language acquisition and a procedural commitment to liberal-democratic rules.

The liberalization of German citizenship law, which was crowned by the introduction of conditional *jus soli* citizenship for second-generation immigrants in 1999, has led to a decoupling of ethnicity and citizenship: one does not have to be ethnoculturally German to become a German citizen. But in contrast to Israel, this does not detract from a person's full political and societal inclusion, as there is no official nationality status[15] separate from citizenship status in Germany. On the contrary, the decoupling of ethnicity and citizenship allowed Germany to become a liberal state in the sense of being inclusive of the people who are residing in her territory, "the state of all of its residents-turned-citizens."

A second respect in which nationality laws have become de-ethnicized is an increasing toleration of dual citizenship. This development is intrinsically linked to the liberalization of access to citizenship, because many states no longer ask citizenship applicants first to divest themselves of their previous citizenship. Dual citizenship breaks with the segmentary logic of the classic nation-state, according to which one could belong to only one state at a time. Witness that the earlier repudiation of dual citizenship had likened it to "bigamy." In U.S. Ambassador George Bancroft's nineteenth-century words, one should "as soon tolerate a man with two wives as a man with two countries" (quoted in Koslowski, 2000:206). This has been enshrined in the 1930 Hague Convention's prescription that "every person should have a nationality and should have one nationality only." Conversely, the toleration of dual citizenship reflects an invasion into the segmentary nation-state domain of the logic of functional differentiation, which endorses and even requires multiple memberships and allegiances. This invasion of functional logic is very visible in the Carnegie Endowment's case for tolerating dual citizenship

(Aleinikoff and Klusmeyer, 2002:29): "Empirically, modern nations in overwhelming proportions tolerate or encourage a wide range of competing loyalties and affiliations in civil society—to family, business, local community, religious denominations, sports teams, nongovernmental organizations promoting both political and nonpolitical causes—and do not treat such allegiances . . . as bigamous or as incompatible with . . . loyalty to the nation-state" (p. 29).

From the point of view of receiving states, the toleration of dual citizenship is part of the trend toward territorial citizenship, which is driven by these states' need to integrate their growing immigrant populations. The linkage between dual citizenship and immigrant integration is explicit in the Council of Europe's new Nationality Convention of 1997, which justifies the departure from its predecessor's strict prohibition of dual nationality in reference to "labour migrations between European States leading to substantial immigrant populations [and] the need for the integration of permanent residents" (Council of Europe, 1997:23). Apart from the immigration angle, dual citizenship is also something the liberal state has to accept if it does not want to discriminate between the sexes. To the degree that all postwar Western states have abolished patrilinear descent rules in response to feminist concerns, dual citizenship has become a sociological reality in them, even before this became linked to the immigration problem.[16]

This is not to deny that dual citizenship is a deeply contested phenomenon, on which there is significant and resilient divergence across European states. In Germany, a government plan in the late 1990s to recognize dual citizenship officially had to be stopped due to massive political and societal opposition. While there was no overtly "ethnic" discourse in this opposition, it is not far-fetched to assume that this was a rearguard battle of the defenders of ethnocultural nationhood (Joppke, 2000)—note that countries with "civic" legacies (such as France, Britain, and the United States) have long tolerated dual citizenship, if not in principle then at least in practice. In addition to being contested, dual citizenship is also a deeply ambivalent phenomenon. Note that, from the point of view of sending states, the toleration of dual citizenship signifies a "re-ethnicization." This has always been the case in Spain, where a reciprocal dual nationality regime with South American states was the main tool to build the *comunidad hispánica*. More recently, migrant-sending states, including Turkey, Mexico, the Dominican Republic, and Colombia, have allowed their emigrants to keep their citizenship even when they naturalize elsewhere, in the interest of retaining materially and politically valued ties with their expatriates.

Dual citizenship is an example of the same global process—increased personal mobility across borders—spurring both the "de-" and "re-ethnicization" of involved states. In some states, the response has been asymmetric, either tolerating only emigrant but not immigrant dual citizenship (as in Germany) or—rather curiously—making dual citizenship an option for immigrants but not emigrants (as in Belgium or pre-2002 Australia). However, in Europe most states have taken a symmetric stance, tolerating both emigrant and immigrant dual citizenship, which entails their simultaneous "de-" and "re-ethnicization" in this respect.[17]

Beyond nationality law, "de-ethnicization" has become the hallmark of Western states' policies of immigrant integration. This is implicit in the very notion of "integration," which has everywhere replaced the older notion of "assimilation" (even in France, see Haut Conseil à l'Intégration, 1993:8). Old-style assimilation meant the complete transformation of the migrant into a serial unit of the receiving nation-state, implying a change of name, dress, and manners. In short, assimilation aimed at eradicating the migrant's ethnicity, her sense of origin. Accordingly, the essence of the first "Americanization" campaign after World War I was to kill the European immigrants' "hyphen" and to transform them into "hundred-percent Americans," in which there was no space for their ethnic origins (Higham, 1955). The difference between "assimilation" and "integration" is perhaps best illustrated by comparing the first with the second "Americanization" campaign, which was launched some eighty years later and addressed the predominantly non-European immigrants arriving since 1965. Americanization now means "the cultivation of a shared commitment to the American values of liberty, democracy and equal opportunity," "rapid acquisition of English," and it even includes the multicultural value of "respect[ing] other cultures and ethnic groups" (U.S. Commission on Immigration Reform, 1997:37, 28).

Originating in UNESCO's recommendation to replace "assimilation" through "integration," since the 1960s the new "integration" idiom has taken hold across Western states. Despite local variations, it everywhere has the same two connotations. First, integration is intransitive, in the sense that the migrant could not be forced into it; integration could only be the result of the migrant's own agency. Respecting the migrant's agency implied that integration had to be a two-way process, in which not just the migrant but the receiving society, too, had to adapt. In the European Commission's recent proposal for a European immigration policy this respect for the actorhood of migrants has taken the curious extreme of conceiving of migrants as "partners" of receiving states.[18] Secondly, and following from this, the migrant was not required to adopt the substantive culture of the receiving society. In this, one sees the operation of the liberal state's public neutrality obligation. The forced imposition of culture became lastingly associated with the negated notion of "assimilation." In turn, the insistence that migrants could keep their "identities" became the general posture across Western states. In historical perspective, this communality by far outshines any "national model" that may have been able to modify locally, but never to alter substantially, the turn from "assimilation" to "integration."

Ironically, but perhaps not surprisingly, in the very moment that Western states desisted from culturally streamlining their immigrants, one can observe a proliferation of "multicultural" recognition claims brought against these states. This indicates a relocation of ethnicity, from the state level to the substate level. Already Daniel Bell (1975) had noticed that the decline of "nationalism" in Western states was accompanied by the flourishing of "ethnicity" at the substate level. Ethnicity is no longer something imposed by the state on society (and especially its newcomers), but mobilized by sections of society against the state. Just as the liberal state was moving in major ways to live up to its neutrality obligation, busily overturning many a narrowly ethnic and "discriminatory" feature in its laws and institutions (including those dealing with citizenship and immigration), it was asked to inscribe glaringly on its forehead the ethnic signature of minority groups and cultures. It is perhaps the central shortcoming of political theories of multiculturalism not to recognize this paradox: not the push by ethnicizing states, but the pull of de-ethnicizing states has helped bring "multiculturalism" into existence. In Kymlicka's influential scenario (1995), minority rights are a compensation for axiomatically assumed strong nation building on part of the contemporary state. Short shrift is given to the fact that the nation-building capacity and ambition of the contemporary state have greatly diminished in the past half-century, at least in the North-Atlantic zone.

If one goes through the official documents in which contemporary liberal states lay out what they expect of their immigrants in terms of "integration," one finds everywhere only two requirements: that they adopt the official language(s) of the receiving society, and that they respect liberal-democratic values and procedures. This is the gist of the second wave of "Americanization." One finds it too in a state that has long denied the reality of immigration and that is known for its ethnic legacy: Germany. In a recent report by the Federal Commissioner for Foreigner Affairs (2000), one can read that there is no "German monolithic culture" that immigrants could be asked to share. Instead, German society is said to consist of a "multiplicity of coexisting life styles." This rules out the possibility that "integration" could mean "assimilation." And when explicating what "integration" is, the usual two suspects are reiterated: "Acceptance of the values of the Basic Law and knowledge of the German language" (ibid., p. 228).

But let us turn to a case with strong nation-building aspirations, in which one might expect that "integration" consist of more than the procedural minimum: Quebec. However, consulting the central document of Quebec's integration policy, entitled *Vision: A Policy Statement on Immigration and Integration,* yields disappointment in this respect (see the discussion by Carens, 1995). It expects immigrants to respect the values of "democracy" and "pluralism," which are not specific to Quebec but generic to all liberal democracies. The only expression of Quebec's "distinct society" pretension is the request that immigrants (like all others) adopt French as the public language. This is the small rest of distinctly cultural adaptation that every liberal state, not just Quebec, asks of its newcomers. As Carens (2000:117) concludes from the case of Quebec, "any defensible version of liberal democracy today entails a commitment to pluralism that inevitably opens the door to multiculturalism in some form."

There are signs that the "differentialist tide" (Brubaker, 2003:41), whose possibility is inherent in the structure of liberal democracy, has passed its peak. In Quebec this has taken the form of more emphasis on the civic communalities of a *citoyenneté québecoise* (Juteau, 2002). In the United States, the very recapture of the "Americanization" term, which previously had been tainted by the racism of its first-time variant, had a similar thrust (see Pickus, 2001), and demographers and sociologists studying second-generation adaptation have recovered the long-discarded "assimilation" concept (see Brubaker, 2003:47–51). In the Netherlands, a champion of multiculturalism in Europe, the previous "ethnic minorities' policy," which had aimed at "emancipating" immigrants within separate but equal institutions, has been replaced by a "civic integration" policy, which makes Dutch-language training and civics classes mandatory for non-EU newcomers (Entzinger, 2003). In Britain,

Europe's second champion of multiculturalism, Labour Home Secretary David Blunkett has declared that it is time to move "beyond multiculturalism," and in unusually blunt words he has told his countries' minorities to learn English, abstain from "forced marriage," and to accept British "norms of acceptability" (see Joppke, 2004: 249–253).

Across Western societies there has been a recent shift from unbridled differentialism toward a stress on civic communalities. Interestingly, while the thrust of these attempts is to bind immigrants here and not elsewhere, into "American," "Dutch," or "British" society, these particularisms are only different names for the same liberal-democratic creed. This is not nationalism (or its current Western variant, right-wing populism) raising its ugly head, but the liberal state becoming more assertive about imposing liberal principles. Consider how the recent British government White Paper (2002) on immigration and citizenship defines the "fundamental tenets" of British citizenship that immigrants are asked to adopt: "that we respect human rights and freedoms, uphold democratic values, observe laws faithfully and fulfill our duties and obligations" (p. 34). There is nothing particularly "British" about this. Similarly, an influential report investigating the causes of severe ethnic riots in northern England stressed that immigrants and their descendants had to adopt "common elements of 'nationhood.'" Yet when spelled out, there was again nothing specifically "British" about these elements of nationhood: "a more visible support for anti-discrimination measures, support for women's rights, a universal acceptance of the English language . . . and respect for both religious differences and secular views" (Cantle Report, 2001:19). This was the universal, nationally anonymous creed of the liberal state.

A particularly telling example of the impossibility of imposing national particularisms on immigrants comes from Germany. A few years ago the conservative opposition party (CDU) made an ill-fated campaign for asking newcomers to accept a "German *Leitkultur*" (dominant culture). Although it was an exact parallel to the civic integration campaigns in other Western states, the concept had to be withdrawn, obviously because in Germany any reference to "national" symbols and rhetoric is still tainted by inevitably illiberal connotations. But when explicating what the German *Leitkultur* was, its proponents could only come up with things that could have been constitutive of a British or Dutch *Leitkultur* as well: the norms of the constitution, the "European idea," equality of women, and the German language.[19] The only national particularism in this is language, which however is also a functional exigency of any state *qua* state.

These examples show the narrow margins for asserting national particularisms in the liberal state. They demonstrate its thorough de-ethnicization, in which the various national labels are only different names for the same thing, the liberal creed of liberty and equality. The de-ethnicization of immigrant integration is the precise complement to the diminishing scope of ethnic selectivity in immigration policy.

. . . and Re-Ethnicization of the Liberal State

States are not just territorial but membership units. If borders become more permeable, and mobility across them increases, this cuts both ways: nonmembers enter, members leave. While the entering of nonmembers triggers the de-ethnicization of the liberal state, the leaving of members unleashes an opposite dynamic of re-ethnicization. This re-ethnicization cuts across the "ethnic" versus "civic" distinction known from the nations and nationalism literature. This is because re-ethnicization feeds upon what a state essentially is. All states are "ethnic" in the sense that birth is the usual way of becoming a member of a state: "states are primarily communities of descent," concede two advocates of liberal citizenship policies for an "age of migration" (Aleinikoff and Klusmeyer, 2002:14). The distinction between *jus soli* and *jus sanguinis* also is secondary to this, because even in *jus soli* states "birth" makes one a member. The ineradicably ethnic quality of the state *qua* membership unit is largely invisible as long as its members stay put, and as long as this immobility applies to other states too. Conversely, there are two moments in which the descent-based, ethnic quality of the state comes into the picture: when nonmembers enter, and when members leave. With regard to the first, even under the most liberal of conditions nonmembers cannot join the citizenry at their discretion, but have to undergo a "naturalization"; its Latin root word *nasci* (to be born) indicates the genealogical dimension of all postbirth entries into the citizenry too. In turn, citizens who leave the territory of their state, even for extended stays, do not thereby lose their citizenship. The state moves with its citizens, and even beyond its territory it continues to exert a "personal sovereignty" over the latter.[20] Moreover, the ethnic quality of the state *qua* membership unit is revealed in the fact that all states, even those that are most deeply committed to civic-territorial principles, allow their members to transmit the good of membership to their offspring born abroad, *jure sanguinis*.

If we live in a world of increased international migration, the often forgotten reverse side of "immigration" is "emigration." This reverse side corresponds to the logic of the state *qua* membership unit, and it is also in the state's best interest (in terms of remittances and influence abroad) to retain ties to its emigrants, even across generations. This is an increasingly topical question, not just for traditionally poor migrant-sending states. Two Council of Europe reports in the 1990s addressed the fact that tens of millions of Europeans were living abroad, while there was no "law of expatriates" in most European states to deal with the complications surrounding this phenomenon (from restrictions on the right to vote to the loss of citizenship) in a consistent way, not to mention the absence of a law of expatriates at international and European levels (Council of Europe, 1994; 1999). This is not bound to last, because with increased emigration all categories of states, and not just migrants, become drawn into the maelstrom of the "deterritorialization of politics" (Council of Europe, 1999:20) that is a mark of contemporary globalization.[21]

Whereas there is nothing new about the re-ethnicizing thrust of retaining links with members abroad, there are today severe constraints on how far contemporary states can go in this direction. Unsurprisingly, the state's parallel inclination to be inclusive to nonmembers on its territory and the liberal norms that frame this inclusion set limits to any desire to be ethnically inclusive with respect to members abroad. A little noticed but telling side effect of the recent introduction of *jus soli* elements in German citizenship law has been to put limits on the possibility of transmitting German citizenship outside the country, *jure sanguinis*. Previously, there was no generational stopping point whatsoever to this transmission abroad. In the new Article 4(4) of the citizenship law of 1999, such a stopping point was introduced in terms of the second ("grandchild") generation born abroad; their German citizenship is no longer automatic but conditional upon their parents' declaration of the fact of birth to a German consulate or embassy within a tight time limit. With this reform Germany adjusted to international standard practice, according to which citizenship should express a "genuine connection" between an individual and her state.[22] Moreover, because the state is fixed to a territory, a "genuine connection" is obviously more likely to be established within than beyond the state's borders. Underneath a highly diverse treatment of the cutting, retaining, or recovering of ties with expatriates, there seems to be an informal consensus among contemporary states that beyond the second foreign-born generation of expatriates the ties of membership either should cease to exist or, where they have been cut already, should not be recoverable in a preferential way. This greatly limits the possibility of emigration-based ethnic (re)migration.

Having said this, the informal second-generation cap[23] on ties with members abroad is not fully exhausted in many contemporary states, not even in those with long-standing emigrant traditions. The reasons for this are manifold and often idiosyncratic. One generic brake, though, is the traditional hostility toward dual citizenship in the international state system, which has only recently given way to its pragmatic toleration. One also has to see that the "emigrant" has always been a twisted figure in the nation-state imagination, and his or her image of carrying the national torch abroad has competed with that of traitor to the national cause—in major emigrant-sending, young nation-states such as Turkey or Mexico, the negative view prevailed until most recently.[24] To the degree that the withering of nationalist interstate rivalry has removed a lingering source of ambiguity surrounding the emigrant, one can observe a growing assertiveness with respect to the sustenance or recovery of ties with emigrant communities abroad.

This has set the scene for increasing clashes between the forces of de- and re-ethnicization, particularly in states that are marked by simultaneous immigration and emigration experiences and legacies. A prominent site for such clashes is citizenship law. In several European states, recent episodes of citizenship reform have been moments in which the forces of de- and re-ethnicization have come to a head. While after the demise of the Communist alternative the distinction between "left" and "right" may have become meaningless in many other respects (see Giddens, 1994), with respect to the conflict between de- and re-ethnicization it still works rather neatly. At the risk of simplification, the political left tends to support the integration of domestic immigrants via de-ethnicized citizenship rules, while the political right carries the torch of emigrant communities abroad, advocating ethnicized citizenship rules. Which side prevails is then a question of who has the political majority in a given time and place.

Let me illustrate this dynamic with two recent examples from France and Italy. The French reform of citizenship in 1993, passed under a Gaullist government, has become known for taking away automatic citizenship at majority age from the France-born children of foreign immigrants, making the granting of citizenship contingent upon their expressed "*volonté*" to become French. A little-noticed but important side plot in this drama was the strengthening of *jus sanguinis* citizenship for French expatriates. The bashing of the immigrant and embracing the emigrant bears the unmistakable signature of the political right. Moreover, this was rightly perceived on the political left as a departure from the Republican legacy of nonethnic citizenship, *jure soli*. On the part of French expatriates, who are formally represented by Senators for the French Abroad in the upper house of Parliament (*Sénat*), a long-standing bone of contention had been provisions in the nationality law that either took away (Article 95) or withheld (Article 144) descent-based citizenship from certain foreign-born children of French emigrants—the condition for this abrogation or denial of citizenship being that their parents had not resided in France for fifty years and that neither the parents nor the offspring in question had a *"possession d'état de français."*[25] Though consistent with the statist-territorial conception of French citizenship, these were undeniably "odious" provisions, which had caused a good deal of individual hardship.[26] On their basis, even someone born and raised in France could be stripped of her citizenship, if after emigrating she did not bother to make contact with a French consulate over a fifty-year stretch (no legal duty this)—not to mention that her offspring would thus forfeit her descent-based citizenship too. The 1993 reform allowed these (first- or second-generation) offspring of French emigrants to reclaim French citizenship through simple declaration, yet with the proviso that they could demonstrate "manifest ties of a cultural, professional, economic, or familial order [with France]" (according to the new Article 21-14 of the *Code Civil*).

This was a smallish measure, of which less than 100 French expatriates would make use between 1995 and 1997 (Baudet-Caille, 2000:58). Yet the combination of strengthening *jus sanguinis* citizenship for expatriates with restricting *jus soli* citizenship for domestic immigrants made it a symbolically charged affair.[27] In a Socialist critic's eye, this combination revealed the existence on the Gaullist side of "a certain conception of the ethnic nation, a conception that we condemn absolutely."[28] This was even admitted on the Gaullist side, in their loud and clear rejection of an amendment that would have treated immigrants and emigrants in a symmetric way. This amendment, proposed by a maverick Gaullist, Pierre Mazeaud, in the National Assembly (the lower house of Parliament), would have made citizenship for the second-generation descendants of French emigrants (more precisely, for the offspring of one French parent abroad who was him- or herself born abroad)[29] contingent upon their expressed *volonté* around majority age.[30] Next to the different foreign(er)-born generations to which this measure was to apply ("first" in the case of immigrants; "second" in the case of emigrants), there was of course one decisive difference in the proposed treatment of both groups: the immigrant did not possess French citizenship before expressing her *volonté*, whereas the emigrant was French at birth *jure sanguinis* yet risked losing her citizenship if she did not express her *volonté* between ages 16 and 21. No wonder that this caused the united wrath of the Senators for the French Abroad, and under their pressure the amendment had to be withdrawn. Yet the more interesting matter was that the Senate commission that recommended the suppression of the amendment brusquely denied that both (immigrant and emigrant) groups should be treated symmetrically. In its view, it was not "acceptable to submit young French born abroad to an obligatory formality . . . like the one that is asked of young foreigners who are born in France of foreign parents."[31] As a Communist senator remarked critically, this view established a "net difference" between both groups: a French by descent was "more French" than a young foreigner born in France and residing in France since her birth. To which the Gaullist side responded: *"Mais oui!" "Par définition!"*[32] In this small but noteworthy instance the rightist forces of re-ethnicization prevailed over the leftist forces of de-ethnicization.[33]

The 1992 reform of Italian citizenship law, passed under Christian Democratic Prime Minister Giulio Andreotti, had a similar gist of embracing emigrants and bashing immigrants. In a striking difference, however, there was not even verbal opposition by the left. Surely, in a country that had seen some 26 million of its inhabitants emigrating between 1876 and 1976, and whose ethnic-origin community abroad is estimated at 50 million, emigrant concerns had always been an important matter. Tellingly, the career of the 1992 Citizenship Law (Law No. 91) began with a December 1988 draft bill by Andreotti, then-Minister of Foreign Affairs who a few weeks earlier had chaired a national meeting of the Italian emigrant community in Rome (see Pastore, 2001:113, n. 26). As in all recent European attempts to bolster ties with emigrants abroad, the range of the respective provisions in the 1992 Italian citizenship law was inconspicuous, and taken alone they would have hardly raised an eyebrow. The law merely extended some emigrant-friendly measures that had already characterized its 1912 predecessor: the second-generation descendants of Italian expatriates were given the option of Italian citizenship "by choice"[34] if certain conditions applied—such as service in the Italian army, employment by the Italian state (even abroad), or a two-year residence in Italy at majority age. A probably wider circle of potential re-migrants was addressed in a parallel reduction of the minimum residence for discretionary naturalization from five to three years for the descendants of expatriates. At the same time, the de facto permission of dual citizenship under the 1912 law was upgraded into an explicit permission. This was not exactly a revolution. The recognition of dual citizenship corresponded to the international trend; the second-generation threshold of citizenship for the foreign-born was not transcended; and the potential of ethnic migration was further reduced by a prior residence requirement in most categories, which made would-be ethnic migrants subject to the normal immigration controls.

As in France, the particular venom of this measure consisted of a parallel tightening of immigrants' access to citizenship, which was a simple result of the conservative parties holding the political majority at the time. First, the minimum residence time for naturalization was doubled, from five to a hefty ten years. Secondly, Italian-born children of immigrants were given the option of Italian citizenship only if they resided in Italy until the age of majority "without interruption."[35] Without bothering to justify why the immigrants had to suffer when the emigrants were handed out a benefit, a Christian-Democratic Senator flatly stated: "Then there is the problem of the immigrants. We have adopted a rather generous regime with respect to the *extracomunitari* . . . [B]ut it is clear that . . . we have to bestow on our co-citizens [*i nostri concittadini*] a favorable treatment. The ties with Italy by emigrants on all continents . . . are so strong that they stay alive across several generations."[36] When the bill was adopted in the *Camera dei Deputati* (the lower house of Parliament), the leader of the Socialist faction meekly gave in: "Surely, there are open questions (for example, the ten-year residence requirement for the *extracomunitari*), but we are altogether convinced that now is not the moment to start this type of discussion."[37] In fact, the bill passed its last hurdle in the lower house without a single "no" vote, even the Socialists and Communists voting in its favor.

If one peruses the justifications given for privileging *i nostri concittadini* abroad in the 1992 Citizenship Law, one is struck by their contemporary-sounding note, invoking themes of globalism and transnationalism, plus a quite ferocious anti-statism. According to Senator Mazzola (the Christian-Democratic *rapporteur* of the bill), this measure responded to a desire of "our foreign communities . . . to increase and strengthen their ties with the mother country within an international community of increasingly rapid, continuous, and dense communications, dialogue, and relationships."[38] The bill's Christian Democratic supporters were anxious to stress that this was not a "politico-nationalist" projection of the Italian state abroad, but instead a measure of purely "cultural recognition," driven by a "vision of the world that transcends the identity of nation-states."[39] In Italy, this was really an old theme because "in Catholic political thinking the nation is prior to the State," as another Christian Democratic Senator refreshed the memory of his peers.[40] Along more contemporary lines, the affirmation of dual citizenship in this law was celebrated as "burying the idea of the State as the only God to whom one owes total and unconditional loyalty."[41] Indeed, the entire debate was permeated by an astonishing (though very Italian) amount of state-bashing by the legislative branch of this very state. Interestingly, the motif of an "ethical obligation" to those who had suffered hardship for helping to "keep up the name of Italy in the world," while not absent, was clearly secondary to the "interest of our national community . . . to retain the tie of citizenship that has an important sentimental and cultural value, beyond its juridical aspects."[42] In short, this was a measure to strengthen the sense of Italian nationhood, separate from and beyond the state, in a world of increased mobility and movement across borders.

Epitomizing the left-right divide behind the de- versus re-ethnicization contest, leftist governments under Romano Prodi and Giulio Amato in the late 1990s sought to undo the hard line on citizenship for foreigners, with Prodi instituting a Commission for Integration Policy that recommended conditional *jus soli* citizenship for the children of immigrants and other measures to facilitate ordinary foreigners' access to citizenship (Pastore, 2001:108–109). However, a first reform proposal by the Minister for Social Solidarity in the Amato government, which was presented in December 2000,[43] was never carried any further, and it became irrelevant after the center-right's election victory in May 2001. Instead, under Berlusconi the concerns of *i nostri connazionali* gained new prominence. This is expressed in the addition to the plethora of Italian state ministries of a Ministry for Italians Around the World, which is headed by a member of the post-fascist Alleanza Nazionale and veteran of Mussolini's Salo government, Mirko Tremaglia. In addition to soliciting a law that allows Italian citizens abroad to vote in national elections, Tremaglia's major feat has been to extend ethnic privileges from citizenship to immigration policy. Note that the ethnic privileges in the 1992 citizenship law were granted in a context of "reduced migratory flows" and the "stabilization of our communities abroad";[44] they were not meant to spur migration. After the recent economic collapse of Argentina, which saw scores of ethnic Italians line up for Italian citizenship, and—one must surmise—in light of a new demographic need for immigrants on the demand side, this has changed.[45] At the behest of Tremaglia, the new immigration law of 2002, which is harsh on *extracomunitari* in any other respect, promptly includes a quota for "workers of Italian origin."[46]

The French and Italian examples, to which more European examples could be easily added,[47] show that emigration is one source of re-ethnicization, and one that is generated by contemporary global processes on an ever larger scale. A second source of recurrent re-ethnicization is the existence of national minorities abroad.[48] At one level, this is an old legacy, rooted in the vicissitudes of post-nineteenth-century nation-state building that produced innumerable losers. A slice of the national minority *problématique* was captured in this study under the "diaspora" rubric. The states involved in it are "ethnic" in a stronger and more specific sense than emigrant states. In a way, emigration reveals all states to be ethnic in a *temporal* sense, because a state *qua* state is a membership unit that reproduces itself across generations. By contrast, the presence of a national minority points to a *spatial* dimension of ethnicity. Not every state is subjected or receptive to it, but only one that historically defines itself as "homeland" of clustered minorities abroad.

While it may be blurred empirically, there is a difference in kind between emigrant- and minority-level coethnics abroad. The first left as individuals, voluntarily, and to a multitude of destinations, whereas the second are often the collective victims of moving state borders, clustering in distinct spaces. Most ethnic migration today is within the latter constellation, and it will persist as long there are "kin states"[49] with a self-given mandate to induce the return of their coethnic minorities abroad.

As I alluded to above, it is tempting to juxtapose these two sources of re-ethnicization in terms of "new" global developments and "old" historical legacies. However, this would be misleading, not only because there is nothing new about emigration in itself; in addition, what a "kin-state" is and does becomes inevitably couched in the discursive and institutional vocabulary of the present time, and its mandate may even be reinforced by contemporary global processes.

A highly instructive case in this respect is the debate surrounding the recent "status law" in Hungary. Like most states in post-Communist central-eastern Europe, Hungary gave itself a constitutional obligation to protect its coethnics abroad. Article 6(3) of Hungary's constitution of 1989 stipulates that "the Republic of Hungary recognizes its responsibilities toward Hungarians living outside the borders of the country and shall assist them in fostering their relations with Hungary." Also as in most east European states, Hungary has two different ethnic communities abroad: those of emigrant origins who were exiled to the West under Communism and shortly thereafter, and national minorities in adjacent states who had seen state borders move above their heads during the twentieth century. In a perceptive analysis of "diaspora politics" in post-Communist Eurasia, King and Melvin (1999/2000:138) found the states in the region altogether more interested in their resourceful Western emigrant communities than in their impoverished Eastern kin-minorities. In terms of return migration, Hungary is no exception, as it allows her Western coethnics to naturalize without residence, while the whole point of the "status law" is to encourage her kin-minorities to stay where they are.

Passed in June 2001, the status law provides Hungary's three million coethnics in six designated neighboring states with seasonal work permits, access to Hungary's institutions of higher education on equal terms with Hungarian citizens, reduced public transport fees in Hungary, and a number of educational benefits (especially for mother-tongue instruction) that are effective in the respective host state. While meant to finally overcome the "Trianon trauma,"[50] that is, Hungary's loss of two-thirds of her territory and one-half of her population after World War I, the interesting feature of the status law is its contemporary fashioning as a response to globalization and Europeanization—an "old" legacy appears here in strikingly "new" cloth.

For Foreign Minister Janos Martyonyi, the status law is about "the slow dissolution of the principles of absolute state sovereignty and absolute territoriality [and] the gradual recognition and acceptance of the possibility and right to belong to multiple communities" (quoted in Fowler, 2002:46). In short, the status law stands for "the value system of a future Europe" (Zsolt Nemeth, quoted ibid.). Nominally to "ensure the free movement of persons and the free flow of ideas" (Article 3d), the status law indeed resembles the European construct in organizing political space along functional rather than territorial lines. By ruling out permanent residence in the kin-state, Hungary creates cyclical cross-border mobility according to function, such as work or study, so that territorial borders become "just lines drawn on a map," as Prime Minister Orban put it (quoted in Fowler, 2002:42).

However, as the governments of Romania and Slovakia have objected, Hungary's postnational stance is hypocritical, because functional mobility is premised on the reassertion of an ethnic difference—the non-Hungarian citizens of Romania and Slovakia, after all, cannot partake in it. To this, and also to a European audience deeply suspicious of state-engineered ethnic distinctions, Hungary built up a second line of defense: not a "blood relationship" but "free choice" makes someone an ethnic Hungarian for the purposes of the status law. On this premise, the Hungarian government even claimed that the status law did "not use ethnicity as a basis for eligibility for claiming benefits under it" (Council of Europe, 2001b:5). In reality, the question of who is an ethnic Hungarian is the most muddled part of the status law. While Article 1 of the status law formally stipulates that it shall apply to all "persons declaring themselves to be of Hungarian nationality," the actual process of ethnic status determination is farmed out to official Hungarian ethnic associations abroad. Further complicating the matter, these associations' status recommendations cannot be overridden by the Hungarian state, but technically they are also non-binding, to avoid the charge that these associations are state agencies operating on foreign territory (ibid., p. 18; Fowler, 2002:45, n. 67).

Hungary's embracing of its kin-minorities stirred massive debate across Europe, and especially Romania and Slovakia, host states of two-thirds of the three million ethnic Hungarians addressed by the status law,[51] have fiercely objected to it. Detecting the old specter of territorial revisionism behind the Euro-jargon, Romanian President Iliescu denounced the law as "a diversion that is provocatory, undemocratic, and discriminatory."[52] More concretely, Romania raised two objections. First, the law discriminated against the members of the titular nation. However, this objection was tantamount to admitting that the Romanian state did not deliver properly to her own citizens, and, tellingly, it could be bought off by allowing all Romanians, irrespectively of their ethnic backgrounds, to work for three months per year in Hungary.[53] A second, more fundamental objection was that the law had extraterritorial effects, being administered by Hungary inside Romanian territory and having legal and material consequences therein. In this respect the status law constituted a "breach inside the citizenship legal relationship."[54] Romania thus defended the modern norm of sovereign statehood against Hungary's express dismissal of it.

To settle the dispute, Romania and Hungary turned to the Venice Commission, the Council of Europe's instrument to steer eastern Europe's transition to democracy. Its *Report on the Preferential Treatment of National Minorities by Their Kin-State,* issued in October 2001, may be read as the dominant international opinion on how far a liberal state can go in protecting its coethnics abroad. Consonant with international law, the Venice Commission reaffirmed the principle that the "home state," not the kin-state, is primarily responsible for minority protection, though supervised by international treaties and conventions. If the kin-state wants to intervene on behalf of its coethnics abroad, the usual way is through international forums or bilateral treaties with the host state. If it nevertheless wants to go further than this, in terms of unilateral domestic legislation, the scope for doing so is limited, among other considerations, by the need to "respect territorial sovereignty" and the "prohibition of discrimination." With respect to sovereignty, the Commission deemed the exercise of state powers outside the national boundaries "not permissible" (Council of Europe, 2001a:13f), thus castigating Hungary's conferral of quasiofficial functions to her ethnic associations abroad. With respect to nondiscrimination, the Commission cautiously intimated that the "difference in treatment" created by the status law "could constitute discrimination—based on essentially ethnic reasons—and be in breach of the principle of non-discrimination" (ibid., p. 16). It all depended on the nature of the discrimination—the latter was tolerable only if its narrow purpose was the fostering of "cultural links" of the minority with the kin-state.

The European verdict on the Hungarian status law reveals the two parameters that shape ethnic migration now and will continue to shape it in the future. On the one hand, the system of states seems to favor ethnic immigration over in situ or "circular" alternatives, which are seen as violation of the principle of territorial sovereignty. On the other hand, human-rights constraints and the principle of nondiscrimination set tight limits for any ethnic discrimination in the liberal state. As a result, there is a space for ethnic migration, but it is constricted by liberal norms that will make this migration always exceptional.

Notes
References
Index

Notes

Preface

1. I am aware that "ethnic migration" has sometimes the opposite meaning of foreignness and noncongruity between migrants and receiving state. This reflects the original meaning of the Greek *ethnos* as "pagan" or "heathen," referring to people "not like us" (see Hutchinson and Smith, 1996:4). However, considering that contemporary migration tends to be equated with *international* (and thus foreign) migration, such a usage of "ethnic" amounts to a redundancy. If "ethnic" is to add something to "migration," it should be reserved to what Brubaker (1998b) has called "migrations of ethnic affinity," and this is the way it is increasingly understood today (see, for example, Münz and Ohliger, 2003). I concede that it would have been more precise to speak of "ethnic-affinity migration" in this book. However, for the sake of conceptual and linguistic economy I decided in favor of the simpler "ethnic migration," also in the hope that *this* (in my view, the only nonredundant) usage of the term will prevail.

1. The Problem of Ethnic Selectivity

1. If not marked otherwise, the terms *immigrant* and *migrant* (as well as immigration and migration) are used interchangeably throughout this book.
2. This is an understatement. The establishment of the unitary Italian state in the late nineteenth century was fought against the fierce opposition of the Vatican; tellingly, the first capital of the Italian Republic was Florence, not Rome.
3. "'Accogliere gli immigrati solo se sono cattolici,'" *la Repubblica*, 25 September 2000.
4. The meeting, in which the author participated, took place on October 16, 2000, at the European University Institute, Florence.
5. See the latest European Commission proposal (2000). The same three selection criteria are deployed at the national level, as in the 2002 German immigration law (*Zuwanderungsgesetz*), which was annulled for procedural reasons by the German Constitutional Court, but reinstated in modified form in 2004.
6. For two opposite views on this, see Soysal (1994) and Joppke (2001a).

7. The matter is certainly more complicated, if one considers that "talent" (as a predisposition for a certain kind of agency) is ascribed rather than achieved. Considering talent as subject to societal redistribution moves John Rawls's theory of justice away from real existing liberalism to socialist-utopian liberalism.

8. Other exceptions, not discussed in this book, are ideological admissions, which were a prominent consideration in Western states' asylum policies during the Cold War period; or reciprocity-based admissions, which are based on interstate treaties and conventions (the latter, however, can overlap with ethnic admissions, as discussed in Chapter 3).

9. In Weber's account, the status of these ethnic markers is ambivalent—they are both "expressive of" and "conducive to" ethnicity, that is, sometimes figuring as answer to the question "How do we know ethnicity when we see it?" and sometimes referring to (by definition nonethnic) factors that favor the formation of common-descent beliefs.

10. Note, however, that Weber mentions as examples for this only neutralized small political communities, such as Liechtenstein or Luxembourg.

11. In Lord Frazer's famous leading speech in *Mandla v. Dowell Lee* (1983), history and culture were the two "essential" criteria that made an ethnic-origin group. In turn, he downscaled "descent from a small number of common ancestors" to one of several "relevant" yet nonessential criteria (see Poulter, 1998:304).

12. See the work by John Meyer and collaborators, most recently Meyer (1999).

13. See also David Miller's (1995:25) similar defense of liberal nationalism, which wants to rule out a national identity based on "biological descent," in which "our fellow-nationals must be our 'kith and kin,' a view that leads directly to racism."

14. He follows Avishai Margalit and Joseph Raz (1990), who argue that only those groups in which membership is a "matter of belonging, not of achievement" (p. 446) qualify for "national self-determination": "[A]t the most fundamental level, our sense of our own identity depends on criteria of belonging rather than on those of accomplishment" (p. 447). This sits oddly with Kymlicka's (1999) distinction between "ethnic" and "cultural" nationalism, defined by their relative closure or openness to nonmembers.

15. The post-September 11 national-origin profiling by U.S. immigration authorities is also in a second sense nonethnic: it applies only to men, not women. See "New Policy Delays Visas for Specified Muslim Men," *New York Times*, 10 September 2002, p. A12.

16. Walzer (1992:101) peculiarly distinguishes between the always ethnic "nation-states" of Europe and the nonethnic United States, which "isn't, after all, a nation-state, but a nation of nationalities."

17. For a similar critique of Walzer's conflation of "state" and "community," see Bader (1995:217-221).

18. Carens derives his case from an internationalization of Rawls's "original position": a rational individual, not knowing into which state she was born, would posit herself as "alien" and advocate the right of free movement. For a similar application of Rawls, see Beitz (1979).

19. But see Rawls's recent application of liberal principles to interstate relations (1999).
20. But see Kymlicka's most recent depiction of the "self-limiting" character of nation building in liberal states (2001). This picture contradicts his justification of minority rights.
21. This blanket statement, made here to bring out a problem with Kymlicka's justification of minority rights, admittedly is in need of qualification. It is not my intention to question the legitimacy of claims of national minority groups for the special recognition of their cultures. Liberal states have actually recognized such claims since the post-World War I Wilsonian minority treaties. What is questionable is only the proliferation of such claims on behalf of all sorts of "minorities"–immigrants, for example (as is conceded by Kymlicka himself, in 1995:63).
22. He borrows this distinction from Ronald Dworkin. Asking whether a liberal state can support art, Dworkin answers "Yes," if "state support is designed to protect structure rather than to promote any particular content for that structure at any particular time" (Dworkin, 1991:233).
23. Note that Carens reversed his earlier position (1987), which had explicitly ruled out immigration restrictions for the sake of "preserving culture."
24. This point is also made by William Galston (1995:522), who concludes from it that liberalism can be about only "the protection of diversity, not the valorization of choice" (p. 523).
25. Tellingly, the other cases of ethnic migration discussed by Carens (1992) are all rejected from a liberal point of view–White Australia, the German and Israeli Laws of Return, and British patriality.
26. This is also his tack on multiculturalism; see Carens (2000).
27. Note that Brubaker (1992), who has done much to popularize the "ethnic" versus "civic" nationhood distinction, cannot be charged with this equation of nationhood and immigration policy. On the contrary, Brubaker held that immigration policies in Germany and France were converging (toward zero immigration), while citizenship laws and policies were persistently divergent. This divergence of approaches to citizenship (and not immigration policy) is then explained in reference to varying nationhood traditions.
28. See in this context Sartori's (1969) brilliant refutation of the traditional view of political parties as reactive to social class cleavages; instead, he shows that political entrepreneurs and parties have proactively created such class cleavages as socially meaningful facts.
29. Although the focus in this study is on English-speaking settler states, Latin American settler states practiced similar forms of national-origin selection and Asian exclusion in the first part of the twentieth century (see Bernard, 1950:219-231).
30. In the different context of ethnoracial group formation in the United States, Yen Le Espiritu (1992) defined "panethnic" as referring to "a politico-cultural collectivity made up of peoples of several, hitherto distinct, tribal or national origins" (p. 2). Since panethnic units "cannot lay claim to a primordial ori-

gin" (p. 9), they are certainly a limiting case of "ethnic." However, if "ethnic" is not to be equated with biological descent, as I suggested earlier, a "pan-ethnic" collectivity is "ethnic" too.

31. In his evaluation of this manuscript, Rogers Brubaker has questioned whether Lusophony (and, by implication, Hispanism) is "ethnic" at all. If one defines *ethnic* in a nonbiological way, in terms of shared history and space, Luso-phony and Hispanism are certainly "ethnic" (or rather "panethnic," as I sug-gest with Le Espiritu [1992]). In fact, in limiting "ethnic" to the return policies that target the descendants of former emigrants, Brubaker implicitly adheres to a biological notion of descent (which is subject to the pitfalls indi-cated earlier). I still agree that qualifying Lusophony as ethnic is only an inch away from illicit "conceptual stretching" (Sartori 1970). By the same token, if Lusophony and Hispanism were indeed nonethnic, as Brubaker suggests, so would be many a policy whose ethnic quality no one would reasonably put in doubt, such as the pre-1965 U.S. national-origins policy that selected on "place of birth" rather than ethnicity proper; even the pre-1992 German *Aussiedler* policy would be potentially nonethnic because descent from a Ger-man parent was not a required selection criterion (see Chapters 2 and 4).

32. For a sophisticated combination of international and domestic-level factors, see Risse, Ropp and Sikkink (1999); also Gurowitz (1999) argues persuasively for combining both levels of analysis.

33. There are at least two other constellations that would merit further atten-tion. The first is the case of minority nations within multinational states, which seek to reproduce themselves by means of ethnically selective immi-gration policies. However, there is only one case in which immigration pow-ers have effectively devolved to the subnational level: Quebec (see Carens, 1995). Catalonia has been asking for such powers, but is unlikely to be ever successful in this. A second possible constellation consists of emigrant-send-ing states (but see the Spanish and Portuguese cases discussed in Chapter 3 and the second half of Chapter 5). This constellation is not pursued here (at least not in the form of a separate chapter) because, upon closer inspection, there is not much that is puzzling. In most cases, genealogical ties do not exceed the second foreign-born generation, so one might equally argue (as British defenders of "patriality" have actually done within a postcolonial context) that this is extended-family migration; and where such ties do exceed the second foreign-born generation, the respective case blends into the "diaspora" constellation.

2. Toward Source-Country Universalism in Settler States: The United States and Australia

1. I borrow this concept from Peter Schuck (1991), especially p. 25.

2. Strictly speaking, in the current U.S. country-based quota system there is still an element of national-origin selection. However, because all country quotas are equally large, there is no formal discrimination involved in this.

3. Between 1825 and 1950, over 80 percent of immigrants to Australia were British; in the same period, the British intake in the United States was just over 11 percent (Bernard, 1950:204).

4. Even Britain, more ostensibly than any other state (particularly its own Dominion states) committed to a nondiscriminatory, free-entry policy, passed an Aliens Act in 1905 to exclude East European and Russian Jews.

5. This has been shown in recent revisionist histories of American immigration, citizenship, and nationhood (see, for example, Jacobson, 1998; King, 2000; Smith, 1997; Gerstle, 2001).

6. For the underlying distinction between ethnicity as (self-) "identification" and race as "classification" (by others), see Banton (1983:106).

7. Therefore UNESCO's programmatic rebuttal of the race concept also clarified that nations, ethnic, and religious groups are not "races": "Les Américains ne constituent pas une race, pas plus d'ailleurs que les Français ou les Allemands. Aucun groupe national ne constitue une race *ipso facto*. Les musulmans et les juifs ne forment pas de race, pas plus que les catholiques ou les protestants . . ." (UNESCO, 1953:12).

8. Before the study of race was transformed into one of "race relations," it consisted of "characterology," the tracing of personality traits of individuals to the physical "races" they belonged to (see Jacobson, 1998:98).

9. Some exceptions were made for diplomats, long-distance traders, academics and other high-skilled professionals, or close family members of already admitted resident immigrants.

10. See Price (1966; 1974); Huttenback (1973; 1976).

11. Australia had always been the proverbial "third choice" of European immigrants after the United States and Canada. Between 1820 and 1930, 61.4 percent of all transoceanic migrants had the United States as their destination; only 11.5 percent and 4.5 percent went to Canada and Australia, respectively (Bernard, 1950:202).

12. In Italy, the noncitizen descendants of Italian turn-of-the-century emigrants, who lined up in January 2002 at the Italian embassies in crisis-plagued Argentina to "recover" Italian citizenship, are perceived as *i nostri connazionali* (our conationals) ("Argentina, la fuga degli italiani," *la Repubblica*, 11 January 2002, p.19).

13. See Lagarde (1984:483–485). Note, however, that there was an Australian "patriality" in reciprocity for British "patriality" between 1973 and 1981.

14. For the notion of official nationalism, see Anderson (1983) and Hobsbawm (1990).

15. This is the claim by Willard (1923:191), convincingly rebutted by Yarwood (1964:24–25).

16. Van den Berghe (1978:78). He quotes Abraham Lincoln, the "Great Emancipator," who was offended when accused of abolitionism: "There is a physical difference between the white and black races which I believe will ever forbid the two races living together on terms of social and political equality" (ibid, p. 79).

17. For this vision, see also Hartz (1955) and Huntington (1981).

18. Hartz (1955) contains only a five-page discussion of "race," safely tucked into the discussion of the "reactionary enlightenment" of the American South (pp. 167–172).

19. See, however, Eugene Weber's (1976) seminal study of state-engineered nation building in nineteenth-century France.

20. But see the interesting account by Eric Kaufmann (2000b), who argued that there had been an "American ethnicity" through "fission from an English Protestant parent stock" all along (p.134). This view, with gives much to the "Anglo-Saxon myth" as expounded in the late nineteenth century by some New England intellectuals (for this, see Solomon, 1956), has to downplay the racial boundaries of the republic, from which only non-Europeans were excluded. Moreover, Anglo-Saxonism was only one interpretation of American nationhood and was particularly prominent in only a specific period.

21. See Iris Chang, "Fear of SARS, Fear of Strangers," *New York Times,* May 21, 2003, p. 31. Chang describes discriminatory health screening procedures against Chinese immigrants in early 1900s San Francisco.

22. The notion of "working class" is perhaps not quite adequate in this context, because it suggests a degree of homogeneity and organization that could not exist in a state half of whose population in the 1850s was foreign-born. Coolidge ([1909] 1969) refers to the rather unsettled constituency driving the anti-Chinese cause as "adventurers" (p. 40) or "alien class" (p. 182).

23. The fracturing of Europeans into a variety of "races" led to conceptual difficulties. The term "race" was no longer available to distinguish the Europeans combined from non-European races; accordingly, Grant conceived of the European "races" as "subdivisions" of the Caucasian "species" (Grant, 1924:21). In this taxonomy there was no shared humanity between Europeans and non-Europeans. But this is perhaps the whole point of racism.

24. From a 1924 House Committee report, quoted in Hutchinson (1981:485).

25. The idea that national-origins quota should represent the entire American people, and not just the foreign-born, was first conceived in a paper by John Trevor, an advisor to the House Committee on Immigration ("Preliminary Study of Immigration Problem," *Congressional Record,* Senate, 3 April 1924, pp. 5469–5470).

26. "Your committee is not the author of any of these books on the so-called Nordic races," said House committee chairman Albert Johnson in the debate on the 1924 immigration bill (*Congressional Record,* House, 5 April 1924, p. 5648).

27. *Congressional Record,* Senate, 3 April 1924, p. 5467.

28. Congressman McReynolds, *Congressional Record,* House, 8 April 1924, p. 5854.

29. In the end, a token quota of 100 was given to independent African states. However, immigration from these quarters was never envisaged. As David Reed said during the Senate debate, "they [the Negro population of the country] do not want, and we do not want, to allow great immigration from

African sources. That is self-evident to all of us" (*Congressional Record*, Senate, 3 April 1924, p. 5468).

30. Western Hemisphere immigrants were quota-free. I discuss their separate treatment in a later section. For the complicated method of computing the quotas, see the statement by chief-statistician Joseph Hill (reprinted in Bernard, 1950:281–288).

31. The so-called "racial prerequisite" cases heard by the Supreme Court shortly before the 1924 immigration act had appositely established that Indians and Japanese were not "white" in the meaning of naturalization law, thus by implication cementing their exclusion from immigration and prefiguring the common "Caucasian" or "white" race into which the fractured Europeans would eventually grow back (see Haney Lopez, 1996).

32. *Congressional Record*, House, 8 April 1924, p. 5864.

33. There is an interesting short exchange over the gap between place of birth and ethnicity or race in the Senate debate over the 1924 immigration bill. For immigration committee leader David Reed, it was a matter of practicality and "common-sense" to define quotas in terms of place of birth: "If we once got into a study of the ethnology involved in this question we could not pass an immigration law in the next 50 years" (*Congressional Record*, Senate, 3 April 1924, p. 5462).

34. For instance, the government of Yugoslavia protested in 1925 that the U.S. authorities classified "citizens of Yugoslavia . . . with names such as Serbian, Montenegrin, Croatian, Slovenian, Dalmatian, Bosnian, Herzogevinian." Probably pressure by Mussolini led to the merging of the two Italian "races" in 1936. American Jewish organizations attacked the "Hebrew race" category, which had to be removed in November 1943. For these and many more examples see Weil (2001a).

35. *Australian Commonwealth Parliamentary Debates* (vol.4), House of Representatives, 12 September 1901, p. 4807.

36. Prime Minister Menzies at the 1950 Citizenship Convention, quoted in Lack and Templeton (1995:43).

37. *Australian Commonwealth Parliamentary Debates* (vol.4), House of Representatives, 12 September 1901, p. 4806.

38. At the behest of Japan, a 1905 amendment replaced the words "an European language" with "any prescribed language."

39. Freeman and Jupp (1992:3). Only Queensland extended assisted passage to the "nordic cousins" from Germany and Scandinavia between the 1870s and 1914 (see Jupp, 1995:211).

40. This was also within the 1901 Immigration Restriction Act, which excluded not just "any person" failing the dictation test but also "idiots," "insane persons," ex-convicts, prostitutes, contract workers, and persons "likely . . . to become a charge" upon the state.

41. Non–British European arrivals more than doubled between 1923 and 1924, from 5,626 to 12,332. This was still only a small fraction of the British entries, which numbered 88,335 in 1924 (Langfield, 1991:2).

42. President Franklin D. Roosevelt, State of the Union message, January 6, 1941, quoted in Burgers (1992:448).

43. *New York Times,* 18 July 1950, p.1.

44. A very good account of this is Tichenor (2002, ch.7). See also Rosenblum (2000).

45. Canada was first in committing itself to source-country universalism in 1962. According to Canadian immigration scholar Freda Hawkins, this change was brought about by "some senior officials" worried about Canada's international standing, and it occurred in the absence of "parliamentary or popular demand" (Hawkins, 1991:39). Yet this was no top-down imposition by international norms, because "Canada was so deeply entrenching itself internationally that domestic changes mirrored international ones and, ultimately, moved beyond them" (Gurowitz, 1999:289).

46. Quoted from President Harry S. Truman's veto message on the 1952 Immigration and Nationality Act (President's Commission on Immigration and Naturalization, [1952] 1971:278).

47. On the status of the principle of nondiscrimination in international law, see Goodwin-Gill (1978, ch. 5; 1990), and Goodwin-Gill, Jenny, and Perruchoud (1985).

48. From a Tokyo broadcast to China in December 1942 (quoted in Riggs, 1950:161).

49. That "racial equality" was a "boomerang argument" is strikingly visible in this exchange between an invited repeal advocate and a member of the House immigration committee during congressional hearings. When answering affirmatively to the question whether he "believe[d] in what is commonly spoken of in this country as social equality among races," the witness was rebuffed: "I thank you for giving your view. You have done your cause more harm than anybody else" (quoted in Riggs, 1950:128).

50. Historian Hugh Davis Graham, cited in Tichenor (2002:179).

51. Senator McCarran, quoted in Divine (1957:191).

52. Both quotes are from a 1950 Senate report recommending the maintenance of national-origin quotas (in Bennett, 1966:129).

53. Bennett (1966:131). Any person with at least 50 percent Asian ancestry was charged against the quota of his or her "titular" country (which was limited to 100 immigrants per year).

54. From a letter by the American Veterans Committee and nine ethnic associations criticizing the pending 1952 legislation, *Congressional Record,* Senate, 23 April 1952, p. 4250.

55. This critique came from Congressman Adam Clayton Powell, a New York Democrat in whose district 150,000 West Indians resided. Quoted in Jacobson (1998:117).

56. Statement by Secretary of State Dean Rusk in *Congressional Record,* House, 11 March 1965, p. 89.

57. From 1954 to 1963, the total of such nonquota immigrants (not including the Western Hemisphere) was 694,643 (*Congressional Record,* House, 2 July

1964, p. 392). Their entry was enabled by no less than thirty-two separate laws passed between 1953 and 1964 that modified the national-origins system (Gimpel and Edwards, 1999:99).

58. Western Hemisphere immigration had been averaging 110,000 between 1955 and 1965, about 70 percent being from Mexico and Canada (*Congressional Record*, House, 8 March 1965, p. 43). Since 1924, Western Hemisphere immigration had filled some of the labor needs that could no longer be satisfied by restricted southern and eastern European immigration. As a partial result of this, already before 1950 the share of northern and western European immigration in total immigration was not 80 percent, as prescribed by the quota law, but only 43 percent (Bernard, 1950:41).

59. Quoted in Skrentny (2002:50). A particularly interesting, though little known, instance of actual policy rushing ahead of "the general letter of the law" concerned the Asia-Pacific Triangle. Since 1961 one was no longer required to indicate one's race and ethnicity on visa applications. Accordingly, it was no longer possible to charge Asian-origin immigrants from outside the triangle (such as those from Latin America) to "their" Asian country (see Bennett, 1966:136).

60. *Congressional Record*, House, 5 August 1964, p. 641.

61. In Congressional hearings in 1964, Cellar laced his proposal for a reformed immigration system with a fictitious story from his multiethnic district: "A fellow goes into a Chinese restaurant and there to his amazement he sees a colored waiter. He says to the colored waiter in the Chinese restaurant, 'What is the specialty of the house?' The colored waiter says, 'Pizza pie.' 'Pizza pie, in a Chinese restaurant?' he says. 'Yes, this is a Jewish neighborhood.' This epitomizes the nature of our society in many of our cities" (*Congressional Record*, House, 11 June 1964, p. 6).

62. *Congressional Record*, House, 2 July 1964, p. 386.

63. "We want to bring our immigration law into line with the spirit of the Civil Rights Act of 1964," said Vice-President Hubert Humphrey on the eve of immigration reform (quoted in Tichenor, 2002:215).

64. *Congressional Record*, House, 2 July 1964, p. 388.

65. Emilio Nunez, in *Congressional Record*, House, 3 September 1964, p. 938.

66. In his State of the Union address in 1964, President Johnson urged Congress to "return the United States to an immigration policy which both serves the national interest and *continues our traditional ideals*. No move could more effectively reaffirm our fundamental belief that a man is to be judged—and judged exclusively, on his worth as a human being" (*Congressional Record*, House, 6 April 1965, p. 164; emphasis added).

67. Four of the seven preference categories established by the 1965 Immigration Act recognized family ties (amounting to 74 percent of annual visas), and only two recognized skills and the economic profile of immigrants (20 percent). The seventh category was for refugees (6 percent). Although the visas in each category were pooled Eastern Hemisphere–wide and granted on a first come, first served basis, no quota country could exceed an annual limit of 20,000 visas.

68. The Western Hemisphere comprises all countries on the North and South American continents.

69. Senator John Box from Texas, quoted in Divine (1957:57).

70. In 1929 the State Department advised its consulates in Mexico to apply these individual-level screening provisions more rigorously to visa applicants; as a result, Mexican immigration dropped from about 40,000 in 1929 to under 13,000 in 1930 (Divine, 1957:63).

71. *Congressional Record,* House, 8 March 1965, p. 42.

72. Ibid., p. 42. A similar exchange unfolded between House committee member Peter Rodino, like Feighan a Democrat beholden to labor interests, and Secretary of State Dean Rusk. "Doesn't this [Western Hemisphere] preference, in effect, raise another question of discrimination?" asked Rodino. Although Rusk conceded that discrimination in the sense of "drawing a distinction" was certainly involved in this preference, it had nothing to do with "those unwelcome, unacceptable, resented kinds of distinctions which come into the narrower sense of the word 'discrimination'" (*Congressional Record,* House, 11 March 1965, p. 96).

73. *Congressional Record,* House, 11 March 1965, p. 98.

74. *Congressional Record,* House, 11 March 1965, p. 27.

75. Ibid.

76. U.S. House of Representatives, *Immigration and Nationality Act Amendments of 1976.* 94th Cong., 2d sess., Report No.94-1553, Washington, D.C., September 1976, p. 9. Perhaps in order to avoid the appearance of offending one's neighbors, the folding of Western Hemisphere countries into the uniform quota system was also presented as in the best interest of their immigrants. As long as the preference categories were not applied to Western Hemisphere countries, their nuclear family immigrants could not be privileged over others, and—because of a heavily oversubscribed Western Hemisphere ceiling by the mid-1970s—they had to wait long periods before their turn arrived. By contrast, immigrant visas were immediately available for family migrants from most Eastern Hemisphere countries. To eliminate these "inequities" was officially presented as the "basic purpose" of the Immigration and Nationality Act Amendments of 1976 (Committee on the Judiciary, House of Representatives, *The 'Immigration and Nationality Act Amendments of 1976' (P.L. 94-571): A Summary and Explanation,* 94th Cong., 2nd sess., Washington, D.C., November 1976, p. 6).

77. See Barbara Solomon, who wrote in the mid-1950s: "(A)lthough no longer tenable, the older ideology of race lingered in the immigration laws of the land, a legacy half-forgotten in its actual content and little understood as a betrayal of the continuing faith in the potentialities of America's democratic people" (Solomon, 1956:209).

78. W. K.Hancock, quoted in Elkin (1945:6).

79. A similar programmatic statement, anticipating the readjustment of the White Australia policy after World War II, is that of Eggleston (1948).

80. *Australian Commonwealth Parliamentary Debates,* House of Representatives, 2 August 1945, p. 4911.

81. Bilateral agreements were made with the Netherlands and Italy (1951); West Germany, Austria, and Greece (1952); Finland, Switzerland, Sweden, Denmark, and Norway (1954); Spain (1958); Turkey (1968); and Yugoslavia (1970). See Jupp (1991:77).

82. See London (1970, ch. 6). According to Gallup polls, a mellowing of majority support for the categorical exclusion of Asians did not occur before the late 1950s (see Rivett, 1962:118f).

83. The only exceptions were the numerically insignificant Australian Communist Party and the right-wing Democratic Labor Party; see London (1970, ch. 4).

84. The 1956 rules are reprinted in Palfreeman (1967:157–163).

85. However, the fifteen-year threshold to permanent residence and naturalization had tangible effects on Asian immigrants: family reunification was denied to them during this period.

86. Mr. Opperman, "Immigration: Ministerial Statement," *Australian Commonwealth Parliamentary Debates,* House of Representatives, 9 March 1966, pp. 68 and 69.

87. See Rivett (1962) and the ex post reflections in Rivett (1992a, b) and Viviani (1992).

88. Even after White Australia was formally abandoned in favor of a nondiscriminatory immigration policy, the IRG still insisted that pragmatic arguments for race selections had "something in them" (Rivett, 1975:1; see also the dissenting statement of an IRG member, ibid., pp. 293–295).

89. Since 1949, Australia was ruled by Liberal Party/National Country Party coalition governments. On the major party stances toward immigration, see Grattan (1993) for Labor, and Rubenstein (1993) for the Liberal Party.

90. *Australian Commonwealth Parliamentary Debates,* House of Representatives, vol. 84, 24 May 1973, p. 2649.

91. Another crucial move was to impose a visa obligation on British immigrants, which had already existed for all other immigrants (see Jordens, 1997:228).

92. "Prior to 1973, persons of non-European descent were ineligible for citizenship until they had been resident in Australia for five years, although many people of European descent could qualify for citizenship after one year's residence. My Government abolished this provision. Non-Europeans qualified for citizenship under the same terms as other migrants, after three years' residence" (Whitlam, 1985:502). In reality, before 1973, European and non-European immigrants were subject to the same five-year rule (with the exception of English-proficient immigrants, who since 1969 could naturalize after three years), and only British immigrants were subject to the one-year rule; and not just non-European, but (non-English-proficient) European immigrants also profited from the new three-year rule. Whitlam's account projects the removal of racial restrictions into that of a positive discrimination between British and "other" immigrants, which as such had nothing to do with the former.

93. "In a family the overall attachment to the common good need not impose a sameness on the outlook or activity of each member, nor need these members deny their individuality and distinctiveness in order to seek a superficial and unnatural conformity" (Al Grassby, *A multi-cultural society for the future* [1973], partially reprinted in Lack and Templeton, 1995:143–144).

94. Canadian multiculturalism postdated the turn to a universalistic immigration policy and is linked to the distinct problem of Francophone Quebec's separatism.

95. See also the valuable critique of the "ambiguous and ephemeral" character of Australian multiculturalism by Castles et al. (1988, ch.4). Among the best short statements on the distinctness of Australian multiculturalism is that of Jupp (1991, ch. 8).

96. The claim that Australia was a "nation of immigrants" first appeared in the booklet *The Evolution of a Policy,* issued in 1971 by the Minister for Immigration (Lynch, 1971).

97. It is perhaps more adequate to call this critique "radical," because it is critical of liberal principles, such as the possibility of impartiality and neutrality. However, it shares with the liberal critique the charge that nondiscrimination is still incomplete in immigration policy.

98. For public opinion, see Simon and Lynch (1999). On the intellectual side, examples of populism are Brimelow (1995) in the United States and Blainey (1984) in Australia; on the political side, marginal politicians such as the independent Pat Buchanan in the United States and Pauline Hanson (a defector from the Liberal Party) in Australia have campaigned on explicitly anti–non-European immigrant platforms.

99. As the Supreme Court held in its *Nishimura Ekiu v. United States* decision in 1892, "it is an accepted maxim of international law, that every sovereign nation has the power, as inherent in sovereignty, and essential to self-preservation, to forbid the entrance of foreigners within its dominions, or to admit them only in such cases . . . as it may see fit to prescribe" (quoted in Chin, 1998:59).

100. The "seventh preference" for refugees under the 1965 Immigration Act only prolonged the ideologically and geographically limited refugee definition under the 1952 Immigration and Nationality Act (Romig, 1985:314).

101. Most systematically, Lennox (1993); see also Ignatius (1993), Johnson (1993), Hughes and Crane (1993), and Little (1998).

102. Besides the literature mentioned in the previous endnote, see Stepick (1982), Helton (1993), and Ortiz Miranda (1995).

103. *Haitian Refugee Center v Civiletti,* 503 F.Supp. 442, 519 (S.D. Fla. 1980); p. 450.

104. In 1992, for instance, the asylum approval rates for Ethiopians and Chinese were 75 and 85 percent, respectively, whereas the approval rates for Salvadorans and Guatemalans were only 28 percent and 21 percent, respectively (Johnson, 1993:26). Before 1990, when a court rule forced the government to reconsider all capriciously denied asylum requests of Salvadorans and Gua-

temalans, their approval rate had been even lower—between 1983 and 1990, 2.6 percent for Salvadorans and 1.8 percent for Guatemalans (Zucker and Zucker, 1992:65).

105. *Hearings before the Subcommittee on Immigration and Refugee Affairs,* U.S. Senate, 100th Cong., 1st sess., S.1611, October 23 and December 11, 1987, pp. 35–36; emphasis in text added (henceforth referred to as *Senate Immigration Hearings 1987*).

106. *New York Times,* 27 November 1988, p. 52.

107. The IIRM, formed in 1986, was centrally involved in shaping all the various incarnations of diversity quotas between 1986 and 1990 (see Jacob, 1992). In Congress the major pro-Irish players were Brian Donnelly in the House and Edward Kennedy in the Senate (both Democrats from Massachusetts).

108. On the origins and development of diversity immigration, see Lawson and Grin (1992), Jacob (1992), Folan Sebben (1992), Aleinikoff, Martin, and Motomura (1995:129–131), Legomsky (1993), Schuck (2003).

109. This is not to say that the IIRM did not have its hand in the permanent diversity program as well. Its influence shows in the doubling of Ireland into Northern Ireland (which is politically a part of the United Kingdom) and the Irish Republic, which ensures a special advantage for the Irish with respect to the "underrepresented country" formula. As the IIRM's chief lobbyist characterized the program, it was "not quite as neutral as it seems" (quoted in Jacob, 1992:318).

110. The two countries that received the most visas in 2001 were Ghana, with 6,333 visas, and Nigeria, with 5,989 (*Migration News* 9(7), July 2002, 4).

111. See the statement by Mark Everson of the INS in *Senate Immigration Hearings 1987*, p. 82.

112. Kennedy statement in *Senate Immigration Hearings 1987*, p. 2.

113. Simpson statement, ibid., p. 3.

114. "[C]ontrary to popular belief, the point system in the Senate bill offers almost no solace to the IIRM and other nationality groups which share our plight" (IIRM leader Donald Martin in *Hearings Before the Subcommittee on Immigration, Refugees, and International Law of the Committee on the Judiciary,* House of Representatives, 100th Cong., 1st sess. on S.358, H.R.672, H.R.2448, and H.R.2646, 1989–90; the quote is from part 1, p. 219. These hearings are henceforth referred to as *House Immigration Hearings 1989* and *House Immigration Hearings 1990*).

115. The IIRM, which represented the only ethnic group without a stake in the family quotas, sought to prevent the wrath of the other (Asian and Hispanic) ethnic groups by stressing the additive (rather than substitutive) nature of diversity immigration. See the statement by Donald Martin in *House Immigration Hearings 1990*, part 1, p. 270.

116. Tichenor (2002:274). For more detail on ethnic-group alignments in the making of the 1990 Legal Immgration Act, see Joppke (1999:38–44).

117. *Senate Immigration Hearings 1987*, p.39.

118. Ibid.

119. Ibid., p.59.
120. Statement by the IIRM, *Senate Immigration Hearings 1987*, p. 309.
121. Donald Martin (IIRM), in *House Immigration Hearings 1989*, part 1, p. 218.
122. Doris Meissner, in *Senate Immigration Hearings 1987*, p. 243.
123. *Senate Immigration Hearings 1987*, p. 536.
124. Joseph Cogo, American Committee on Italian Migration, in *Senate Immigration Hearings 1987*, p. 471.
125. On the politicians' side, liberal Democrats Edward Kennedy and Daniel Moynihan; on the experts' side, for instance, Michael Teitelbaum, one of America's most quick-witted immigration experts (who argued that the 1965 reforms unintentionally "discriminate[d] against would-be immigrants from Europe and Africa, and discriminate[d] in favor of immigrants from Asia and Latin America," in *House Immigration Hearings 1989*, part 1, p. 389).
126. *Senate Immigration Hearings 1987*, p. 57.
127. *Senate Immigration Hearings 1987*, p. 161.
128. Ibid., p. 161.
129. Ibid., p. 180.
130. Within Australia's universal visa scheme, which applies to all aliens of all nationalities wishing to enter Australia, a pertinent example is the "risk factor" control measure vis à vis applicants for a visitor visa. It was introduced in the early 1990s in the context of a campaign against overstayers and a deluge of on-shore change-of-status claimants. If certain "risk factors" for overstaying were present in the applicant (such as a certain nationality, gender, or age), the visa could be denied. Although this was "the first occasion since 1900 on which Australia has explicitly named particular nationalities as targets for specific immigration controls" (Cronin, 1993:96), this was still justifiable in reference to the "basic statistical fact" (ibid.) that people with certain characteristics (certain nationalities being among them) were more likely to overstay their permits.
131. Such was Labor Prime Minister Bob Hawke's negative response to Cambodian boat people in the 1980s, and the same distaste for "jumping the resettlement queue" has motivated the conservative Howard government in the 1990s to automatically detain asylum-seekers and other illegal entrants under extraordinarily harsh conditions in remote prisonlike camps (Nicholls, 1998:76–77).
132. For public opinion, see Betts (1996) and Goot (2000).
133. Department of Immigration and Multicultural and Indigenous Affairs (2002b:6).
134. The impact of the "ethnic lobby" on Australian immigration policy is in dispute. According to the critical accounts of Birrell and Birrell (1987) and Betts (1988), its impact has been significant, at least in certain moments and respects. From a more apologetic perspective, Jupp (1993:217) finds that, to the degree that a concerted "ethnic lobby" existed at all, it had "more influence (and [was] more interested) in settlement and cultural issues than in immigration policy."

135. This is the subtitle and *Leitmotiv* of the Fitzgerald Report of 1988.
136. "Immigration Program: Ministerial Statement," *Australian Commonwealth Parliamentary Debates,* House of Representatives, 30 May 1984, p. 2460. This statement was given at the peak of the first debate on "too many Asians."
137. Mr. Hodgman, in *Australian Commonwealth Parliamentary Debates,* House of Representatives, 30 May 1984, p. 2468.
138. Mr. Hodgman, in *Australian Commonwealth Parliamentary Debates,* House of Representatives, 7 March 1984, p. 644.
139. Max Harris, in *The Australian,* 2 July 1988, quoted in Jayasuriya and Sang (1992:53).
140. Department of Immigration and Multicultural and Indigenous Affairs (2002b:28–31); author's calculations.
141. Whitlam's Labor government held friendly relations with the North Vietnamese Communists, bestowing diplomatic recognition on Hanoi in 1973. In addition, Labor feared that the "Yellow Croats" would steer the electorate to the right, as the influx of eastern European anti-Communist refugees had done after World War II (Viviani, 1984:56).
142. Lobbied by southern and eastern European ethnics, already the late Frazer government had introduced a new category, "C," within the family unification stream, which was for adult brothers and sisters and nondependent children. In 1983, Hawke's Labor government further eased their entry by abolishing a (point-based) priority for English speakers and entrants with "skills in demand"; all that sufficed now was a job offer (see Betts, 1988:158). This requirement was easily fulfilled by many a small (Asian) shopkeeper, and the "job offers" issued within the C category were quickly suspected to be a façade for extended-family migration. See the detailed analysis of family migration in the 1980s by Birrell (1990).
143. "Immigration Policy Questioned," *Warrnambool Standard,* 19 March 1984 (reprinted in Singer, 1984).
144. "Migrant Poll Shock," *The Herald,* 19 May 1984 (reprinted in Singer, 1984).
145. Interestingly, the shift from skill-focused to family-focused immigrant selection was justified in economic terms, namely "that in times of economic recession our first commitment would be to honor responsibilities to those migrants already in Australia" (Immigration Minister West, "Migration Program 1983–84: Ministerial Statement," *Australia Commonwealth Parliamentary Debates,* House of Representatives, 7 March 1984, p.640). See Appleyard (2001:64), who argued that the tying of family-focused selection to "periods of recession" had a long pedigree in Australia.
146. The quotes are from "Migration Program 1983–84: Ministerial Statement," *Australia Commonwealth Parliamentary Debates,* House of Representatives, 7 March 1984, pp. 640 and 643. The Immigration Minister's rebuttal of a "deliberate Asianisation" of the immigration program was given shortly before the Blainey intervention; the latter only brought to the open what had been a latent opposition charge against Hawke's Labor government since its arrival in 1983.

147. "UK migrant figures prove no bias: Hawke," *The Australian,* 11 May 1984 (reprinted in Singer, 1984).

148. "In relation to family reunion . . . there is bipartisanship," said the Shadow Immigration Minister Hodgman (*Australian Commonwealth Parliamentary Debates,* House of Representatives, 30 May 1984, p. 2469). With respect to refugee resettlement, the opposition even criticized the (politically motivated) "diversification" of source countries (which now included El Salvador and Chile) under Hawke (ibid, pp . 2472–2473).

149. Mr. Hodgman (Shadow Immigration Minister) in *Australian Commonwealth Parliamentary Debates, House of Representatives,* 8 May 1984, p. 2008.

150. Mr. Hodgman (Shadow Immigration Minister) in *Australian Commonwealth Parliamentary Debates,* House of Representatives, 30 May 1984, p. 2472.

151. Shadow Prime Minister Peacock: "What he [the immigration minister] has to do is not reduce the Asian element . . . but redress the imbalance by increasing the European element that has been allowed to slip . . ." (*Australian Commonwealth Parliamentary Debates,* House of Representatives, 8 May 1984, p. 2028).

152. This was revealed by the same Gallup poll that had shown the public in opposition to increased Asian immigration ("Migrant poll shock," *The Herald,* 19 May 1984; reprinted in Singer, 1984).

153. "Asian entry threatens tolerance: Blainey," *The Age,* 19 March 1984 (reprinted in Singer, 1984). Only in this indirect way did the notion of "Asianisation" slip into the debate; Blainey had never himself used it.

154. This was part of a larger "One Australia" campaign and critique of multiculturalism led or made throughout the year, spurred by the 1988 Bicentennial celebrations, whose logo was "Commitment to Australia" (see Spillman, 1997, ch. 4).

155. Though he never officially retracted his one-time gaffe, the ostracized Howard would later admit: "If I had the opportunity to rephrase something I have said in my political career, I would rephrase that" (Betts, 1999:287).

156. In 1985–86, Category C (for siblings and nondependent children) was reconnected to English-language competence and skills (in addition to the "firm job offer" requirement). Soon thereafter, it was replaced by a new "Independent/Concessional" category, which (in order to appease the European ethnic lobby) notionally expanded the field of eligibles to nephews and nieces but, in also including applicants without family ties and further strengthening the skill component, "represented a form of backdoor expansion of the skills programme, dressed up in the more politically palatable family reunion context" (Birrell and Birrell, 1987:292).

157. It must be pointed out that in numerical terms the leading recipients of sibling visas between 1985 and 1988 were the United Kingdom and Ireland (Birrell 1990:18); however, this was only due to their vastly larger population share.

158. A national telephone poll found a staggering 77 percent of respondents in agreement with Howard's statement that "Asian immigration to Australia should be slowed down" (see Betts, 1999:293).

159. This rebuttal appeared in *The Age,* 9 September 1988, and is partially reprinted in Lack and Templeton (1995:244–248).

160. *Australian Commonwealth Parliamentary Debates,* House of Representatives, 8 October 1996, p. 4858. Howard's refusal to condemn Hanson directly was still widely criticized; in the most complimentary reading, this was "not [to] dignify with his attention a backbench independent whom the Liberals had tossed out" (Grattan, 1998:80).

161. Quoted in National Multicultural Advisory Council (1999).

162. If there was any "Hanson effect" at all, it was that "her targeting of Asian migration made it more difficult to review migration issues rationally" (Birrell, 1996:58), and some early measures of the incoming Howard government to tighten family reunion were stalled as a result.

163. "Australia Is Striving to Be Asian, but How Asian?" *New York Times,* 16 August 1992, p. L3.

164. In 1971, eastern and southeastern Asia had received 39 percent of Australia's exports and provided 21 percent of imports; by 1994, these figures had increased to 62 and 41 percent, respectively (Huntington, 1996:151).

165. "A National Identity Crisis," *The Economist,* 14 December 1996, p. 66.

166. These figures are from Department of Immigration and Multicultural and Indigenous Affairs (2002a:17).

167. For instance, in 1996 China-born residents had three to four times higher divorce rates than Australia-born persons, which suggests a widespread practice of "white marriages" (Birrell and Rapson, 1998:8).

168. In 2000–01, ten of the eleven leading source countries of foreign students were Asian, and they accounted for 56 percent of all student visas granted (the only leading non-Asian source country was the United States, which received 9 percent and thus ranked just behind the number one source country, China, which received 10 percent of visas that year); see Department of Immigration and Multicultural and Indigenous Affairs (2002a:44).

169. In this category the Asian component is less predonderant but still significant (see Department of Immigration and Multicultural and Indigenous Affairs, 2002a:48–49).

3. Europe's Postcolonial Constellations, Northwestern and Southwestern

1. Between 1500 and 1960, some 61 million Europeans participated in the intercontinental migration that was enabled by European overseas expansion; between 1945 and 1960, less than 3.5 million non-Europeans migrated to the European states (estimates by Emmer, 1992:3–4).

2. Both postcolonial migrations are insufficiently distinguished in the few existing studies (Miège and Dubois, 1994; A. Smith, 2003; and the excellent

synopsis by Etemad, 1998). This perhaps reflects a certain tendency of decolonizing European states to lump together both (native and European-origin) migrations as "repatriation." Building on Miège and Dubois (1994:18), Etemad (1998:464–465) estimates that 3.3 to 4 million of the 5.4 to 6.8 million "repatriates-expatriates" migrating from the colonies to the European states between 1945 and 1985 were "European," whereas only 2.1 to 2.8 million were "non-European." However, these are imprecise and misleading figures. Consider, for instance, that 170,000 of the 300,000 "repatriates" from the Dutch East Indies (now Indonesia) were of mixed descent (see Obdeijn, 1994:52), even though they were officially perceived and classified as "European" and apparently figured as such in Etemad's (1998:465) calculation.

3. "Historical and cultural ties" is the notion routinely invoked by Spain to justify its preference scheme for Ibero-Americans ("Hispanics").

4. The notions of "northwestern" and "southwestern" are shorthand for saying that, with respect to ethnicity and postcolonial immigration, Britain and France combined are different from Spain and Portugal combined. No claim is made that other than the cases considered here may easily fit these notions.

5. "Family connections" is the favorite notion used by the defenders of patriality.

6. The post-World War II preference for European over postcolonial immigrants in France only prolonged the interwar pattern (see Lewis, 2000, ch. 7).

7. Britain's rejection of labor migration, exceptional in postwar Western Europe, was certainly made possible by the free availability of Irish labor migrants, the single biggest yet strangely invisible immigrant group to Britain after World War II (see Paul, 1997).

8. Sir David Maxwell Fyfe, quoted in Hansen (2000:50).

9. Enoch Powell, *Parliamentary Debates,* House of Commons, 8 March 1971, col. 77.

10. The notion of "belonging" was introduced in Home Secretary Butler's presentation of the Commonwealth Immigrants Act to Parliament: "[E]xcept from control [are] . . . persons who in common parlance belong to the United Kingdom" (*Parliamentary Debates,* House of Commons, 16 November 1961, col. 695).

11. The Commonwealth Immigrants Act's actual impact on Old Commonwealth entries was minuscule, because those numbers were low already before its passing, and they subsequently were absorbed mostly by Category B of the Act's employment voucher system, which was for skilled immigrants. In addition, there were positive discriminations in the implementation of the act. Shorthand typists, for example, were put into Category B because the majority of them were women from the Old Commonwealth. In addition, many Old Commonwealth immigrants entered as "working holiday-makers" who, though admitted as visitors, took up employment (see Paul, 1997:173).

12. *Parliamentary Debates,* House of Commons, 8 March 1971, col. 45.

13. Home Secretary Maudling, ibid.

14. Home Secretary Maudling, quoted in Macdonald (1972:16).

15. David Steel (Liberal Party), *Parliamentary Debates,* House of Commons, 8 March 1971, col. 113.
16. *Parliamentary Debates,* House of Commons, 8 March 1971, col. 46.
17. Home Secretary Maudling, *Parliamentary Debates,* House of Commons, 8 March 1971, col. 46.
18. Kenneth Clarke, *Parliamentary Debates,* House of Commons, 8 March 1971, cols. 126–127. Identical reasoning can be found in a variety of *Times* editorials, for instance, "The Price We Pay for Hypocrisy" (22 November 1972).
19. *Parliamentary Debates,* House of Commons, 8 March 1971, col. 113.
20. When the Immigration Rules implementing the 1971 Immigration Act were finally approved in February 1973, the Labour Party openly endorsed the positively discriminatory aspect of patriality: "[W]e recognize the need for a special link with citizens of [New Zealand, Australia and Canada]" (Peter Shore, *Parliamentary Debates,* House of Commons, 21 February 1973, col. 580).
21. *Parliamentary Debates,* House of Commons, 8 March 1971, col. 80.
22. *Parliamentary Debates,* House of Commons, 21 February 1973, col. 627.
23. The liberal part of this odd coalition was heavily lobbied by the National Council for Civil Liberties, which opposed patriality in toto ("Liberty Powell," *Times,* 8 April 1971).
24. The next logical step was to remove this sex discrimination for non-Commonwealth aliens as well, as brought forward in a motion by Liberal David Steel (*Parliamentary Debates,* House of Commons, 16 June 1971, col. 459–460). State Secretary Sharples in the Home Office retorted: "[Mr. David Steel] asked whether it was intentional that there should be discrimination in favor of Commonwealth citizens. The answer is a clear 'Yes'" (ibid., col. 464).
25. Home Secretary Maudling, during the third reading of the Immigration Bill (*Parliamentary Debates,* House of Commons, 17 June 1971, col. 770).
26. Enoch Powell *Parliamentary Debates,* House of Commons, 22 November 1972, col. 1396.
27. *Parliamentary Debates,* House of Commons, 22 November 1972, col. 1442.
28. Russell Kerr, *Parliamentary Debates,* House of Commons, 22 November 1972, cols. 1396–1397.
29. Bryant Godman Irvine, ibid., col. 1436.
30. Robert Carr, ibid., col. 1374.
31. As stressed in the closing statement by Foreign Secretary Alec Douglas-Home, ibid., col. 1447.
32. Ibid, col. 1395.
33. *Parliamentary Debates,* House of Commons, 21 February 1973, col. 598.
34. Ibid, cols. 592–593.
35. Technically, it was not within government's authority to undo the legislative ban on grandparental Commonwealth patriality by means of an administrative rule change. What the government reinstated was a weaker form of grandparental patriality for Commonwealth citizens, who (unlike other

patrials) remained subject to deportation, whose entry clearance could be refused, and—most important—whose privilege could be withdrawn by means of another (nonlegislative) rule change. The most precise (though mocking) definition of this "new privileged elite" is "non-patrial Commonwealth citizens with a United Kingdom grandparent" (Arthur Davidson, ibid., col. 622).

36. Home Secretary Carr, ibid., col. 598.

37. See the exchange between Williams and Carr in *Parliamentary Debates,* House of Commons, 25 January 1973, cols. 657 and 659. In the early 1970s only one of 200 requests for a permanent residence permit by Old Commonwealth citizens was rejected (figure provided by Foreign Secretary Douglas-Home, *Parliamentary Debates,* House of Commons, 22 November 1972, col. 1448). One may reasonably assume that their treatment at citizenship registration would be equally generous.

38. In late summer 1972, a Tory government admitted some 28.000 Asian British passport holders threatened by ethnic cleansing in Uganda—in marked contrast to a Labour government that had rejected Kenyan Asians four years earlier.

39. This is how the *Economist* (27 January 1973) titled its report on Home Secretary Carr's double-edged immigration statement before Parliament.

40. The main food for this critique was the abolishment, in the 1981 Nationality Act, of unconditional jus soli and its replacement by a mixed jus sanguinis and jus soli regime. However, with this reform Britain only abandoned an anomaly that had stemmed from its feudal past and been prolonged by the experience of empire, while embracing the continental European norm of citizenship that mixes elements of jus sanguinis and jus soli (a good overview of the present scene in Europe is Hansen and Weil, 2001).

41. Etemad (1998:465) estimates that in Britain between 380,000 and 500,000 "Europeans" moved to the United Kingdom from 1945 to the early 1990s, whereas the corresponding figure for "non-Europeans" is between 1,350.000 and 1,750.000; in France, the proportion of "Europeans" and "non-Europeans" is the opposite, 1.4 million to 1.7 million Europeans versus 350,000 to 500,000 non-Europeans. The high number of European "repatriates" in France largely consisted of the Algerian *pieds-noirs,* one million of whom fled to France under dramatic circumstances in 1962.

42. The first French empire, in the Americas, had collapsed without any traces in the early 1800s.

43. The Law of 7 May 1946 (*Loi Lamine Guèye*) declared all natives in the overseas territories, including Algeria, "citizens on the same basis as French nationals of the metropole" (quoted in Marshall, 1973:222).

44. French Union citizenship was relevant only for the members of associated states and protectorates, which had their own nationality laws (such as Indochina, Morocco, and Tunisia). See Lampué (1950).

45. See the heated debate over Michèle Tribalat's (1995) rather cautious (and in its stress on "assimilation" impeccably "Republican") landmark survey of France's ethnic minority population (Le Bras, 1998). See also the discussion of French "color blindness" in Bleich (2001b).

46. Traces of ethnic selectivity can still be found in a decree implementing the nationality *Ordonnance* of 19 October 1945, which was replaced only in 1973 (see Weil, 1995c:30).

47. This is expressed in making the holding of a work contract the precondition for a residence permit.

48. ONI is France's official immigration authority, charged with the recruitment and supervision of immigrant labor and situated within the Ministry of Work.

49. Michel Massenet (ONI) on 30 November 1970, quoted in Viet (1998:269).

50. Portuguese migrant workers also faced severe exit hurdles, particularly after the Junta suspended organized emigration in May 1967. After this, Portuguese migrant workers had to enter as false tourists, or even illegally, and then apply for "regularization" of their status.

51. In 1970 Morocco surpassed Spain as immigrant-importing country number two, after Portugal.

52. The last of France's guest-worker intakes, Turkish immigration really took off only in the early 1970s.

53. The French governor-general of Algeria, quoted in Lustick (1993:111).

54. Article 55 of the French Constitution establishes that in the legal hierarchy international treaty norms and provisions precede domestic law.

55. For unequal treatment of Algerians in postcolonial nationality law, see Lagarde (1973;1995); for an (aborted) policy of forced repatriation in the late 1970s, which was based on reneging on the French-Algerian Accord, see Weil (1995a:158–211); for excluding Algerians from common-regime reforms, see GISTI (2000). However, with respect to the latter, a revision of the French-Algerian Accord in July 2001 adjusted the status of Algerians to that of common-regime immigrants. Algerians, particularly those of the second generation, were also central to France's protracted conflict over citizenship and immigrant integration since the mid-1980s (see Brubaker, 1992, ch. 8, and Feldblum, 1999).

56. Quoted in *Migration News Sheet*, November 1999, p.2.

57. Even in the Spanish and Portuguese languages, there is next to no legal or social science literature available on the Hispanic and Lusophone preference regimes.

58. I will henceforth refer to it as *comunidad hispánica*.

59. Spiritual *Hispanidad*, essentially an inferiority complex turned into a source of pride, survived even into the post-Franco era. Its dichotomy of "materialism" versus "spiritualism" (the latter being the distinct virtue shared by the "Hispanic family") was, for instance, fully present in the welcome speech of King Juan Carlos (Franco's designated successor) to Mexico's President Lopez Portillo in October 1977 (see Pike, 1986:86).

60. This change of emphasis is symbolized in the renaming of the *Instituto de Cultura Hispanica* into *Instituto de Cooperación Iberoamericana* (Wiarda, 1989:313; Grugel, 1995:143).

61. F. Gonzalez "Die Kraft des Wir: Hispanische Welt und Globalisierung [The power of us: Hispanic world and globalization]," *Frankfurter Allgemeine Zeitung*, 6 January 2001, p. 43.

62. "García Márquez dice que no volvera a España mientras se exija visado a los colombianos. *El País,* 18 March 2001, p. 22.

63. In addition, Article 20 of the 1954 reform of the Civil Code allowed the privileged foreigners to naturalize after two (instead of ten) years of residence. These dual-nationality and naturalization privileges remain in force today, though the groups/countries entitled to them have subsequently expanded. With respect to the reduced naturalization requirement, the 1982 reform of the Nationality Law added Andorra, Equatorial Guinea, and Sephardic Jews as privileged countries (or groups).

64. *Ley de 15 de julio de 1954 (Boletín Oficial del Estado,* 16 July 1954, p. 483).

65. Interestingly, there was some opposition to the "countries of Iberian culture" formula that had appeared in an earlier version of this clause, because it was seen as diluting the centrality of Spanish language for the ties to be sanctioned by it; but this opposition did not succeed (Garrido Falla, 1980:154).

66. Article 42 stipulates: "The state shall pay special attention to safeguarding the economic and social rights of Spanish workers abroad and shall direct its policy towards their return."

67. The second novelty of Article 11.3 is to grant the possibility of dual nationality even in the absence of a treaty, as long as the "particular tie" condition is fulfilled. The respective states are listed in Article 23 IV (now Art. 24.2) of the Civil Code: all Latin American states, Portugal, Andorra, the Philippines, and Equatorial Guinea. There is legal ambiguity as to whether the unilateral dual nationality provided by Article 23 IV (now 24.2) of the Civil Code is an alternative or a complement to the dual-nationality treaties. According to Virgós Soriano (1990), this clause constitutes "a complement that operates when the Treaties cannot" (p. 244), because otherwise the underlying idea of a "community of Spanish-American states" would be defeated.

68. Article 1 of the 1958 Dual Nationality Convention with Chile, the model for most other conventions that followed, says: "Los españoles *nacidos en España,* y récíprocamente los chilenos *nacidos en Chile,* podrán adquirir la nacionalidad chilena o española, respectivamente, en las condiciones y en la forma prevista por la legislación en vigor en cada una de las Altas Partes contratantes, sin perder por ello su anterior nacionalidad" (emphasis supplied).

69. This article, along with other protections for Spaniards abroad, was removed in 1990.

70. *Ley Orgánica 7/1985, de 1 de julio, sobre derechos y libertades de los extranjeros en España (Boletín Oficial del Estado,* no. 158, 3 July 1985, p. 153).

71. Would-be immigrants must apply for a visa at a Spanish consulate in their country of origin, with a job offer by a Spanish employer on hand that is subsequently checked by the Ministry of Labor for the availability of prioritized local (Spanish and EU) workers—a daunting and de facto unsurpassable hurdle in the context of double-digit unemployment rates throughout the 1980s and 1990s (see Mendoza, 2000:5).

72. The precise meaning of the clause on work permits in the 1969 law is debated among jurists. Some argue that it exempts its beneficiaries from the need to

hold a work permit; others argue that it makes the concession of a work permit mandatory (see Alvarez Rodriguez, 1994:363, fn. 3).

73. *Ley de 30 diciembre de 1969* (*Boletín Oficial del Estado*, no. 313, 31 December 1969, pp. 2297–2298).

74. Dissenting votes in two Supreme Court decisions on February 25, 1991, and July 10, 1991, which upheld the legality of the 1986 regulation in this respect, argued that the capricious exclusion of Iberoamericans from Article 38 violated the spirit of the 1985 preamble, thus rendering the entire regulation illegal (see Miquel Calatayud, 1993:892–897; Adroher Biosca, 1996:1886–1887).

75. Quoted from the *Convenio de doble Nacionalidad con Chile* of 1958. The conventions with Nicaragua, Bolivia, and Costa Rica do not contain this specifying clause, and courts have not derived any further work or residence rights from them (Alvarez Rodriguez, 1990:5).

76. See the discussion in Alvarez Rodriguez (1990) and Miquel Calatayud (1993).

77. *Real Decreto 511/1992* of May 14, 1992, which created a new Interministerial Foreigner Commission, defined as one of its purposes the "promotion of the special consideration to the particularities of the Iberoamerican immigrant population" (quoted from Adroher Biosca, 1996:1897–1898).

78. *Situación de los extranjeros en España: Lineas basicas de la politica española de extranjería* (Comunicación del Gobierno al Congreso de los diputados), Madrid, December 1990. A copy is on file with author.

79. On the impact of Schengen, see Delgado (1993). Spain was helped in this rupture of the *comunidad hispánica* by the other side. In the early 1990s some Latin American countries (such as Peru and the Dominican Republic) introduced a visa obligation for Spaniards, in retaliation for the increased denial of entrance into Spain of their nationals. In 1991, before the introduction of these visas, only 0.9 percent of arriving Latin Americans were denied entry; however, no less than 20 percent of Dominicans and 25 percent of Peruvians were rejected, mostly because they did not have sufficient money in their pockets (see Ulmer, 1997:184).

80. The only remaining explicit reference to Iberoamericans is Article 46 of *Ley Orgánica 8/2000*, which reintroduces their exemption from work-permit taxes (which had been suppressed by its short-lived predecessor). *Ley Orgánica 4/2000*, which was approved in an urgency procedure, includes no preamble—the usual place to indicate fundamental policy changes. Its successor contains a preamble, but one that only justifies the swift reform of the reform.

81. Cited in *El País*, 18 March 2001, p. 5. Perhaps not by accident, this statement was given in an interview with a regional newspaper in Catalonia, where immigration (especially of Muslim origins) is widely perceived as a threat to Catalan language and culture.

82. "Social, cultural, and religious racism" is the wholesale accusation by the (Communist dominated) United Left (*Izquierda Unida*) against the Aznar

government ("Llamazares exige a Zapatero que recurra ya la Ley de Extranjería," *El País,* 13 March 2001).

83. Xavier Vidal-Folch, "Dios, Idioma, Imperio," *El País,* 18 March 2001, p. 5. See also the critique by the leading columnist and intellectual Andres Ortega, "En Madrid no hay negros," *El País,* 2 April 2001.

84. Note, however, that the Ombudsman (*Defensor del Pueblo*), Enrique Mugica, a member of the Socialist Party, also argued in favor of preferring immigrants from Latin America, for "reasons of cultural affinity" (*El País,* 22 December 1990, p. 27). Appointed by (and apparently close to) conservative Prime Minister Aznar, Mugica is a controversial figure, who is criticized by pro-immigrant associations for neglecting his official function of bringing civil society concerns to bear on government and judiciary.

85. "Defensa planea reclutar 2.000 inmigrantes anuales 'para paliar el déficit' de soldados," *El País,* 20 March 2001, p. 13. At first obviously ignorant of European Community constraints, the minister later added that this offer had to be extended to all EU member state nationals. It became law in 2002.

86. "Latinoamérica crece," *El País,* 22 December 2000, p. 27.

87. The open letter is reprinted in *El País,* 19 March 2001, p. 22.

88. "El Principe pide en Lorca la incorporación de extranjeros al trabajo 'con arreglo a ley'," *El País,* 18 January 2001.

89. "España negocia reservar a ecuatorianos hasta un 30% del cupo anual de inmigrantes," *El País,* 22 January 2001.

90. The full text of the agreement can be found at http://www.reicaz.es/extranjeria.

91. "Una delegación de parlamentarios de Ecuador rechaza por 'inviable' el convenio de inmigración," *El País,* 31 January 2001.

92. "Trabajo descubre una finca en Huelva donde 100 inmigrantes sin papeles vivian como esclavos," *El Mundo,* 27 April 2001.

93. "De inmigrante irregular a semiesclavo sin salir de Huelva," *El Mundo,* 27 April 2001.

94. "Rouco Varela exige la regularización de todos los 'sin papeles'," *El País,* 13 March 2001.

95. Centro de Investigaciones Sociológicas (2001:3).

96. Among the 9.1 percent of respondents who favored preferential treatment for some immigrant nationalities, 59.6 percent favored Ibero-Americans and only 4.4 percent favored "Moroccans, Algerians, etc." (Centro de Investigaciones Sociológicas, 2001:8).

97. "De Derechos y Libertades," *El País,* 5 January 2001.

98. "El Gobierno propone a los ecuatorianos sin papeles que regresen a su país en busca de visado," *El País,* 12 January 2001.

99. "Las Asociaciónes critican la propuesta del Gobierno de devolver a su país a los 'sin papeles' ecuatorianos," *El País,* 12 January 2001.

100. These are the words of the secretary for immigration of the Workers' Unions (*Comisiónes Obreras*), quoted in "Los ecuatorianos rechazan la oferta del Gobierno de viajar a su país para regularizarse," *El País,* 13 January 2001.

101. By the first week of February 2001, over 60 Algerians were reported to have taken advantage of the paid repatriation offer ("Colombia negocia con España un convenio similar al de Ecuador," *El País*, 7 February 2001).
102. "Fernández-Miranda dice que no pagara a todos los inmigrantes ecuatorianos el viaje a su país," *El País*, 8 March 2001.
103. "El Ministerio del Interior inicia la regularización urgente de 21.000 ecuatorianos," *El País*, 7 May 2001.
104. After all, the estimated 50,000 illegal Ecuadorians who had not accepted the paid repatriation offer did not qualify for the in-country regularization to which the government eventually resorted ("El Ministerio del Interior inicia la regularización urgente de 21.000 ecuatorianos," *El País*, 7 May 2001). Note also that Spain acquiesced in December 2002 to Ecuador's inclusion in the European Union's "black visa list," as a result of which the January 2001 bilateral agreement between the two states is null and void (*Migration News Sheet*, January 2003, p. 1).
105. "Madrid y Rabat pactan regular el flujo de trabajadores estables," *El País*, 30 March 2001.
106. Quoted in Brettell (1993:59).
107. See also Russell-Wood's (1992) authoritative account of the Portuguese empire, which makes "movement and mobility" its central theme (p. 6).
108. Freyre (1986) cites approvingly the observations of James Bryce, an English traveler in colonial South America: "In the case of the Spaniard and the Portuguese, religion, as soon as the Indians had been baptized, made race differences seem insignificant" (p. 189). Focusing on the relationship between colonizers and imported slaves, Tannenbaum (1947) is the classic elaboration of this common element of "Latin" (as against "Anglo Saxon") colonization.
109. In contrast to Brazil, within which Freyre develops his effusive "lusotropicalism" scenario, there has been much less miscegenation and "racial democracy" in Portuguese Africa; for the particularly well-studied case of Angola, see Bender (1978) and Castro Henriques (1995).
110. On the embrace of Freyre's "lusotropicalism" by Salazar in the 1950s and 1960s, see Enders (1997) and Leonard (1997).
111. Quoted from Salazar's speech to the First Congress of his National Unity Party (*União Nacional*) on May 26, 1934 (http://www.cphrc.org.uk/sources/so-ns/26may34.htm).
112. It is no surprise that under the reign of prewar Portuguese colonial ideology, which—like all European colonialisms at the time—espoused a hierarchy of races and civilizations with the Europeans on top, the reception of Freyre was rather reserved. This changed only after World War II, when hierarchical race reasoning had lost its legitimacy (see Leonard, 1997).
113. Freyre had been a student of Boas at Columbia University.
114. The Portuguese colonizing principles as laid out by Caetano (1951) reflect the turn toward a more centralist administration of the empire following the new Constitution of 1951. As is visible in the relabeling of the "colonies" into "overseas provinces," Portugal now embraced the French model of unitary

stateness, according to which "Angola and Goa are integrated in the national territory just like the metropolitan provinces of Algarve or the adjunct islands of the Azores" (ibid., p. 32). However, this change was interlaced with elements of British "indirect rule" (also widely practiced by the French in sub-Saharan Africa and Indochina). In addition, there was a strong sense of civilizing mission, yet under the umbrella (in this form unknown in France or Britain) of "carry[ing] the Christian gospel to the people living in the darkness of paganism" (ibid., p. 34). As in the French empire, colonial natives in the majority of African colonies (as well as Timor) had Portuguese "nationality," whereas full "citizenship" was reserved to a small category of "*assimilados.*" In 1950 there were 30,000 of the latter in Angola (out of a population of about four million), and just 4,000 in Mozambique (out of five million) (Chamberlain, 1985:71). In Cape Verde, India, and Macao no such distinctions between "citizens" and "aborigines" were made, and all enjoyed unitary citizen status.

115. Against the many UN resolutions defending the right of self-determination in the colonies and against the repeated UN condemnations of Portugal's intransigence, Salazar retorted, in a speech of February 18, 1965, that "we are fighting proudly alone" (Gomes Canotilho, 1996:49). This stance was tacitly condoned by the United States, which came to value the Portuguese presence in West Africa as a bulwark against Communism in the region. On Portugal's shifting stances toward colonial self-determination see Galvão Teles and Canelas de Castro (1996).

116. B. Sousa Santos, quoted in Trenz (1999:75).

117. *Público,* 3 February 1993, quoted in Trenz (1999:105).

118. "Political unity" is the first of four "principles of colonial administration" as laid out by Caetano (1951:32): "Portugal is a unitary state with only one territory, only one population and only one Government."

119. See the critique by Moura Ramos (1978:186). For the French *reconnaissance* procedure, which granted the entire post-independence colonial populations a virtual French citizenship, see Lagarde (1973, 1995).

120. Minister of Internal Affairs, Exposition of Law Proposal no. 29/II: Sobre Nacionalidade. *Diário da Assembleia da República,* Série I, num.53, 22 April 1981; quote on p. 2022.

121. CPHRC. Annual emigration from Portugal, 1900-1988. http://www.cphrc .org.uk/sources/so-stat/stat2.htm (accessed July 2001).

122. Lloyd-Jones, Stewart. Portugal's history since 1974. www.cphrc.org.uk (accessed July 2001). This may explain why the massive return of over 500,000 settlers (the so-called *retornados*) after the independence of Mozambique and Angola in 1975 did not create any adjustment problems (see Lewis and Williams, 1985).

123. See Feldman-Bianco (1992:148–149). *Diaspora* is the official government term to designate Portuguese émigrés (see Poinard, 1988).

124. In addition, Article 59.2 obliges the state to "[protect] the working conditions and [guarantee] social benefits of workers abroad"; Article 74.2 is to "ensure instruction in Portuguese language and access to Portuguese culture for the

children of emigrants." Note that, in contrast to the Spanish constitution, these provisions do not oblige the state to solicit the return of emigrants.

125. A recent count is just under 10 million Portuguese living in Portugal and 4.8 million Portuguese living abroad (OECD, 2000).

126. In addition, those who had lost their Portuguese nationality as a result of the dual-nationality prohibition in the 1959 law were given the possibility to re-acquire it through declaration (Article 31).

127. When the 1994 reform of nationality law added the proof of "an effective link to the national community" to the catalog of conditions for naturalization, the enumerated categories were exempted from this requirement too. Moura Ramos (2001:229, n. 29) criticized the addition of the "effective link" re-quirement as "pleonastic" because it was already taken care of by the resi-dence and language requirements. The purpose of the new requirement was obviously to put the burden of proof firmly on the applicant.

128. To put the 1981 Nationality Law into perspective, one must also consider that the transmission of Portuguese nationality abroad was made contingent upon the (vicarious) declaration of the willingness to become Portuguese, or upon registering the birth in the civil Portuguese register (Article 1 b). This was symmetric to the declaration of will in the new conditional *jus soli* provi-sion and shows the overall intention of the Portuguese lawmakers to strengthen the voluntaristic component of citizenship.

129. In the early 1990s the number of illegal immigrants was estimated at 70,000, the great majority of them (70 percent) from Portuguese-speaking Africa—the so-called PALOP states (*países africanos de língua oficial portuguesa*). Most of them had entered on temporary (tourist) visa and then overstayed. See Rocha-Trindade and Oliveira (1999:285).

130. In fact, the treaty with Mozambique, which, along with the Angolan treaty, is the weakest treaty with a PALOP state, expressly adjusts the status of Mozam-biquans and Portuguese residing in the other state to that of other nonnationals (as against nationals, as is the case in the Brazilian treaty). See Article 4 of the General Cooperation Treaty between Mozambique and Portugal (*Diário do Governo*, 1 Série, no. 286, 12 December 1975, p. 2000).

131. *Diário do Governo*, 1 Série, no. 302, 29 December 1971, p. 2028.

132. *Diário do Governo*, 9 February 1979, p. 214.

133. *Diário do Governo*, 1 Série, no. 286, 12 December 1975, p. 1999.

134. Quoted in Trenz (1999:107).

135. The quotes are from the 1825 Treaty of Rio (in Trenz, 1999:40).

136. For instance, between 1850 and 1950, 1.54 million Italian immigrants stood against 1.48 million Portuguese immigrants (Bender, 1978:24).

137. This still makes Brazilians the second-largest immigrant group in Portugal to-day, after Cape Verdeans (40,100 in 1998) and ahead of Angolans (16,500). The total number of legal immigrants in 1998 was 177,800 (OECD, 2000:343).

138. A certain assimilation regarding civil and social rights (with the exception of the all-important employment priority for nationals) is also provided by the

treaties with Cape Verde and Guinea-Bissau, whose logic—as in the Luso-Brazilian treaty—is the assimilation of the respective nonnationals to nationals (see Moura Ramos, 1990–93:598–599).

139. Unlike the civil and social rights regulated by the "general" part of the 1971 statute, the enjoyment of political rights according to its "specific" part is contingent on five years of permanent residence. All of these rights are not granted automatically, but have to be explicitly requested.

140. One Council of Europe document (1999:21) promptly refers to the "'Luso-Brazilian' model of citizenship" as "a source of inspiration for an extended form of European citizenship."

141. The Immigration Law of March 3, 1993 (*Decreto-lei* 59/93), which was necessitated by Portugal's joining of the Schengen Convention and which acknowledged Portugal's new situation as "immigration country within the (European) Community space," concedes the possibility of "special regimes" on the basis of international treaties and conventions (Article 4) (the quote is from the preamble of the law, *Diário da Republica*, 1 Série-A, no. 52, 3 March 1993, p. 929). A modification of the law in 1998 (*Decreto-lei* 244/98) states that the "special regime" proviso "especially" applies to treaties or conventions with Portuguese-speaking countries (Article 1.2).

142. Such visa-free entries do not even require a passport, only the provision of a national ID card.

143. Of the 177,800 legal immigrants residing in Portugal in 1998, 48,200 originated from other European Union states (OECD, 2000:343).

144. 68 percent of respondents expressed "sympathy" with Brazilians, whereas only 61.2 percent expressed sympathy with "other Europeans." Note that the sympathy expressed for Spaniards was below that of "Blacks" (56.7 as against 61.1 percent) (Marques, 1999:202).

145. I rely on the detailed account given by Trenz (1999:96–112).

146. The word *mulatinha* connotes "prostitute" in Brazilian Portuguese.

147. Both acts went into effect on the same day: March 3, 1993.

148. *Público,* 3 February 1993 (in Trenz, 1999:105).

149. *Público,* 5 February 1993 (in Trenz, 1999:106).

150. 19 February 1993 (in Trenz, 1999:108).

151. *Seminário,* 6 March 1993 (in Trenz, 1999:107).

152. For a particularly blunt statement, see José Leitão (1997). At the time, Leitão was the High Commissioner for Ethnic Minorities and Refugees in the Portuguese government.

153. An extreme right does not exist in Portugal.

154. Quoted in Trenz (1999:58).

155. *Diário da Assembleia da República,* 1 Série, no. 44, 27 March 1992, pp. 1363–1400.

156. This is in specific defense of exempting Lusophones who had entered Portugal before June 1, 1986, from proving their continued residence since then (ibid., p. 1366).

157. Ibid., p.1367.

158. Ibid.
159. *Diário da República*, 1 Série-A, no. 235, 12 October 1992, p. 4756.
160. *Diário da República*, 1 Série-A, no. 121, 24 May 1996, p. 1254.
161. An interesting aspect of these figures is the decrease of the Lusophone share between 1992–93 and 1996, despite the increase of formal privileges for Lusos in the 1996 regularization. This points to an increasing diversity of the illegal migrant population in Portugal. For instance, the share of regularized Asians increased from 5.3 percent in 1992–93 to 14.3 percent in 1996 (Malheiros, 1998:175).
162. OECD (2000:343).
163. Ibid.
164. Portuguese is the seventh most-spoken official language in the world, ahead of French.
165. *Declaração Constitutiva da Comunidade dos Países de Língua Portuguesa*, Lisbon, 17 July 1996, http://www.cplp.org/documentos/1 capitulo/I/declaracao.html (accessed July 2001).
166. The *Estatuto Cidadão Lusófono* is reprinted in the *CPLP Bulletin* of January 1998 (http://www.cplp.org/boletim/jan 98/b jan98 6.html).
167. Such permits would be granted for one year and could be renewed for a maximum of five years. After this period the respective immigrant would have to either leave the country or receive a permanent residence permit.
168. These Eastern European immigrants are highly coveted by Portuguese construction firms for their skills and work discipline (*Migration News Sheet*, August 2000, p. 4).
169. The only such reference came from a Social Democratic (PSD) deputy, who (unsuccessfully) proposed an alternative scheme of bilateral agreements with immigrant-sending states, "preferentially CPLP countries" (*Diário da Assembleia da República*, 1 Série, No. 89, 27 July 2000, p. 3567).
170. Ibid., pp. 3559 and 3562. That the measure would sanction "slave labor" had been the earlier charge of the bill's opponents (which included the Social Democrats [PSD], Communist Party [PCP], and Greens), and it was turned around by the Interior Minister as a measure to combat just that.
171. "I came to get gold, not till the soil like a peasant," said the young conquistador Hernán Cortés when he landed in Cuba in the early sixteenth century (Finer, 1997:1379).
172. The term *Creole*, commonly used in a Latin American context but not in the United States, means born in the colonized country but descended from the colonizing nation or from later settlers rather than from the indigenous peoples.
173. Comparing Brazil and the United States, Degler (1971) would later encapsulate the greater malleability and fluidity of the Brazilian race structure in the figure of the distinct and upwardly mobile "Mulatto," who offered an "escape hatch" for the "Negro" at the bottom, whereas in the dualist race structure of the United States mixed-race people were regarded as black and subjected to discrimination.

174. The Dutch anthropologist Hoetink (1967:54) recognized the moral "feeling of guilt" driving the U.S.-Latin contrast: "The North American seems to have a psychic need to hold up to himself the mirror of a society which 'proves' that the relations between Negro and white can be different." This was complemented by the Latin American scholar's "inferiority complex (turned) inside-out" (Marx, 1998:34), as in the work of Gilberto Freyre, who celebrated Luso-Brasilian "tolerance" as a substitute for the lack of "development" there. As a result of both, "[i]n the same way as one speaks of the *leyenda negra*, the legendary image formed of the Spanish *conquista*, one might also speak of the *leyenda brasileira*, the Brazilian myth of extremely liberal race relations and very easy upward mobility for the Negro" (Hoetink, 1967:55).

175. This perception is widespread in Portugal. A survey of primary and secondary school children in 21 Ibero-American states (including Portugal and Spain) found that almost 70 percent of Portuguese respondents considered their colonialism a "huge civilizing work," whereas only 28 percent considered it a "genocide." Spanish school children were more ambivalent, almost half of them considering Spanish colonialism a "genocide." Predictably, outside Spain and Portugal the majority of respondents considered these colonialisms a "genocide" (63 percent). As the author concludes, "Portugal appears as the country with the most positive view of colonization" (Calvo Buezas, 1998:175).

176. See also Tannenbaum (1946:65), who distinguishes between three "slave systems" in the West: the uniquely harsh "British-American-Dutch-Danish" system, the more benign "Spanish-Portuguese" system, and "in between" the French system, which shared with the former the lack of an indigenous slave tradition and law but with the latter the inclusionist Catholic faith.

177. Article 64.1 of French nationality law waves the five-year residence requirement for naturalization in the case of any person who "belongs to the French cultural and linguistic entity." The latter was defined in 1973 as French being the applicant's "mother language" and the official language in her state of origin (see Lagarde, 1973).

178. De Gaulle characterized the relationship of France with its recently independent colonies as a "politics of cooperation" (Viet, 1998:263).

179. M. Deniau, *Assemblée Nationale,* séance du 25 Mai 1972, p. 1908.

180. "Whoever next? Britain?" asked *The Economist* ("French Blows Its Horn," 22 November 1997, p. 99). The latest count of the Francophone network is 55 states. On the current list of states interested to join are Armenia, Serbia, Croatia, the Dominican Republic, Austria, Lichtenstein, Angola, and Ukraine ("Francophonie," *Le Figaro,* 28 October 2002).

181. See the official statement, "La Francophonie," on the Web site of the French Ministry of Foreign Affairs (www.france.diplomatie.fr/francophonie/francophonie.html; accessed June 30, 2004).

182. This difference is particularly plastic regarding language. In the Latin Caribbean societies, Spanish or Portuguese became the "commonly spoken and

written language" (Hoetink, 1967:178), whereas in the British, Dutch, and French Caribbean the official European language came to coexist with creole languages that evolved among the descendants of slaves.

183. Note that the 2002 reform of Spanish nationality law includes a general acceptance of dual nationality. This removes a major legal stronghold of postcolonial preferences in Spain, in this case through "upgrading" (rather than "downgrading," as was the case in immigration law).

184. Interestingly, immigration privileges are not part of the original dualnationality and equal-rights regimes, and they became added on only later (for instance, in the form of bilateral agreements over the suppression of visas). This is because these regimes were crafted when immigration control was not yet an issue, and free movement between the respective states was simply presumed.

185. See, for instance, the anticolonial, even explicitly "socialist" rhetoric in the Preamble and Article 7 of Portugal's present Constitution.

4. Resilience versus Demise in the Diaspora Constellation: Israel and Germany

1. Münz and Ohliger (2003) even equate "ethnic" with "diaspora" migration.

2. See, however, Cohen (1997:26), who points to a pre-Jewish, Greek notion of *diaspora* as a "sowing," colonizing enterprise, whose meaning was "hijacked" at a later point by the Jewish experience to describe a "forcible dispersal." From here one may draw the license to apply a more elastic notion of diaspora. Accordingly, Cohen distinguishes between "victim," "labour," "trade," "imperial," and "cultural" diasporas. This is a definitional decision that cannot be argued about. However, to capture the strong "return" provisions that can be found in the immigration and nationality laws of some states, and to distinguish the migrations engendered by them from other types of ethnic migration, it makes sense to reserve the notion of diaspora to what Cohen has called "victim diasporas."

3. As an Israeli jurist put it: "[I]f the Law of Return is to be considered a form of repatriation, it can certainly not be considered discriminatory" (Klein, 1997:56 n. 15).

4. It goes without saying that, in a post-imperial age, this redressing of noncongruent nation and state boundaries is in the *inward* direction of adjusting national to state boundaries rather than vice versa.

5. The full text of this article is: "Special measures taken for the sole purpose of securing adequate advancement of certain racial or ethnic groups, or individuals requiring such protection as may be necessary in order to ensure such groups or individuals equal enjoyment or exercise of human rights and fundamental freedoms shall not be deemed racial discrimination, provided, however, that such measures do not, as consequence, lead to the maintenance of separate rights for different racial groups and that they shall not be continued after the objective for which they were taken has been achieved."

6. There is, of course, a rub in couching ethnic "return" migration as based on a positive discrimination on the part of the receiving state: in international as well as domestic law positive discrimination is usually taken to be a measure by the state in which a minority actually resides, and not by the state to which the minority is deemed to belong. However, what matters here is not the legal correctness of the term, but the perception and justificatory rationale on the part of the receiving state.

7. This raises the question why ethnic migration within the postcolonial constellation, which likewise occurred only after World War II, could get away without a persecution or minority-protection rationale. One answer is that postcolonial entry privileges were generally weaker than those in the diaspora constellation, and they were embedded within a restrictive context of "immigration" law and policy.

8. See also Kasher's (1985) defense of the Law of Return as "affirmative action" for Jews. For a critique, see Gans (2003:ch.6)

9. Under the pressure of its Soviet-*cum*–Third World majority, the United Nations General Assembly declared Zionism a form of "racism" in 1975 (this was repealed only in December 1991). See Dayan (1993:96).

10. Witness the ritual text that accompanies the Orthodox conversion procedure to Judaism: "What induces you to join us? Do you not know that in these days the Israelites are in trouble, oppressed, despised and subjected to endless suffering?" (in Abramov, 1976:310). But see the thorough normative discussion by Kasher (1985:112), who argues that the reaching of a "viable majority" of Jews in Israel would be the moment in which at least the automatic citizenship component of the Law of Return would cease to be legitimate.

11. The "ethnic" versus "civic" distinction is one of the main themes in the nations and nationalism literature. For standard accounts, see Smith (1986) and Brubaker (1992). For critical accounts, see Yack (1996), Brubaker (1999), and—most recently—Peters (2002).

12. Consider the opening passage of Israel's Proclamation of Independence of May 14, 1948: "The Land of Israel was the birthplace of the Jewish people. Here their spiritual, religious and political identity was shaped. Here they first attained to statehood, created cultural values of national and universal significance and gave to the world the eternal Book of Books." http://www.knesset.gov.il/docs/eng/megilat_eng.htm (accessed July 1, 2004).

13. Other possibilities would have included Russia, Hungary, Slovakia, and Greece.

14. This pairing has actually been done, in both apologetic and critical perspectives. For the former, which considers Israel as an instance of new nation building through immigration, see Eisenstadt (1955); for the latter, which considers Israel as an instance of the European colonization of the world, see Shafir (1989).

15. The natural-law construction of the Law of Return enabled this Jewish preference to be reconciled with the parallel commitment, also articulated in the Declaration of Independence, that "[i]n its positive acts . . . the state would

always maintain strict equality between its Jewish and non-Jewish citizens" (Peled, 1992:435).

16. Quoted in Moshe Zak, "The Rationale of Return," *Jerusalem Post*, 5 September 1994.

17. Article 4 of the Law of Return says: "[E]very Jew who was born in this country, whether before or after the coming into force of this Law, shall be deemed to be a person who has come to this country as an *oleh* under this Law."

18. Ariel Sharon, "Beyond Democracy," *Jerusalem Post*, 2 June 1993.

19. Amnon Rubinstein, quoted in Liebman and Don-Yehiya (1983:96).

20. See Amos Elon (1996:22), who called the Zionist new beginning a "*risorgimento* for Jews."

21. Conversion to Judaism is, of course, possible, but it is always exceptional, especially in the Orthodox branch, which is predominant in Israel.

22. "Similar" but not "identical" prerogatives, because only the Jewish, not the Christian or Muslim, authority over family law was regulated and sanctioned in a state law (the Chief Rabbinate of Israel Law).

23. See Shafir and Peled's (2002, ch. 1) excellent discussion of the many faultlines in Israeli state and society that are *not* captured by the "Jewish state" versus "Western-style democracy" opposition.

24. This is implicitly acknowledged in the distinction between Israeli "citizenship" and a variety of Jewish and non-Jewish "nationalities" (*leom*) in Israeli law, which is unknown in France and other "normal" nation-states.

25. The two best accounts of the Arab minority *problématique* in Israel are Lustick (1980) and Kretzmer (1990). Landau (1993) is informative but apologetic ("The Arabs in Israel should recognize Israel as a state with a Jewish majority, eager to preserve its dominant national identity", p. 196).

26. "Kleiner bill would limit PM candidacy to Jews," *Jerusalem Post*, 2 February 1997.

27. "Israeli parliament removes 'racist' bill from agenda," *Agence France Presse*, 4 February 1997. The rejection of the bill is hypocritical, if one considers the universal shunning of Arab Israelis in the Knesset, where no Arab has ever served as a cabinet minister and Arab parties have never been part of a government coalition (Arian, 1998:137–138).

28. "Legislative distractions," *Jerusalem Post*, 5 February 1997.

29. Rouhana (1997, 1998), Yiftachel (1997, 1999), Ghanem (1998).

30. Lustick (1989) argued, prematurely, that this turn toward consociationalism was actually happening from the 1980s on. This is because against the backdrop of "Jewish polarization" (into the religious-nationalist and peace camps) the Arab vote was becoming increasingly attractive for the peace camp. However, fishing for the Arab vote is one thing; institutionalized sharing of power is quite another.

31. In the imposed absence of Arab immigration, this stable share of the Arab Israeli population (and its numerical increase from 156,000 in 1948 to 875,000 in 1991) is due to a significantly higher fertility rate (Landau, 1993:6–7).

32. This act, in force until 1992, compensated the expellees for lost property and damages (see Schillinger, 1988).

33. Quoted in the third reading of the Federal Expellee Bill (*Deutscher Bundestag,* 254. Sitzung, 18 March 1953, p. 12237).

34. Expellee Minister Lukaschek (CDU), quoted during the second reading of the Federal Expellee Bill (*Deutscher Bundestag,* 250. Sitzung, 25 February 1953, p. 11971).

35. In addition, the expellees were well represented within the political system. Eighteen percent of the deputies in the first *Bundestag* of 1949 were expellees (Patton, 1999:60). This roughly corresponded to their population share.

36. Expellee Minister Lukaschek, second reading of the Federal Expellee Bill (*Deutscher Bundestag,* 250. Sitzung, 25 February 1953, p. 11972).

37. Member of Parliament de Vries (FDP), ibid., p. 11985.

38. Ibid.

39. de Vries, ibid.

40. In official perception, *Aussiedlung* was to enable the entitled ethnic migrants to "live as Germans among Germans" ("Aufnahme und Eingliederung der Aussiedler," *Deutscher Bundestag,* 11. Wahlperiode, Drucksache 11/3465, 23 November 1988, p. 1). When the Commissioner for Foreigner Affairs (*Ausländerbeauftragte*) of the current Red-Green government qualified *Aussiedlung* as an "aspect of immigration policy," members of the conservative opposition party (CDU/CSU) interrupted her in parliament: "*Rückführung nennen wir das!* [We call that 'guided return']" (*Deutscher Bundestag,* 14. Wahlperiode, 95. Sitzung, 23 March 2000, pp. 8831–8832).

41. As by a conservative jurist who claimed that the Federal Republic was "a state created by the German people for the German people with the purpose of national reunification" (Uhlitz, 1986:145).

42. This was Zuleeg's (1987:188) response to Uhlitz (1986).

43. Article 79 (3) of the Basic Law immunizes Articles 1 to 20 from future revision.

44. The *Siebenbürger Sachsen* formed their first colony in what is today Romania in the twelfth century.

45. This was one of "four considerations" to be taken into account by the so-called "Sages of Israel" in the first "who is a Jew" debate of 1958 (see subsequent discussion in text).

46. For overviews of the protracted "who is the Jew" debate in Israel, see Abramov (1976, ch. 9), Kraines (1976), Zucker (1973, ch. 12), and Samet (1985; 1986).

47. According to the Halacha, one does not stop being a Jew after converting to another religion; apostates are "sinners" but still Jews.

48. Judge M. Silberg, who wrote the court's majority opinion (quoted in Abramov, 1976:287–288).

49. Ibid., p. 288.

50. Justice Landau, quoted in Abramov (1976:288–289).

51. Justice Silberg, quoted in Kraines (1976:25).

52. The Orthodox groups acquiesced in the *Rufeisen* decision, "presumably because it was a matter of excluding a dubious Jew rather than including one" (Alter, 1970:56).

53. Technically, the definition of "Jew" under the Population Registry Law served as a basis for defining the term under the Law of Return and any other law (Richmond, 1993:107).

54. The March 1958 Interior Ministry order to its population registry department stipulated: "[A]ny person declaring in good faith that he is a Jew, shall be registered as a Jew" (quoted in Abramov, 1976:290).

55. The text of the letter is available at Jewish Agency for Israel (1998), item 18.

56. However, the majority of addressed "Sages" were known to support a religious-traditionalist position, so that "[i]t is difficult to avoid the impression that Ben-Gurion had accepted the NRP's stand and was looking for an honorable way out and for constraints that would justify the surrender to 'religious coercion'" (Samet, 1985:90).

57. This comparison with the unquestioned Jewishness of an anti-Jewish terrorist drew additional acumen from the fact that Shalit was a career officer in the Israeli Defense Forces.

58. A summary of the Supreme Court judges' individual opinions in the *Shalit* case can be found in Jewish Agency for Israel (1998), item 20. A sensitive account of the court's division between secular subjectivists and religious objectivists (with Chief Justice Agranat uncomfortably in the middle) is Lahav (1997, ch. 12).

59. The coalition crisis caused by the *Shalit* decision coincided with a looming military confrontation with Egypt over the Suez Canal, which was then under Israeli control.

60. Section 4B of the Law of Return, as amended in 1970 (Law of Return, Amendment No.2, 5730-1970).

61. Section 4A of the Law of Return, as amended in 1970, reads: "(a) The rights of a Jew under this Law . . . are also vested in a child and a grandchild of a Jew, the spouse of a Jew, the spouse of a child of a Jew and the spouse of a grandchild of a Jew, except for a person who has been a Jew and has voluntarily changed his religion. (b) It shall be immaterial whether or not a Jew by whose right a right under subsection (a) is claimed is still alive and whether or not he has immigrated to Israel."

62. According to Article 1.2.3 of the Federal Expellee Law, the nominally expelled were the so-called *Aussiedler*.

63. "Schriftlicher Bericht des Ausschusses für Heimatvertriebene (22. Ausschuss) über den Entwurf eines Gesetzes über die Angelegenheiten der Vertriebenen und Flüchtlinge (Bundesvertriebenengesetz)" (*Deutscher Bundestag*, 1. Wahlperiode 1949, Drucksache 3902, 1 December 1952, p. 3).

64. "Entwurf eines Gesetzes über die Angelegenheiten der Vertriebenen und Flüchtlinge" (*Deutscher Bundestag*, Drucksache 2872, 26 November 1951, p. 7).

65. They are reprinted in Liesner (1988:97–107).

66. Ibid, p. 102.
67. Member of Parliament Kohl (KPD), during the second reading of the Federal Refugee Law, *Deutscher Bundestag,* 250. Sitzung, 25 February 1953, p. 11977.
68. Ibid., p. 11978.
69. Expulsion Pressure Guidelines, in Liesner (1988:99).
70. FAC decision of 20 October 1987, *BVerwG 9 C 266.86,* p. 149.
71. From an FAC decision of 1977, quoted in the Expulsion Pressure Guidelines (Liesner, 1988:99).
72. See Alexy (1989:2851). This practice lasted until 1992, when a reform of Article 6 of the Federal Expellee Law required direct descent from a German ancestor as a separate and necessary recognition criterion (at least for ethnic claimants born after 1923).
73. Before the occupation of Poland in September 1939, more than ten million people had already been "Germanized" this way in Austria and Czechoslovakia (Otto, 1990:64).
74. Membership in and commitment to the Zionist movement (including immigration to Israel) also did not count as an indicator against German *Volkszugehörigkeit.*
75. Referred to in *BVerfG 59,* 139.
76. *BVerfG 59,* 128 (decision of 16 December 1981).
77. Ibid., p. 159.
78. Federal Administrative Court, Decision of 10 November 1976 (*BVerwG VIII C92.75*), p. 309.
79. "Der Familienverband vermittelt den Bekenntniszusammenhang" (ibid., p. 305).
80. Decision of 12 November 1996 (*BVerwG 9 C 8.96*).
81. Ibid, p. 220.
82. Decision of 19 October 2000 (*BVerwG 5 C 44/99*).
83. "Gesetzentwurf der Fraktionen SPD und Grüne, Entwurf eines Gesetzes zur Klarstellung des Spätaussiedlerstatus" (*Deutscher Bundestag,* Drucksache 14/6310, 19 June 2001), pp. 1 and 5.
84. Ibid., p. 1.
85. But see also the critique of the centrality of language in the new Late Resettler Status Law (*Spätaussiedlerstatusgesetz*) by Silagi (2001).
86. Shafir and Peled (2002), Kimmerling (2001), Dowty (1998), *The Economist* (1998).
87. As Daniel Patrick Moynihan, in his capacity as American ambassador to the UN, objected to the UN General Assembly resolution that "Zionism is a form of racism and racial discrimination," this "drained the word 'racism' of its meaning" (quoted in Skrentny, 2002:65).
88. A 1980 amendment to the citizenship law retroactively granted Israeli citizenship to all returning Palestinians (including their children) who were left stateless after 1948. The 1952 citizenship law had granted automatic Israeli citizenship on the basis of residence, but only if three cumulative conditions

were met: residency, presence in Israel after the establishment of the state in 1948, and registration in the 1951 Population Registry. The cumulative nature of these conditions was meant to exclude all Palestinians who first left their homes and then returned illegally.

89. This is the subject of Anton Shammas's gloomy "the morning after" scenario (1988).

90. "No 'right of return' for non-Jewish spouses," *Jerusalem Post*, 6 March 1998.

91. "Interior Ministry iron fist makes gentiles feel unwelcome," *Ha'Aretz*, 26 January 2001.

92. See Israeli philosopher Yael Tamir (1993:160): "[T]he Israeli 'Law of Return' . . . would only be justified if the largest minority in the state, namely the Palestinians, would also have a national entity in which they could enact a similar law."

93. See the critical discussion of this intervention in Hazony (2000:57–58).

94. Conversely, the defenders of the Law of Return questioned the premise that "normality" had arrived. As Natan Sharansky, the Soviet dissident and leader of the fastest-growing immigrant group in Israel, objected to the "post-Zionists": "As long as the process of ingathering major Jewish communities continues, Israel remains, in an important sense, *a state-in-the-making, not yet complete*" ("Why they close the gates," *The Jerusalem Report*, 19 October 1995; emphasis supplied).

95. It would actually be more appropriate to label this position "anti-Zionist." However, both in the eye of the critic (Pappe, 1997; Silberstein, 1999) and of the meta-critic (Wurmser, 1999; Hazony, 2000) the "original sin" position (as articulated mostly by Israel's' 'new historians' and' 'critical sociologists') is subsumed under the "post-Zionism" label.

96. In Kelman's vision, a reduced Law of Return would be tied to actual persecution (1998:50).

97. The notion of "Green Line" refers to Israel's quasiofficial borders after the 1949 armistice.

98. An Arab Israeli shopkeeper in Jerusalem, quoted in *The Economist*, special section "After Zionism," 25 April 1998, p. 6.

99. The other narrative is "security" (Kimmerling, 2001, ch. 6).

100. Neuer (1998:2).

101. On Israel's "constitutional revolution," see Neuer (1998), Hirschl (1998), and Shafir and Peled (2002, ch. 10).

102. David Weinberg, "Change the Law of Return," *Jerusalem Post*, 5 December 1999.

103. Ibid.

104. Between 1974 and 1989, there were no less than nine attempts by orthodox-religious parties to add to the Law of Return's conversion clause the "according to the Halacha" proviso. Israel's electoral arithmetic helped turn this practical nonissue into a highly salient stake of political conflict that would make or break entire coalition governments. Since Likud's historic victory of 1977, which ended three decades of uncontested Labour hegemony, Israel's

political forces were about evenly divided between the "nationalist" and the "peace" camps. In this parity situation, the orthodox-religious parties, which were consistently gaining in strength, were often in the role of king-makers—routinely making the promise of a halachic-conversion proviso in the Law of Return their price for supporting Likud.

105. Judy Dempsey, "Israeli government shaken by row over who is a Jew," *Financial Times,* 24 January 1998.

106. Tovah Lazaroff, "Who's that knocking at our door?" *Jerusalem Post,* 14 December 2001.

107. Haim Shapiro and Nina Gilbert, "Narrowing of law of return passes Knesset committee," *Jerusalem Post,* 25 June 2002.

108. Herb Keinon, "Deri: Law of Return must be made tougher," *Jerusalem Post,* 20 July 1990.

109. Herb Keinon, "Proposed change in Law of Return would require one Jew in each family," *Jerusalem Post,* 11 July 1991.

110. As the Sephardic chief rabbi explained his request: "Twenty times the number of Christmas trees were sold this year compared with previous years, and the churches are being filled" (quoted in Dan Itzenberg, "Chief rabbis support changing Law of Return," *Jerusalem Post,* 27 December 1994).

111. Haim Shapiro and Nina Gilbert, "Narrowing the Law of Return passes Knesset committee," *Jerusalem Post,* 25 June 2002.

112. This is an Interior Ministry estimate from 1999 ("The Jewish people's law," *Jerusalem Post,* 3 December 1999).

113. "Who is an Oleh?" *Jerusalem Post,* 24 July 1990.

114. Netty Gross, "What are they doing here?" *Jerusalem Report,* 26 August 2002.

115. "The Jewish people's law," *Jerusalem Post,* 3 December 1999.

116. Herb Keinon, "Make room for the remnants of the lost tribes," *Jerusalem Post,* 2 September 1994.

117. Jonathan Rosenblum, "Save the Zionist dream," *Jerusalem Post,* 23 October 1998.

118. Orit Shohat, "Who decides who's Jewish?" *Ha'Aretz,* 26 November 1999.

119. Jonathan Rosenblum, "Save the Zionist dream," *Jerusalem Post,* 23 October 1998.

120. Yair Sheleg, "The staggering inequities of the Law of Return," *Ha'Aretz,* 2 December 1999.

121. Ben Lynfield, "Israelis ask to change Law of Return," *United Press International,* August 23, 1994.

122. "No letup in heated debate over Namir's call for 'selective aliya,'" *Mideast Mirror* (UK), 5 October 1994.

123. Michael Parks, "Call to Limit Russian Jews in Israel Hits Discordant Note," *Los Angeles Times,* 7 October 1994.

124. Barak had made the election pledge, "[T]here will be an interior minister for whom all those eligible under the Law of Return will in fact be considered

eligible by him" (quoted in Dalia Shehori, "Barak: Law of Return will stay as is," *Ha'Aretz*, 29 November 1999).

125. Both quotes from Prime Minister Barak are in Heidi Gleit and Danna Harman, "Prime Minister rips Shas demands to amend Law of Return," *Jerusalem Post*, 29 November 1999, p. 2.

126. Natan Sharansky, quoted in "Immigrant group assails Law of Return," *Jerusalem Post*, 3 December 1999.

127. Marilyn Henry, "Burg warns against Law of Return debate," *Jerusalem Post*, 16 November 1995. Throughout the entire debate surrounding the Law of Return in the 1990s, the Jewish Agency has persistently defended the law in its currently expansive form. It is driven to this position by organizational interest, because its funds are contingent upon the number of "Jews" (however loosely defined) whom it manages to recruit for immigration to Israel.

128. *Jerusalem Post*, 1 July 2002, p. 1.

129. Chancellor Helmut Kohl (CDU), *Deutscher Bundestag*, 11. Wahlperiode, 108. Sitzung, Bonn, 22 November 1988, p. 7446.

130. *Frankfurter Rundschau*, 7 November 1988, p. 1.

131. Ibid.

132. Both flows were of approximately the same size: between 1988 and 1996, there were 2.3 million resettlers and 2 million asylum seekers (Koopmans, 1999:640).

133. M. Horacek (Greens), *Deutscher Bundestag*, 10. Wahlperiode, 129. Sitzung, Bonn, 28 March 1985, p. 9570.

134. Ibid., p. 9570 and p. 9569, respectively.

135. Mrs. Olms (Greens), *Deutscher Bundestag*, 11. Wahlperiode, 91. Sitzung, Bonn, 8 September 1988, p. 6265.

136. *Deutscher Bundestag*, 11. Wahlperiode, 102. Sitzung, Bonn, 26 October 1988; p. 7005.

137. Erika Trenz, "Einwanderung gestalten," *Das Parlament*, 25 August 1989.

138. SPD proposal, "Beendigung des Neuerwerbs des Vertriebenenstatus und bundeseinheitliche Anwendung des Staatsangehörigkeitsrechts" (*Deutscher Bundestag*, Drucksache 11/6311, 24 January 1990, p. 2).

139. Mrs. Hämmerle (SPD), *Deutscher Bundestag*, 11. Wahlperiode, 146. Sitzung, Bonn, 1 June 1989, p. 10920.

140. "Lafontaine gegen Aussiedler-Zuzug," *Frankfurter Allgemeine Sonntagszeitung*, 25 February 1996.

141. "Keine Stimmungsmache gegen Aussiedler zulassen" (*Deutscher Bundestag*, Drucksache 13/3892, Bonn, 28 February 1996).

142. Greens leader Jürgen Trittin, *Süddeutsche Zeitung*, 28 February 1996.

143. This is a background figure driving (SPD-ruled) Lower Saxony's current initiative to further curtail the entry of Russian resettlers ("Niedersachsen will Zuzug der Spätaussiedler begrenzen," *Frankfurter Allgemeine Zeitung*, 20 February 2002).

144. Cem Özdemir (Greens), Debate on Green proposal "No Polemics Against Aussiedler," (*Deutscher Bundestag*, Plenary Protocol 13/105, Bonn, 10 May 1996), p. 9300.

145. Ibid.
146. Klaus Bade, "Aussiedler und Einwanderungspolitik," *Süddeutsche Zeitung*, 29 February 1996.
147. The law was later annulled for procedural reasons by the Federal Constitutional Court, and in modified form reintroduced in July 2004.
148. In 1989, the average pension for male resettlers was 1,778 DM, 221 DM higher than the average pension of male natives (Otto, 1990:298).
149. H. Lukaschek (CDU), *Deutscher Bundestag*, 260. Sitzung, 16 April 1953, p. 12660.
150. Proposal by CDU/CSU and FDP on "Acceptance and Integration of *Aussiedler*," (*Deutscher Bundestag*, Drucksache 11/3465, 23 November 1988), pp. 1–2.
151. W. Schäuble (CDU), in: *Deutscher Bundestag*, 11. Wahlperiode, 152. Sitzung, Bonn, 22 June 1989, p. 11449.
152. Declaration by Horst Waffenschmidt (CDU), parliamentary state secretary in the Interior Ministry, *Bundesrat*, 649. Sitzung, Bonn, 27 November 1992, p. 612.
153. "Ergebnisse der Verhandlungen zu Asyl und Zuwanderung," *Süddeutsche Zeitung*, 8 December 1992, p. 5. The ties with later-generation emigrants were cut only in the reformed Citizenship Law of 1999; see Chapter 5.
154. Horst Waffenschmidt (CDU), *Deutscher Bundestag*, 13. Wahlperiode, 203. Sitzung, Bonn, 13 November 1997, p. 18353.
155. Horst Waffenschmidt (CDU), *Bundesrat*, 707. Sitzung, Bonn, 19 December 1996, p. 713.
156. Horst Waffenschmidt (CDU), *Bundesrat*, 704. Sitzung, Bonn, 8 November 1996, p. 555.
157. Jochen Welt (SPD, the current SPD/Green government's *Aussiedler* commissioner), *Deutscher Bundestag*, 14. Wahlperiode, 95. Sitzung, Bonn, 23 March 2000, p. 8829.
158. Max Stadler (FDP): "The right of free movement does not mean that there is a right to social benefits independently of where one resides in the Federal Republic" (*Deutscher Bundestag*, plenary protocol 13/84, 2 February 1996, p. 7418).
159. Max Stadler (FDP), *Deutscher Bundestag*, 14. Wahlperiode, 95. Sitzung, Berlin, 23 March 2000, p. 8834.
160. Ibid.
161. H. Koschyk (CDU), *Deutscher Bundestag*, 14. Wahlperiode, 177. Sitzung, Berlin, 22 June 2001, p. 17503.
162. In the former Soviet Union and Russia, the offspring of mixed-nationality parents had or have the option to identify with the nationality of either parent.
163. When, in the mid-1990s, the Federal Administrative Court became amazingly tolerant of nationality changes that occurred just when an application for resettlement was filed (such changes were then considered a "confession" to German peoplehood), the government tightened the ethnicity clause of the Federal Expellee Law, excluding applicants who had previously self-identified

in terms of a non-German (mostly Russian) nationality for domestic purposes. See SPD and Green Factions of the Bundestag, "Entwurf eines Gesetzes zur Klarstellung des Spätaussiedlerstatus" (*Deutscher Bundestag,* Drucksache 14/6310, Berlin, 19 June 2002, p. 6).

164. *Migration News Sheet* (Brussels), November 2002, p. 4.

165. This is a highly simplifying assumption. The generally promigrant attitude of liberal challengers forces them to embrace ethnic migration too, though the effect of removing ethnic quotas and other privileges would be to stop *this concrete* ethnic migration. There is thus something hypocritical about *Aussiedler* (*qua* minority)-friendly Greens, whose plea for a "comprehensive" and ethnically neutral migration policy implies having *this* particular migration stopped. Conversely, restrictive challengers (particularly in Israel) surely want "false" coethnics out but may still be strong advocates of "true" coethnic migration.

5. The Liberal State between De- and Re-Ethnicization

1. "Opening the door," *The Economist,* 2 November 2002, p. 11.

2. An outraged reader found *The Economist*'s suggestion "smack[ed] of an imperialist attitude," and he continued: "What you are advocating sets the rules for an exclusive 'westerners only' club" (*The Economist,* 7 December 2002, p. 20). Any immigration policy honoring "cultural affinities" must reckon with multicultural sensibilities that are violated by it.

3. In fact, at the level of intellectual debate this constraint already *has* made itself felt in Israel, as in Kasher (1985). The notion that the Law of Return is a remedial, affirmative-action type of measure is shared by many of its less differentiated defenders (such as Steinberg, 2000).

4. Interestingly, the only parallel to this is the family unit. No wonder that national belonging has often been couched in family terms (as in Zolberg's [1999:84] notion of modern nations as "familylike bodies").

5. Until 1952, birth in the United States was the only access to U.S. citizenship for Asians.

6. "The internment rationale, upheld by the U.S. Supreme Court, was national security, but the question of confining German or Italian-Americans never arose. The real reasons were clearly racist" (Christopher Reed, "US Agonises Over Scandal of Japanese Internment," *The Guardian,* 17 February 1992).

7. "New Policy Delays Visas For Specified Muslim Men," *New York Times,* September 10, 2002, p. A12.

8. "U.S. Plan to Monitor Muslims Meets With Widespread Protest," *New York Times,* January 15, 2003, p. A9.

9. For the distinction between "Hobbesian" America and "Kantian" Europe, see Kagan (2002).

10. The denounced statement was made by Italian Prime Minister Silvio Berlusconi (*Associated Press,* September 27, 2001).

11. Lorenz Jäger, "Auf allen Karten abseits," *Frankfurter Allgemeine Zeitung,* 14 August 2002.

12. "Mind your language—Jacques Toubon," *Financial Times,* 29 November 1994, p. 20.

13. For a more detailed account, see Joppke and Morawska (2003:3–20).

14. This is enshrined in Article 1 of the 1930 Hague Nationality Convention: "It is for each State to determine under its own law who are its nationals."

15. "Nationality" in the ethnic sense of the Hebrew word *leom.*

16. One has to distinguish here between two different access routes to dual citizenship: attribution at birth versus naturalization. Even states that have notionally remained opposed to dual citizenship have to tolerate dual citizenship at birth if they do not want to discriminate between the sexes. Their opposition has therefore centered on disallowing dual citizenship via naturalization.

17. This last group of states includes France, Greece, Ireland, Italy, the Netherlands, Portugal, and Britain.

18. The notion of "partnership with migrants" was contained in a European Commission draft paper discussed on October 16, 2000, at the European University Institute in Florence. Obviously responding to the oddity of this notion (which was brought up during this discussion), the final document (European Commission, 2000) contains it only in a weaker form, in the notion that there should be "partnership with countries of origin."

19. Friedrich Merz, "Einwanderung und Identität," *Die Welt,* 25 October 2000.

20. "Personal sovereignty" in international law means that the state may unilaterally grant rights and impose obligations on its members, even outside its territory (Hailbronner and Renner, 2001:83).

21. The literature on "transnationalism" has largely ignored the role of the state in this process (see Joppke and Morawska, 2003:26–29). But see the exception by Nina Glick Schiller (1999).

22. "Genuine connection" is the notion coined in the International Court of Justice's famous *Nottebohm* decision, according to which the absence of a "genuine connection" forfeited a state's right of diplomatic protection. The notion has since been redeployed within a human rights context, referring to a state's duty to confer citizenship to people on its territory who have a "genuine connection" to that state (see Orentlicher, 1998:320).

23. If one counts the actual emigrants as "first" generation, the informal cap in question is a "third"-generation cap. In the following, the notion of "second" generation will refer to the second foreign-born generation.

24. In pre-1989 Eurasia, a variant of this was to consider emigrants (as "exiles") traitors to the Communist cause.

25. The "*possession d'état de français*" is a sociological concept with juridicial consequences. Someone is considered French by public authorities, for instance, on the basis of a valid passport, electoral registration, inscription in a French consulate, or any other contact with French authorities. Conversely, a person living abroad who fails to renew his passport or make contact with French authorities in any other way over a period exceeding ten years loses his or her "*possession d'état de français.*" See Lagarde (1997:116).

26. See the statement by Jacques Habert, Senator for the French Abroad, *Sénat*, séance du 16 juin 1993, p. 1376.

27. See Lagarde's (1993:558) critique of the "totally exorbitant" strengthening of *jus sanguinis* over traditional *jus soli* in the 1993 reform of nationality law.

28. Statement by Jean-Luc Mélenchon, *Sénat*, séance du 15 juin 1993, p. 1304.

29. Limiting this measure to children of *one* French parent betrays the intention to treat emigrants and immigrants symmetrically with respect to *volonté*— immigrant children with one French parent, after all, were French *jure sanguinis*.

30. *Assemblée Nationale*, 2nd Session of 12 May 1993, p. 419. The Mazeaud amendment resembled closely a recommendation of the Long Commission (Long, 1988:178–180).

31. *Sénat*, séance du 15 juin 1993, p. 1303.

32. Ibid.

33. Note that the Socialists and Communists also voted against the Mazeaud amendment, but with the broader intent of rejecting "elective" nationality for all groups, the immigrants included.

34. Citizenship "by choice" means as-of-right citizenship, without the need to naturalize, established by mere declaration of the entitled individual.

35. Previously no such continuous residence was required for second-generation immigrants born in Italy.

36. Senator Toth, *Senato della Repubblica*, 10th Legislature, 524. Session, 23 May 1991, p. 524.

37. Silvia Barbieri, *Camera dei Deputati*, 10th Legislature, First Commission, Meeting of 9 January 1992, p. 79.

38. Senator Mazzola, *Senato della Repubblica*, 10th Legislature, Disegni di legge e relazioni, documenti 1460 e 1850-A, p. 41.

39. Senator Mazzola, *Senato della Repubblica*, 10th Legislature, 524th Session, 23 May 1991, p. 15.

40. Senator Toth, ibid., p. 43.

41. Senator Strik Lievers, ibid., p. 10.

42. Senator Mazzola, *Senato della Repubblica*, 10th Legislature, Documents 1460 and 1850-A., 31 July 1989.

43. "Piu facile diventare italiani," *la Repubblica*, 22 December 2000, p. 1.

44. Senator Mazzola, *Senato della Repubblica*, 10th Legislature, designi di legge e relazioni, documenti 1460 e 1850-A, p. 4.

45. "Argentina, la fuga degli italiani," *la Repubblica*, 11 January 2002, p. 19.

46. "Italian origin" is defined in Article 17 of the new immigration law as having at least a "third-degree [Italian] ancestor in the direct line" (*Senato della Repubblica*, 14th Legislature, Disegno di legge N. 795-B).

47. For Portugal, see my discussion of its 1981 nationality law reform in Chapter 3; for a more recent episode of nationality law reform in Spain, see Joppke (2003:452–454). All of these countries are admittedly classified in a Council of Europe report on "Europeans living abroad" (1999:8) as "proactively" courting their emigrant communities abroad, in contrast to the "laissez-faire"

approach prevailing in northern Europe. However, the report also states that to the degree that there is movement across these categories, it is from "laissez-faire" toward a more "proactive" approach.

48. It is not my claim here that "emigration" and "national minorities abroad" are the *only* sources of re-ethnicization in the contemporary liberal state. For a third important source of re-ethnicization—the existence of domestic rivals to the titular nation—see the discussion of Israel in Chapter 4. An exhaustive treatment of the "re-ethnicization" *problématique* is beyond the scope of this chapter. My purpose here is more modest: to make it plausible that certain types of ethnic migration are likely to persist, even in the ambit of the liberal state.

49. "Kin-state" is the term most often used in the literature to denote the "ethnic homelands" of minorities abroad (King, 1998:1). It has also been officially adopted by the Council of Europe's (2001a) Venice Commission.

50. Zsolt Nemeth, Political State Secretary in the Foreign Ministry and architect of the status law, quoted in Fowler (2002:38).

51. According to recent census data, there are 1,627,021 ethnic Hungarians in Romania and 567,296 in Slovakia (Council of Europe, 2001b:19).

52. "Ungarn wehrt sich für das Statusgesetz," *Neue Zürcher Zeitung,* 4 July 2001, p. 2.

53. "Ungarn und Rumänien legen Streit bei," *Frankfurter Allgemeine Zeitung,* 24 December 2001, p. 5.

54. The quote is from the Government of Romania position paper before the Venice Commission (in Fowler, 2002:54).

References

Abramov, S. Zalman. 1976. *Perpetual Dilemma: Jewish Religion in the Jewish State.* Jerusalem: The World Union for Progressive Judaism.

Adroher Biosca, Salomé. 1996. Los iberoamericanos en el Derecho español. *Revista Crítica de Derecho Inmobiliario* 72(636), 1867–1903.

Aguiar, Manuela. 1998. Comunidades lusófonas. In: *Interculturalismo e cidadania em espaços lusófonos. Cursos da Arrabida.* Ed. M. B. Rocha-Trindade. Lisbon: Europa-America.

Aleinikoff, T. Alexander. 2002. *Semblances of Sovereignty.* Cambridge, Mass.: Harvard University Press.

Aleinikoff, T. Alexander, and Douglas Klusmeyer. 2002. *Citizenship Policies for an Age of Migration.* Washington, D.C.: Carnegie Endowment for International Peace.

Aleinikoff, T. Alexander, David Martin, and Hiroshi Motomura. 1995. *Immigration: Process and Policy.* St. Paul, Minn.: West Publishing.

Alexy, Hans. 1989. Rechtsfragen des Aussiedlerzuzugs. *Neue juristische Wochenschrift* 45, 2850–2859.

Alter, Robert. 1970. The *Shalit* Case. *Commentary* 50(1), 55–61.

Alvarez Rodriguez, Aurelia. 1990. Regimen juridico de algunos iberoamericanos en el ordenamiento español. *La Ley* (Madrid), 30 November, 4–8.

———. 1994. Los nacionales de los países iberoamericanos ante el ordenamiento juridico español. In *La frontera, mito, y cultura americana, curso de literatura y cultura americana.* Universidad de Leon.

Anderson, Benedict. 1983. *Imagined Communities.* London: Verso.

Andrade, Antonio Alberto de. 1961. *Many Races—One Nation.* Lisbon.

Andreas, Peter. 2001. *Border Games.* Ithaca, N.Y.: Cornell University Press.

Appleyard, R. T. 2001. "Post-war British Immigration." In: *The Australian People.* Ed. J. Jupp. Cambridge: Cambridge University Press.

Arango, Joaquin. 2000. Becoming a country of immigration at the end of the twentieth century: the case of Spain. In: *Eldorado or Fortress? Migration in Southern Europe.* Ed. R. King, G. Lazaridis, and C. Tsardanidis. Basingstoke: Macmillan.

Arian, Asher. 1998. *The Second Republic: Politics in Israel.* Chatham, N.J.: Chatham House.

Auerbach, Frank L. 1955. *Immigration Laws of the United States*. Indianapolis: Bobbs-Merrill Company.

Bader, Veit. 1995. Citizenship and exclusion. *Political Theory* 23(2), 211–246.

Baganha, Maria, José C. Marques, and Graca Fonseca. 2000. *Is an ethclass emerging in Europe? The Portuguese case*. Lisbon: Luso-American Foundation.

Banton, Michael. 1983. *Racial and Ethnic Competition*. Cambridge: Cambridge University Press.

Barkan, Elazar. 1992. *The Retreat of Scientific Racism*. Cambridge: Cambridge University Press.

Barraclough, Geoffrey. 1967. *An Introduction to Contemporary History*. Harmondsworth: Penguin.

Barreto, Antonio. 1994. Portugal, a Europa e a democracia. *Analise Social* 29(129), 1051–1069.

Barrière, Louis-Augustin. 1995. Le puzzle de la citoyenneté en Algérie. *Plein Droit* 29–30, 92–96.

Baudet-Caille, Véronique. 2000. *La nationalité française*. Paris: Editions ASH.

Beitz, Charles. 1979. *Political Theory and International Relations*. Princeton, N.J.: Princeton University Press.

Bell, Daniel. 1975. Ethnicity and social change. In: *Ethnicity: Theory and Experience*. Ed. N. Glazer and D. P.Moynihan. Cambridge, Mass.: Harvard University Press.

Bender, Gerald J. 1978. *Angola under the Portuguese*. London: Heinemann.

Benedict, Ruth. 1934. *Patterns of Culture*. Boston: Houghton Mifflin.

Bennett, Marion T. 1966. The Immigration and Nationality (McCarran-Walter) Act of 1952, as amended to 1965. *Annals of the American Academy of Political and Social Science* 367, 127–136.

Bernard, William, ed. 1950. *American Immigration Policy*. New York: Harper and Brothers.

Betts, Katharine. 1988. *Ideology and Immigration: Australia 1976–1987*. Melbourne: Melbourne University Press.

———. 1996. Immigration and public opinion in Australia. *People and Place* 4(3), 9–20.

———. 1999. *The Great Divide*. Sydney: Duffy and Snellgrove.

Betts, Raymond. 1961. *Assimilation and Association in French Colonial Theory, 1890–1914*. New York: Columbia University Press.

Bigo, Didier. 2001. Migration and security. In: *Controlling a New Migration World*. Ed. V. Guiraudon and C. Joppke. London: Routledge.

Birrell, Robert. 1990. *The Chains that Bind: Family Reunion Migration to Australia in the 1980s*. Canberra: Australian Government Publishing Service.

———. 1992. Problems of immigration control in liberal democracies. In: *Nations of Immigrants*. Ed. G. P. Freeman and J. Jupp. Melbourne: Oxford University Press.

———. 1995. *A Nation of Our Own*. Melbourne: Longman.

———. 1996. Managing the cost and scale of family reunion. *People and Place* 4(4), 58–67.

——. 1999. The 1999–2000 immigration program. *People and Place* 7(2), 48–59.

——. 2001. Immigration on the rise: the 2001–2002 immigration program. *People and Place* 9(2), 21–28.

Birrell, Robert, and Katharine Betts. 1988. The FitzGerald report on immigration policy. *Australian Quarterly* 60(3), 261–274.

Birrell, Robert, and Tanya Birrell. 1987. *An Issue of People: Population and Australian Society.* 2nd ed. Melbourne: Longman Cheshire.

Birrell, Robert, and Virginia Rapson. 1998. The 1998–99 immigration program. *People and Place* 6(2), 1–14.

Blainey, Geoffrey. 1984. *All for Australia.* North Ryde (Australia): Methuen Hayes.

Bleich, Erik (with Jill Parsons). 2001a. The legacies of history? From colonization to integration in Britain and France. Paper presented at the conference, The Legacy of Colonization and Decolonization in Europe and the Americas, University of Paris I (Sorbonne), 22–23 June.

Bleich, Erik. 2001b. The French model: colour-blind integration. In: *Color Lines.* Ed. J. D. Skrentny. Chicago: University of Chicago Press.

Boes, Mathias. 1993. Ethnisierung des Rechts? *Kölner Zeitschrift für Soziologie und Sozialpsychologie* 45(4), 619–643.

Borjas, George. 1990. *Friends or Strangers.* New York: Basic Books.

Bourdieu, Pierre. 1974. *Sociologie de l'Algérie.* 5th ed. Paris: Presses universitaires de France.

——. 1991. Elements for a critical reflection on the idea of region. In: *Language and Symbolic Power.* Cambridge: Polity Press.

Boxer, Carl R. 1963. *Race Relations in the Portuguese Colonial Empire, 1415–1825.* Oxford: Clarendon Press.

Brawley, Sean. 1995a. *The White Peril.* Sydney: University of New South Wales Press.

——. 1995b. The Department of Immigration and abolition of the 'White Australia' policy reflected through the private diaries of Sir Peter Heydon. *Australian Journal of Politics and History* 41(3), 420–434.

Brettell, Caroline B. 1993. The emigrant, the nation, and the state in 19th and 20th century Portugal. *Portuguese Studies Review* 2(2), 51–65.

Brigagão, Clóvis. 1996. Comunidade dos países de língua portuguesa. *Política Internacional* 1(13), 13–24.

Brimelow, Peter. 1995. *Alien Nation.* New York: Random House.

Brubaker, Rogers. 1992. *Citizenship and Nationhood in France and Germany.* Cambridge, Mass.: Harvard University Press.

——. 1995. Comments on 'Modes of immigration politics in liberal democratic states.' *International Migration Review* 29(4), 903–908.

——. 1996. *Nationalism Reframed.* New York: Cambridge University Press.

——. 1998a. Myths and misconceptions in the study of nationalism. In: *The State of the Nation.* Ed. J. Hall. Cambridge: Cambridge University Press.

——. 1998b. Migrations of ethnic unmixing in the "New Europe." *Internation-*

al Migration Review 32(4), 1047–1065.

———. 1999. The Manichean myth: rethinking the distinction between 'civic' and 'ethnic' nationalism. In: *Nation and National Identity*. Ed. H. Kriesi et al. Zürich: Rüegger.

———. 2002. Ethnicity without groups. *Archives européennes de sociologie* 43(2), 163–189.

———. 2003. The return of assimilation? In: *Toward Assimilation and Citizenship*. Ed. C. Joppke and E. Morawska. Basingstoke: Palgrave Macmillan (originally published in *Ethnic and Racial Studies* 24(4), 2001, 531–548).

Brückner, Peter. 1978. *Versuch, uns und anderen die Bundesrepublik zu erklären.* Berlin: Wagenbach.

Brunschwig, Henri. 1986. De l'assimilation à la décolonisation. In: *Les chemins de la décolonisation de l'empire colonial français*. Ed. C.-R. Ageron. Paris: Editions du Centre National de la Recherche Scientifique.

Burgers, Jan Herman. 1992. The road to San Francisco. *Human Rights Quarterly* 14, 447–477.

Caetano, Marcelo. 1951. *Colonizing Traditions, Principles and Methods of the Portuguese*. Lisbon: Ministerio do Ultramar.

Cairns, Alan C. 1999. Empire, globalization, and the fall and rise of diversity. In: *Citizenship, Diversity, and Pluralism*. Ed. A. C. Cairns. Montreal and Kingston: McGill-Queen's University Press.

Calavita, Kitty. 1998. Immigration, law, and marginalization in a global economy: notes from Spain, *Law and Society Review* 32(4), 529–566.

Calvo Buezas, Tomás. 1998. *La patria común iberoamericana*. Madrid: Ed. Cauce.

Cantle Report (UK). 2001. *Community Cohesion*. London: Government Printing Office.

Carens, Joseph. 1987. Aliens and citizens: the case for open borders. *Review of Politics* 49(2), 251–273.

———. 1992. Migration and morality: a liberal egalitarian perspective. In: *Free Movement*. Ed. B. Barry and R. Goodin. New York: Harvester.

———. 1995. Immigration, politial community, and the transformation of identity: Quebec's immigration policies in critical perspective. In: *Is Quebec Nationalism Just?* Ed. J. Carens. Montreal and Kingston, Ontario: Mc-Gill–Queen's University Press.

———. 2000. *Culture, Citizenship, and Community*. Oxford: Oxford University Press.

Carr-Saunders, A. M. 1936. *World Population*. Oxford: Clarendon Press.

Castles, Stephen, et al. 1988. *Mistaken Identity: Multiculturalism and the Demise of Nationalism in Australia*. Sydney: Pluto Press.

Castro Henriques, Isabel de. 1995. *Commerce et changement en Angola au XIX siècle. Vol. 1*. Paris: L'Harmattan.

Centro de Investigaciones Sociológicas. 2001. Barómetro de febrero. Estudio no. 2.409. Febrero 2001. Available at: http://www.cis.es/File/ViewFile.aspx?FileId=1642 (PDF document; accessed June 29, 2004).

Chamberlain, M. E. 1985. *Decolonization*. Oxford: Blackwell.

Chin, Gabriel J. 1996. The civil rights revolution comes to immigration law. *North*

Carolina Law Review 75, 273–345.

———. 1998. Segregation's last stronghold: race discrimination and the constitutional law of immigration. *UCLA Law Review* 46(1), 1–74.

Cohen, Erik. 1983. Ethnicity and legitimation in contemporary Israel. *Jerusalem Quarterly* 28, 111–124.

———. 1989. The changing legitimations of the State of Israel. In: *Israel: State and Society, 1948–1988*. Ed. P. Y. Medding. New York: Oxford University Press.

Cohen, Robin. 1997. *Global Diasporas*. London: University College of London (UCL) Press.

Cohen-Almagor, Raphael. 1995. Cultural pluralism and the Israeli nation-building ideology. *International Journal of Middle East Studies* 27, 461–484.

Coleman, Jules L., and Sarah K. Harding. 1995. Citizenship, the demands of justice, and the moral relevance of political borders. In: *Justice in Immigration*. Ed. W. F. Schwartz. Cambridge: Cambridge University Press.

Condorcet, Antoine-Nicolas de. [1795] 1955. *Sketch for a Historical Picture of the Progress of the Human Mind*. Tr. June Barraclough. Westport, Conn.: Hyperion.

Coolidge, Mary Roberts. [1909] 1969. *Chinese Immigration*. Reprint, New York: Arno Press and the New York Times.

Corkill, David, and Martin Eaton. 1998. Multicultural insertions in a small economy: Portugal's immigrant communities. *Southern European Society and Politics* 3(3), 148–168.

Cornelius, Wayne. 1994. Spain. The uneasy transition from labor exporter to labor importer. In: *Controlling Immigration*. Ed. W. Cornelius, P. Martin, and J. Hollifield. Palo Alto, Calif.: Stanford University Press.

Council of Europe. 1997. *European Convention on Nationality and Explanatory Report*. Strasbourg: Council of Europe Publishing, European Treaty Series No. 166.

——— (Parliamentary Assembly). 1994. *Europeans Living abroad*. Strasbourg: Council of Europe, Doc. 7078.

——— (Parliamentary Assembly). 1999. *Links between Europeans Living abroad and Their Countries of Origin*. Strasbourg: Council of Europe, Doc. 8339.

———(Venice Commission). 2001a. *Report on the Preferential Treatment of National Minorities by their Kin-state*. Strasbourg: Council of Europe, CDL-INF (2001) 19.

———(Venice Commission). 2001b. *Paper containing the position of the Hungarian government in relation to the act on Hungarians living in neighbouring countries*. Strasbourg: Council of Europe, CDL (2001) 80.

Cronin, Kathryn. 1993. A culture of control. In: *The Politics of Australian Immigration*. Ed. J. Jupp and M. Kabala. Canberra: Australian Government Publishing Service.

Danese, Gaia. 2001. Participation beyond citizenship: migrants' associations in Italy and Spain. *Patterns of Prejudice* 35(1), 69–89.

Das Gupta, Jyotirindra. 1975. Ethnicity, language demands, and national development in India. In: *Ethnicity: Theory and Experience*. Ed. N. Glazer and D. P.Moynihan. Cambridge, Mass.: Harvard University Press.

Dayan, Arie. 1993. The Debate over Zionism and racism: an Israeli view. *Journal of Palestine Studies* 22(3), 96–105.

Debré, Robert, and Alfred Sauvy. 1946. *Des Français pour la France*. Paris: Gallimard.

de Castro y Bravo, Federico. 1948. La doble nacionalidad. *Revista española de derecho internacional* 1, 77–107.

Degler, Carl N. 1971. *Neither Black nor White: Slavery and Race Relations in Brazil and the United States*. New York: Macmillan.

de Groot, Gérard-René. 1989. *Staatsangehörigkeitsrecht im Wandel*. Cologne: Heymanns.

Delgado, Isabel Lirola. 1993. Spanish viewpoints and problems with the Schengen Convention, Free Movement of Persons and Aliens Law. In: *Free Movement of Persons in Europe*. Ed. H. G. Schermers et al. Dordrecht: Martinus Nijhoff Publishers.

Department of Immigration and Multicultural and Indigenous Affairs (DIMIA). 2002a. *Population Flows: Immigration Aspects*. Canberra: Australian Government Publishing Service.

———. 2002b. *Australian Immigration: Consolidated Statistics No. 21, 1999–00*. Canberra: Australian Government Publishing Service.

Deutchman, Iva Ellen, and Anne Ellison. 1999. A star is born: the roller coaster ride of Pauline Hanson in the news. *Media, Culture and Society* 21, 33–50.

Dietz, Barbara, and Peter Hilkes. 1994. *Integriert oder isoliert?* Munich: Olzog Verlag.

Divine, Robert. 1957. *American Immigration Policy, 1924–1952*. New Haven, Conn.: Yale University Press.

Dowty, Alan. 1998. *The Jewish State: A Century Later*. Berkeley: University of California Press.

———. 1999. Is Israel democratic? *Israel Studies* 4(2), 1–15.

Doyle, Michael. 1986. *Empires*. Ithaca, N.Y.: Cornell University Press.

Dudziak, Mary. 1988. Desegregation as a Cold War imperative. *Stanford Law Review* 41, 61–120.

Dummett, Ann, and Andrew Nicol. 1990. *Subjects, Citizens, Aliens and Others*. London: Weidenfeld and Nicolson.

Dumont, Louis. 1986. *Essays on Individualism*. Chicago: University of Chicago Press.

Dupraz, Paule, and Francine Vieira. 1999. Immigration et "modernité": le Portugal entre heritage colonial et intégration européenne. *Pôle Sud*, 11, pp. 38–54.

Dworkin, Ronald. 1978. Liberalism. In: *Public and Private Morality*. S. Hampshire, Ed. Cambridge: Cambridge University Press.

———. 1991. Can a liberal state support art? In: *A Matter of Principle*. Ed. R. Dworkin. Oxford: Oxford University Press.

Eggleston, F. W. 1948. Australia's immigration policy. *Pacific Affairs* 21(4), 372–383.

Eisenstadt, Shmuel Noah. 1955. *The Absorption of Immigrants*. New York: The Free Press.

Elkin, A. P. 1945. Re-thinking the White Australia policy. *Australian Quarterly*, September, 6–34.

Elon, Amos. 1996. Israel and the end of Zionism. *New York Review of Books*, 19 December, 22–30.

Elster, Jon. 1989. *Nuts and Bolts for the Social Sciences*. Cambridge: Cambridge University Press.

Emerson, Rupert. 1968. Colonialism: political aspects. In: *International Encyclopedia of the Social Sciences*. Ed. D. Sills. New York: Macmillan.

Emmer, P. C. 1992. European expansion and migration. In: *European Expansion and Migration*. Ed. P. C. Emmer and M. Moerner. Oxford: Berg.

Enders, Armelle. 1997. Le lusotropicalisme, théorie d'exportation. *Lusotopie* 5, 201–210.

Entzinger, Han. 2003. The rise and fall of multiculturalism: the case of the Netherlands. In: *Toward Assimilation and Citizenship*. Ed. C. Joppke and E. Morawska. Basingstoke: Palgrave Macmillan.

Espósito, Carlos. 1991. Los títulos de odontólogo expedidos por terceros estados. *Revista Española de Derecho Internacional*, 43, 285–287.

Etemad, Bouda. 1998. Europe and migration after decolonisation. *Journal of European Economic History* 27(3), 457–470.

European Commission. 2000. *Communication from the Commission to the Council and the European Parliament on a Community Immigration Policy*. COM (2000) 757, 22 November 2000, http://europa.eu.int/eur-lex/en/com/cnc/2000/com2000_0757en01.pdf (accessed July 27, 2004).

Falcão, José A. 1997. Racismo: as nossas desculpas. In: Coloquio Internacional, *Portugal na Transição do Milênio*. Lisbon: Fim de Século.

Favell, Adrian. 1998. *Philosophies of Integration*. Basingstoke: Macmillan.

Favell, Adrian, and Randall Hansen. 2002. Markets against politics: migration, EU enlargement and the idea of Europe. *Journal of Ethnic and Migration Studies* 28(4), 581–602.

Federal Commissioner for Foreigner Affairs. 2000. *Vierter Bericht zur Lage der Ausländer in der Bundesrepublik Deutschland*. Berlin: Government Printing Office.

Feldblum, Miriam. 1999. *Reconstructing Citizenship: the Politics of Nationality Reform and Immigration in Contemporary France*. Albany: State University of New York Press.

Feldman-Bianco, Bela. 1992. Multiple layers of time and space. In: *Towards a Transnational Perspective on Migration*. Ed. N.Glick Schiller, L. Basch, and C.Blanc-Szanton. New York: The New York Academy of Sciences.

Ferro, Marc. 1997. *Colonization*. London: Routledge.

Finer, Samuel E. 1997. *The History of Government, vol. 3*. Oxford: Oxford University Press.

Fitzgerald, Stephen. 1988. *Immigration: A Commitment to Australia. The Report of the Committee to Advise on Australia's Immigration Policies*. Canberra: Australian Government Publishing Service.

Folan Sebben, Patricia. 1992. U.S. immigration law, Irish immigration and diversity. *Georgetown Immigration Law Journal* 6, 744–771.

Ford, Christopher. 1994. Administering identity. *California Law Review* 82, 1231–1285.

Fowler, Brigid. 2002. Fuzzing citizenship, nationalising political space: a framework for interpreting the Hungarian "Status Law" as a new form of kin-state policy in central and eastern Europe. Economical and Social Research Council, One Europe or Several? Working Paper 40/02, University of Sussex, http://www.one-europe.ac.uk/pdf/w40fowler.pdf (accessed July 7, 2004).

Francis, Emerich. 1965. *Ethnos und Demos*. Berlin: Duncker and Humblot.

Fransman, Laurie. 1983. Patriality. *New Law Journal,* 5 August, 691–692, 707.

Freeman, Gary P. 1995a. Modes of immigration politics in liberal democratic states. *International Migration Review* 29(4), 881–902.

———. 1995b. Rejoinder. *International Migration Review* 29(4), 909–913.

Freeman, Gary P., and James Jupp. 1992. Comparing immigration policy in Australia and the United States. In: *Nations of Immigrants*. Ed. G. P. Freeman and J. Jupp. Melbourne: Oxford University Press.

Freeman, Gary P., and Robert Birrell. 2002. Divergent paths of immigration politics in the United States and Australia. *Population and Development Review* 27(3), 525–551.

Freyre, Gilberto. 1940. *O mundo que o Português criou*. Lisbon: Livros do Brasil.

———. 1986. *The Masters and the Slaves*. Berkeley: University of California Press.

Galanter, Marc. 1963. A dissent on Brother Daniel. *Commentary* 36(1), 10–17.

Galston, William A. 1995. Two concepts of liberalism. *Ethics* 195, 516–534.

Galvão Teles, Miguel, and Paulo Canelas de Castro. 1996. Portugal and the right of peoples to self-determination. *Archiv des Völkerrechts* 34, 2–46.

Gans, Chaim. 2003. *The Limits of Nationalism*. Cambridge: Cambridge University Press.

Garrido Falla, Fernando. 1980. *Comentarios a la constitución*. Madrid: Editorial Civitas.

Gerstle, Gary. 2001. *American Crucible*. Princeton, N.J.: Princeton University Press.

Ghanem, As'ad. 1998. State and minority in Israel. *Ethnic and Racial Studies* 21(3), 428–448.

Giddens, Anthony. 1994. *Beyond Left and Right*. Cambridge: Polity Press.

Gillette, Alain, and Abdelmalek Sayad. 1984. *L'immigration algérienne en France*. Paris: Éditions Entente.

Gil-White, Francisco. 1999. How thick is blood? *Ethnic and Racial Studies* 22(5), 789–820.

Gimpel, James G., and James R. Edwards, Jr. 1999. *The Congressional Politics of Immigration Reform*. Boston: Allyn and Bacon.

Ginossar, Shalev. 1970. Who is a Jew: A better law? *Israeli Law Review* 5(2), 264–267.

GISTI (Groupe d'information et de soutien des immigrés). 2000. Les droits des

Algériens en France. http://bok.net/pajol/gisti/brochalg1-2000/intro.html (accessed June 28, 2004).

Glick Schiller, Nina. 1999. Transmigrants and nation-states. In *Handbook of International Migration: the American Experience*. Ed. C. Hirschman, P. Kasinitz, and J.DeWind. New York: Russell Sage Foundation.

Goldscheider, Calvin. 2002. Ethnic categorizations in censuses. In: *Census and Identity*. Ed. D. Kertzer and D. Arel. New York: Cambridge University Press.

Gomes Canotilho, José Joaquim. 1996. Offenheit vor dem Völkerrecht und Völkerrechtsfreundlichkeit des portugiesischen Rechts. *Archiv für Völkerrecht* 34, 47–71.

Goodwin-Gill, Guy S. 1978. *International Law and the Movement of Persons Between States*. Oxford: Clarendon Press.

———. 1990. The status and rights of nonnationals. In: *Constitutionalism and Rights*. Ed. L. Henkin and A. Rosenthal. New York: Columbia University Press.

Goodwin-Gill, Guy S., R. K. Jenny, and Richard Perruchoud. 1985. Basic humanitarian principles applicable to non-nationals. *International Migration Review* 29(3), 556–569.

Goot, Murray. 2000. More 'relaxed and comfortable': public opinion on immigration under Howard. *People and Place* 8(3), 46–59.

Grant, Madison. 1924. *The Passing of the Great Race*. London: G. Bell and Sons.

Grattan, Michelle. 1993. Immigration and the Australian Labor Party. In: *The Politics of Australian Immigration*. Ed. J. Jupp and M. Kabala. Canberra: Australian Government Publishing Service.

———. 1998. Pauline Hanson's hijack of John Howard. In: *Two Nations: The Causes and Effects of the Rise of the One Nation Party in Australia*. Ed. T. Abbott et al. 1998. Melbourne: Bookman.

Greenfeld, Liah. 1992. *Nationalism*. Cambridge, Mass.: Harvard University Press.

Grossman, David. 1993. *Sleeping on a Wire: Conversations with Palestinians in Israel*. New York: Farrar, Straus and Giroux.

Grugel, Jean. 1995. Spain and Latin America. In: *Democratic Spain*. Ed. R. Gillespie, F. Rodrigo, J. Story. London: Routledge.

Guendelsberger, John. 1988. The right to family unification in French and United States immigration law. *Cornell International Law Journal* 21(1), 1–102.

Gurowitz, Amy. 1999. Mobilizing international norms. Ph.D. diss., Cornell University.

Hailbronner, Kay, and Günter Renner. 2001. *Staatsangehörigkeitsrecht*. Munich: Beck.

Hampton, Jean. 1995. Immigration, identity, and justice. In: *Justice in Immigration*. Ed. Warren Schwartz. New York: Cambridge University Press.

Handlin, Oscar. 1951. *The Uprooted*. Boston: Little, Brown, and Company.

Haney Lopez, Ian F. 1996. *White by Law*. New York: New York University Press.

Hansen, Randall. 1999. The Kenyan Asians, British politics, and the Commonwealth Immigrants Act, 1968. *The Historical Journal* 42(3), 809–834.

———. 2000. *Citizenship and Immigration in Post-war Britain*. Oxford: Oxford University Press.

———. 2001. *Issue Definition, Political Discourse and the Politics of Nationality Reform in France and Germany.* Manuscript.

Hansen, Randall, and Patrick Weil, eds. 2001. *Towards a European Nationality.* New York: Palgrave.

Hartz, Louis. 1955. *The Liberal Tradition in America.* New York: Harcourt.

Hartz, Louis, ed. 1964. *The Founding of New Societies.* New York: Harcourt, Brace and World.

Hattam, Victoria. 2001. Immigration and empire: rethinking ethnicity and race in the United States, Conference on The Legacies of Colonization and Decolonization on the Integration of Migrants in Europe and the Americas, University of Paris (I), Sorbonne, 22–23 June 2001.

Haut Conseil à l'intégration. 1993. *L'intégration à la française.* Paris: La documentation française.

Hauteville, Laure d'. 1995. Algériens: feu la libre circulation. *Plein Droit* 29–30, 87–89.

Hawkins, Freda. 1991 *Critical Years in Immigration: Canada and Australia Compared.* 2nd ed. Montreal and Kingston: McGill-Queens University Press.

Hazony, Yoram. 2000. *The Jewish State.* New York: Basic Books.

Heffernan, Michael. 1995. French colonial migration. In: *The Cambridge Survey of World Migration.* Ed. R. Cohen. Cambridge: Cambridge University Press.

Helton, Arthur C. 1993. The United States government program of intercepting and forcibly returning Haitian boat people to Haiti. *New York Law School Journal of Human Rights* 10, 325–349.

Hennessy, Alistair. 2000. Ramiro de Maeztu: *Hispanidad* and the search for a surrogate imperialism. In: *Spain's 1898 crisis.* Ed. J. Harrison and A. Hoyle. Manchester: Manchester University Press.

Herzl, Theodor. 1997. *The Jews' state.* Northvale, N.J.: Jason Aronson Inc.

Higgott, Richard. 1994. Closing a branch office of empire: Australian foreign policy and the UK at century's end. *International Affairs* 70(1), 41–65.

Higham, John. 1955. *Strangers in the Land.* New Brunswick: Rutgers University Press.

Hirschl, Ran. 1998. Israel's "constitutional revolution." *American Journal of Comparative Law* 46, 427–452.

Hobsbawm, Eric. 1990. *Nations and Nationalism since 1780.* Cambridge: Cambridge University Press.

Hoetink, H. 1967. *The Two Variants in Caribbean Race Relations.* Oxford: Oxford University Press.

Hollinger, David A. 1998. National culture and communities of descent. *Reviews in American History* 26, 312–328.

Holmes, Stephen. 1995. *Passions and Constraint.* Chicago: University of Chicago Press.

Holt, H. E., et al. 1953. *Australia and the Migrant.* Sydney: Angus and Robertson.

Horowitz, Donald. 1975. Ethnic identity. In: *Ethnicity: Theory and Experience.* Ed. N. Glazer and D. P. Moynihan. Cambridge, Mass.: Harvard University Press.

Hughes, Joyce A., and Linda R. Crane. 1993. "Haitians: seeking refuge in the United States. *Georgetown Immigration Law Journal* 7, 747–794.

Huntington, Samuel P. 1981. *American Politics: the Promise of Disharmony.* Cambridge, Mass.: Harvard University Press.

———. 1996. *The Clash of Civilizations and the Remaking of World Order.* New York: Simon and Schuster.

Hutchinson, Edward P. 1981. *Legislative History of American Immigration Policy 1798–1965.* Philadelphia: University of Pennsylvania Press.

Hutchinson, John, and Anthony D. Smith, eds. 1996. *Ethnicity.* Oxford: Oxford University Press.

Huttenback, Robert A. 1973. No strangers within the gates. *Journal of Imperial and Commonwealth History* 1(3), 271–302.

———. 1976. *Racism and Empire.* Ithaca: Cornell University Press.

Ignatius, Sarah. 1993. Haitian asylum-seekers: their treatment as a measure of the INS asylum officer corps. *Georgetown Immigration Law Journal* 7, 119–146.

Jackson, Robert H. 1984. Ethnicity. In: *Social Science Concepts.* Ed. G. Sartori. London: Sage.

Jacob, Walter P. 1992. Diversity visas: muddled thinking and pork barrel politics. *Georgetown Immigration Law Journal* 6, 297–343.

Jacobson, Matthew Frye. 1998. *Whiteness of a Different Color: European Immigrants and the Alchemy of Race.* Cambridge, Mass.: Harvard University Press.

Jalles, Isabel. 1984. Nationalité et statut personnel dans le droit de la nationalité portugaise. In: *Nationalité et statut personnel.* Ed. M. Verwilghen. Brussels: Bruylant.

James, Harold. 2001. *The End of Globalization.* Cambridge, Mass.: Harvard University Press.

Jaspers, Karl. 1960. *Freiheit und Wiedervereinigung.* Munich: Piper.

Jayasuriya, Laksiri, and David Sang. 1992. Asian immigration to Australia. In: *From India to Australia.* Ed. S. Chandrasekhar. La Jolla, Calif.: Population Review Books.

Jewish Agency for Israel. Department for Jewish Zionist Education. 1998. The Law of Return and the Law of Citizenship as expressions of the Jewish and democratic nature of the State of Israel. http://www.jafi.org.il/education/50/act/shvut/ (accessed July 2, 2004).

Johnson, Carol. 1998. Pauline Hanson and One Nation. In: *The New Politics of the Right.* Ed. H.-G. Betz and S. Immerfall. New York: St. Martin's Press.

Johnson, Kevin R. 1993. Judicial acquiescence to the executive branch's pursuit of foreign policy and domestic agendas in immigration matters. *Georgetown Immigration Law Journal* 7(1), 1–37.

———. 1998. Race, the immigration laws, and domestic race relations. *Indiana Law Journal* 73, 1111–1159.

———. 2000. Race matters. *University of Ilinois Law Review* No.2, 525–558.

Joppke, Christian. 1999. *Immigration and the Nation-State: the United States, Germany, and Great Britain.* Oxford: Oxford University Press.

———. 2000. Mobilization of culture and the reform of citizenship law. In: *Chal-*

lenging Immigration and Ethnic Relations Politics. Ed. R. Koopmans and P. Statham. Oxford: Oxford University Press.

———. 2001a. The legal-domestic sources of immigrant rights. *Comparative Political Studies* 34(4), 339–366.

———. 2001b. Multicultural Citizenship: a critique. *Archives européennes de sociologie* 42(2), 431–447.

———. 2003. Citizenship between de- and re-ethnicization. *Archives européennes de sociologie* 44(3), 429–458.

———. 2004. The retreat of multiculturalism in the liberal state: theory and policy. *British Journal of Sociology* 55(2), 237–257.

———. 2005. Exclusion in the liberal state: the case of immigration and citizenship policy. *European Journal of Social Theory* (forthcoming).

Joppke, Christian, and Zeev Rosenhek. 2002. Contesting ethnic immigration: Israel and Germany compared. *Archives européennes de sociologie* 43(3), 301–335.

Joppke, Christian, and Ewa Morawska. 2003. Integrating immigrants in liberal nation-states. In: *Toward Assimilation and Citizenship.* Ed. C. Joppke and E. Morawska. Basingstoke: Palgrave Macmillan.

Joppke, Christian, and Elia Marzal. 2004. Courts, the new constitutionalism, and immigrant rights: the case of the French *Conseil Constitutionnel. European Journal of Political Research* 43, 825–846.

Jordens, Ann-Mari. 1997. *Alien to Citizen: Settling Migrants in Australia, 1945–75.* Sydney: Allen and Unwin.

Jupp, James. 1991. *Immigration.* Melbourne: Oxford University Press.

———. 1993. The ethnic lobby and immigration policy. In: *The Politics of Australian Immigration.* Ed. J. Jupp and M. Kabala. Canberra: Australian Government Publishing Service.

———. 1995. From "White Australia" to "part of Asia." *International Migration Review* 29(1), 207–228.

———. 2001. Changes in immigration patterns since 1972. In: *The Australian People.* Ed. J. Jupp. Cambridge: Cambridge University Press.

Juteau, Danielle. 2002. The citizen makes an *entrée*: redefining the national community in Quebec. *Citizenship Studies* 6(4), 441–458.

Kagan, Robert. 2002. Power and weakness. *Policy Review* 113 (June-July). http://www.policyreview.org/JUN02/kagan.html (accessed July 7, 2004).

Kasher, Asa. 1985. Justice and affirmative action: naturalization and the Law of Return. *Israel Yearbook on Human Rights* 15.

Kaufmann, Eric. 2000a. Liberal ethnicity: Beyond liberal nationalism and minority rights. *Ethnic and Racial Studies* 23(6), 1086–1119.

———. 2000b. Ethnic or civic nation? Theorizing the American case. *Canadian Review of Studies in Nationalism* 27, 133–154.

Kedar, Alexandre. 2000. "A first step in a difficult and sensitive road": preliminary observations on *Quaadan v. Katzir, Israel Studies Bulletin,* Fall, 3–11.

Keller, Morton. 1994. *Regulating a New Society.* Cambridge, Mass.: Harvard University Press.

Kelly, Paul. 1992. *The End of Certainty*. Sydney: Allen and Unwin.

———. 1998. Hanson—symptom of a deeper problem. In: *Two Nations: The Causes and Effects of the Rise of the One Nation Party in Australia*. Ed. T. Abbott et al. Melbourne: Bookman.

Kelman, Herbert C. 1998. Israel in transition from Zionism to post-Zionism. *Annals of the American Academy of Political and Social Sciences* 555, 46–61.

Kennedy, John F. 1964. *A Nation of Immigrants*. New York: Harper and Row.

Kertzer, David, and Dominique Arel, eds. 2002. *Census and Identity*. New York: Cambridge University Press.

Khalidi, Rashid I. 1992. Observations on the Right of Return. *Journal of Palestine Studies* 21(2), 29–40.

Kimmerling, Baruch. 2001. *The Invention and Decline of Israeliness*. Berkeley and Los Angeles: University of California Press.

Kind, Hansgeorg, and Michael Niemeier. 2002. Das Spätaussiedlerstatusgesetz— eine notwendige Klarstellung. *Zeitschrift für Ausländerrecht* 5–6, 188–192.

King, Charles. 1998. *Nations Abroad*. Boulder, Colo.: Westview Press.

King, Charles, and Neil J. Melvin. 1999/2000. Diaspora politics. *International Security* 24(3), 108–138.

King, Desmond. 1999. *In the Name of Liberalism*. Oxford: Oxford University Press.

———. 2000. *Making Americans*. Cambridge, Mass.: Harvard University Press.

Klein, Claude. 1987. Israel as a nation-state and the problem of the Arab minority. Working paper, International Center for Peace in the Middle East, Tel Aviv, December.

———. 1997. The Right of Return in Israeli law. *Tel Aviv University Studies in Law* 13, 53–61.

Koopmans, Ruud. 1999. Germany and its immigrants. *Journal of Ethnic and Migration Studies* 25(4), 627–647.

Koslowski, Rey. 2000. Demographic boundary maintenance in world politics. In: *Identities, Borders, Orders*. Ed. M. Albert, D. Jacobson, and Y. Lapid. Minneapolis: University of Minnesota Press.

———. 2001. Personal security and state sovereignty in a uniting Europe. In: *Controlling a New Migration World*. Ed. V. Guiraudon and C. Joppke. London: Routledge.

Kraines, Oscar. 1976. *The Impossible Dilemma: Who is a Jew in the State of Israel?* New York: Bloch.

Kretzmer, David. 1990. *The Legal Status of the Arabs in Israel*. Boulder, Colo.: Westview Press.

Kuttab, Jonathan. 1990. Why the immigration of Soviet Jews must be opposed. *Middle East International* 30, 30 March, 16–17.

Kymlicka, Will. 1989a. *Liberalism, Community and Culture*. Oxford: Clarendon Press.

———. 1989b. Liberal individualism and liberal neutrality. *Ethics* 99, 883–905.

———. 1995. *Multicultural citizenship*. Oxford: Clarendon Press.

———. 1998. *Finding Our Way*. Toronto: Oxford University Press.

———. 1999. Misunderstanding nationalism. in: *Theorizing Nationalism*. Ed. R. Beiner. Albany: State University of New York Press.

———. 2001. Territorial boundaries: a liberal egalitarian perspective. In: *Boundaries and Justice: Diverse Ethical Perspectives*. Ed. D. Miller and S. H. Hashmi. Princeton, N.J.: Princeton University Press, pp. 249–275.

Lack, John, and Jacqueline Templeton, eds. 1995. *Bold Experiment*. Melbourne: Oxford University Press.

Lagarde, Paul. 1973. La rénovation du Code de la nationalité par la loi du 9 janvier 1973. *Revue Critique de Droit International Privé* 62, 431–469.

———. 1984. Nationalité et filiation. In: *Nationalité et statut personnel*. Ed. M. Verwilghen. Brussels: Bruylant.

———. 1993. La nationalité française rétrécie. *Revue Critique de Droit International Privé* 82(4), 535–563.

———. 1995. Décolonisation et nationalité. *Plein Droit* 29–30, 83–86.

———. 1997. *La nationalité française*. Paris: Dalloz.

Lahav, Pnina. 1997. *Judgment in Jerusalem*. Berkeley: University of California Press.

Lampué, Paul. 1950. La citoyenneté de l'Union française. *Revue juridique et politique de l'Union française* 4, 305–336.

Landau, David. 1996. *Who is a Jew? A Case Study of American Jewish Influence on Israeli Policy*. New York: The American Jewish Committee.

Landau, Jacob M. 1993. *The Arab Minority in Israel, 1967–1991*. Oxford: Clarendon Press.

Langfield, Michele. 1991. "White aliens": The control of European immigration to Australia 1920–30. *Journal of Intercultural Studies* 12(11), 1–14.

———. 1995. To restore British migration: Australian population debates in the 1930s. *Australian Journal of Politics and History* 41(3), 408–419.

Lawson, Miguel, and Marianne Grin. 1992. The Immigration Act of 1990. *Harvard International Law Journal* 33, 255–276.

Le Bras. Hervé. 1991. *Marianne et les lapins: L'obsession démographique*. Paris: Olivier Orban.

———. 1998. *Le démon des origines*. Paris: Éditions de l'Aube.

Le Espiritu, Yen. 1992. *Asian American Panethnicity*. Philadelphia: Temple University Press.

Legomsky, Stephen H. 1993. Immigration, equality, and diversity. *Columbia Journal of Transnational Law* 31(2), 319–335.

Leitão, José. 1997. The Portuguese immigration policy and the new European order. In: *Immigration in Southern Europe*. Ed. M. Baganha. Oeiras (Portugal): Celta Editora.

Lennox, Malissia. 1993. Refugees, racism, and reparations: a critique of the United States' Haitian immigration policy. *Stanford Law Review* 45, 687–724.

Leonard, Yves. 1997. Salazarisme et lusotropicalisme, histoire d'une appropriation. *Lusotopie* 5, 211–226.

Levy, Daniel. 1999. Remembering the nation. Doctoral diss., Columbia University, New York.

Lewis, Jim R., and Allan M. Williams. 1985. Portugal's *retornados*. *Iberian Studies* 14(1–2), 11–23.

Lewis, Mary D. 2000. The company of strangers: immigration and citizenship in interwar Lyon and Marseille. Ph.D. diss., New York University.

Lie, John. 1995. From international migration to transnational diaspora. *Contemporary Sociology* 24, 303–306.

Liebman, Charles S., and Eliezer Don-Yehiya. 1983. *Civil Religion in Israel*. Berkeley: University of California Press.

Liesner, Ernst. 1988. *Aussiedler*. Herford: Maximilian Verlag.

Lipset, Seymour M. 1963. *The First New Nation*. New York: Basic Books.

Little, Chery. 1999. Beyond/between colors: intergroup coalitions and immigration politics. *University of Miami Law Review* 53, 717–741.

London, H. I. 1970. *Non-white Immigration and the "White Australia" Policy*. New York: New York University Press.

Long, Marceau. 1998. *Être français aujourd'hui et demain: rapport de la Commission de la Nationalité*. Paris: Olivier Orban.

Luhmann, Niklas. 1980. *Gesellschaftsstruktur und Semantik*, vol. 1. Frankfurt: Suhrkamp.

Lustick, Ian S. 1980. *Arabs in the Jewish State*. Austin: University of Texas Press.

———. 1989. The political road to binationalism: Arabs in Jewish politics. In: *The Emergence of a Binational Israel*. Ed. I. Peleg and O. Seliktar. Boulder, Colo.: Westview Press.

———. 1993. *Unsettled States, Disputed Lands*. Ithaca, N.Y.: Cornell University Press.

———. 1999. Israel as a non-Arab state. *Middle East Journal* 53(3), 417–433.

Lynch, Phillip. 1971. *The Evolution of a Policy*. Canberra: Australian Government Publishing Service.

Macdonald, Ian. 1972. *The New Immigration Law*. London: Butterworths.

Machado, Fernando Luís. 1997. Contornos e especificidades da imigração em Portugal. *Sociologia: Problemas e Práticas* 24, 9–44.

Malheiros, Jorge Macaísta. 1998. Immigration, clandestine work and labour market strategies: the construction sector in the metropolitan region of Lisbon. *Southern European Society and Politics* 3(3), 169–185.

Mann, Michael. 1993. Nation-states in Europe and other continents. *Daedalus* 122(3), 115–140.

———. 1999. The dark side of democracy. *New Left Review* 235, 18–45.

Margalit, Avishai, and Joseph Raz. 1990. National self-determination. *The Journal of Philosophy* 87(9), 439–461.

Marot, Nadia. 1995. L'évolution des accords franco-africains. *Plein Droit* 29–30, 96–99.

Marques, M. Margarida. 1999. Attitudes and threat perception: unemployment and immigration in Portugal. *Southern European Politics and Society* 4, 184–205.

Marques, M. Margarida, et al. 1999. Between the "Lusophone community" and European integration. Paper presented at the conference Citizenship: Comparison and Perspectives, Carnegie Endowment for International Peace, Lisbon, June.

Marshall, D. Bruce. 1973. *The French Colonial Myth and Constitution-making in the 4th Republic*. New Haven: Yale University Press.

Marx, Anthony W. 1998. *Making Race and Nation*. Cambridge: Cambridge University Press.

Mauco, Georges. 1932. *Les étrangers en France*. Paris: Armand Colin.

Maxwell, Kenneth. 1995. *The Making of Portuguese Democracy*. Cambridge: Cambridge University Press.

McRae, Kenneth D. 1964. The structure of Canadian history. In: *The Founding of New Societies*. Ed. L. Hartz. New York: Harcourt, Brace and World.

Meaney, Neville. 1995. The end of "White Australia" and Australia's changing perceptions of Asia, 1945–1990. *Australian Journal of International Affairs* 49(2), 171–189.

Mendoza, Cristobal. 2000. The role of the state in influencing African labor outcomes in Spain and Portugal. The Center for Comparative Immigration Studies, working paper no. 3, University of California at San Diego.

Meyer, John W. 1999. The changing cultural content of the nation-state. In: *State/ culture*. Ed. G. Steinmetz. Ithaca, N.Y.: Cornell University Press.

Miège, Jean-Louis, and Colette Dubois, eds. 1994. *L'Europe retrouvée: Les migrations de la décolonisation*. Paris: L'Harmattan.

Miller, David. 1995. *On Nationalism*. Oxford: Clarendon Press.

Miquel Calatayud, José Antonio. 1993. El régimen preferencial en materia de extranjeráa y los nacionales iberoamericanos. *Revista Crítica de Derecho Inmobiliario* 69(616), 875–933.

Morita, Keiko. 1999. Asians for Australia's identity. *Asia-Pacific Review* 5(3), 105–122.

Motomura, Hiroshi. 1996. Whose alien nation? Two models of constitutional immigration law. *Michigan Law Review* 94, 1927–1952.

Moura Ramos, Rui Manuel. 1978. Note: Décret-loi no.308-A/75 du 24 juin 1975. *Revue Critique de Droit International Privé* 67, 183–186.

———. 1990–93. La double nationalité et les liens spéciaux avec d'autres pays. Les développements et les perspectives au Portugal. *Revista de Direito e Economia* 16–19, pp. 577–605.

———. 2001. Migratory movements and nationality law in Portugal. In: *Towards a European Nationality*. Ed. R. Hansen and P. Weil. New York: Palgrave.

Münz, Rainer, and Rainer Ohliger. 1998. Deutsche Minderheiten in Ostmittel- und Osteuropa, Aussiedler in Deutschland. Berlin: Humboldt University, Chair for Demography.

———, eds. 2003. *Diasporas and Ethnic Migrants: Germany, Israel and Post-Soviet Successor States in Comparative Perspective*. London: Frank Cass.

Myrdal, Gunnar. 1944. *An American Dilemma*. New York: Harper.

Nassehi, Armin. 1990. Zum Funktionswandel von Ethnizität im Prozess gesellschaftlicher Modernisierung. *Soziale Welt* 41(4), 261–282.

National Multicultural Advisory Council. 1999. *Australian Multiculturalism for a*

New Century: Toward Inclusiveness. Canberra: Australian Government Publishing Service.

Nesis, Lawrence S. 1970. Who is a Jew? *Manitoba Law Journal* 4, 53–88.

Neuer, Hillel. 1998. Aharon Barak's revolution. *Azure* 3, 1–31.

Ngai, Mae M. 1999. The architecture of race in American immigration law. *The Journal of American History*, June, 67–92.

Nicholls, Glenn. 1998. Unsettling admissions: asylum seekers in Australia. *Journal of Refugee Studies* 11(1), 61–79.

Norton, Philip. 1976. Intra-party dissent in the House of Commons. *Parliamentary Affairs* 29(4), 404–420.

Obdeijn, Herman. 1994. Vers les bords de la mer du nord: les retours aux Pays-Bas induits par la décolonisation. In: *L'Europe retrouvée: Les migrations de la décolonisation.* Ed. J.-L. Miège and C. Dubois. Paris: L'Harmattan.

OECD. 2000. *Trends in International Migration. SOPEMI 2000 Edition.* Paris: Organisation for Economic Co-operation and Development.

Orentlicher, Diane F. 1998. Citizenship and national identity. In: *International Law and Ethnic Conflict.* Ed. D. Wippman. Ithaca, N.Y.: Cornell University Press.

Ortiz Miranda, Carlos. 1995. Haiti and the United States during the 1980s and 1990s. *San Diego Law Review* 32, 673–744.

Otto, Karl A. ed. *Westwärts-Heimwärts?* Bielefeld: AJZ Verlag.

Pagden, Anthony. 1995. *Lords of All the World: Ideologies of Empire in Spain, Britain and France, c. 1500–c. 1800.* New Haven, Conn.: Yale University Press.

Palfreeman, A. C. 1957. Some implications of Asian immigration. *Australian Quarterly*, March, 26–38.

———. 1958. The end of the dictation test. *Australian Quarterly*, March, 43–50.

———. 1967. *The Administration of the White Australia Policy.* Melbourne: Melbourne University Press.

Pappe, Ilan. 1997. Post-Zionist critique on Israel and the Palestinians. *Journal of Palestine Studies* 26(2), 29–41.

Parsons, Talcott. 1971. *The System of Modern Societies.* Englewood Cliffs, N.J.: Prentice-Hall.

———. 1975. Some theoretical considerations on the nature and trends of change of ethnicity, In: *Ethnicity: Theory and Experience.* Ed. N. Glazer and D. P. Moynihan. Cambridge, Mass.: Harvard University Press.

Pastor, Robert A. 1984. U.S. immigration policy and Latin America. *Latin American Research Review* 19(3), 35–56.

Pastore, Ferruccio. 2001. Nationality law and international migration: the Italian case. In: *Towards a European Nationality.* Ed. R. Hansen and P. Weil. New York: Palgrave.

Patton, David F. 1999. Aussenseiter der Republik. *Sozialwissenschaftliche Informationen* 28(1), 52–63.

Paul, Kathleen. 1997. *Whitewashing Britain.* Ithaca, N.Y.: Cornell University Press.

Peled, Yoav. 1992. Ethnic democracy and the legal construction of citizenship:

Arab citizens of the Jewish state. *American Political Science Review* 86(2), 432–443.

Perera, Suvendrini, and Joseph Pugliese. 1997. "Racial suicide": the re-licensing of racism in Australia. *Race and Class* 39(2), 1–19.

Peres, Hubert. 1999. L'Europe commence à Gibraltar. *Pôle Sud* 11, 8–23.

Perry, Stephen R. 1995. Immigration, justice, and culture. In: *Justice and immigration*. Ed. W. F. Schwartz. Cambridge: Cambridge University Press.

Peters, Wilfried. 2000. Die Entwicklung des Vertriebenen- und Aussiedlerrechts von 1993 bis 1999. *Neue Verwaltungswissenschaftliche Zeitschrift (NVwZ)* 12, 1372–1375.

Peters, Bernhard. 2002. A new look at 'national identity.' *Archives européennes de sociologie* 43(1), 3–32.

Pickus, Noah. 2001. Which America? Nationalism among the nationalists. In: *One America? Political Leadership, National Identity and the Dilemma of Diversity*. Ed. S. A. Renshon. Washington, D.C.: Georgetown University Press.

Pike, Frederick B. 1980. Latin America. In: *Spain in the twentieth-century world*. Ed. J. W. Cortada. London: Aldwych Press.

———. 1986. Spanish-Latin American relations: two centuries of divergence—and a new beginning. In: *The Iberian–Latin American connection*. Ed. H. Wiarda. Westview Press.

Pires, Francisco Lucas. 1997. *Schengen e a comunidade de países lusófonos*. Coimbra: Coimbra Editora.

Plender, Richard. 1988. *International migration law*. 2nd ed. Dordrecht: Nijhoff.

Poinard, Michel. 1988. La politique d'un pays d'origine: le Portugal. *Revue Européenne des Migrations Internationales* 4(1/2), 187–200.

Pollack, Benny (with Graham Hunter). 1987. *The Paradox of Spanish Foreign Policy*. London: Pinter.

Poulter, Sebastian. 1998. *Ethnicity, Law and Human Rights*. Oxford: Clarendon Press.

President's Commission on Immigration and Naturalization. [1952] 1971. *Whom We Shall Welcome*. Reprint, New York: Da Capo Press.

Price, Charles A. 1966. "White" restrictions on "coloured" immigration. *Race* 7(3), 217–234.

———. 1974. *The Great White Walls are Built*. Canberra: Australian National University Press.

———. 1998. Post-war immigration: 1947–98. *Journal of the Australian Population Association* 15(2), 115–129.

———. 1999. Australian population: ethnic origins. *People and Place* 7(4), 12–16.

Puskeppeleit, Jürgen. 1996. Der Paradigmenwechsel der Aussiedlerpolitik. In: *Forschungsfeld Aussiedler*. Ed. I. Graudenz and R. Römhild. Frankfurt: Peter Lang.

Rawls, John. 1971. *A Theory of Justice*. Cambridge, Mass.: Harvard University Press.

———. 1993. *Political Liberalism*. New York: Columbia University Press.

———. 1999. *The Law of Peoples*. Cambridge, Mass.: Harvard University Press.

Resek, José Francisco. 1978. Aspectos elementares do estatuto da igualdade. *Boletim do Ministerio da Justiça* 277, 5–12.

Richmond, Nancy Caren. 1993. Israel's Law of Return. *Dickinson Journal of International Law* 12, 95–133.

Riggs, Fred. 1950. *Pressures on Congress: a Study of the Repeal of Chinese Exclusion*. New York: Columbia University Press.

Risse, Thomas, Stephen C. Ropp, and Kathryn Sikkink, eds. 1999. *The Power of Human Rights*. Cambridge: Cambridge University Press.

Rivett, Kenneth. 1992a. From White Australia to the present. In: *From India to Australia*. Ed. S. Chandrasekhar. La Jolla, Calif.: Population Review Books.

———. 1992b. The Immigration reform movement. In: *The Abolition of the White Australia policy*. Ed. Nancy Viviani. Asia Papers No.65, Centre for the Study of Australia-Asia Relations, Griffith University.

———, ed. 1962. *Immigration: Control or Colour Bar*. Melbourne: Melbourne University Press.

———, ed. 1975. *Australia and the Non-white Migrant*. Melbourne: Melbourne University Press.

Rocha-Trindade, Maria Beatriz, and Manuel Armando Oliveira. 1999. Portugal. In: *Asylum and Migration Policies in the European Union*. Ed. S. Angenendt. Bonn: Europea Union Verlag.

Rodier, Claire. 1995. Des familles selon les besoins. *Plein Droit* 29–30, 79–82.

Roe, Michael. 1995. *Australia, Britain, and Migration, 1915–1940*. Cambridge: Cambridge University Press.

Romig, Jeffrey L. 1985. Salvadoran illegal aliens: a struggle to obtain refuge in the United States. *University of Pittsburgh Law Review* 47, 295–335.

Rosecrance, Richard. 1964. The radical culture of Australia. In: *The Founding of New Societies*. Ed. L. Hartz. New York: Harcourt, Brace and World.

Rosenblum, Marc. 2000. International politics and immigration. In: *Encyclopedia of American Immigration*. Ed. J. Ciment. Armonk, N.Y.: M. E. Sharpe.

Rosenhek, Zeev. 1999. The exclusionary logic of the welfare state: Palestinian citizens in the Israeli welfare state. *International Sociology* 14(2), 195–215.

Rosenne, Shabtai. 1954. The Israel Nationality Law 5712-1952 and the Law of Return 5710-1950. *Journal du droit international* 81, 4–63.

Rouhana, Nadim. 1997. *Palestinian Citizens in an Ethnic Jewish State*. New Haven, Conn.: Yale University Press.

———. 1998. Israel and its Arab citizens. *Third World Quarterly* 19(2), 277–296.

Rubinstein, Amnon. 1967. State and religion in Israel. *Journal of Contemporary History* 2(4), 107–121.

———. 1976. Israel nationality. *Tel Aviv University Studies in Law* 2, 159–189.

———. 2000. *From Herzl to Rabin: the Changing Image of Zionism*. New York: Holmes and Meier.

Rubenstein, Colin. 1993. Immigration and the Liberal Party of Australia. In: *The Politics of Australian Immigration*. Ed. J. Jupp and M. Kabala. Canberra: Australian Government Publishing Service.

Ruddock, Philip. 1999a. Population options for Australia. *People and Place* 7(1), 1–6.

———. 1999b. The Coalition government's position on immigration and population policy. *People and Place* 7(4), 6–12.

Russell-Wood, A. J. R. 1992. *A World on the Move: the Portuguese in Africa, Asia, and America 1415–1808.* Manchester: Cancarnet Press.

Sahlins, Peter. 1989. *Boundaries.* Berkeley: University of California Press.

Salyer, Lucy E. 1995. *Laws Harsh as Tigers.* Chapel Hill: University of North Carolina Press.

Samet, Moshe. 1985. Who is a Jew? (1958–1977). *The Jerusalem Quarterly* 36, 88–108.

———. 1986. Who is a Jew? (1978–1985). *The Jerusalem Quarterly* 37, 109–139.

Santos, Miguel. 1995. Portugal. In: *New Xenophobia in Europe.* Ed. B. Baumgartl and A. Favell. Dordrecht: Kluwer Law International.

Sartori, Giovanni. 1969. From the sociology of politics to political sociology. In: *Politics and the Social Sciences.* Ed. S. M. Lipset. New York: Oxford University Press.

———. 1970. Conceptual misformation in comparative politics. *American Political Science Review* 54(4), 1033–1053.

Sassen, Saskia. 1998. The de facto transnationalizing of immigration policy. In: *Challenge to the Nation-State.* Ed. C. Joppke. Oxford: Oxford University Press.

Schillinger, Reinhold. 1988. Der Lastenausgleich. In: *Die Vertreibung der Deutschen aus dem Osten.* Ed. W. Benz. Frankfurt: Fischer.

Schneider, William H. 1990. *Quality and Quantity: The Quest for Biological Regeneration in 20th Century France.* Cambridge: Cambridge University Press.

Schuck, Peter. 1991. The emerging political consensus on immigration law. *Georgetown Immigration Law Journal* 5(1), 1–33 (esp. 25).

———. 2003. *Diversity in America.* Cambridge, Mass.: Harvard University Press.

Scott, James C. 1998. *Seeing Like a State.* New Haven, Conn.: Yale University Press.

Segev, Tom. 1986. *1949: The first Israelis.* New York: Free Press.

———. 1993. *The Seventh Million: the Israelis and the Holocaust.* New York: Hill and Wang.

Shachar, Ayelet. 1999. Whose republic? Citizenship and membership in the Israeli polity. *Georgetown Immigration Law Journal* 13(2), 233–272.

Shafir, Gershon. 1989. *Land, Labor and the Origins of the Israeli-Palestinian Conflict, 1882–1914.* Berkeley: University of California Press.

Shafir, Gershon, and Yoav Peled. 1998. Citizenship and stratification in an ethnic democracy. *Ethnic and Racial Studies* 21(3), 408–427.

———. 2002. *Being Israeli.* New York: Cambridge University Press.

Shammas, Anton. 1988. The morning after. *New York Review of Books,* 29 September, 47–52.

———. 1989. "Your worst nightmare." *Jewish Frontier* 56(4), 8–10.

Silagi, Michael. 2000. Der Status der Vertriebenen und Spätaussiedler nach Par. 7 StAG und Par. 40 a StAG. *Zeitschrift für Ausländerrecht* 1, 3–7.

Silberstein, Laurence J. 1999. *The Postzionism Debates*. New York: Routledge.

Simmel, Georg. 1992. *Soziologie: Untersuchungen über die Formen der Vergesellschaftung*. Frankfurt: Suhrkamp.

Simon, Rita, and James Lynch. 1999. A comparative assessment of public opinion toward immigrants and immigration policies. *International Migration Review* 33(2), 455–467.

Singer, Renata. ed. 1984. *The Immigration Debate in the Press*. Richmond (Australia): The Clearing House on Migration Issues.

Skrentny, John. 1998. The effect of the Cold War on African-American civil rights. *Theory and Society* 27, 237–285.

———. 2002. *The Minority Rights Revolution*. Cambridge, Mass.: Harvard University Press.

Slaughter, Anne-Marie. 1997. The real new world order. *Foreign Affairs* 76(5), 183–197.

Smith, Andrea L., ed. 2003. *Europe's Invisible Migrants*. Amsterdam: Amsterdam University Press.

Smith, Anthony D. 1981. *The Ethnic Revival*. Cambridge: Cambridge University Press.

———. 1986. *The Ethnic Origins of Nations*. Oxford: Blackwell.

———. 1995. Zionism and Diaspora nationalism. *Israel Affairs* 2(2), 1–19.

Smith, Rogers M. 1993. Beyond Tocqueville, Myrdal, and Hartz: the multiple traditions in America. *American Political Science Review* 87(3), 549–566.

———. 1997. *Civic Ideals*. New Haven, Conn.: Yale University Press.

Smooha, Sammy. 1978. *Israel: Pluralism and Conflict*. London: Routledge and Kegan Paul.

———. 1990. Minority status in an ethnic democracy: the status of the Arab minority in Israel. *Ethnic and Racial Studies* 13(3), 389–413.

———. 1997. Ethnic democracy: Israel as an archetype. *Israel Studies* 2(2), 198–241.

Solomon, Barbara Miller. 1956. *Ancestors and Immigrants*. Cambridge, Mass.: Harvard University Press.

Sousa Santos, Boaventura de. 1994. *Pela mão de Alice*. Porto: Edições Afrontamento.

Sowell, Thomas. 1983. *The Economics and Politics of Race*. New York: William Morrow.

Soysal, Yasemin. 1994. *Limits of Citizenship*. Chicago: University of Chicago Press.

———. 2002. Locating Europe. *European Societies* 4(3), 265–284.

Spillman, Lyn. 1997. *Nation and Commemoration*. Cambridge: Cambridge University Press.

Spire, Alexis. 2001. D'une colonie à l'autre. Conference on The Legacy of Colonization and Decolonization in Europe and the Americas, University of Paris I (Sorbonne), 22–23 June.

Starr, Paul. 1992. Social categories and claims in the liberal state. In: *How Classification Works*. Ed. M. Douglas and D. Hull. Edinburgh: Edinburgh University Press.

Steinberg, Gerald M. 2000. "The poor in your own city have precedence": a critique of the Katzir-Quaadan case and opinion. *Israel Studies Bulletin* 116, 12–18.

Stepick, Alex. 1982. Haitian boat people. *Law and Contemporary Problems* 45(2), 163–196.

Sternhell, Zeev. 1998. *The Founding Myths of Israel*. Princeton, N.J.: Princeton University Press.

Stichweh, Rudolf. 1988. Inklusion in Funktionssysteme der modernen Gesellschaft. In: *Differenzierung und Verselbständigung*. Ed. R. Mayntz, B. Rosewitz, U. Schimank, and R. Stichweh, Frankfurt and New York: Campus.

Stone-Sweet, Alec. 2000. *Governing with Judges*. Oxford: Oxford University Press.

Tamir, Yael. 1993. *Liberal Nationalism*. Princeton, N.J.: Princeton University Press.

Tannenbaum, Frank. 1946. *Slave and Citizen: the Negro in the Americas*. New York: Vintage Books.

Tapinos, Georges. 1975. *L'immigration etrangère en France, 1946–73*. Paris: Presses Universitaires de France.

The Economist. 1998. A survey of Israel: after Zionism. 25 April.

Tichenor, Daniel J. 2002. *Dividing Lines: the Politics of Immigration Control in America*. Princeton, N.J.: Princeton University Press.

Ting, Jan. 1995. "Other than a Chinaman": how U.S. immigration law resulted from and still reflects a policy of excluding and restricting Asian immigration. *Temple Political and Civil Rights Law Review* 4, 301–315.

Tocqueville, Alexis de. [1835–1840] 1969. *Democracy in America*. New York: Doubleday.

Todd, Emmanuel. 1994. *Le destin des immigrés*. Paris: Seuil.

Torregrosa, José R. 1996. Spanish international orientations: between Europe and Iberoamerica. In: *Changing European Identities*. Ed. G. M. Bleakwell and E. Lyons. Oxford: Butterworth-Heinemann.

Trenz, Hans-Jörg. 1999. Mobilizing collective identities: the public discourse on immigration in Portugal and Germany. Dissertation filed at the European University Institute, Florence.

Tribalat, Michèle. 1995. *Faire France*. Paris: La Decouverte.

Twaddle, Michael. 1994. British nationality law, Commonwealth immigration and the ending of the British Empire. In: *L'Europe retrouvée: Les migrations de la décolonisation*. Ed. J.-L. Miège and C. Dubois. Paris: L'Harmattan.

Uhlitz, Otto. 1986. Deutsches Volk oder "multikulturelle Gesellschaft." *Recht und Politik* 22(3), 143–152.

Ulmer, Eva Carolin. 1997. Spain and the challenge of immigration. Doctoral diss., Trinity College, Oxford University.

UNESCO. 1953. *Le concept de race*. Paris.

U.S. Commission on Immigration Reform. 1997. *Becoming an American*. Washington, D.C.: Government Printing Office.

Van den Berghe, Pierre. 1978. *Race and Racism*. 2nd ed. New York: Wiley.

———. 1981. *The Ethnic Phenomenon*. New York: Elsevier.

Vanel, Marguerite. 1951. La notion de nationalité. *Revue critique de droit international privé*, 3–39.

Viet, Vincent. 1995. Qu'affluent les bras aux manches retroussées! *Plein Droit* 29–30, 22–26.

———. 1998. *La France immigrée*. Paris: Fayard.

Viñas Farre, Ramón. 1998. Los régimenes especiales de Extranjería en la Ley Orgánica 7/1985, de 1 de julio. *Revista de la facultad de ciencias jurídicas de la Universidad de las Palmas de Gran Canaria* 3, 295–310.

Virgós Soriano, Miguel. 1990. Nationality and double nationality principles in Spanish private international law system. In: *Nation und Staat im Internationalen Privatrecht*. Ed. E. Jayme and H.-P. Mansel. Heidelberg: C.F. Müller Juristischer Verlag.

Viviani, Nancy. 1984. *The Long Journey: Vietnamese Migration and Settlement in Australia*. Melbourne: Melbourne University Press.

———, ed. 1992. *The abolition of the White Australia Policy*. Australia-Asia Papers No.65, Centre for the Study of Australia-Asia Relations, Griffith University, Queensland.

Walzer, Michael. 1983. *Spheres of Justice*. New York: Basic Books.

———. 1990. What does it mean to be an "American"? *Social Research* 57(3), 591–614.

———. 1992. Comment. In: *Multiculturalism*. Ed. C. Taylor et al. Princeton, N.J.: Princeton University Press.

Warner Parker, A. 1924. The quota provisions of the Immigration Act of 1924. *American Journal of International Law* 18(4), 737–754.

Weber, Eugene. 1976. *Peasants into Frenchmen*. Palo Alto, Calif.: Stanford University Press.

Weber, Max. 1976. *Wirtschaft und Gesellschaft*. Tübingen: Mohr.

Weil, Patrick. 1995a. *La France et ses étrangers*. Paris: Gallimard.

———. 1995b. Racisme et discrimination dans la politique française de l'immigration, *Vingtième Siècle*, 77–102.

———. 1995c. Naturalisations: le bon grain plutôt que l'ivraie. *Plein Droit* 29–30, 27–30.

———. 1998. The transformation of immigration policies. Working Paper, European University Institute, Florence.

———. 2001a. Races at the gate. *Georgetown Immigration Law Journal* 15, 625–648.

———. 2001b. Access to citizenship. In: *Citizenship Today*. Ed. T. A. Aleinikoff and D. Klusmeyer. Washington, D.C.: Carnegie Endowment for International Peace.

———. 2002. *Qu'est-ce qu'un Français?* Paris: Grasset.

Weiner, Justus R. 1996. The Palestinian refugees' "right to return" and the peace process. *Boston College International and Comparative Law Review* 20(1), 1–57.

Wheelan, Frederick G. 1988. Citizenship and freedom of movement. In: *Open Borders? Closed Societies?* Ed. M. Gibney. New York: Greenwood Press.

White Paper (UK). 2002. *Secure Borders, Safe Haven*. London: Government Printing Office.

Whitlam, Gough. 1985. *The Whitlam Government 1972–1975*. Melbourne: Viking.

Wiarda, Howard J. 1989. *The Transition to Democracy in Spain and Portugal*. Washington, D.C.: American Enterprise Institute for Public Policy Research.

Willard, Myra. 1923. *History of the White Australia policy to 1920*. Melbourne: Melbourne University Press.

Willke, Helmut. 1992. *Ironie des Staates*. Frankfurt: Suhrkamp.

Winkelmann, Rainer. 2001. *Immigration Policies and Their Impact: the Case of New Zealand and Australia*. Working Paper No.29, Center for Comparative Immigration Studies, University of California at San Diego.

Wurmser, Meyrav. 1999. Can Israel survive post-Zionism? *Middle East Quarterly* March, 1–12.

Yack, Bernard. 1996. The myth of the civic nation. *Critical Review* 10(2), 193–211.

Yarwood, A. T. 1964. *Asian Migration to Australia: the Background to Exclusion, 1896–1923*. Melbourne: Melbourne University Press.

Yiftachel, Oren. 1992. The concept of "ethnic democracy" and its applicability to the case of Israel. *Ethnic and Racial Studies* 15(1), 125–136.

———. 1997. Israeli society and Jewish-Palestinian reconciliation. *Middle East Journal* 51(4), 505–519.

———. 1999. "Ethnocracy": the politics of Judaizing Israel/Palestine. *Constellations* 6(3), 364–390.

Zappala, Gianni, and Stephen Castles. 2000. Citizenship and immigration in Australia. In: *From Migrants to Citizens*. Ed. T. A. Aleinikoff and D. Klusmeyer. Washington, D.C.: Carnegie Endowment for International Peace.

Zolberg, Aristide. 1997. The great wall against China. In: *Migration, Migration History, History*. Ed. J. Lucassen and L. Lucassen. Bern: Peter Lang.

———. 1999. Matters of state: theorizing immigration policy. In: *The Handbook of International Migration: The American Experience*. Ed. C. Hirschman, P. Kasinitz, and J. DeWind. New York: Russell Sage Foundation.

Zucker, Norman L. 1973. *The Coming Crisis in Israel*. Cambridge, Mass.: MIT Press.

Zucker, Norman L., and Naomi Flink Zucker. 1992. From immigration to refugee redefinition: a history of refugee and asylum policy in the United States. *Journal of Policy History* 4(1), 54–70.

Zuleeg, Manfred. 1987. Der unvollkommene Nationalstaat als Einwanderungsland. *Zeitschrift für Rechtspolitik* 20(6), 188–191.

Index

Selecting by Origin

Selecting by Origin

*Ethnic Migration in
the Liberal State*

Christian Joppke

Harvard University Press

Cambridge, Massachusetts, and London, England | 2005

Library of Congress Cataloging-in-Publication Data

Joppke, Christian.
   Selecting by origin: ethnic migration in the liberal state / Christian Joppke.
      p. cm.
   Includes bibliographical references and index.
   ISBN 0-674-01559-2
   1. Emigration and immigration—Government policy. 2. Ethnic groups—
Government policy. 3. Multiculturalism. 4. Nationalism. I. Title.
JV6038.J65 2005
   325'.1—dc22   2004052276

For Benjamin and Nicolas

Contents

Preface

In a world divided into mutually exclusive sovereign states, each encaging a distinct national subset of the human species, international migration constitutes a fundamental anomaly and disturbance. As Aristide Zolberg (1999:84) describes the source of the trouble, "modern nations have come to be perceived by most of their members as family-like bodies, with a common ancestry and a common destiny." International migration stirs up the national order of things, as people do not just break out of their own ancestry and destiny nexus but, by necessity, break into another one, which is always differently configured. No wonder that, to cushion the impact of migration, there is an intrinsic inclination in modern nation-states to select newcomers in light of their proximity to the particular ancestry and destiny definitions they happen to adhere to. The result is ethnic migration.[1]

The purpose of this book is twofold: to map out the different forms that ethnic migration has taken in different geographic-historical constellations, from "settler state" to "postcolonial" and "diaspora"; and to point to a general trend away from ethnically selective toward nonethnic, universalistic immigration policies across Western states. This trend is due to the fact that such states are not just nation-states, embodiments of historically particular collectivities with distinct ancestry and destiny definitions, but also liberal states in which public policies that distinguish between people, be they citizens or aliens, along the ascriptive lines of ethnicity, national origin, or race are in conflict with fundamental liberal precepts, such as public neutrality and equality. This raises the question of why these liberal precepts, born in the European Enlightenment three centuries ago, became unambiguously embodied in Western states only much later, arguably not before the 1960s. The answer is both simple and complex (and, as a complex one, lies outside the purview of this study):

the rise of a world-spanning human rights culture after the Holocaust and decolonization.

Ethnic migration is a prominent site in which the tension between the national and liberal vocations of the modern state has come to a head. On the one hand, this is a migration that is everywhere waged for national "identity" reasons, and the policies that enable it are decoupled from the interest-driven political economy matrix in which the contemporary immigration function is usually located (for the latter, see Freeman, 1995a). On the other hand, if the diminishing scale of ethnic migration across Western states is any measure, liberal-universalistic principles and forces are steadily gaining ground over the parochially national ones. This leads to a paradox: Although it is notionally the foremost expression of a state's sovereignty, immigration (as well as citizenship) policy is no longer at the service of reproducing historically particular nationhood.

This does not mean that ethnic migration has come to an end, nor that it will come to an end any time soon. The contemporary state is in the crossfire of countervailing trends and forces, some furthering its "de-ethnicization," others instead pushing for its "re-ethnicization." Both trends, as opposite as they are, are often generated by the same global processes. An example is globalization-induced migration itself, whose immigration and emigration sides work toward the involved states' de- and re-ethnicization, respectively. Whether ethnic migration happens then depends on the contingent concatenation of de- and re-ethnicizing forces in a certain time and place. However, *when* it happens, ethnic migration is likely to be constrained by liberal norms: that is, it is likely to be based on a positive discrimination that redresses a disadvantage to a "minority" group; to be nested within a nonethnic frame of immigrant selection *or* to be notionally decoupled at all from "immigration" policy; and not to generate a concrete loser in domestic society who is capable of effective mobilization.

In looking at state policies and laws in the context of societal contestation, this book lies at the intersection of sociology, political science, and legal studies. Because the focus is on the policies and legal provisions that generate ethnic migration, the book will disappoint the sociologist who expects to hear more about the migration and the migrants themselves. Because it gives much to the cultural factor of nationhood (in, however, critical and qualified ways) and to the justifications and sociopolitical pressures surrounding ethnic migration policies, it will disappoint the political scientist who may expect a more technical and rigorous account of the policy process. Not to mention that the legal scholar will immediately recognize the dilettante. Some twenty-five years ago Aristide Zolberg and Gary Freeman started to look at international migration as a process shaped by states, within a broad historical and cross-national perspective. This book is meant to be a contribution to that program. There are signs that, in light of new kinds of circular and market-regulated migration, especially in Europe, "nation-state"-centered conceptions of immigration and citizenship have run their course (see Favell and Hansen, 2002). Then this book may be one of the last of its kind. However, in shifting the focus from the "nation-state" to the "liberal state," it comes to a quite similar conclusion, though from a statist angle.

I began working on this book during my last three years in service at the European University Institute in Florence and finished it as a Visiting Scholar at the Russell Sage Foundation in New York. At the European University Institute, I am grateful to the EUI Research Council for generously funding this project between 2000 and 2002. At Russell Sage, my thanks go to Eric Wanner, without whose kind invitation I might have spent many more years on a seemingly endless project. A group of extremely capable, amazingly multilingual research assistants in Florence helped me to compile and sift the primary parliamentary and legal documents on which much of this study is based. Elia Marzal, Mercedes Fernandez, Pablo Jáuregui, and Oscar Molina were indispensable for getting especially the Portuguese and Spanish cases done; Emmanuelle Ryon procured and organized the parliamentary records and documents on which the discussion of the French and Italian citizenship debates in Chapter 5 is based; and Elke Viebrock provided me with tall stacks of German parliamentary and government materials. Zeev Rosenhek of the Hebrew University, Jerusalem, familiarized me with the Israeli case. The architecture of Chapter 4 owes much to an article we conceived and published together (Joppke and Rosenhek, 2002), but it is based on a second round of independent research done at Russell Sage in the fall of 2002. My thanks go to Sabina Neem and the superb library service at Russell Sage for getting this chapter done. As so often in the past, I profited from a razor-sharp report on the entire manuscript by Rogers Brubaker. Rainer Bauböck is also to be thanked for a meticulous reading of Chapter 1.

Because it takes so long to write a book, it is always a period in one's life. This period coincided with the arrival of Benjamin at the beginning and that of Nicolas toward the end. This book shall be dedicated to them, big boys by now, bigger travelers still, *fiorentini per la vita*.